Racial Revolutions

A JOHN HOPE FRANKLIN CENTER BOOK

A BOOK IN THE SERIES

Latin America Otherwise: Languages, Empires, Nations

SERIES EDITORS: WALTER D. MIGNOLO, DUKE UNIVERSITY

IRENE SILVERBLATT, DUKE UNIVERSITY

SONIA SALDÍVAR-HULL, UNIVERSITY OF CALIFORNIA AT LOS ANGELES

Racial Revolutions

Antiracism and Indian Resurgence in Brazil

JONATHAN W. WARREN

Duke University Press   Durham and London 2001

© 2001 Duke University Press   All rights reserved

Printed in the United States on acid-free paper ⊛

Typeset in Quadraat by Tseng Information Systems, Inc.

Library of Congress Cataloging-in-Publication Data

appear on the last printed page of this book. Royalties

from this book will be donated to the Indians of Eastern

Brazil. Initial funds will support Projecto Arana.

About the Series

Latin America Otherwise: Languages, Empires, Nations is a critical series. It aims to explore the emergence and consequences of concepts used to define "Latin America" while at the same time exploring the broad interplay of political, economic, and cultural practices that have shaped Latin American worlds. Latin America, at the crossroads of competing imperial designs and local responses, has been construed as a geocultural and geopolitical entity since the nineteenth century. This series provides a starting point to redefine Latin America as a configuration of political, linguistic, cultural, and economic intersections that demand a continuous reappraisal of the role of the Americas in history, and of the ongoing process of globalization and the relocation of people and cultures that have characterized Latin America's experience. *Latin America Otherwise: Languages, Empires, Nations* is a forum that confronts established geocultural constructions, that rethinks area studies and disciplinary boundaries, that assesses convictions of the academy and of public policy, and that, correspondingly, demands that the practices through which we produce knowledge and understanding about and from Latin America be subject to rigorous and critical scrutiny.

In *Racial Revolutions: Antiracism and Indian Resurgence in Brazil* Jonathan Warren analyzes the complexities of race in Brazil by contrasting the Maxakali Creation Story, the inauguration of Brasília in the 1960s, and the ideology of modernization and development that defined the first twenty-five years of the Cold War. The Brazilian state found itself in a new world order and, like the rest of Latin America, challenged by indigenous peoples.

Through the emblematic scene of the Pataxó Indian Galdino Jesus dos Santos, who found himself lost in the city of Brasília on the eve of its thirty-seventh anniversary and ended up brutally murdered, Warren weaves socioeconomic conflicts with hegemonic social discourses, the latter of which also justifies exploitation of labor and discriminatory appropriation of land by claiming white entitlement to both. Warren's narrative and argument clearly demonstrate that the built-in complicity between colonialism and racism can only be understood by examining each specific country in the context of modern and colonial world systems. The racial configuration of Brazil in the past fifty years therefore cannot be understood within the confines of national history alone.

To France Winddance Twine,

& in memory of my grandfather,

Frederick A. Roberts (1913–1968)

Contents

Illustrations

Acknowledgments

This book would not have been possible without the support and guidance that I received from a number of faculty members at the University of California at Berkeley. During the past three decades, Troy Duster, my dissertation chair, almost single-handedly kept antiracist scholarship alive in the sociology department and thus created the institutional space for me to pursue this project. I am also thankful to Troy for both his insightful feedback on earlier drafts of this manuscript and the letters of reference he wrote that enabled me to secure a Fulbright Student Program award to finance the bulk of the research.

I am especially indebted to Russell Thornton for having been one of a handful of sociologists in the United States who made Indians a valid topic of study within the discipline. Moreover, Russell reviewed versions of *Racial Revolutions*, never wavered in his enthusiasm for this project, and generously allowed me to use his office at a time when I had neither computer nor work space. His letter of support was also key to my reception of a Social Science Research Council Predissertation Fellowship, which allowed me to conduct preliminary research for this manuscript in 1992.

Despite his numerous obligations, Pedro Antonio Noguera always made time to meet with me, write letters of recommendation, offer suggestions on various drafts of this manuscript, or have me over to his home for dinner and family celebrations. His commitment to bridging the academic and nonacademic worlds inspired me to attempt the same in this book. Gerald Vizenor, a professor in Native American studies, gave me a healthy irreverence for the social sciences as well as a deeper appreciation for the significance of irony, humor, and a good story. I think anyone familiar with his scholarship will quickly notice the important influence he has had on *Racial Revolutions*.

In 1989, I had the good fortune to meet Brackette Williams when she was a visiting scholar at Berkeley. Besides her extraordinary generosity—both pedagogically and materially—I am most grateful to Brackette for introducing me to the logic of symbols, demonstrating through example the significance of language play, and offering an invaluable critical overview of the social scientific study of race, nation, and class. She was also kind enough to review several chapters of this manuscript in their later versions. Then, too, there were a few other faculty at Berkeley whose scholarship, teaching, and support helped make this project possible and so deserve some mention: Gerald Berreman, Margaret Conkey, Peter Evans, Jerome Karabel, Linda Lewin, Kristin Luker, and Jack Potter.

Especially in the early phases of this book, many friends and colleagues were just as vital to my survival and success as were the faculty who mentored me. Many thanks to the following individuals for their affection, intellectual stimulation, material assistance, and appreciation of a good time: Eric Avila, Ricky Bluthenthal, Chris Dunn, Frieda Ekotto, Gilbert Ekotto, Stephen Epstein, Anthony de Falco, Brian Folk, Maria Franklin, Derrick Gilbert, Phil Gorsky, Nathaniel Hill, Arnell Hinkel, Dan Hoffman, Yumi Iwai, Donna Jones, Vandana Kohli, Natasha Kirsten Kraus, Paul Lopes, Jelani Mahiri, Imar Moreira, Sherrie Morford, Kenny Mostern, Ruth Mostern, Sarah Murray, Trisha Newland, Lowell Noble, Jodi O'Brien, Selma Oliveira, Jennifer Pierce, Phara Pietre, Tim Riera, Marlon Riggs, Darrell Robinson, Glen Switzke, Amber Tally, Guy Tally, Patricia Vattoune, Ara Wilson, John Wolfe, and Abdul-Aleem Zaid.

I would like to give special thanks to Dr. Larry Casalino, who at a time when I was desperately broke provided me with the physical examination required by the Fulbright Student Program free of charge; the late Tom McGlinn, who rescued me from disaster and gave me shelter on numerous occasions; Luis Absuaid Garcia, whose charm, intellect, and brotherhood kept me going; and Naheed Islam and Raihan Zamil, who offered me wonderful meals and company, allowed me to use their home as a refuge and their car for transportation, and commented on drafts of the manuscript.

In Brazil, I would first like to extend my deepest gratitude to everyone who agreed to be interviewed, many of whom will remain nameless to protect their privacy. The willingness of these individuals to share their stories with a stranger represented a tremendous act of faith and trust.

I worked hard not to betray this confidence by attempting to present their remarks, ideas, experiences, histories, and sentiments in a manner that was respectful and faithful to their responses. I believe that I have succeeded in this regard and hope that they agree.

A number of Brazilians taught me the meaning of hospitality. Time after time, I would arrive in a city or small town, virtually penniless and with only the name of a contact, and on every occasion I would be taken into people's homes and treated as if I were kin. Such acts of generosity can never be adequately thanked; nonetheless, I would like to extend my deepest appreciation and gratitude to these individuals for their warmth, friendship, faith, humor, and kindness: Antônia de Lourdes Alves, Garanga Barreto, Carla Simone Barbosa de Brito, Maria Lira Marques Borges, Maria and Domingos das Braes, Antônia Rita da Conceição, Eva Maria de Cruz, Eliane Rodrigues da Graça and her daughter Helena, Tomoya Inyaku, Ana Lidia Ivo, Jerry Adriane de Jesus and his mother and grandmother, Geralda and Claudia Santana Leão, Maria Ferreira Lopes, Terezinha de Oliveira Moreira and her family, Nando Neves and his parents, Benvinda and Eugenio Pankararu and their family, Cleonice Wakire Pankararu, Bekoy Pataxó, Karakana Pataxó, Puhuí Pataxó, Bruna Santos, Maria Santos, Selma Santos, Wilson Dias Santos, Maria das Dores Barbosa dos Santos, Patricia and Roberto dos Santos, Valdi Ferreira da Silva, Sonia Maria Vieira da Silva, Dale Robertson Fernandes Soares, Geralda Chaves Soares, Regina Helena Vianna and her parents, Claudio Cesar Vianna, Isabella Vianna, Daniella Vianna, and Lilian Nunes Vieira.

Two scholars were pivotal to my success in Brazil. Antônio Carlos de Souza Lima was supportive of my research from its earliest stages. Ever encouraging and enthusiastic, he went out of his way to thoroughly and patiently note the scholars, activists, and scholarship that he thought might be helpful. Thanks to Antônio Carlos, I felt at home at the Museu Nacional in Rio de Janeiro. The other key scholar was Geralda Chaves Soares. If there is anyone who deserves an honorary Ph.D., it is Geralda. A tireless researcher and activist, she has conducted almost two decades of fieldwork and published a number of groundbreaking books on Indians in Minas Gerais. This project would not have been realized without her insights, references, and general support.

The transcribers were Martha Marques Alves, Carla Simone Barbosa de Brito, Claudia Santana Leão, Nivea Mendes Ribeiro, and Wilson Dias Santos. They did an outstanding job, oftentimes simply on the promise of one day receiving payment—a promise that was eventually fulfilled.

Brazilian institutions that were extremely helpful to me were the Museu Nacional (special thanks to Luis Fernando Dias Duarte for establishing this affiliation), Estudos Afro-Asiáticos (thanks here to Beluce Belucci, Carlos A. Hasenbalg, Ana Senna, and Sonia Maria Vieira da Silva), Instituto Brasileiro de Análises Sociais e Econômicas (my gratitude to Carla Simone Barbosa de Brito, Tomoya Inyaku, Atila Roque, and Cleide Quiteria dos Santos), Centro de Documentação Ely Ferreira da Silva, Conselho Indigenista Missionario Leste (special thanks to Luís Lobo), the federal universities of Brasília, Minas Gerais, Pernambuco (special thanks to Silvia Martins and Ivson Ferreira), and Rio de Janeiro (my appreciation to João Pacheco de Oliveira), the "Indian Tent" at the Environmental Summit 1992 (my thanks to Ed Burnstick), the Ford Foundation in Rio de Janeiro (thanks to Eddie Telles), and the Comissão Fulbright in Rio de Janeiro and Brasília (my gratitude to Marco Antônio da Rocha and Terry V. McIntyre).

The research for this project would not have been possible without the financial support of the Fulbright Student Program award, and an International Predissertation Fellowship from the Social Science Research Council and American Council of Learned Societies, with funds provided by the Ford Foundation. I want to also express my appreciation to the restaurants (Broadmoor and New South Wales in Colorado Springs, La Fleur and Simpatico in Seattle) that provided employment on my returns from Brazil. The camaraderie that I had with my colleagues in those restaurants was a welcome and needed complement to the solace of the time I spent writing.

Besides UC Berkeley, three other U.S. institutions of higher education greatly facilitated this project. The Colorado College—and in particular, the Department of Sociology—took me under its wing, providing an affiliation and, most important, an office. My special appreciation goes out to Margie Duncombe, Norma Flemming, Jeff Livesay, and Michael Siddoway. The Department of Sociology at the University of California at Santa Barbara also supported me for one quarter as a visiting professor. Thanks to Rich Appelbaum, Chris Allen, Kum-Kum

Bhavnani, Bill Bielby, Denise Bielby, Susan Dalton, Mitch Duneier, Dick Flacks, John Foran, Avery Gordon, Harvey Molotch, Chris Newfield, Constance Penley, Cedric Robinson, Beth Schneider, Jane Ward, and Nancy Willstater.

The Henry M. Jackson School of International Studies at the University of Washington was my institutional and intellectual base during most of the writing of this book, and thus deserves much of the credit for its realization. My gratitude to those colleagues who were especially supportive: Jennifer Aradanas, Jere Bacharach, Tani Barlow, Chuck Berquist, Johnella Butler, Mary Callahan, Aaron Fox, Christoph Giebel, Lauren Goodlad, Marilyn Ivy, Lucy Jarosz, Susan Jeffords, Gene Hunn, Resat Kesaba, Charles Keyes, Victoria Lawson, Joel Migdal, Alicia Palacio, John Pemberton, Camillo Penna, Gigi Petterson, Denise Pruitt, Sabrina Ramet, Matt Sparke, Cynthia Steele, and Madeleine Yue Dong. I also had the pleasure of working with a number of outstanding students at the University of Washington who were kind enough to offer feedback on various drafts or help with translations: Becky Anerued, Emily Arfin, David Carlson, Sandra Hernandes, Dawn Hewett, Leila Lehnen, Molly Robertson, Heidi Shultheis and her partner Francisco C. Amaral dos Santos, Christi Sue, and Mark Vasquez.

A few individuals need to be singled out for their emotional support at crucial moments and, in most cases, invaluable editorial advice: Jere Bacharach, Ingrid Banks, Howie Becker, Elizabeth Cook-Lynn, William Darity, John Foran, Maria Franklin and her parents, Jan French, Avery Gordon, Ruth Simms Hamilton, Gail Hanlon, Martha Heller, Patricia Mickelberry, Valerie Millholland, Sabrina Ramet, José Augusto Laranjeiras Sampaio, Ana Flavia Santos, Pauline Escudero Shafer, Audra Simpson, Nikhil Pal Singh, Paulette Thompson, Stefano Varese, Howard Winant, the late Joe Wood, and Leon Zamosc. My appreciation as well to the two anonymous reviewers of *Racial Revolutions* for their excellent suggestions.

With regard to my family, let me begin by thanking my mother, Janice Roberts Wilbur, and stepfather, Michael Wilbur. If it had not been for their passion for learning, faith in my abilities, commitment to social justice, and insistence on pursuing one's vision, then I would never have entered graduate school, let alone completed this book. My other mother, Mamie Lois Twine, was invariably reliable in providing useful words of wisdom. I could always count on her keen wit and charm to bring a smile to my face. In addition to this, she came through with an emergency loan from time to time despite having little herself. My father, Win Warren, has been consistently behind me through some difficult times. His love, willingness to accept collect calls and make emergency loans, and respect for my decisions even when he did not agree made the difference between utter ruin and my ability to continue on. For this I am of course extremely thankful. My grandparents—Wava Roberts, Melvin Warren, and Pauline Warren—have been supportive of my endeavors since I was born, and this project proved no exception. To them, all of my love and respect. Let me also mention the names of my other family members, who I am sure had no idea what I have been doing for the past several years, but nonetheless have continued to love and support me: Britney Abbott, Marsha Berry, Catherine Brownley, Dave Brownley, D. J. Brownley, Aerian Saxon, Stacy Saxon, Paul Christopher Twine, Joe Twine, Christine Warren, Jessica Warren, Mitchell Warren, and Terry Warren. Finally, a special thanks to my uncle Richard Warren, who gave me a one thousand dollar gift that helped me survive one summer during the writing of this book.

The person most responsible for the fruition of this book is my partner, France Winddance Twine. Winddance and I began and endured graduate school together. We have worked in tandem on several projects, and this one proved no exception. She was key in the conceptualization and development of this book. Her belief in the worthiness of this project sustained me through a number of difficult times. Winddance was the one person I could depend on for affection and humor. Moreover, Winddance kept all in order while I was in Brazil conducting research. Remarkably, she did this while completing her first book and launching her professional career as an assistant professor, enabling us to eat, keep a roof over our heads, and pay the bills. For this, somehow my deepest gratitude and love seem pathetically inadequate.

Abbreviations

CEB: Comunidade Eclesial de Base (Ecclesiastical Base Community), a grassroots Catholic organization inspired by liberationist Christianity. The aim is to facilitate both religious and socio-political involvement by linking faith to life, by relating concrete societal and political problems to religious themes. Promoted by numerous bishops in Brazil and in other parts of Latin America, thousands of these communities exist throughout the region.

CEDEFES: Centro de Documentação Ely Ferreira da Silva (Ely Ferreira da Silva Center for Documentation), a small, nongovernmental organization founded in 1985, is based in Belo Horizonte. Its stated objective is "to help strengthen popular movements by documenting the history of the people and supporting them in their struggles in order to build a more humane society."

CEDI: Centro Ecumenico de Documentação e Informação (Ecumenical Center for Documentation and Education), a nongovernmental organization, has been a major supporter of the indigenous movement, indigenous communities, and research on issues relevant to Indians.

CIMI: Conselho Indigenista Missionário (Indigenous Missionary Council), a Catholic organization institutionally under the jurisdiction of the CNBB, was founded in 1972 with "the general objective of helping to build the autonomy of Indians as peoples who are ethnically and culturally different, and to contribute to the strengthening of their organizations and alliances in both Brazil and the continent."

CNBB: Conferência Nacional dos Bispos do Brasil (National Conference of Brazilian Bishops).

CPT: Comissão Pastoral da Terra (Pastoral Land Commission). "Founded in 1975 by a group of Catholic Bishops whose Dioceses are located in the northern Amazonian areas where there are intense land conflicts, the C PT is now a nationwide lay and clerical organization linked to the National Conference of Brazilian Bishops. C PT functionaries monitor and tabulate data on the various aspects of the Brazilian agrarian question, particularly violent land conflicts, and typically assist unions around the countryside to establish themselves" (Maybury-Lewis, *The Politics of the Possible*, 100).

FU NAI: Fundação Nacional do Índio (National Foundation for the Indian) is the government agency responsible for Indian affairs— much like the Bureau of Indian Affairs in the United States. F U N A I replaced s P I (the previous Indian agency) in 1967 at the height of the military dictatorship with the principal objective of national security. The agency currently employs more than five thousand individuals.

N G O: Nongovernmental organization. The Portuguese acronym is O N G (Organização Não-Governmental).

s P I: Serviço de Proteção aos Índios (Indian Protection Service), the first government agency dedicated to the protection of Indians, was founded in 1910 with the guiding principle of "fraternal protection." It was abolished and replaced by F U N A I in 1967.

U N I: União das Nações Indígenas (Union of Indigenous Nations), founded in 1978, became the first nationwide indigenous organization in Brazil.

Racial Revolutions

Antiracism and Indian Resurgence in Brazil

Primary Research Areas

State Boundaries

City

State Capital

Indigenous Areas

Officially Recognized

Officially Recognized
(off scale)

Not officially recognized

G Guarani
Ge Geren
K Krenak
Kx Kaxixó
M Maxakali

P Pataxó
Ph Pataxó Hã Hã Hãe
Pk Pankararu
T Tupiniquim
X Xacriabá

Introduction: Maxakali Creation Story

Long ago, in the time of the ancient Maxakali, Topar, the creator, gave the Maxakali an otter. Topar said, "This otter is to help you fish so that you always have something to eat. But remember, you must always give the three biggest fish to the otter. You are welcome to all of the rest. You may fill your sacks full of the little fish so that the whole community can eat, so that no one goes hungry. The three biggest fish, however, are the otter's." And this is how it was done for many years.

And in that time of the ancient Maxakali, the son-in-law of the guardian of the otter decided that he would like to go fishing with the otter. He said, "Hey grandfather, I'd like to fish with the otter. Would you loan it to me?" The old man replied, "Sure, but remember this otter belongs to the community and that we have an agreement with Topar that the three biggest fish must be given to the otter. If you do not do this, then everything will come to an end."

This man, the son-in-law, took the otter and went down to the river. When he got there, he threw the otter into the water. The otter dove in and after a few minutes came out of the water with three enormous fish. The otter tossed the fish onto the riverbank and quickly dove back into the water in search of more fish. The otter brought back more and more fish, until the man almost had his sack filled. But the son-in-law could not keep his mind off the three enormous fish that the otter had first brought out of the river. He thought to himself, "I'm not going to give those three big fish to the otter. I'm going to take them for myself. Besides, he's not going to notice. That otter doesn't know any better." So when the otter was making one of his last dives for fish, the son-in-law put those enormous fish into his sack and left for the village.

The otter returned to find that his fish had been taken. So the otter dove back into the river and swam away downstream. On his way back to the village, the man began to rethink his decision. He quickly returned to the river and started yelling, "Otter! Otter! Please return! I'll give you the enormous fish! Please come back, otter! I promise, I'll give you the fish!" He kept calling to the otter, but the otter no longer understood his language.

The man then returned to the village. His sack was full of fish but he was sad. He went up to the old man and explained, "Oh grandfather, I've done something very wrong. I kept the three biggest fish and so the otter has gone away." The grandfather said, "Oh no! You've really made a serious mistake. Tonight we are going to suffer a terrible punishment. The otter was given to the community to ensure that we would never go hungry."

The son-in-law then returned to his hut, sad and preoccupied. When night fell, it started to rain and rain and rain. Everyone became very frightened. News of what had happened had spread throughout the community, and so they knew that this could be their punishment. They woke to find everything flooded. So they ran for the woods. They climbed the trees to get out of the water. But the rain kept coming and coming. It rained and rained. Eventually, the water became so high that it swept the trees away with the people on them.

But the son-in-law was clever. He had decided not to seek refuge in the trees. Instead he decided to hide. So as the waters were rising, he quickly grabbed some deerskin, crawled inside a log, and sealed himself there.

Eventually the rain stopped and the waters receded. But the man was so weakened after having spent so many days in the log that he didn't even have enough strength to pull himself from the log. Then the creator returned with a friend to see how the Maxakali were doing. This time Topar, the creator, returned as a beetle. As he was buzzing around, talking with his friend, the Maxakali in the log started yelling, "Topar! Topar! Get me out of here, Topar! I'm trapped in here! Get me out of here!" Finally, Topar heard the faint sounds and followed them to the log.

Topar pulled the Maxakali from the log. That Maxakali was ugly. He was white, skinny, and covered with shit. He was a mess. Topar said, "Don't worry, I'll save you." So he made a fire and began to roast the Maxakali the way one would a chicken. That helped the Maxakali to warm up. "Now I'm going to give you *your* food," Topar declared. He gave the Maxakali bananas, manioc, honey, peanuts, melon, and watermelon.

This is why, to this day, the Maxakali still don't care for beans and other foods of the white.

After the Maxakali ate and began to feel better, Topar said, "Fine, let's go. I'll take you with us." The Maxakali said, "No, I'm not going with you. I'm not God. I'm going to stay here. I want to stay here." The Maxakali was afraid to go with Topar. And Topar said, "But what are you going to do here all alone? There aren't any women. There are only animals." But the Maxakali was determined to stay and so replied, "No, I'm not going. I want to stay here."

Time passed, and the Maxakali was becoming quite discouraged. He was feeling extremely sad. Everyone was gone; all the Maxakali had died in the flood. Then one night, feeling lonely, sitting next to the fire making arrows, he heard some voices in the distance. He became very still so that he could better hear the voices. He recognized them. They were human voices. He became excited because they were speaking Maxakali.

So he went in the direction of the voices. Finally he arrived at a small house and there was a woman inside cooking. But she wasn't really a human. She was a deer. He said, "Good evening, is your husband around?" She said, "No, I'm afraid he's out working in the fields. But come in and have a seat." He said, "No, I think I'll go out and introduce myself to your husband." So he left with his bow and arrows.

There in the field the buck was working hard. He was tilling the soil and pulling out weeds. He was working so hard that he didn't even notice the Maxakali. And while that buck was working hard, the Maxakali carefully aimed his arrow and shot the buck dead. So he murdered the deer's husband and returned calmly to the house. He told her that he couldn't find her husband out in the field. So she said, "Well, let's wait for him to return. He probably went hunting." They waited and waited, but he never returned.

When the buck never returned, the Maxakali and the deer decided to wed. The problem was that the Maxakali didn't know how to have sex with a deer. So first he had sex with her toes and she grew a baby in her leg—that is where the potato in the back of our leg comes from. Then he tried having sex in various other places, but the babies would never grow in his wife's stomach. Well, Topar had been watching everything and decided to help the Maxakali out. He said, "I'm going to show you how it works." So he grabbed a small machete and cut the deer open between her legs to make her sex. Then he showed the Maxakali how to have sex with his wife so that they could have children. After that, the Maxakali people were born—anew.

1. Posttraditional Indians

At mid-century, the consensus among those who worked with indigenous groups in Brazil was that native populations would soon be extinct or completely assimilated into the national society. However, more recent appraisals suggest that Brazil's indigenous population has not only survived, but has grown threefold in the last fifty years, in an "Indian demographic turnaround."
—David Kennedy and Stephen Perz, "Who Are Brazil's Indígenas?"

Conceived from the miscegenation of socialist architects and developmentalist politicians, Brasília was to have been Brazil's new beginning. This capital city was imagined as an "exemplar, enclave, beachhead, or blueprint radiating change" from which a great society was to emerge. Its planners "believed it possible not only to generalize [Brasília's] innovations throughout the nation, but moreover to propel [Brazil] into a planned future, causing it to skip predicted but undesired stages in its historical development." [1] Thus the audacious creators of Brasília, acting as if they were endowed with the powers of Topar, built their modernist city on the conviction that it would spare Brazil from the wrath of its own history.

In the early hours of 20 April 1997, the eve of the thirty-seventh anniversary of Brasília, the Pataxó Indian Galdino Jesus dos Santos found himself lost in this city constructed to birth a new Brazil. The forty-four-year-old man had come to Brasília in pursuit of a different vision from the municipality of Pau Brasil, located hundreds of miles away in the southern tip of Bahia. He and five other Pataxó Hã-Hã-Hãe had journeyed to the airplane-shaped capital to pressure the government to follow through with the removal of *fazendeiros* (ranchers or plantation owners) who were illegally occupying 788 hectares of their land. [2] Thirteen of their colleagues had been killed over this land since 1986, and they wanted to ensure that no one else from their community of 1,723 died in the conflict.[3]

Late at night, after a full day of meetings and demonstrations, and in an unfamiliar city that is notoriously difficult to navigate, dos Santos had trouble finding his hostel. It was well after midnight by the time he located the place where he was to have stayed. He rang the doorbell, but no one answered. No doubt exhausted, he headed for a bench at the bus stop on Avenue 3W South, between the quadrants 703 and 704, and there he went to sleep.[4]

In the early hours of the morning, Max Rogério Alves, Antonio Novely Cardoso da Vilanova, Eron Chaves de Oliveira, Tomás Oliveira de Almeida—all age nineteen—and a sixteen year old whose name was withheld because he was a juvenile, were driving around, as they later said, "looking for something to do."[5] According to these young men, at approximately 4:00 A.M. they spotted dos Santos asleep on the bench. This gave these white, upper-middle-class teenagers an idea for breaking the morning's boredom, and off they sped to the nearest gas station.[6]

The gasoline station attendant would later explain that the men "were not nervous at all. There was no music in the car and they seemed very calm. They hadn't been drinking. Given how relaxed they were, it seems like it was not the first time that they had done something like that."[7] In fact, thirteen other such burnings of street people had taken place during the previous two years.[8] Whether or not this was the first such "joke" they had played, the young men returned to the bus stop, where they dosed the sleeping man with two liters of gasoline and then each threw a match, "hoping to scare the man," as they claimed afterward.[9]

Dos Santos must have awakened in shock—at first wondering what was happening. Was someone pissing on him, playing a prank? And then in that eternal instant when he became aware of the scent of gasoline, saw the matches being lit and thrown his way, smelled the stench of his burning body, and caught a glimpse of the men running away, the mixture of horror, disbelief, and terrific pain must have been overwhelming. The young men drove away as dos Santos, a human fireball, ran desperately into the street for help.

Until his death later in a hospital, dos Santos remained conscious. He suffered burns over 85 percent of his body, so severe that muscle and bones as well as skin were badly scorched. The youth were quickly found and, on arrest, exclaimed in their defense that they thought the man had been a *mendigo* (a homeless or street person). Forgetting or never appreciating that race and class are intimately entwined in Brazil, editorialists would seize on this statement to reassure their readers in the subsequent weeks that albeit a heinous crime, at least the "racial democracy" was still intact since dos Santos "was not burnt for being Indian or black, but because he was 'homeless.' " [10]

Eventually, the young men were brought before Judge Sandra de Santis Mello, who ruled that the youth had not intended to kill but only frighten: "The accused were attempting to commit a *savage joke*, they were trying to set on fire that which they presumed to be a homeless person, but they never believed that it would result in death" (emphasis added).[11] Murder charges were reduced to manslaughter, for which the maximum allowable sentence would have been twelve years in prison. The youth were given two years in prison with a chance of parole in only four months.

Some declared that justice had been served because the law remained above popular sentiment. But such sanctimonious claims rang hollow for others who knew all too well the truth of dos Santos's mother's assertion that had the roles been reversed, a very different verdict would have been reached. In Minervina Santos's words, "If it had been my son that had burnt one of those children . . . , I would like to have seen my son not go to prison." [12] In a world where the police routinely moonlight as child assassins, in a society warped by conquest, slavery, and some of the most extreme inequities of wealth in the world, it was a victory of sorts that anyone believed or at least dared to hope that justice could be served at all.[13]

Immediately following the murder of dos Santos, journalists were quick to argue that these "monsters," "animals," "trash," "rats of Brazil," and so forth were the product of a moral breakdown in the nation.[14] How else to explain how these "educated and calm [boys who] had never caused any problems" could define and experience the burning of a human being as a joke? [15] In these reporters' view, Brazil had become too materialistic, too fixated on consumption, too hedonistic, too far removed from the church. Television, computers, automobiles, and capitalism, as well as neoliberal economic policies, were to blame for this moral decay.[16] As one retired professor, Maria José Campos, put it in an editorial that echoed other social analysts at this time: "The youth of today only want the 'shopping center.' They only want pleasure. They're the monsters fabricated by television."[17]

But such contentions are based on short memories. With the church's blessing, countless monsters terrorized Brazil in an era that predated computers, neoliberalism, television, automobiles, and shopping centers. The problem, then, is not that certain morals have been destroyed in the quixotic quest for modernity. To the contrary, one of the most disturbing aspects of dos Santos's horrific death was how it indicates that certain values—forged in the time of conquest, slavery, and colonialism—have yet to be undone.

Indian Resurgence

The torture and killing of dos Santos with impunity suggests that the architects of Brasília failed in their efforts to break with tradition and create a new nation unencumbered by history. Yet it would be a mistake to interpret this "savage joke" as evidence of an unchanged Brazil. In fact, there is one aspect of this story, one subtle facet of the dos Santos biography, that hints at an altered Brazil: he was from southern Bahia, a region, as I will explain below, where Indian populations were presumed to be extinct.

Southern Bahia is where the Portuguese first landed, by pure chance, in Brazil in 1500. Thirteen Portuguese ships en route to India via Cape Horn were driven hundreds of miles off course by the winds of fate. For the Portuguese, this proved to be an extremely fortuitous mishap because the newly "discovered" land fell within an area allotted to Portugal—to the east of a line drawn by Pope Alexander VI, and negotiated between Spain and Portugal in the Treaty of Tordesillas on 7 June 1494.

This was, of course, a less fortuitous moment for the peoples of the lands that were about to become known as Brazil. For soon after this discovery, King João III began setting in motion the colonization of those vast stretches of the Atlantic littoral that the pope had determined fell under the sovereign of the Portuguese Crown. The basis of the fledgling colonial economy—as well as the origin of the colony's name—was *pau brasil* (brazilwood).[18]

Eugenio Pankararu taking a break from the midday sun in aldeia Apukaré. All photographs courtesy of the author.

Ever since the twelfth century trees that yielded a red dye were known as *brasile*, from the Latin for red. And hardwood found in the new continent produced a powerful dye that ranged from maroon to ochre exports. . . . The dye [from this "redwood"] was not particularly stable, but reds were fashionable, especially at the French court, and the profits from the brazilwood trade were attractive enough to justify the risks involved in the ocean crossing.[19]

The brazilwood trade combined with sugar production, which began flourishing in the 1540s, spawned an ever growing demand for labor. Not surprisingly, the colonists' appetite for Indian workers steadily increased. So the white settlers, given their conception of the indigenous people as heathens and their acceptance of slavery as merely "one of the conditions of man," resorted to Indian slavery as a "natural" solution to their labor "needs."[20]

Slaves had been sent back to Portugal since the first ships visited Brazil, but by the mid–sixteenth century, Indian slavery was rapidly becoming institutionalized as part of the Brazilian way of life. For example, in the captaincy of Itamaracá to the north of Pernambuco, one of the original fourteen captaincies established by King João III, "there was no white man, however poor, who did not have twenty or thirty of those darkies [Indians] to use as slaves, and the rich had whole villages."[21] The population of San Vicente in 1548, which included 600 free persons and 3,000 Indian slaves, offers yet another illustration of how quickly Indian slavery had become embedded in Brazilian society.[22]

By the mid-1550s, the trade in "red gold" had become a robust business that was to flourish for generations to come.

[The Jesuit missionary] José de Anchieta reckoned that slaving expeditions out of Bahia brought down an average of two or three thousand Indians a year. [The chronicler] Vincente do Salvador told how António Dias Adorno was sent inland to search for minerals but returned with 7,000 Tupinguen and how Luis Álvares Espinha, who marched out of Ilhéus on a punitive raid, "was not content with capturing all those villages: he went on inland and brought down infinite heathen." The Indians of the coast north of Sergipe became so terrified by Portuguese victories that "they allowed themselves to be tied up by the whites like sheep or ewes. These therefore went along those rivers in boats which they sailed back loaded with Indians to sell for 2 cruzados or 1 milreis each, which is the price of sheep." [23]

Indian slavery, as I detail in chapter 3, did not come to an end in eastern or northeastern Brazil until the mid–twentieth century. Thus, for almost five centuries, Indian slavery and colonization, the accoutrements of European civilization, have been key features of the cultural landscape of the Brazilian littoral. Given the duration, degree, and horrific brutality of European discoveries in this region, it is understandable why many believed that the Indian had vanished from the original colonies of Brazil. For instance, Charles Wagley wrote in the early 1950s that "unlike the situation in the plantation and mountain regions, where the Indian disappeared very early as an active element in the population, in the Amazon region the Indian and the mestizo are important elements of the modern social and racial scene." [24] Twenty years later, the Brazilian anthropologist Darcy Ribeiro made a similar assessment of this region's racial geography when he noted, "They are living their last days, those remnants of the Indians from the interior of the northeast who have somehow managed to extend themselves into the twentieth century." [25]

Dos Santos, then, was from an area where Indians were thought to be on the verge of extinction, irrelevant, or even nonexistent. So was this slain man a "remnant" of an Indian community that once existed in southern Bahia? Was he a sort of Ishi figure, the last surviving member of his people, who in another context would have spent the remaining years of his life as a janitor in a university museum? [26] Surprisingly, given the demographic predictions cited above, the answer to these questions is "no." Rather than declining into nonexistence, the indigenous population in "the plantation and mountain regions" of Brazil has rapidly increased over the past three decades.

Indeed, one of the primary goals of this book is to put forth an explanation as to why there has been an indigenous resurgence in recent times. Why has the centuries-long trend of de-Indianization been brought to a halt and even reversed in a region presumed free of Indians? In the late 1960s, for example, in the states of Minas Gerais and Espírito Santo, there were probably at most a few hundred individuals who self-identified as Indian—and even fewer who were recognized by the government as Indian. Yet in a period of some twenty-five years, the Indian population has increased from a couple of *aldeias* (villages or communities) and two Indian penal colonies to ten officially acknowledged indigenous territories and at least two communities, those of the Kaxixó and Aranã, that are struggling to be recognized.[27] Moreover, peoples thought to be on the verge of extinction have experienced rapid upsurges in populations (for instance, the Pataxó). Several "new" Indian peoples (e.g., Xacriabá, Tupinikim, Kaxixó, and Aranã) have also emerged since the 1970s, and the population in eastern Brazil on the aldeias alone is now estimated to be between 15,000 and 20,000.[28]

A similar increase has taken place in northeastern Brazil. As José Augusto Laraneiras Sampaio noted in the mid-1980s, in a little over ten years, a number of "groups" have surfaced "that until recently had been considered extinct—the Pataxó, the Karapotó"—or were previously "unknown in the literature, such as the Kapinawá, Tingui-Botó, Pankararé, Wasu.... From eleven groups with around 13,000 individuals aided by *postos indígenas* in 1975, there are today in the area from northern Bahia extending to Piauí approximately seventeen ethnic groups with a population of about 17,000." [29]

The following comments made by the secretary of the 1995 Assembleia dos Índios de Leste/Nordeste (Assembly of the Indians from the East and Northeast) underscores the impact of this trend over the next decade.

> At the first assembly in 1987, only twelve peoples were represented. At every subsequent assembly, five or six new peoples have attended, whom nobody believed existed anymore. This year it's to the point where we have thirty-five peoples represented.[30]

Thus, in eastern and northeastern Brazil, there are now approximately forty different peoples or tribes, and the total population is estimated to be between 60,000 to 70,000.[31]

As some recent data suggest, the increase in the Brazilian Indian population in the east and northeast may be part of a larger national trend. For instance, in 1995, a random sample survey of racial attitudes among urban Brazilians was conducted by *Folha de São Paulo* and published under the title *Racismo Cordial* (*Cordial Racism*). In total, 5,000 individuals were interviewed in 120 different cities throughout Brazil. Of

Claudio Pankararu with his son, Iuri, in aldeia Apukaré.

A Xacriabá family in Belo Horizonte: (left to right) Claudia Santana Leão, Geralda Santana Leão, Neuza Nunes Marcedo, and Welbert Gilhermo Leão (up front).

these urban Brazilians, 49.95 percent self-identified as white, 12 percent as black, 28.80 percent as *pardo* (brown or mestizo), 2.79 percent as Asian, and 6.46 percent as Indian.[32] An Indian population of 6.46 percent is considered extraordinarily high given that most previous estimates have been around .2 percent. One should keep in mind, however, that the earlier figures are suspect because they are based on survey and census data of questionable quality. In a recent review of the demographic research on Brazilian Indians, Marcio Ferreira da Silva complained that in Brazil "systematic demographic studies of indigenous people are still rare to this day."[33] One of the principal sources of survey data in the past thirty years has been the federal Indian bureau, the National Foundation for the Indian (FUNAI), which enumerated 325,000 Indians in 1995 (or approximately .2 percent of the Brazilian population). Since FUNAI tends *not* to count self-identified Indians who either live outside a federally recognized indigenous territory or are not officially viewed as Indian, its figures would exclude many of the rural Indians who appear in this book—such as the Pankararu, Kaxixó,

Cristiano Xacriabá works at a macaroni factory in Belo Horizonte.

Arana, or other descendants of mission Indians in Minas Gerais. FUNAI also typically undercounts, if not completely misses, urban Indians who constitute approximately one-quarter of the Indian population according to some estimates.

The federal census, conducted by the Brazilian Institute of Geography and Statistics (Instituto Brasileiro de Geografia e Estatística, or IBGE), has been another crucial source of survey data on Indians. Prior to the 1970 census, when no figures were taken on race, individuals were considered Indian only if their primary language was indigenous. Yet "because many indigenous persons primarily [speak] Portuguese," due in large measure to forced acculturation, "the indigenous population was misreported and underenumerated."[34] In the 1980 census, anyone who self-identified as Indian was racially classified as pardo. In response to criticisms that indigenous people were basically erased from the 1980 census, IBGE created a new category, indígena, which it added to the skin color/race variable.[35] Even though census enumerators were instructed to classify individuals as indígenas based on self-identification, there are reports that they did so only if that person possessed a FUNAI identity card. Those who did not have such a card were allegedly enumerated as pardo.[36] As such, "if reporting of indígenas depended less on self-identification" than on whether the person had an identity card or "looked Indian" to the enumerator, then "reporting of indígenas will be biased toward enumerations that underestimate the true population size."[37]

Whether the findings from the Folha de São Paulo, IBGE, or FUNAI prove to be an accurate reflection of how Brazilians currently self-identify will depend on what future censuses and surveys uncover. Without doubt, there will continue to be great variability in the estimates of the actual number of Indians in Brazil until many of the above-noted problems with enumeration are resolved. Nonetheless, on one matter there has been a remarkable degree of consensus: ethnographers as well as survey researchers have all observed and documented a dramatic upsurge in the Brazilian Indian population over the past few decades. In fact, some estimate that it has increased by 300 percent since the 1950s.[38]

The demographic resurgence that has taken place in eastern and northeastern Brazil has thus been paralleled at the national level.

Furthermore, there is solid evidence that this increase has been matched by similar ones elsewhere in the Western Hemisphere. In the United States, for instance, the Indian population experienced a 74 percent increase between 1970 and 1980 while the general population grew by only 11 percent.[39] Even though the pace of the increase slowed to 37 percent in the 1990s, this still represents a growth rate approximately four times that of the total population.[40]

The rates of these population increases are simply too accelerated to be accounted for exclusively in terms of the fundamental demographic processes of births, deaths, and migration; nor can this demographic trend merely be attributed to changed enumerating techniques.[41] Although these factors have no doubt played a role in spurring so-called indigenous population recoveries, it is evident that one of the primary variables responsible for Indian resurgence has been racial identity shifts. In other words, one of the driving forces behind the swift increase in the indigenous population has been the increased tendency of individuals who had previously self-identified as non-Indian, or whose parents did not have Indian subjectivities, to now self-identify as Indian.

One example of the type of identity transformation to which I am referring, albeit from a different national and historical context, is that of N. Scott Momaday's mother, Mayme Natachee. In his memoir *The Names*, Momaday tells us that his mother was born in 1913 and that her father, Theodore, raised her alone after his wife died in the great influenza of 1918.[42] Mayme, "a raving beauty who had very black hair and very blue eyes; her skin was clear and taut, of an olive complexion, and her bones were fine and well shaped," had been brought up a "Southern belle" (that is, white).[43] It can probably be safely assumed that her father, despite being one-quarter Cherokee "by blood," was white (at least in his public life, given that he was sheriff in Trenton County in the Jim Crow South—a position rarely held by nonwhites at the time).

Then, for reasons unknown or unexplored by Momaday, Mayme began to reimagine herself. At the age of sixteen, she experienced a shift in her racial identity.

> In 1929 my mother was a Southern belle. . . . It was about this time that she began to see herself as an Indian. That dim native heritage became a fascination and cause for her, inasmuch, perhaps, as it en-

abled her to assume an attitude of defiance, an attitude which she assumed with particular style and satisfaction; it became her. She imagined who she was. This act of imagination was, I believe, among the most important events of my mother's early life.[44]

Mayme was atypical of her generation, for until recent decades, the predominant trajectory of acts of racial imagining had been toward whiteness. That is, in most parts of the Americas, the prevailing movement in racial formation had been away from Indian subjectivities toward non-Indian ones. In Latin America, this gravitation is widely known and referred to as "whitening." And until a short while ago, this whitening movement seemed so inevitable that it prompted numerous depictions of a racial future not unlike the one foreseen in 1975 by the Brazilian anthropologist, Paulo Marcos de Amorim.

> The tribal groups [in northeastern Brazil] have been reached by a progressive proletarization process. [Because there are few employment opportunities on the reserve, Indians must] sell their manpower [sic] to the white man, the only way to assure the indispensable acquisition of money. [Consequently] the loss of ethnic identity will gradually continue . . . , since the ones who are forced to look for a job outside of their tribal setting will [shed their Indianness] in order not to be stigmatized by the various prejudices against Indians.[45]

Yet despite such predictions, the erosion of tribal subjectivities has not continued. Dos Santos is not the last of his people. "The Indian" in eastern Brazil, as is the case throughout much of the Americas, is not "losing his identity hour by hour." [46] In fact, the exact opposite appears to be the case. The age-old tendency for Indians to be absorbed and assimilated into non-Indian subjectivities and communities has seemingly been reversed. Suddenly, for reasons to be explored in subsequent chapters, an undercurrent of "Indianning" has welled up against the mainstream of whitening.

Survivors of the Flood

The creation story of the Maxakali told in the introduction is obviously about many things, including their genesis, the origins of their cuisine, and the ethics of individualism versus community. Given my research interests, I brought yet another reading to the tale. When I first heard of the origins of the Maxakali, I immediately thought of the Indian communities in Minas Gerais, Espírito Santo, and southern Bahia (eastern Brazil) that are the focus of this book.[47] To me, the condition of the father of the contemporary Maxakali when he was pulled by Topar from the log is analogous to the present-day state of the Kaxixó, Pataxó, Krenak, Tupinikim, Pankararu, Xacriabá, Arana, and others. These peoples are metaphorically just emerging from their "logs," barely alive and not in the best of shape. Their communities have been fragmented and scattered, their numbers greatly reduced. Yet instead of simply assimilating into the Brazilian nation, instead of simply "leaving with Topar," they have decided to rebuild their communities anew. To accomplish this task, they have been forced to mate and live not with "deer" but with people from various parts of the globe. In order to reconstitute their communities, they have had to alter the "race" of these foreigners, as the story suggests the Maxakali altered the "sex" of the beast he encountered.

I choose to refer to these survivors of the flood as posttraditional Indians. Posttraditional Indians live in the rubble of tradition. Many, if not most, of their tribal traditions, epistemologies, languages, religions, stories, and philosophies have been crushed by conquest rather than water. José, a forty-four-year-old subsistence farmer and Xacriabá leader I interviewed in 1995, quantified the degree of this fragmentation as having "lost 90 percent of what we were." Thus, the traditions of posttraditional Indians are not complete languages but sometimes only sets of words, not intact religions but only the memory of a sole trickster figure or ceremonial dance, not a comprehensive knowledge of all the vegetation in an area but the understanding of the medicinal use of a few local plants, not a family heirloom but a pottery shard found in an abandoned field or the story of a battle lost.

Salvinho Pataxó, a subsistence farmer and community leader, described the posttraditional condition in the following manner:

> The Indian from the east and northeast is an Indian who has always endured massacres. We have been going through this carnage way before those Indians in the Amazon, who live there in Roraima. The

A Kaxixó field hand for neighboring fazendeiros near Martinho Campos.

invasion of their land, the expropriation of gold, of timber—that's just happening to them today. We've already lost everything. We've already lost the timber. We've already lost the gold. We've already lost our culture. Many lives were destroyed. So we've already lost all of this. But still the people say that we're not real Indians because we wear shorts, sneakers, put a watch on our arms. But in reality, all of this is meaningless. What matters is the root that comes from there [he points to the ground], underneath our community, the root that comes from our ancestors.[48]

As Salvinho Pataxó's comments illustrate, posttraditionality is not simply a question of living in the ruins of tradition, for such an individual might be nontraditional or antitraditional. There is instead another component to posttraditionalism: the meanings that one ascribes to these ruins. To be a posttraditional Indian is to regard these fragments and shadows of tradition as relevant or important, to embrace, privilege, and value them. It is to define one's indigenous ancestral roots as essential to one's identity, to make them the anchor of one's dreams and future, and to work toward their recovery. In Salvinho Pataxó's words:

Our dream is always to fight to defend our *parente* [kin], to unite our community. To try and recover my language, my culture, and my history, this is the future that I'm working toward. This is the future of my dreams.

I use posttraditional, then, as a way both to describe the experience of the dramatic shattering of tradition and to refer to a longing, an orientation, that involves an active attempt to rediscover, recuperate, and reinvigorate that which has been dismembered. That is, posttraditional Indians look to tradition, or what is left of it, as a central point of reference.

As in the following example by Sampaio, conventional academic lexica consider terms such as *assimilated*, *integrated*, or *acculturated* adequate to describe this state of posttraditionality:

After nearly three hundred years of intensive contact with European civilization, without speaking any other language besides Portuguese, with a phenotype which is so highly assimilated (to the point of there being no differences from the surrounding regional population) and given that they are also profoundly wrapped up in the regional economy and culture, configures to make these communities an extreme case of what is classified as "integrated Indians." [49]

I, however, prefer not to use terms like *integrated Indian* or *assimilated Indian* precisely because these categories are already imbued with a number of meanings that I wish to avoid. First, they imply a one-way process of acculturation whereby the culture into which one is assimilated is unaffected. This language presumes that the colonizer is not transformed by the colonized and the process of colonization. It is precisely why Mary Louise Pratt, in her book *Imperial Eyes*, uses the concept "contact zone" to refer to the "colonial frontier."

> By using the term "contact" the aim is to foreground the interactive, improvisational dimensions of colonial encounters so easily ignored or suppressed by diffusionist accounts of conquest and domination. A "contact" perspective emphasizes how subjects are constituted in and by their relations to each other. It treats relations among colonizer and colonized not in terms of separateness or apartheid but in terms of copresence, interaction, interlocking understandings and practices, often within radically asymmetrical relations of power. [50]

The vocabulary of integration is also troublesome because it calls forth the idea that one's desired or inevitable orientation is in the direction of the colonial culture. This, therefore, would be a grave mischaracterization of posttraditional Indians. As I stated above, the individuals in this study whom I classify as posttraditional use tradition as an important referent. Far from desiring integration, eastern Indians are constantly struggling to maintain an ethnic boundary. I repeatedly heard comments like, "The Indians have maintained their customs!" expressed with a mixture of pride and bravado—not the sort of statement and affect one would expect if their orientation were one of assimilation.

Finally, the nomenclature of integration tends to reinscribe essentialist notions of tradition in which "authenticity" only applies to "those Indians who have somehow short-circuited four centuries of history and thus represent a direct line from the pre-Colombian past to the Indian present." [51] This language is laden with the modernist colonial logic that asserts if Indians change, they are contaminated, less authentic, and hence less Indian. As David Frye observes in his study *Indians into Mexicans:*

> Indian cultures . . . are granted two historical paths. . . . They can continue unchanged (in fact or in essence) or they can disappear, be "lost." Mexquitic, which was considered a pueblo de indios for two and half centuries, from its foundation until the mid-nineteenth century, is now a mestizo town. Therefore, the logic goes, it must have lost its Indian culture to the influence of the dominant culture of San Luis. When we think with this contemporary colonial logic (and, I suggest we all do so, in the United States and in Mexico), we seldom concern ourselves with the obvious fact that the non-Indian (Spanish, I suppose), urban culture of San Luis has no more remained unchanged than the rural culture of Mexquitic. . . . [A]ccording to our common perceptions progress (hence, change of any sort) is by definition "European" or, if you prefer, modern: "Indian" is equally identified with tradition. If an Indian pueblo has changed, we think, it can no longer be entirely Indian, since by changing it must have lost something. . . . The "Spanish" culture of urban Mexico, on the other hand, change as it will, cannot be lost to any outside influence — unless, of course, it is to that of the more powerful North American culture (again, always, the vocabulary of power).[52]

My use of tradition, then, is not meant to invoke this notion of static, timeless, primordial Indians positioned in opposition to the most current constructions of modernity. Nor do I wish to imply that posttraditional Indians are inauthentic or less authentic Indians. In other words, I am not suggesting a view of traditional that implies an underlying schema in which real Indians are *only* those who have putatively remained "securely located outside modern societal boundaries" and as such, are able to be considered biologically and culturally "pure." [53]

Mais civilizados (more civilized) is the term most Brazilians — including Indians — use to describe posttraditionality. As Gumercino Pataxó, a fifty-eight-year-old Pentecostal from southern Bahia, explains:

> The Indian was independent. The Indian lived in the forest and didn't depend on a hospital. The doctor of the Indian was God, family, and

the forest. He [sic] didn't use clothes. Everything that he needed was in the forest. But today, unfortunately, the white has taken over everything. So the Indian has become more civilized, but at the same time he has maintained his customs. Because it happens from one generation to the next. My children already live in the rhythm of the white. I have one son who is a mechanic and another that's a truck driver.

It is significant that even though posttraditional Indians often refer to themselves as mais civilizados, they never say that they are "civilized" or "civilized Indians." Instead they were "more civilized," which acknowledges that they have become more like "the civilized," while simultaneously implying that differences persist. I, however, choose not to use the expression "more civilized" because of its colonial or racist connotations.[54]

There is also the question of whether or not an analytic differentiation is even necessary. That is, I could opt to make no distinction at all between posttraditional and traditional Indians. This has been one of the directions taken of late by some scholars. Motivated, at least in part, by an attempt to avoid some of the pitfalls outlined above, a number of Latin Americanists have tended to shy away from such distinctions.[55] Beginning from the premise that ethnicity is "a notion only existing in a context of oppositions and relativities," Indian culture is then reduced to being "inversely derivative of colonial culture rather than continuous with an indigenous past."[56] Indian cultures become analytically undifferentiated. All indigenous cultures, be they traditional or posttraditional, are equalized, for all are an artifact of colonization.

Yet all indigenous cultures are not equal. Colonialism has not been monolithic. While it has been a central facet of indigenous life in eastern Brazil for hundreds of years, it has only indirectly touched a number of peoples living in certain parts of the Amazon. Furthermore, the material and cultural repertoire that Indian communities have had available to negotiate European discoveries has varied greatly. The point is that although colonialism has affected all indigenous peoples, its impact has in no way been uniform.

This truism is reflected in the language and thoughts of Brazilians. As we have seen, laypeople distinguish between more or less civilized and academics talk about integrated Indians. And as we shall discover, the category into which an Indian is put can greatly influence how he or she is seen by Indians and non-Indians, determine whether an Indian is socially recognized or legitimated by the state as authentic, and dramatically impact the options that an Indian has at his or her disposal to construct and reproduce his or her community. These distinctions are, if nothing else, a sociological reality that should not be ignored.

Índios Mesmos

The overwhelming majority of the indigenous people portrayed in this book are officially recognized by the Brazilian government as Indians.[57] Yet few are socially recognized as índios mesmos ("real" Indians). Instead, they are racially positioned as *caboclos* (see glossary), *pretos* (blacks), *brancos* (whites), *morenos* (see glossary), and so forth. For instance, a number of Brazilians who viewed photographs I had taken of these communities remarked remorsefully at how *bem civilizados* (well civilized) they appeared. They were, of course, politely suggesting that these Indians were not Indians. In their minds, I had spent months in Brazil and had only been able to locate faux Indians.

Further proof of how unrecognizable most posttraditional Indians are to non-Indians are these Indians' repeated testimonies as to how they must constantly defend their identity claims. The following passage is taken from an interview with a nineteen–year–old Canoeiro Indian, Karakana, who worked as a nanny in Belo Horizonte and was studying to complete her high school equivalencies in the evenings.

> I'm very proud to be Indian. There are persons who say that I don't appear to be Indian, but I am, period. I fought this one guy because he said that I wasn't Indian. I showed him my documents. He said that they were false. So I got even angrier. [It's] because of my appearance. Lots of times they believe that an Indian has to walk nude. I become insistent with persons who say that I'm not Indian. I tell them that I'm Indian, period. Then suddenly many of them become interested in the history, and I tell it to them. When I get to the end of the story, these people turn around and say that I don't look like an Indian. I get so angry. And then there are other people who say that the Indian is a pig that doesn't like to work. Lots of people be-

lieve this. For example, the other day there was a woman in the house of a friend of mine, and she asked if I was really an Indian because I walked and ate just like she did. She was doubtful of my Indianness.

The reasons individuals such as Karakana are not considered authentic Indians can be attributed to a combination of three factors: the intermixture of indigenous and nonindigenous cultures, phenotype, and caricatures of Indianness.

INTERMIXING

First, as posttraditional Indians themselves note, many of the cultural distinctions that used to exist between themselves and non-Indians have been reduced since European colonization began to influence this region almost five hundred years ago. Thus, as Catholics and *Crentes* (Protestants, usually fundamentalists), speakers of Portuguese, participants in mainstream cultural events such as Carnival, workers and consumers in a "global economy," non-Indian Brazilians are not readily distinguishable by custom from posttraditional Indians, as illustrated in the above quote.

The erosion of distinctions is partly a consequence of the expansion of capitalism and technologies that have lessened cultural variations throughout the world. These forces, coupled with nation building, have also not surprisingly generated a more uniform national culture. Moreover, when individuals interact they affect and influence one another. Indians and non-Indians have thus incorporated and adopted many of one another's tastes, habits, knowledge, values, and so on.[58] For instance, Europeans of centuries past came from societies in which people bathed infrequently, whereas Indians were noted for their cleanliness. As "Yves d'Evreux remarked, [in 1613], '[the Indians] are very careful to keep their bodies free of filth. They bathe their entire bodies very often . . . rubbing all parts with their hands to remove dirt and other filth. The women never fail to comb themselves frequently.' "[59] John Hemming argues that "this is one of the Indians' legacies to modern Brazil, a nation whose people take frequent showers and are never without a comb."[60]

The waning of cultural distinctions is also attributable to the conventions of Indian "exorcism" discussed here in chapter 3. Many facets

(From left to right) Geralda Soares, Ivan Pankararu, Karakana Canoeiro, and Dery-Valdo Pankararu in Contagem, a suburb of Belo Horizonte.

of the cultures of eastern Indians—such as language, religion, architecture, art, and so on—have been ravaged by massacres, economic coercion, forced assimilation, and religious crusades. Consequently, as I have already stated, all that remains of many tribal traditions are cultural shards and ruins.

PHENOTYPES

A second reason that eastern Indians are unrecognizable as such is because most Brazilians subcribe to certain tenets of "racialisms" developed by nineteenth-century scientists such as Samuel Morton, Johann Blumenbach, Robert Knox, and Josiah Nott.[61] These men of science promulgated the notion that there were three to five racial types. Morton identified "five different races" based on putative distinctions in "cranium capacities": Caucasian, Mongolian, Malay, American, and Ethiopian.[62] These races were considered to be culturally as well as biologically distinct because biology, in their opinion, determined culture. "Race is everything," wrote Knox, "literature, science, art, etc.—in a word, civilization depends on it."[63] He then went on to contend that since Indians are "destined by the nature of their race to run, like all

A Crente Pataxó with Oswaldo Pataxó in aldeia Guarani.

other animals, a certain limited course of existence, it matters little how their extinction is brought about." [64] Although most Brazilians would probably reject the genocidal conclusions and justifications purported by these scholars, they would still concur with their central premise that Indianness is a question of blood.[65]

More specifically, most Brazilians are taught and come to believe that an Indian is one who has "pureblood." For example, children are instructed in school that an individual who has both European and Indian blood is a *mameluco*, whereas someone with African and Indian blood is a *cafuso*. These definitions are deemed official facts that must be committed to memory. Thus when asked, "What is the race of a person who is the descendant of an African and an Indian?" most Brazilians will struggle to recall the racial multiplication tables they were supposed to have memorized in school. If they fail to remember the "correct" answer, they frequently offer an embarrassed "*esquecí*" ("I forget").

In everyday life, however, most Brazilians regard a mameluco as either a white or moreno (a "dark-skinned white," in this case). And cafusos are typically considered either blacks, mulattoes, or morenos (in this context, a "light-skinned black"). The point is that most "mixed bloods" of indigenous descent do not exhibit the somatic features associated with Indianness and so are rarely recognized as Indian.[66] This creates problems for eastern Indians since most of them are *mestizos* (that is, of indigenous, African, and European descent). As Cleonice Pankararu, a twenty-four-year-old nurse in 1995, says,

> There's been a mixture of the two groups: Indians and blacks. My race was Pankararu when they were herded onto the reservation. At that time lots of Indians fled, and when they fled they encountered other races. Also a lot of black slaves came to our communities fleeing. And they stayed with us, and with this there was a lot of mixing. But the Pankararu race continues.[67]

José Xacriabá, the forty-four-year-old farmer who discussed how the Xacriabá had lost most of their culture also expresses concern over misconceptions about his identity due to phenotype.

> I'm not recognized as Indian by people who don't know me as Indian because I'm very mixed with *negro*. I have dry hair, so I'm already very mixed. I already have curlier hair, so I need to show a document to be recognized.

Given the degree to which Indianness is somatically constructed, mestizos who self-identify as Indian tend not to be viewed as índios mesmos by non-Indians.

CARICATURES

The third reason eastern Indians are not perceived as "real" is because most notions of what constitutes Indianness are caricatures or simulations.

> How ironic that the most secure simulations [of Indianness] are unreal sensations, and become the real without a referent to an actual tribal remembrance. Tribal realities are superseded by simulations of the unreal, and tribal wisdom is weakened by those imitations, however sincere.[68]

One example of these caricatures is the binary framework still used to categorize, homogenize, and define Indianness. Clearly echoing nineteenth-century models of the so-called primitive, a number of contemporary literary scholars continue to argue that Indians are "more communal" or "less individualistic" than "Westerners." Arnold Krupat, for one, writes that Indians have a sense of self that

> would seem to be less attracted to introspection, integration, expansion, or fulfillment than the Western self appears to be. [Indians] would seem relatively uninterested in such things as the "I-am-Me" experience, and a sense of uniqueness or individuality. More positively, one might perhaps instantiate an I-am-We experience as descriptive of the Native sense of self, where such a phrase indicated that I understand myself as a self only in relation to the coherent and bounded whole of which I am part.[69]

One of the many problems with employing such notions to describe and define Indian communities and subjectivities is that they tend to bear so little connection to either past or contemporary tribal realities. In short, these models are built on extremely suspect data. For instance, David Brumble attempts to make the same argument as Krupat regarding "Indian" and "Western" thinking, utilizing as proof a two-page letter by Albert Hensley (a Winnebago) in the nineteenth century to the white superintendent of his daughter's Indian boarding school. Hensley's letter, written in a context of highly unequal power relations to a director of a colonial institution who was in a position to significantly affect his daughter's life, is used to demonstrate that Indians have no "unified idea of [themselves] as an individual."[70] After having illustrated "the Indian sense of self" with Hensley's letter, Brumble then quickly travels to the other end of the continuum of colonial/racial power—white, elite, male intellectuals in Washington, D.C., and Paris —in search of an example for the modern/Western pole of his binary.

> [John] Adams and [Jean-Jacques] Rousseau are typical of modern autobiographers, then, in that they are aware of themselves as individuals, and in their complex awareness that they might have been otherwise. On the other hand, an Indian living in the old way had little sense of an individual self apart from the tribe or clan, little sense that he [sic] might have been a different self had he been born in a different lodge, or had he, say, spent more time learning about plants and less time hunting.[71]

As if the above were not enough to underscore the disconnection between simulated ideas of the native and tribal realities, the absurdity of this binary is further evidenced by how effortlessly one could turn the argument on its head. Take a practice such as naming. Almost all known Indian communities have names, be they sacred or nicknames, that are extremely specific to the particular individual. As such, naming in indigenous communities is highly personalized and individualized. So-called Western names, in contrast, are neither distinctive nor unique. Most non-Indian Brazilians have names such as Maria, João, Regina, José, and so forth. If one were so inclined, then, one could simply reverse the binary and maintain just as effectively that Westerners are marked by their lack of individuality and like-mindedness.

The predicament, however, is not that most of the categorizations of Indians are erroneous but that these simulations are often used to prove the inferiority of Indians and/or to measure the degree of an individual's Indianness. It is a cruel irony indeed that índios mesmos are simulations of Indiannesses that have no connection to tribal realities. As I will discuss in chapter 7, such faux Indians are the romanticized savages of colonial nostalgia; they are the projections of what non-Indians believe posttraditional Indians are not, or what they should ideally become. The only índios mesmos, in the minds of most Brazilians, are savages frozen in a fictive past, somehow unaffected by the centuries of slavery, colonization, war, forced assimilation, friendships, religious crusades, technological change, intermarriage, and disease that followed the arrival of Europeans and Africans to the Americas.

In the next chapter, I discuss how I came to this project via my study of race and racism in a small town in rural Rio de Janeiro. I also detail a number of the methodological issues that underlie my empirical findings and analyses. In chapter 3, I begin to formulate a response to one of the central questions of this book: Why has there been a sudden change in the direction of racial imaginings? The focus in this chapter is on the role of the state in Indian formation. I call into question a popular version of the "racial huckster" thesis, which purports that individuals are gravitating toward Indian identities due to state-provided material incentives. Instead, I identify equally compelling disincentives such as state-nurtured terrorism and forced acculturation. The emphasis of chapter 4 is on the material costs and benefits of being Indian as compared to being a mestizo of a similar class. I find that except for land, popular theories of "material incentives for being Indian" do not satisfactorily explain this demographic shift. In chapter 5, I argue for a strong causal relationship between nongovernmental organizations and Indian resurgence. I also underscore how such a relationship in no way inauthenticates these communities' claims to Indianness, although this has been alleged by many opponents of Indians.

Chapter 6, is the first of two chapters that analyze the linkages between the growing indigenous population and the discursive terrain. Here the emphasis is placed on how posttraditional Indians have constructed alternative notions of Indianness and how these reimaginings may be key factors behind an indigenous resurgence. In chapter 7, I move to an examination of the role of academics, in particular anthropologists. I map out how changing conceptualizations of ethnicity in the 1960s have helped to spawn expanded definitions of Indianness, concomitantly creating an ideological and institutional space for certain communities to redefine themselves as Indian—if they so choose.

In the final chapter, I explore whether this trend toward being Indian has consequences for the broader politics of race in Brazil. The central question I investigate is whether Indian subjectivities are entwined with a different racial politic. Surprisingly, given that scholars of race have all but ignored Indians, I find that Indians are proving to have much more success in upsetting white supremacy than other racial subalterns.

I wish to underscore that this book represents more than a search to discover why the centuries-long trend of Indians becoming non-Indians has seemingly come to a halt. This book is about more than dismantling the prison of racism that slavery and conquest have built throughout the hemisphere. Both concerns, however, serve to contextualize the story of what it means to be a posttraditional Indian in eastern Brazil. As such, this study also offers documentation of the recent histories of posttraditional Indians, exploring the issues and challenges they confront in contemporary Brazil. It is an analysis of how non-Indians imagine Indianness, and how posttraditional Indians negotiate these imaginings. As Domíngos Pataxó, a forty-four-year-old government employee, says below, this book is a testimonial put forth in the hopes of creating a more just Brazil in the only way possible: by acknowledging and examining, rather than denying or ignoring, Brazilian history and the society it has birthed.

> We just want the power to be able to resolve our lives just as whites want to be able to control their lives. There are people who still come to kill off the rest of the Indians. We talk in the hopes that it will help to explain how it is for Indians living in Brazil today without any justice and only a little piece of land in a country so large, in a country that once was ours and now it's a place where the Indian has no justice, no means of being independent, of being able to resolve our own problems. If we were equal to whites, more powerful, we wouldn't let anyone take control. . . . They have taken everything. Today it's no longer our country. We don't have anything . . . we don't even have the means of solving our own problems. They have massacred the Indians, killed the whole world. So we appreciate the opportunity to be able to talk with people who come to see how the Indian really is. If we didn't do this, tomorrow or the day after they could come and finish us all off, and then there wouldn't even be any records about what that race of Indians was like who once ruled the whole country.[72]

2. Methodological Reflections

Racial subalterns in Brazil, rather than mistrusting a white researcher, may instead be more likely to identify with them. — France Winddance Twine, *Racing Research, Researching Race*

Until recently, most studies of Brazilian Indians — especially those done by non-Brazilians — began with a stylized form of arrival story. The study would open in a city in Brazil, usually Rio de Janeiro or São Paulo, juxtaposing it to the even more "modern" location (say, New York) that the researcher had just left. The remainder of the introduction would be spent detailing the long, arduous journey — "from modern metropole to primitive hinterland" — that the ethnographer had to negotiate to arrive at the research site.[1] The researcher's geographic movement away from "modern" spaces demonstrated how far removed he or she was from "civilization," thereby "proving" the authenticity of the Indians under study.[2]

My own entrée into so-called Indian country proceeded in much the opposite direction: from rural to urban Brazil. During the first half of 1992, I had been conducting ethnographic research with my partner, France Winddance Twine, in a small town, Vasalia (a pseudonym), situated in the coffee-growing highlands of northwestern Rio de Janeiro near the borders of Minas Gerais and Espírito Santo.[3] In July 1992, seven months after I had first arrived in Brazil, the International Environmental Summit was held in Rio de Janeiro. Given the summit's significance and how relatively close we were to the city (approximately seven hours by bus), we decided to venture out from *o interior* to the Brazilian metropolis to attend.[4]

When we attempted to enter the indigenous area to hear that day's discussions, we were informed that only reporters and indigenous people were allowed in. Winddance, not missing a beat, told them that she

Cleonice Pankararu in aldeia Apukaré.

was an American Indian and therefore should be permitted entrance. Given that phenotypically she is considered *negra* or *mulata* in Brazil, the guards did not believe her. They told her that she would have to speak with the coordinator, and we were escorted in to meet with Ed Burnstick (a Cree from Canada). Winddance explained that she was an enrolled member of the Muskogee nation. He hesitated for a moment and then, while handing us both entrance passes, affected a western drawl, "Well, I guess you just can't tell anymore who's an Indian."

It was in the indigenous tent that I met and eventually befriended two of the delegates representing indigenous communities in eastern Brazil—Cleonice Pankararu and Puhuí Pataxó. During our first few conversations, I was struck by how in terms of phenotype, they physically resembled many of the individuals we had interviewed in Vasalia, yet their subjectivities were notably different from the Vasalians. For example, Vasalians maintained a deep conviction that Brazil, or at least the community in which they resided, was free of racism despite overwhelming evidence to the contrary.[5] Cleonice and Puhuí, in contrast, spoke freely and comfortably about racism in Brazil. Furthermore, they seemed to have distinct interpretative frameworks from Vasalians when questioned about such matters as Brazilian history, definitions of racism, and personal genealogies. Unlike Vasalians, for instance, Cleonice and Puhuí did not tell of family histories free of racism, nor did they emphasize their white ancestors.

Needless to say, I became extremely curious about their identities and consciousness. I wanted to know why their thoughts on a range of matters seemed so remarkably different from the Vasalians I knew. I was also interested in discovering whether Cleonice and Puhuí were representative of their communities. Discussing my observations with them, I asked if it would be possible to spend some time in their communities and interview others there about their lives. They seemed enthusiastic about the prospect of my coming to conduct research and graciously extended an open invitation, which I was able to accept two and half years later.

Eastern Indians

In January 1995, I returned to Brazil hoping to reevaluate my initial impressions of Cleonice and Puhuí, and to ascertain, if possible, how typical they were of the other indigenous people in their region. As well, if there were indeed substantive differences between Indians and non-Indians in terms of racialized discourses, symbolic orders, and practices, I wanted to map the specificities of these distinctions and explore their potential consequences for Brazilian society—aims that eventually became the focus of this book.

I spent most of 1995 in the rural and urban areas of Minas Gerais and Espírito Santo.[6] According to official geographic demarcations, these states belong to the region of southeastern Brazil, which also includes the states of Rio de Janeiro and São Paulo. Given that the Indians who were interviewed for this book resided (or had resided) in Minas Gerais, the extreme southern tip of Bahia, or Espírito Santo, and that I had done some previous research in Rio de Janeiro, I originally conceived of this project as a study of "southeastern Indians." I even attempted to establish contact with Indians in the city of São Paulo. For example, I tried without success to visit the Pankararu who live in the favela Real Parque adjacent to Morumbi, one of the wealthiest neighborhoods in São Paulo.[7]

After some time, however, I realized that the Indians in Minas Gerais and Espírito Santo did not define themselves in terms of conventional regional divisions. Rather than being southeastern Indians, they saw and referred to themselves as *eastern* Indians. In addition, they clearly felt more closely allied with northeastern Indians than with those in São Paulo and Rio de Janeiro. For example, the regional organizations to which eastern Indians belonged and the conferences they attended usually included the Indians of the northeast, but rarely those from São Paulo or Rio de Janeiro.[8] Taking my cue from their regional categories, then—coupled with a number of logistical issues, such as the feasibility of studying *all* of southeastern Brazil—I came to focus this project on analysis of eastern Indians.

Race in the Field

It is difficult to overstate the degree of privilege afforded to whites in Brazil. As numerous qualitative and quantitative researchers have documented, whiteness is closely associated with descriptions such as "attractive," "modern," "intelligent," "valued," and the like. To take but one example, Vera Moreira Figueira discovered in interviews with 204 *Cariocas* (city of Rio de Janeiro residents) of color that "positive qualities are liberally attributed to whites a high percentage of the time." In 75 percent of the cases, she found that whiteness was linked to words like "friend," "studious," "intelligence," "beauty," and "wealth." Blacks, in contrast, were associated with terms such as "jackass," "pig," and "thief."[9]

Such a favorable symbolic field offers white researchers several methodological advantages.[10] It can enhance, for instance, an ethnographer's access to individuals or communities because her or his credentials and intentions as a researcher are more likely to be taken seriously.[11] Moreover, given the prestige hierarchies in which whiteness is valorized, Brazilians—including Brazilians of color—sometimes prefer to be interviewed by whites.[12] In Vasalia, it was my experience that non-Indian Brazilians were often more amenable to being interviewed by me, a white North American, rather than my research partner, a U.S. black who, as I mentioned, is also enrolled in the Muskogee nation.[13]

In general, as compared to my experiences interviewing whites, blacks, and pardos, I felt that my whiteness presented a greater handi-

The author grinding coffee in aldeia Guarani.

cap with eastern Indians because, as I detail in chapters 6 and 8, most of them operate with symbolic orders that privilege Indianness over whiteness.[14] While whiteness may take neutral and sometimes negative connotations for these Indians, it certainly does not acquire positive ones. In turn, a white researcher cannot depend on having the same level of symbolic capital in obtaining access to Indian interviewees. I am fairly certain that had I been coded as Indian, in some cases it would not have taken as long for me to build the degree of rapport required for a successful interview. In a few of the interviews where I failed in my efforts to move beyond a superficial level, I believe that the interviewees would have been less guarded had I been considered a racial insider.[15]

Having mentioned that my racial position may not have been the optimal one for facilitating my research within Indian communities, I want to add that my project was also met with widespread enthusiasm. For instance, toward the end of an interview, as a way of bringing the discussion to a close, I would often ask what someone thought about the questions I had posed, and why they had agreed to share their stories, experiences, and perspectives with me. One of the more frequent responses I received was that the interviewee had decided to take a risk and participate in this project because of its potential to serve an antiracist/anticolonial function. Individuals expressed the hope that their words might "raise consciousness," thereby weakening traditional practices of domination. Cleonice Pankararu's comments were typical of this sentiment.

> I think that Brazilians should have a consciousness of what happened because the majority of Brazilians don't know what happened, how colonization occurred. They believe that colonization was something good—growth occurred, progress took place—something that helped a lot. But they don't realize what happened, for instance, when Paulo Afonso made the electric dam. He had to murder lots of Indians. To make the Trans-Amazon highway, how many Indians were killed? They think that these are good things, necessary things, but no one realizes what was done, how many were killed. They need to recognize this. If they have consciousness of all this, perhaps it could help avoid some future massacres. And this would be a very good thing.

Another commonly cited motive for taking part in this project was linked to the fact that eastern Indians tend to feel invisible. Residing in a region that has been declared Indianless, and because most of them do not fit the image of what an Indian is, eastern Indians have received little media attention—as compared to Indians in the Amazon region, for example. Moreover, and probably for similar reasons, virtually no academic research has focused on these communities. Not surprisingly, then, a number of eastern Indians believed that speaking with me might counter this invisibility and make known their opinions. That is, many who participated in this project felt that by documenting and telling me about their lives and struggles, they could make their existence known as well as leave a record of "their side of the story" for posterity.

The Research Sites

I decided early on to explore a few indigenous communities in-depth, rather than spend a short amount of time in a number of aldeias. Given my decision, I strove to select aldeias that were as varied as possible. Aldeia Guarani is located a few miles outside the small town of Carmésia in a region that reminded me of Vasalia because of its coffee production history, climate (humid and cool in the winter), and deforested, knob-hilled topography. The local economy is based primarily on agricultural production and some tourism from Belo Horizonte, which is approximately five hours away by bus (200 km). The aldeia is nestled in a narrow, wooded valley that in the nineteenth and early twentieth centuries had been a prosperous coffee plantation with numerous slaves. When the landholder died without an heir, the estate became the property of the state of Minas Gerais. In the 1970s, FUNAI was given control of the land, eventually converting it into the Center for the Reeducation of Rebellious and Disobedient Indians — that is, an indigenous penal colony for political prisoners.[16] In the 1980s, with no lands to return to, the former prisoners fought successfully to have the area converted into an indigenous reserve. Thus, most of the residents of Guarani are descendants of the former prisoners or were invited to the reserve by the families of these prisoners.

Because the prisoners were brought from various indigenous communities throughout eastern and northeastern Brazil, Guarani (population 250) was the most ethnically heterogeneous of the aldeais I visited. When I was there, the Pataxó and Krenak were the most numerous. The Krenak have since succeeded in getting the courts to return some of their land. Consequently, many of the Krenak have left during the past two years to live on their reserve near the Doce River. The other tribes represented at Guarani include the Pankararu, Kaingang, Maxakali, and Guarani.

The fact that Guarani was once a major plantation that had, like all *fazendas*, been made possible by the appropriation of Indian lands and bodies, gave it the atmosphere of a ghost town. The former "big house," which at one time overlooked the nucleus (*sede*) of the fazenda from its elevated perch, has since been reduced to its foundations where a few stray animals like to graze during the day and, according to some of the residents, the screams of dead slaves can sometimes be heard at night. Although dilapidated, many of the plantation edifices still serve as homes for the residents of Guarani. These buildings line the narrow road that cuts through the heart of the aldeia and connects one mile to the south with the road that goes to Carmésia and in the other direction dead-ends in the hills approximately two miles to the north. Some of the older structures were beyond repair, so villagers have destroyed them

Aruara and Valdi Pataxó, the parents of Puhuí, are the couple with whom I lived in aldeia Guarani. Like the other Pataxó, they had been driven out of southern Bahia by anti-Indian violence and the appropriation of their lands. In this picture, they have just purchased two chickens from a traveling vendor to prepare a special meal for me.

A Guarani Indian, married to a Krenak, preparing for an all-night hunting excursion in the forests of aldeia Guarani.

Ritual cabana and satellite dish, aldeia Guarani. In the foreground are some of the ruins from the former plantation.

and built new ones in their place — sometimes using a standing wall, the old foundation, or the materials from the former structure. Several new homes have cropped up beyond the bounds of the original sede in both directions along the aldeia's road. The aldeia, then, is concentrated in terms of its population and the number of buildings in the nucleus of the former fazenda, but the settlement density has been stretched out since its days as a plantation.

The village also consists of a Pataxó ritual cabana, communal garden, soccer field, dried-up lagoon (a failed attempt at creating a fish farm), and *casa de artesenato* (house of arts and crafts), situated near the former big house. The artesenato house, which was just being completed when I was there, serves as an artistic workshop as well as a place to display and sell arts and crafts to visiting tourists.

On the old center square (*terreiro*) of the former fazenda stands the massive, two-story administration building from the former plantation along with two newer structures built in the past thirty years: a schoolhouse and the former Catholic Church, now home to a few families who had to leave their houses because they had deteriorated to the point of being dangerous. When fazenda Guarani was a penal colony, the main

Washing laundry beside the administrative building in aldeia Guarani.

building was used as a jail and center for indigenous "reeducation." It is now where the FUNAI administration for the aldeia is located; as well, the FUNAI administrator, a Krenak, lives with his family on the second floor.

At the time of my study, most people in the sede of the aldeia had electricity and about half had televisions—the main form of nightly entertainment. Three homes had satellite dishes. Only a few homes had running water, and of these, only two had hot water. Women cooked meals on woodstoves and washed clothes by hand in a pool near the creek that ran alongside the administrative building. Only one resident owned a car, and that was in poor repair. In fact, the automobile was so noisy that villagers could hear it five minutes before it arrived and so referred to it as "the plane" ("o avião").

THE APUKARÉ ALDEIA

The Pankararu aldeia, named Apukaré, was built on a parcel of land that an Italian bishop, who resides in the neighboring town of Araçuaí, donated to the Pankararu in 1994. The land is in the municipality of Coronel Murta, which the Indians sometimes sarcastically refer to as Coronel Morto (Colonel Death), in part because he was an infamous

Te Pataxó washing dishes in the pond behind the home where I resided.

Cleide Pankararu bathing her youngest son, Wayrokrã, in aldeia Apukaré. Helping are his brother, Bany-Nari, and Krenak cousin, Iara (squatting).

Cleide Pankararu and Wayrokrã after his bath.

Indian slaver. Situated in the Jequitinhonha Valley in northeastern Minas Gerais, the terrain is an expansive, semidesert landscape more similar to the Brazilian *sertão* (arid wilderness) than the moister, cooler highlands. The local economy—based on ranching, mining, agriculture, and a few eucalyptus plantations—is weak. In fact, the valley is considered one of the poorest regions in Brazil, and as a result, many young men leave in search of employment elsewhere. *Vaqueiros* (cowboys), who speak with a Bahian accent, are plentiful, and many of them don leather hats similar to but much smaller in circumference than U.S. cowboy hats. There is also a vibrant organic arts culture in this region that includes wood carvers, songwriters, sculptors, painters, and others. A certain religious fervor was articulated in a manner that reminded me more of medieval Catholicism than late-twentieth-century evangelicalism; for example, week-long processions to particular holy sites replete with displays of self-flagellation were more evident than the Protestant churches and born-again worshipers that I frequently encountered in Vasalia, aldeia Guarani, and the working-class neighborhoods in Rio de Janeiro and Belo Horizonte.

During the bulk of my stay at Apukaré, the homes of the Pankararu had yet to be constructed; thus, I lived with the four founding families

Some days in aldeia Apukaré, we would spend hours playing in this river—badly polluted by chemicals used in mining and the lack of a sewage system in the upstream town (Coronel Murta). (From left to right) Dimas Pataxó, Paulo Pankararu, Ivan Pankararu, César Pataxó, and Dery-Valdo Pankararu.

in a small, run-down house that had been abandoned by a local cowboy. The house, surrounded by a cornfield when I arrived, sat on a hill on the banks of a small river where the young men of the village spent many hours daily swimming and relaxing. The home had no amenities except for a *fugão* (woodstove). Evenings were like large slumber parties in which the older people would sometimes tell stories, and we would play games by candlelight, talk about the day's events, and tease one another. Because there was no electricity to dim the night skies and it was quite arid, we would on occasion sit outside and observe the stars. For someone like myself from a more temperate climate, the seasons seemed reversed. During the summer, the vegetation would turn completely brown from the intense heat (in the mid-nineties) and lack of rain. The terrain returned to green in the winter, and a number of tarantulas and scorpions surfaced—a constant concern for parents since their sting can be lethal for children. A small irrigation system, set up while I was there, provided enough moisture to enable people to grow bananas, melon, sweet potatoes, manioc, corn, sugarcane, pumpkin, beans, and other things. Even though the living quarters were tight, with many people having to sleep on the concrete floors, I was fortunate to be there at that time; it provided me with an opportunity to observe an aldeia being created from scratch and witness its impact on the surrounding community.

THE KAXIXÓ COMMUNITY

The other indigenous community I visited was that of the Kaxixó. Their land is located on the Pará River, one of the headwaters of the São Francisco River about five hours west of Belo Horizonte by bus (160 km). The terrain in this region is more savannalike: drier than the Guarani region, but not nearly as arid and treeless as the Jequitinhonha Valley. Martinho Campos is the name of both the county and nearest town, separated from the aldeia by a wide, bridgeless river and approximately ten miles of poorly maintained dirt roads.

The community is clustered on top of one of many gradually elevated hills, which seemed to have been created through erosion rather than by glaciers or the collision of the earth's templates. Most of the Kaxixó, who spoke with a Paulista accent, earned less than the minimum wage (one hundred U.S. dollars per month) working as field hands or *empregadas* (servants) for the local landholders, laboring on corporate eucalyptus plantations, or burning wood to make charcoal. At the center of the aldeia there was a general store, pool hall, pay phone, Catholic Church, and primary school; new housing appeared in what seemed to be randomly chosen locations.

Many of the Kaxixó did not live in the center of the community but were instead dispersed over a fairly large territory, oftentimes living adjacent to the land of the large landholders for whom they worked. I stayed in one of the homes located outside the center of the community. Like most of the other houses on the aldeia, it had no running water or electricity. The family I stayed with raised some livestock; most of their staples were purchased at the general store, and all the cooking was done on the fugão. Their home, bordering the property of one of the landholders with whom the Kaxixó had had conflicts, was separated from the village center by about an hour's walk. If the moonlight was dim, however, the hike could take much longer because care must be taken to avoid stepping on a snake. We also had to cross through part

Antonieta Francisca da Silva, the grandmother of Jerry Kaxixó, cleaning beans in front of their home—the residence where I stayed while in the Kaxixó community.

of the landholder's property that included an area, the Kaxixó told me, where slaves had once been punished, tortured, and killed.

Kaxixó was the only aldeia I visited that was not recognized by the government. Moreover, unlike the other two aldeias, this community was encountering intense, sometimes violent opposition from local fazendeiros. Part of the reason for the antagonism had to do with the fact that landholders stood to lose some of their property if the Kaxixó were recognized as Indian. This would also usurp some of their labor, they feared, because the Kaxixó would not be as dependent on them for a livelihood, and thus, could negotiate more effectively their salary and working conditions. Then, too, the landholders in the region were accustomed to controlling the Kaxixó and other peasants—which included a *quilombo*—with an iron fist.[17] As such, unlike the other aldeias I visited, a palpable fear of violence seemed to weigh on people, influencing many of their decisions, and inhibiting their conversations with me and one another.

BELO HORIZONTE

My final principal research site was a working-class neighborhood in Belo Horizonte, where most of the people I met worked as telephone operators, sales clerks, low-paid factory workers, mechanics, maids, beauticians, evening security guards, and so on. Most adults earned between $200 and $400 per month. The majority had health care, but it was of substandard quality. Workers could nonetheless earn more there than in the countryside, and more important, the educational opportunities, although still dismal, were better than in the rural parts of the state.

Situated about one hour by bus from the city center, this residential community was little different in appearance from other working-class neighborhoods I have visited in major metropolitan areas of Brazil. Because mortgages are not available to average citizens, houses have to be built gradually rather than on credit. As a result, throughout the community, homes seemed to be perpetually "in progress." Most structures were not visible from the street since houses were defended by cement walls with broken glass lining the tops. Watchdogs prowled the inner courtyards as a second line of defense. Consequently, the streets felt like roofless tunnels, occasionally broken up by a storefront or small bars.

Even though running water, gas, and electricity were commonplace, telephones were still a rarity. As on the reserves, except for the owner of "the plane," no one I met owned a car. Sewage was dumped untreated into what must have been a creek at one time. The smells and smoke of burning rubbish often saturated the air, and the treeless streets were littered with candy wrappers, empty cigarette cartons, dog feces, and other assorted trash.

On the main arteries, there were various kinds of stores that served the community: bakeries, stationers' shops, and small groceries. There were also numerous bars and churches, primarily Evangelical Protestant. In total, there were six indigenous households in this neighborhood—one Maxakali, one Pataxó, and four Xacriabá. I did not live in any of these homes but instead stayed in nearby Contagem, approximately ten minutes distance by taxi, yet sixty minutes by bus (my principal means of transportation) because of its circuitous route.

The Research Parameters

Although television, newspapers, magazines, and school textbooks —as well as academic, government and nongovernment literature— served as data for this book, my primary sources of information were my field notes and the transcripts from the formal interviews I conducted with 122 individuals (50 Indians and 72 non-Indians).[18] All of the interviews were tape-recorded in a private setting and structured around an interview schedule. Appendix A is the schedule I used for the 1995 and 1997 interviews, and appendix B is the exemplar that was used during the two trips to Vasalia in 1992 and 1994. Although everyone was asked the same general set of questions, the emphasis and particular direction of the interview varied from person to person.[19]

My technique for selecting interviewees in a given community was quota sampling. I would actively attempt to interview individuals who fit certain categories, such as tribe, color, age, urban/rural, education, class, gender, and religion. Class diversity was difficult to achieve in the Indian subsample because I met only one Indian who could be considered middle class. I also persistently sought to interview those who were less accessible and amenable to being interviewed. Furthermore, I actively searched for individuals who seemed as if they might present a different perspective than those persons whom I had already interviewed, or whose experiences might be a departure from a particular idea or theory that was emerging from my findings.

Since my method of sampling was nonprobability, I cannot claim that either sample, the Indian or non-Indian, is representative. I am, however, much more certain about the generalizability of my findings regarding non-Indians because of how closely they resonate with the literature on this population. In other words, my observations concerning how non-Indians think about race and Indianness differ little from those of other scholars. With respect to Indians, I am much less sure that my results are representative. I did not have the sense that my sample was atypical or unusual for the eastern Indian population; nonetheless, I cannot be certain about the generalizability of these findings for the simple reason that there is no literature within which to situate my data and conclusions. That question, then, will have to remain unanswered until further research is conducted with Indians in eastern Brazil.

3. The State of Indian Exorcism

Let us seek to fulfill the objectives fixed by President Geisel, so that, through concentrated work among various Ministries, within ten years, we can reduce to 20,000 the 220,000 Indians existing today in Brazil, and within thirty years, all of them shall be duly integrated into the national society. —Rangel Reis, Minister of the Interior, 1976

I returned to the Guarani aldeia from the United States for a brief visit in September 1997. While I was there, a number of Pataxó excitedly told me about "a researcher from your country named Oscar" who had spent a few weeks on the aldeia earlier that year. They asked me if I knew him, explaining what a wonderful person he was and how he had interviewed a number of elderly people about their knowledge of the medicinal uses of various plants. When I visited Belo Horizonte, one hundred and twenty miles southeast of the Guarani aldeia, I asked other colleagues if they knew of Oscar, somewhat concerned that he might be a bioprospector for a pharmaceutical company. I hoped instead that he was a fellow academic. Given how few scholars have conducted research with Indians in eastern Brazil, I was enthusiastic about the possibility of sharing insights and observations with a colleague who had visited one of the communities I had studied.

I eventually discovered that Oscar was an anthropologist who is not from the United States after all but from Italy. He was a visiting professor at the Federal University of Minas Gerais. I called to make arrangements to see him, and the day of our meeting, I took along my dissertation in hopes that Oscar would find time to read it and offer some feedback. While a photocopy of the manuscript was being made, Oscar and I went for a *cafezinho*. He asked me about my conclusions on the subject of indigenous resurgence in eastern Brazil. In a tone that implied he was merely stating the obvious, he went on to add, "Most of them are not real Indians. That's what everyone here thinks. They are just identifying as Indians for instrumental reasons. By 'being Indian' they receive vaccinations, ambulance service, and general health care—things they couldn't otherwise get."

Oscar was voicing what I refer to as the "racial huckster thesis" of Indian formation. The logic is straightforward: many individuals are increasingly asserting Indian identity not because they are in fact Indians but because there are benefits to be had, and it is generally suggested that the benefits are material in nature. Although this analysis may not be as widely shared as Oscar claimed, it is one that some academics and many laypeople hold. Indeed, it has proven to be a conventional thesis about so-called Indianization not only in Brazil but in other national contexts as well.[1] Sharlotte Neely characterized a subsection of the Cherokee community in North Carolina in a similar manner, as illustrated in this passage:

> Legally the residents of Tomotla are Indians; physically they mostly look white. [T]hey can choose whether to be Indian or white. This phenomenon has . . . much to do with economics. Tomotla is in a position to ask itself, is there more advantage to being Indian or white? Depending on the times and situation, either identity can be more to its advantage. At present, there is a continuing continent-wide movement for the improvement of Native American status and self-image. And, locally, there are more economic advantages to being Indian: tribal-supported employment, and health, educational, and housing opportunities. The Tomotla community has found a way to tap these opportunities by asserting its Indian identity and seeking and acquiring power within tribal government.[2]

Neely, like others who subscribe to this racial huckster theory, argues that the contemporary Mayme Natachees are racial accountants who are merely reimagining themselves as Indian for material gain. More and more individuals are gravitating toward Indian identities, these social analysts allege, because they can now "tap" into educational, health, housing, and employment opportunities. In other words, "that dim native heritage" has increasingly become "a fascination and a cause" principally (if not exclusively) for instrumental reasons.[3]

One of the shortcomings of this rational choice model of human action is that it assumes individual ontologies that are overly determined by market logics. It presumes a common sense like the one that underpinned Urcenio Bucelli's confused response to the terror sweeping through the Putamayo region of Colombia in the early twentieth century. After seeing "drunken company officials dousing Indians in kerosene and burning them alive during a birthday party," Bucelli was at a loss as to how to account for these atrocities. In bewilderment he exclaimed, "These Indians bring in so much rubber but still they are killed!" as if the murders would have been comprehensible had the Indians not been a source of profit.[4] But, as Michael Taussig observes, the brutality of colonization cannot be satisfactorily squeezed into the official logic of political economy.[5] In Taussig's words, the attempt to create "capitalist sense from the raw material of the terrible cruelty meted out to the Indians" serves to reinscribe, if not naturalize, the rationality of business.

> This cost-accounting way of building sense presuppose[s] and hence reinforce[s] as eternal verities the notions of market pressure, the capital-logic of commodities, and the rationality of business. Thus even in blaming the market, its mode of appropriating reality and creating intelligibility [is] upheld.[6]

Just as Taussig maintains that the terror of the Putamayo cannot be adequately explained via a "market-price way of understanding social events," I contend that it is overly simplistic to reduce racial formation to the rationality of business.[7] To assume that individuals select racial identities in the same manner that they might balance their financial accounts can only provide a shallow knowledge of Indian resurgence. This does *not* therefore mean that a cost-benefit analysis holds no explanatory value; it does suggest, though, that a market-rational-based model is likely to yield only a limited picture of Indianization. Yet this cost-accounting way of making sense of Indian identity has appropriated reality to such a degree that it is difficult to counter it. Increasingly, alternative symbolic orders and moral codes have been rendered implausible, even invisible, as the logic of capital gains strength.

Before outlining and analyzing the many factors behind Indianization that fall outside the purview of capitalist sense making, I will address the concerns of racial huckster theorists directly. What are the advantages and disadvantages of being Indian, and how do they compare to those asserting non-Indian identities? Is there any truth, however limited, to the claim that a great number of individuals are adopting Indian identities like racial accountants? Might there be linkages between the putative benefits of Indianness and the recent Indian resurgence?

The Race-Making State: Carrots or Sticks?

Those who make the racial huckster contention often imply that the state and its role, or changing role, in shaping material incentives is largely responsible for Indianization. Ironically, it was Pierre van den Berghe, one of the foremost proponents of a biological basis to racial formation, who was one of the first scholars to formulate this argument for me. After viewing some slides I had presented in conjunction with a talk on posttraditional Indians at the University of Washington in 1996, he scolded me for my foolishness, explaining that the individuals I had photographed were clearly not Indians "given their phenotypes" and were no doubt feigning Indianness so as "to claim the goodies of the state."

This theory is reminiscent of the "new ethnicity" theories developed by disillusioned North American social scientists in the 1970s.[8] Assuming that unhyphenated white identities did not constitute racial/ethnic identities, these scholars claimed that in postindustrial societies, the "welfare state" creates more material incentives to organize and identify racially than did the prewelfare states of the Jim Crow and antebellum eras.[9] Similarly most racial hucksters theorize the state as the principal actor in racial/ethnic formation through its structuring of material incentives. The state is believed responsible for producing a material terrain so that when individuals ask themselves, as Neely suggests they do, whether there is "more advantage to being Indian or white," the answer will be Indian.

In 1994, Maria Hilda Baqueiro Paraiso, an anthropologist at the University of Bahia, was hired by FUNAI to determine whether or not the Kaxixó were Indians. After having spent just one day in the Kaxixó community, where she interviewed briefly only a handful of individuals, Paraiso felt able to dismiss not only the Kaxixó's claim but archeological evidence and the opinions of other Indians in the state who recognize the Kaxixó as such. To buttress her contention that the Kaxixó were "not Indians," Paraiso also invoked the state-as-goods-provider hypothesis:

> We cannot characterize the Kaxixó as the remnants of an Indian people that form a distinct community . . . even though beginning at a certain moment—with the instigation of CPT [Pastoral Land Commission] and other entities of assistance—they began to make demands as Indians. We can affirm, however, that the option for this path of political action, the affirmation of an indigenous identity, was taken because (based on the expectations and hopes transmitted by entities of assistance) it might prove successful in their search for government protection to avoid the losses of land on which they work. They are, nevertheless, once again the great victims of the process of the dispute over power and prestige between nongovernmental organizations and the government. . . . We have concluded that the so-called Kaxixó is a group that is looking to articulate its political aims behind an ethnic identity. . . . At the moment they are not an Indian community according to judicial or anthropological thinking. We would say that they constitute a political entity that is seeking to guarantee their physical survival by giving the most effective performance that will ensure the protection of a state organization, in this case, FUNAI. [10]

To reiterate, one of the greatest weaknesses of the state-as-carrot-provider thesis (and racial hucksterism in general) is that it is overly determined by capitalist epistemologies. It is presumed that individuals select racial identities using cost-benefit analyses. The potential significance of broader discursive shifts regarding Indianness and non-Indianness or the possibility that individuals might be motivated by nonmarket logics is precluded by this model. Yet what is most troubling about the work of Paraiso and others is that they, like the new ethnicity theorists, fail to scrutinize the state's role in structuring disincentives to identify as Indian.

This emphasis is particularly suspect given that in several of the cases where the indigenous population has increased dramatically, this has not been paralleled by an increase in material benefits but rather by a sig-

Djalma Vicente de Oliveira, cacique of the Kaxixó, showing me an archeological site of a village where some of his ancestors once lived.

nificant curtailing of the state's involvement in anti-Indian violence and forced assimilation, or what I refer to as Indian exorcism. For instance, the Indian population in Canada began to flourish when the government's "termination policies" were slowed or brought to a standstill.[11]

> For the first time, the Canadian Government has formally apologized to its 1.3 million indigenous people for 150 years of paternalistic assistance programs and racial residential schools that devastated Indian communities as thoroughly as any war or disease. Along with the formal apology the Government promised today to establish a $245 million "healing fund" for the thousands of Indians who were taken from their homes and forced to attend the schools where they were sometimes physically and sexually abused. . . . The [residential school] system began in 1849. . . . The Government took thousands of youths from their families and forced them to attend schools where they could not speak their languages or practice their customs or beliefs.[12]

When these "exorcist programs" began to be scaled back in the 1950s, the aboriginal population in Canada increased by 33 percent—compared to a 2 percent growth rate in the 1940s. In the 1960s, the indigenous population increased by 42 percent, and in the subsequent decade by 57 percent. While the rate of growth declined to 28 percent in the 1980s, it was still well ahead of the ratio of births to deaths.[13]

Perhaps it is merely coincidence that the Indian population began to grow in Canada as boarding schools (and other products of exorcist policies) were being dismantled. It is difficult to argue either for or against such a causal link because the scholastic attention in this area has been on the state-influenced benefits of being Indian. As a result, any understanding of how state-induced disincentives may be related to Indian resurgence is limited.

The Racist State and Its Bloody Sticks

All societies are built on stories, and the racial democracy narrative is one of Brazil's bedrock tales. Gilberto Freyre, one of Franz Boas's students, is probably most responsible for the solidification of this myth in Brazilian thought, in large part through his romanticization of Brazilian history, as seen in the following description of Brazilian race relations during slavery:

> Of the female slave or "mammy" who rocked us to sleep. Who suckled us. Who fed us, mashing our food with her own hands. The influence of the old woman who told us our first tales of ghosts and *bicho* [bogeyman]. Of the mulatto girl who relieved us of our first *bicho de pé* [jigger], of a pruriency that was so enjoyable. Who initiated us into physical love and, to the creaking of a canvas cot, gave us our first sensation of being a man. Of the Negro lad who was our first playmate.[14]

Such an arcadian portrait of Brazilian slavery belies its documented horrors: the seven-year life expectancy of slaves, forced "miscegenation," deadly whippings, mouth plugs, starvation, back-breaking work, shackles, and torturous murders. Despite this history, even North American scholars have been known to embrace Freyre's idyllic images, arguing mimetically that Portuguese discoveries, colonization, and slavery were "more benign" than those of the Spanish, French, or English. Harry Hutchinson, for example, contends that

> slaves and their masters, on [Brazilian] plantations, formed two distinct social groups, but it is distinctive of the region that their relations were intimate and warm. . . . Slavery was not a humane institution in Brazil or elsewhere, but in Brazil relations between the slave and the master were of a more personal nature than in other regions where slavery existed in the New World.[15]

Mem de Sá, the third royal governor of Brazil (1558–1572), led several brutal military campaigns against Indians who resisted forced acculturation and slavery.[16] Whenever I read his account of the massacre that he carried out against the Tupinikim—a Tupi tribe that resided in the area between Porto Seguro and Ilheus, Bahia[17]—I am dismayed by Freyre and others' bucolic characterization of Brazilian colonization and slavery.

> Before morning, at two o'clock, I attacked the village [that was several leagues from Ilheus] and destroyed it and killed all who tried to resist. On the return I came burning and destroying all the villages

that lay behind. The heathens assembled and were following me all along the beach. I made some ambushes against them in which I surrounded them, and they were forced to plunge swimming into the sea of the open coast. I ordered other Indians and chosen men to follow them for almost two leagues. They fought there in the sea in such a way that no Tupinikim remained alive. And they brought them all on to land and placed them along the beach in order, and their bodies occupied almost one league [four miles]. I made many other sorties in which I destroyed many strong villages, and I fought with them on other occasions on which many were killed or wounded. They now dared only to live in the hills and forests where they ate dogs and cocks. Forced by necessity, they came to beg for mercy. I granted them peace on condition that they must be subjects of His Majesty and pay tribute and rebuild the mills. They accepted everything.[18]

Because there are no surviving accounts of these battles from the Tupinikim point of view—at least to my knowledge—it is difficult to know how and to what degree Mem de Sá may have embellished his military prowess. Nonetheless, what is certain is that there are no longer any self-identified Tupinikim living in southern Bahia. The only remaining Tupinikim reside in Espírito Santo, a neighboring state to the south. The Pataxó, however, do live in this same region, and their testimonials—like that of Gumercino, a fifty-five-year-old Pataxó who grew up in Bahia[19]—paint a strikingly similar picture to that of Mem de Sá.

When there was an uprising on the Pataxó reservation—that was in '51—there arrived some whites from outside saying that they were employees of the government and were there to help Indians. The only problem was they were crooks.

After these men had been on the reservation for three days, they went to a place called Corumbão, on the same reservation. That's where the businessman was—the big businessman called Teodomiro. They attacked his store. They took him and tied him up and robbed everything, everything that he had. He was attacked by these two men that claimed to be helping Indians.

[The news spread quickly]: "The Indians attacked Teodomiro!" So they returned to the exterior to call people . . . and everyone came.

They attacked Barra Velha, they set fire to everything. . . . They killed many Indians there on the reservation. The Indians all scattered.

All the Indians were imprisoned in a little jail they had there, between 100 to 200 Indians. So the soldiers took the Indians to bathe and there they raped the girls, they committed much debauchery. Then [a federal official] arrived and ordered their release.[20] He said, "I have a cacao plantation and I'm losing cacao because of these Indians. So you let those Indians loose, but do the following: Don't let them return to the reservation! Each one of you should take an Indian back with you to your plantation." So they divided up all the Indians. Indians went in every direction so that today there are Indians spread throughout the entire world. Many simply died. . . . Every fazendeiro took control of an Indian. So they made a slave agreement. They made the Indians slaves once again.[21]

In '52 or '53, some anthropologists from Rio de Janeiro came and took some pictures of the whole aldeia, the way it was, totally destroyed, no one else lived there. At that time I was fourteen or fifteen years old. They interviewed everyone. They took pictures. So they invaded the land and took control of it. The whites, the governor of the state of Bahia, created a park, a nature reserve, right in the middle of the indigenous territory. The Indians didn't have the right to collect firewood, to even take crabs out of the swamp. It was absurd. And at that time Indians couldn't travel. If they left the aldeia, they were caught and put in prison.

So the Indians went to Brasília where their government made an agreement.[22] They asked, "Would four hundred hectares be good for you?" The Indians responded, "That's fine." So they made a division. They left the bad land for the Indians. And on the other part they defended the fazendeiros as if they were good people. They even took the most precious things that the Pataxó had: the swamp where we got our shellfish and other things to eat. We were dependent on these things for survival. So with this there was little land, and so the Pataxó became scattered.

It is interesting that in most Pataxó accounts of this event, one of the primary concerns is with establishing the naïveté and concomitant innocence of the two Indians who participated in the robbery of Teodomiro. For example, during my interview with Gumercino, he went out of his way to describe the two Pataxó who "helped the crooks" as individuals who "didn't know any better, [they] were innocent." This detail affords a glimpse of how notions of culpability and accountability were racialized during this era. According to the letter and spirit of Brazilian law, if individual members of a community are found responsible for a robbery, there is no legal or moral justification for punishing or killing other members of the same community.

Yet clearly a different code of justice applied to Indians. Neighboring plantation owners, their employees, and the county police saw the ransacking of the local businessman's store as a justifiable reason for destroying the Pataxó community. Furthermore, when the federal authorities arrived, they validated the fazendeiros' actions. Instead of reigning in these vigilantes, SPI, the Forestry Service (*Serviso Florestal*) and other government officials legitimated and furthered their exorcist ways.[23] They sided with the fazendeiros "as if they were good people." Far from condemning the massacre, the federal authorities facilitated the disbanding of the community, enslavement of the surviving Indians, and succession of most of their territories to the national forestry service.

Exorcising Missions

In 1553, Brazil became the Jesuits' first foreign province. This militant vanguard of the Counter-Reformation almost immediately became the advance guard of Brazilian Indian colonization. Filled with missionary zeal, and assigned the task of pacifying and Christianizing Indians by the king of Portugal, these religious crusaders quickly tired of the pace of spiritual conversion in the budding colony.[24] They became convinced that "conversion could take place only if Indians were uprooted from their homes and moved to large new mission aldeias."[25] As one Jesuit in favor of this policy of "reduction" explained, "Some means are sought so that larger numbers of Indians can be taught and indoctrinated with greater ease in the matters of Faith. . . . The first step, which is already a great success, is to concentrate the Indians from scattered villages into one large village."[26]

This reduction was greatly facilitated by the brutal military campaigns being carried out by the colonial government, such as the one led by Mem de Sá. As the survivors of the butchering rapidly began to fill the newly founded missions, the Society of Jesus chose not to condemn the atrocities but rather praised God that their strategy of congregating Indians into large aldeias was being realized. "One Jesuit wrote in 1561 that chiefs were coming to his settlement near Bahia from distances of over a hundred miles. 'They come in such humility that it is something for which to praise the Lord.' " [27]

As Mem de Sá recognized, the Indians' "humility" was "forced by necessity," as the Jesuits too were well aware. Consequently, they not only turned a blind eye to the atrocities committed by colonial monsters but even went so far as to "condone force as the only way to make the Indians accept the move" into the mission aldeias.[28] The leader of the Brazilian Jesuits, Father Manoel da Nóbrega, for example, expressed this sentiment in more paternalistic, yet no less ominous terms:

> By experience we see that their conversion by love is a very difficult business, whereas, being a servile people, they do anything from fear. . . . They are people with whom one can do whatever one wishes by custom and by upbringing with subjection—which would not be possible by reasoning and arguments.[29]

The missions were about much more than indoctrinating Indians in matters of faith. They also functioned as institutions of de-Indianization, to change their entire way of life. The goal was to eradicate tribal languages, stories, marriage practices, aesthetics, clothing styles, artistic expressions, and so on. As John Hemming observes, the Jesuits were committed to "the complete overthrow and suppression of Indian culture. Such destruction today is called ethnocide, and its effects on the will to survive can be almost as deadly as genocide." [30]

The Jesuits were driven from Brazil in 1759, but their legacy in the form of mission aldeias endured.[31] Diretórios (directors), who were usually Capuchin priests, replaced the Jesuits, but the objective of Indian exorcism continued and even intensified. In exchange for a percentage of the fruits of Indian labor, the directors were obliged by the Crown to de-Indianize the aldeias under their tutelage. "[The directors'] duties were to help convert and civilize the Indians, to teach the Portuguese language, try to eliminate drunkenness, encourage mixed marriages, and help parish priests or missionaries." [32] Diretório missions also carried on the Jesuit tradition of providing a pool of slave labor for the surrounding plantations.

The Indians were still obliged to work for the settlers and of course on public works for the Crown. Their chiefs and the directors were to see that half the eligible Indians, all males aged between thirteen and sixty, were working for the settlers at all times. They were to do this "even to the detriment of the best interests of the Indians themselves!"[33]

As late as the concluding decades of the nineteenth century, numerous tribes were still being faithfully "congregated" into large mission settlements in eastern Brazil. For instance, in 1870, two Capuchin priests founded a mission in Itambacuri.[34] The mission existed until 1920, during which time the Capuchins worked "to congregate, miscegenate, work, and civilize the Indians all in order to evangelize them."[35] The excerpt below taken from Domigos Ramos Pacó's 1918 history of the founding of the Itambacuri mission testifies to this. His writings offer a rare and fascinating look at the implementation of the reduction policy as well as the missions' termination methods from the perspective of one of its converts. Here, Pacó, born in Itambacuri in 1869, penned the following out of fear that the Indians of Itambacuri would vanish from Brazilian history without even a record of their existence.[36]

In 1870, the imperial government asked the General Commission of Capuchin Missionaries to establish several [indigenous] catechisms. . . . Subsequently, the president of Minas Gerais entrusted Fray Serafim de Gorízia and Fray Ângelo de Sassoferrato with the responsibility for creating an indigenous catechism in Mucuri.[37] On 7 June 1872, following the instructions they received from Ouro Preto, the Frays left for Teófilo Otoni.

On arriving in Teófilo Otoni, Fray Serafim ordered Fray Ântonio to open up a road between Teófilo Otoni and Itambacuri. Frey Ântonio sent Senhor Félix [a translator and friend of chief Pohóc] to communicate with Captain Pohóc to immediately round up one hundred Indian workers to help with the building of the road. . . . Then Fray Serafim ordered the building of houses, a church and a small plaza. Trees were felled so as to plant coffee and sugarcane. . . . The first reading lessons were given to Indian boys and girls. The center of Itambacuri was inhabited solely by Captain Pohóc's aldeia, which numbered eight hundred men. . . .

[O]n the orders of Fray Serafim, Captain Pohóc along with Félix Ramos called the tribes who lived outside the aldeia to come and form a large indigenous aldeia. The tribes that were transported to Itambacuri are the following: Kraccatã, Cujãn, Jeruñhim, and Nerinhin that are from Poté, Trindade, Pontarat. They numbered about three hundred men in addition to women and children. The other tribes are the following: Hén, Jukût, Remré, Krermum, Nhãn-Nhãn, Cânmir, Pmacjirum, that are from Cressiúma, Potão, São Mateus, Pézinho, Bananal, Maurício, Catolé Grande and São João. These tribes numbered twelve hundred, and all of them came to inhabit Itambacuri because of their friendship with Captain Pohóc.

Pacó continued on in this vein, listing various other tribes that were incorporated into the mission. He also mentioned a number of instances in which particular communities resisted the advances of the Frays, killing several of the Frays' soldiers. Finally, Pacó detailed the pedagogical efforts that he and others carried out at Itambacuri.

For years in Itambacuri, it was necessary to expound morality and civilized religion in the savage language, because the savage Indians don't have a religion. . . . During [my] tenure [as a teacher, I] always recommended that the parents order their children to attend school and teach them religious morality.[38] [I] always spoke with the parents in the indigenous language about the morality of good citizens and to have great esteem for the fathers, executive agents, general directors, and governors of the country. [I] imprinted in their hearts the love for country and obedience to authorities — both civic and ecclesiastical.

Pacó, the grandson of Captain Pohóc, had been taken away from his parents at a young age by the Capuchins in order to instill in him a "Christian education" and then use him to spearhead Indian exorcism. Since the time of the first Jesuit missions, this had been a preferred colonial strategy. Hemming notes that Indian youth would oftentimes become so indoctrinated by the Jesuits that they would use "their European education to dominate and patronize their parents. They behaved like youth organizations of modern totalitarian regimes."[39] From the above passage, it is impossible to determine whether Pacó was domineering or condescending, but it is evident that he had devoted himself to "civilizing" the "faithless savages." Despite having been one of the mission's agents, however, late in life Pacó became unsettled by the effectiveness of the termination policy. He was particularly disturbed by the fact that the catechized Indians "were denying their tribe, language, and customs," and was afraid that his people would vanish without a trace given that "no one at Itambacuri wants to be an Indian anymore."[40] With an irony that he did not appear to grasp, Pacó then wrote against the social transformation he himself had helped nurture.[41]

WHITENING MISSIONS

With the establishment of the Brazilian republic in 1889, Indian colonization increasingly fell under the rubric of the state. Missions became known as "Indian reserves" and "Indian posts." State bureaucrats replaced priests, and the ultimate goal was no longer to transform Indians into Christians, but to create "national workers."

The primary government institution established to handle indigenous affairs was SPI. Its responsibility was to assist Indians' "progress through" what were conceived of as "stages of development."[42] Indians were to be "modernized" without being allowed to fall victim to the numerous pitfalls that "primitives" supposedly encountered when "advancing up" the evolutionary ladder to "civilization." Thus, "SPI was to help mediate the transition from 'hostile Indian' to 'national worker' " in such a way as "to avoid producing a 'demoralized,' 'addicted,' or 'low-life' Indian."[43]

Despite the secularization of the mission system and the positivist language, little changed with respect to the policy of Indian exorcism. Indigenous lands continued to be appropriated through the technique of relocating or "assembling" (agremiação) Indians into large communities. SPI worked to "spatially dislocate and geographically concentrate" Indians into areas now called reserves "around an administrative nucleus [indigenous post]."[44] Thus assembled, Indians were still to be de-Indianized, "domesticated," and exploited as a source of cheap labor for neighboring plantations and ranches. To this end, the secular missions sought to transform Indians' mode of production, change the geographic structure of their communities, instill in them different conceptions of property and trade, teach them the Portuguese language, and discourage their migration to urban centers.[45]

Although it is not addressed in the academic literature on SPI, one of the more significant distinctions between the secular and ecclesiastical missions was the intensification of efforts to erase Indians biologically through miscegenation. As mentioned above, one of SPI's responsibilities was to assist Indians in becoming not just workers but national workers. Indian exorcism, then, was to be carried out with an emphasis on "Brazilianizing," rather than Christianizing, savages. Both Jesuits and Capuchins had encouraged miscegenation in their efforts to colonize, catechize, and exorcise Indians, although as far as I have been able to discern, so-called racial mixing was never defined as a requirement of the civilizing process.

By the early twentieth century, with the rise of scientific racism in Brazil, nation building demanded racial transformation imagined in biological terms. Progress, modernization, and the fate of the nation, in the minds of the Brazilian elite, were not simply questions of establishing particular institutions or political systems; they were instead questions of having a certain kind of blood. Race, conceived of in a biological sense, was believed to determine culture and civilization. As a result, efforts to allegedly civilize Indians into national subjects required more than a cultural transformation. They required a racial or biological change.

Having accepted the idea that civilization and progress could only be produced by those with "Caucasian blood," the Brazilian elite faced a demographic problem in that nonwhites, as defined by the racial categories of the day, represented the numerical majority. If race qua biology determined the fate of nations, and if Brazil was indeed composed of inferior races, then it was doomed to being an inferior country. Interestingly, rather than rejecting scientific racism altogether and the bleak future it portended for Brazil, the elite chose to work within its surreal confines.

In addition to financially subsidizing European immigration (instead of assisting the former slaves in making the transition to freedom), the Brazilian elite altered one of the key tenets of conventional scientific thought. Preeminent North American and European scientists of race had argued for well over half a century that "miscegenation" produced degenerates. For example, in 1844, the internationally renowned North American scientist Dr. Josiah C. Nott declared that "wherever in the history of the world the inferior races have been conquered and mixed in with the Caucasian, the latter have sunk into barbarism. This adulteration of blood is the reason why Egypt and Barbary States never can again rise, until the present races are exterminated and the Caucasian substituted."[46]

The elite rejected the notion that racial mixing was ruinous, determined not to succumb to the fate that biology had seemingly assigned to Brazil. Instead of pulling Caucasians into barbarism, they asserted that it lifted nonwhites up into whiteness. As Thomas Skidmore notes, between 1889 and 1914, the Brazilian elite came to believe that "miscegenation did not inevitably produce 'degenerates,' but could forge a healthy mixed population growing steadily whiter, both culturally and physically."[47]

> The Director of the Museu Nacional, João Batista de Lacerda, delivered a paper ("The Métis, or Half-Breeds of Brazil") at the First Universal Races Congress in London in 1911. . . . Lacerda even went so far as to assert that in Brazil the "children of métis have been found, in the third generation, to present all physical characters of the white race. . . . In virtue of this process of ethnic reduction, it is logical to expect that in the course of another century the métis will have disappeared from Brazil." . . . Martím Francisco, a prominent Republican politician and writer, agreed with Lacerda's timetable. He wrote in his diary during a trip abroad in 1913 that although the Negro had been indispensable in Brazil's agricultural growth the "caucasian blood" was "stronger" and therefore was now "dominating the Ethiopian. . . . It will win out within a century, and will later conquer the Indian."[48]

Unlike North Americans and Europeans, Brazilians imagined "white blood" as more potent. The third or fourth "mixture" would result in a generation of Caucasians—the implication being, of course, that Brazil could become a white, and therefore great, nation through racial mixture. The 1943 writings of Fernando de Azevedo, a widely honored educational reformer who occupied the chair of sociology at the University of São Paulo and directed the state's public school system, underscore how these ideas of race mixing and nation building held sway with the Brazilian elite well beyond the initial decades of the twentieth century.

If we admit that Negroes and Indians are continuing to disappear, both in the successive dilutions of white blood and in the constant process of biological and social selection, and that immigration, especially that of Mediterranean origin, is not at a standstill, the white man [sic] will not only have in Brazil his major field of life and culture in the tropics, but be able to take from old Europe—citadel of the white race—before it passes to other hands, the torch of western civilization to which the Brazilians will give a new and intense light—that of the atmosphere of their own civilization.[49]

It seems likely, then, that SPI put more of an emphasis on race mixing than did the religious missions. Historically, as discussed earlier, one of the methods of Indian exorcism was to "persuade" Indians to accept and even seek out concubinage with non-Indians. This was considered an effective means of undermining the tribal identities and affiliations of the individuals (usually women) involved in such relationships, as well as those of their offspring. Yet, at the turn of the twentieth century, with the widespread acceptance of scientific racism and emergence of the whitening ideology, the employees and directors of SPI likely understood their task in more eugenic terms than had the exorcists of previous eras. Hence, efforts to miscegenate Indians probably intensified under SPI in the hope of generating mestizoness en route to whiteness so that primitives could become national workers and Brazil would one day be able to take the torch of Western civilization.

THE LONG WALK

According to the eastern Indians I interviewed, the SPI policy of assembling Indians onto indigenous reserves in order to Brazilianize them was still in effect in eastern Brazil well into the 1950s. Approximately one hundred miles south of Itambacuri lies the Krenak aldeia on the banks of the Sweet River.[50] As Geralda Chaves Soares explains, "The same methods" were applied to the Krenak

that had been used with success to physically and culturally eliminate the Indians of Itambacuri. [The government had attempted to]
transform the Indians into workers. However, the Krenak resisted.
They didn't accept fieldwork. They wouldn't abandon their way of life
based on hunting and collecting fruit. . . . They prevented SPI from
opening roads in order to avoid the encroachment of whites and their
ambushes.[51]

Despite the resistance of the Krenak, by the 1930s, SPI had established an indigenous post on their territory. Almost immediately there-
after,

> SPI employees started to interfere with the Krenak's principal ritual.
> They forced them to perform their ritual in a fixed location — some-
> thing that was against custom. They also helped in the theft of the
> Totem Jonkyon. With this the Krenak were fundamentally trauma-
> tized and ceased performing their religious rituals.[52]

A mica mine was discovered on the reserve in the 1950s. With this,
the anti-Indian violence of colonists intensified and the political pressure to annul Krenak land claims increased. SPI, in conjunction with
the police from the Forestry Service, decided to convert Krenak territory
into a state forest preserve that would in effect open the land up for mining and settlement. To this end, the Krenak were forced to relocate to
various other indigenous reserves.

Some of the Krenak resisted removal, but the majority capitulated
out of fear. Júlia Krenak, who was just a girl at the time, offers a glimpse
of the difficult decision that the Krenak people were required to make.

> The police told us if we didn't leave, they would kill us. My father
> said, "And if you murder? I'm not leaving. I'm not living outside of
> the land. If you want to leave, then that is your decision." And then
> my mother said, "The police are going to kill us. They're going to fin-
> ish us off. I'm not staying. I'm going to try to catch a piece of that
> train and we're gone." Papa stayed. The rest of us left for Maxakali.[53]

A number of the Krenak were relocated to the Maxakali aldeia situated nearly two hundred miles to the north. The conditions for the assembled Krenak on this aldeia were abysmal. As Maria Krenak reports,

"There wasn't anything. We didn't have anything to eat. We went hungry for days. People were so weak that they began to get sick. My daughter died from hunger. I became very ill, too." [54] Júlia Krenak paints a similar picture: "When we arrived there, everyone became sick. Eugênio de Mariazinha died because there it's cold. Chica died. The son of Chica died. Adults died. Two of Pedrim's children died. Mother died. My sister died." [55] Sônia Krenak adds,

> There it was impossible to plant anything. We lived in a little hay shack. There were these little cockroaches that bit like a dog. They ate us so bad that it itched everywhere. They lived in the hay. They ate us all day. The children itched constantly. There were cockroaches everywhere! They were so hungry! [56]

The situation became so desperate that the Krenak broke off into various groups and attempted to return to the Sweet River by foot. Sônia explains the decision to leave this way: "My father [Teófilo] said, 'Let's get out of here. These bugs are too much! We're going to die here! Let's leave! Let's just start walking!' And that is what we did." [57] In a 1997 interview with me, Maria Krenak tells a comparable story:

> We stayed there two months and then finally my sister-in-law said, "I'm not staying here to watch everyone die. Let's see if we can take back our land!" And my husband then said, "Let's get out of here! Let's just walk back! Don't say anything to the *chefe* [head] of the post. Let's get out of here!" But I said, "How am I going to return by foot? I'm so sick. I'm almost dying." My husband said, "I can't find work here so that I can buy you medicine. It's better if we leave. You'll get stronger if we leave." I was dying from hunger on that aldeia. We stayed there two months until we walked away.

All of the Krenak who attempted to return to their aldeia vividly remembered having "to walk and walk and walk and walk" for several months. Sick, suffering from hunger, and trying to care for dying children, they slept alongside the road, and scavenged and begged for food as they walked. The moments from the "long walk" told in greatest detail are those in which they were given food by strangers, underscoring the terrible hunger they endured. As Maria Krenak told me,

We walked for six months. It was a sacrifice. It was difficult. It was not easy. We walked always begging, just like a gypsy, for a little bit of food so that we wouldn't die of hunger. It's one of most ugly things on earth: having to beg. I remember one place where those fazendeiros helped us. We were waiting underneath some trees when they asked us, "Where are you from?" "We're Krenaks and we're dying of hunger. Could you give us some help?" They said, "Let's go there to the house." When we got to the house, the fazendeiro said, "Woman, make some coffee and milk! Give everyone a piece of cheese! Give them whatever they want because they're dying of hunger!" We ate a huge lunch. We ate and we ate. And when we left, they gave the children bread for the trip. They gave us farina, almost a whole sack of dried meat, and a big container of coffee and milk.

The trek ended for most in Governador Valadares, some two hundred miles southeast of the Maxakali aldeia and approximately fifty miles upstream from Krenak territory. Maria Krenak went on to explain that

in Valadares, the forestry police came as we were asking for food. They photographed all the Indians. Then a truck came and took us to the battalion. We stayed two weeks eating and drinking. They gave medicine to the children. They took us to the doctor. They did everything for us. Everyone was given clothing because we had been walking without clothing, without anything. We didn't have anything. Then the police told us, "You should go to Rio de Janeiro to talk with the Dom (seigneur/boss/lord) who took your land." So we were wanting to talk with Captain Pinheiro, the man with a white mentality [cabeça branca]. We arrived in Rio de Janeiro at 9:00 A.M. We went and knocked on Pinheiro's building. Once again he was very upset with us. "What are you doing here? You have to return to Maxakali! You don't have any more land! Your land belongs to the [Serviço] Florestal now!" [58]

Maria and the other Krenak that were with her were then resettled on the Kaingang aldeia in São Paulo, where another band of Krenak had been relocated when their aldeia was turned into a forest preserve. She and her husband worked awhile on the peanut and cotton plantations in São Paulo, and were later moved to Matto Grosso and then to the in-

Gonçaga Krenak, an ambulance driver in aldeia Guarani, sitting in front of the prison, now the office space for FUNAI, where his relatives were incarcerated by Captain Pinheiro.

digenous penal colony on the fazenda Guarani. In the mid-1990s, the courts ruled that the Krenak land had been illegally appropriated and therefore had to be repatriated to the Krenak people. The government began removing the fazendeiros from Krenak territory in 1997, and by the end of that same year, Maria and the other Krenak, whom "Pinheiro had dispersed throughout Brazil," were moving back to their aldeia on the Sweet River.

Indigenous Penal Colonies

When SPI was abolished in 1967 and FUNAI established in its place, it was supposed to represent an end to the centuries-long government policy of Indian exorcism. But this was not to be the case for another decade. As late as the mid-1970s, the Brazilian government was still relocating and imprisoning Indians. Indigenous people continued to be targeted and removed to what FUNAI euphemistically referred to as the Center for the Reeducation of Rebellious and Disobedient Indians (Centro de Reeducação de Índios Rebeldes e Infratores). In reality, Geralda Chaves Soares argues, these reeducation centers were "indigenous penal colonies in the old military tradition of forced labor, solitary confinement, violence, torture, and assassinations." [59]

According to the accounts of both Indians who were imprisoned or the relatives of those who were taken prisoner, it appears that the authorities specifically targeted Indian leaders on a number of different aldeias. Whole communities were no longer being assembled, resocialized, and miscegenated, but individual community leaders and activists were. Once identified as "disobedient Indians," leaders were relocated without even the pretense of a trial to a distant penal colony. As Cleonice Pankararu says of her family's move to Minas Gerais,

> We came here because of my grandfather. He was part of the leadership of the old aldeia and he was involved in the conflict over the land. Then there were deaths, so the government imprisoned him. This was in the late 1960s. He eventually killed an invader. He got involved in the land conflicts. They wanted to take the land. The invaders lost in the courts, but they returned again, and now I don't know if they're going to succeed in taking all the land. . . . They took my grandfather

away because he was part of the leadership. . . . It was he who led the movement of resistance of our people. So they brought him here. And there the movement stalled; they weren't able to get our land back. So they brought my grandfather here to Minas Gerais along with other Indians. At the time, my mother said that we weren't going to stay here more than two years, and we've stayed till today. He died, but my mother didn't want to return to the aldeia. Eventually, the prison became the aldeia Guarani. That's where they put Indians from various places, from Goias, Pará, Maranhão, Bahia. In 1980, it was registered as an Indian reserve and no longer as an Indian prison. That happened in 1980.[60]

I am aware of at least two Indian prisons that were established in the state of Minas Gerais between 1966 and 1972: the fazenda Guarani mentioned above and another situated on a section of the dismantled Krenak aldeia. These Indian penal colonies crested during the height of the military dictatorship in the late 1960s and early 1970s. Like similar institutions in the nineteenth-century United States (for instance, the Indian penal colony in Pensacola, Florida), such prisons housed Indians from all over Brazil.[61] These prisoners underwent a military-type training: their hair was cut, marching drills were constantly conducted, and they were forced to perform menial labor. Furthermore, there is evidence to suggest that many of them were tortured and murdered.[62]

There were Indians from various tribes: Kaingang, Maxakali, Terena. The Captain . . . said they had robbed on their aldeias. Others were said to have killed. Others were brought because of *cachaça* [rum]. So they put every type there in that area. There were times when there were twenty-nine and thirty Indians from other places. They stayed there. The police ordered them around. They made them work.

They brought one Indian from Mato Grosso. That Indian didn't know how to speak Portuguese. He was tricked into leaving. . . . They shot at him. They would show him a gun and say they were going to kill him. That Indian was afraid he was going to die.

When I arrived home they were shooting . . . shooting. The police arrived shouting that two Indians had fled. They were unloading their machine gun on those Indians. . . . They were able to get one of them. They beat him so badly . . . that his eyes were like ashes from a fire. They wanted to crush him with their blows. He slept tied up the whole night. His arms and legs were bound to the cold floor! The whole night![63]

The prisoners, and oftentimes their families who moved to be near them, had to suffer the traumas of relocation and exile. They had to adjust to a completely different climate and diet. I was repeatedly told that many of the older adults who had relocated from southern Bahia and Pernambuco to the highlands of Minas Gerais had died from *saudades* (a profound homesickness or nostalgia) for the warmer weather, ocean, and cuisine.[64]

Laissez-faire Terminations

The most blatant manifestations of state-fostered exorcisms were the military massacres, de-Indianizing missions, and reeducation centers. Although these methods had a dramatic impact on eastern Indians, perhaps the most devastating termination policy was tacit support of anti-Indian terrorism. This laissez-faire approach meant that the state could encourage Indians to flee their communities and shed or conceal their Indian subjectivities without the use of overt force. The government simply allowed the surrounding non-Indian communities to murder and enslave Indians, resocialize them, steal their land, and destroy their communities without any threat of prosecution.

Throughout the nineteenth century, the government continued to subsidize colonists' exorcisms in eastern Brazil. In 1808, for instance, the regional government intensified the massacre of Indians of the Jequitinhonha and Mucuri Valleys with a two-pronged strategy. First, it ordered the formation of a civilian militia to fight a war against the "savages of the Jequitinhonha," and then it provided "incentives for the settlement of forests. Anyone who settled an area in northeastern Minas Gerais was freed from paying taxes for ten years and the repayment of debts to the government could be deferred for six years."[65]

Due at least in part to government incentives, the degree of anti-Indian violence quickly escalated. Soon after the implementation of the above-mentioned policy, "the number of murdered Indians was enormous in the Mucuri and Jequitinhonha regions."[66] There existed hundreds of cases like the following description of a raid against a tribe in 1839. Teófilo Benedito Otoni—the namesake of the largest city in northeastern Minas Gerais—told of how the well-armed colonists of Calhua, guided by two Indians—Cró and Crahy—occupied the aldeia at night:

> [They] murdered the old ones, the women and children, sparing only those who could be sold into slavery, and some adults to carry the baggage and ammunition of the assassins. And along the way back, if they could dispense with one of these beasts of burden, they would have him shot in the forehead. They called this "Kill an aldeia," a feat that they repeated on several occasions. It's a technical phrase that the hunters of savages use. They murdered aldeias in the Jequitinhonha, Mucuri, and Sweet River Valleys, in Minas [Gerais], and in Espírito Santo. The traffickers in Indian slaves hunted the indigenous people as if they were ferocious animals. They said that to train their dogs to hunt Indians, they let them eat the corpses of slain Indians.[67]

Countless peoples were eliminated in this manner. The massacres were so intense that

> one is tempted to believe that the Indians were exterminated in a brutal war motivated by colonists who wanted their land. But this is just part of the truth. The massacres were frequent, but they were not the only, not even the principal instrument of Indian liquidation. . . . This struggle did not take place on the battlefield, but on the plantations and in the houses of the colonists, where many Indians were transformed into fieldworkers and "Brazilians." The survivors of the massacres—probably the majority of the Indians in the Jequitinhonha and Mucuri Valleys—suffered a massacre much more sophisticated: they were obliged to accept civilization.[68]

Using tactics strikingly similar to those of the ecclesiastical and secular missions, colonists actively worked to transform Indians into non-Indians via relocation, enslavement, miscegenation, reeducation, and so on.

Teófilo Benedito Otoni actually pioneered a form of colonization that later government and priests used. . . . He hired a technician to demarcate the Indian land, made sure they stayed in their territory, and instructed them in agriculture. The remaining lands were then transformed into large plantations and individual homesteads. Otoni tried to teach Indians modern notions of law, work, money, and property. He greatly admired Cacique Poton because he had converted many Indians into field hands by instituting the norm: "Whoever doesn't work, doesn't eat." The Indians were taught to plant, and then in their spare time they could work on the plantations of the arriving "Portuguese" colonists. The first large plantations in the Mucuri Valley—plantations Universo, Monte Cristo, and Mestre do Campo— were cultivated in this way, with Indian labor.[69]

After 1820, colonists could no longer use the phrase "Indian slavery" because the government had abolished it.[70] Subsequently, they began referring to their indigenous slaves as "capacitated" ("*capacitações*"). To capacitate meant that the Indians were "being trained in how to do fieldwork and the chores of the plantation"; in actuality, they were "imprisoned on the plantation, and constantly submitted to physical and cultural violence."[71] Indians were tortured and ridiculed for refusing to abandon tribal traditions. As Eduardo Magalhães Ribeiro remarks, "there was an enormous stigma attached to indigenous languages and customs that led to great embarrassment for anyone who did not abandon them."[72]

The lengthy passage below is taken from an interview with Dorinha, an elderly Maxakali woman whose two long braids, vibrant personality, and enthusiasm for life always led me to think of her as a young schoolgirl. She resides in a working-class neighborhood of Belo Horizonte, and pieces together a living by working part-time as a maid for the Catholic Church and also selling arts and crafts.[73] In 1995, at the time of this interview, she was sixty years old and lived with her husband (who died in 1997), six of her nine children, a number of grandchildren, and several adopted stray animals. Her family's history in northeastern Minas Gerais details a number of the colonists' methods of Indian exorcism discussed earlier: anti-Indian terrorism; capacitation of the victims of terror; countless pressures to abandon or at least hide tribal language, customs, and identity; and the push to assimilate and intermarry.

My strongest memory was that massacre of the Indians there on the reserve, when I saw the children in the hammocks dripping with blood. This never leaves my mind. This is etched in my mind. I was a child there and I saw that horror. This is marked in my mind . . . , and I don't like to think about it. There were so many people there that came to destroy. It was the dead of night when they entered killing. . . . This was the horror of my childhood.

At that time, we had lots of land on the reserve. But the big land-holder there demarcated the land, taking meter after meter . . . of manioc. So he made the horrible divide right through the middle of our community. Everyone became very upset. . . . Then he let his cattle out on that land and they stepped on all the manioc that was ready to be harvested . . . , and destroyed it all. . . . They should liberate that land, they should demarcate that land for the Indians. They robbed that land. . . . They destroyed everything.

The whites let loose the cattle on our crops, and so the Indians killed those cattle. . . . So one day they arrived and they murdered many Indians. It was an awful massacre. A brother of my father was killed. A sister also died there. So the people were dying. The elderly were dying because they had no tranquillity. My grandfather died. He was so distressed that he died. And also because of this, my grand-mother died. She was so upset because she had no peace.

That's when that boy that's in charge of the city, the governor, said that no more Indians were going to be permitted to leave there, to come to the city to sell things. And no more whites would be allowed on the reserve to help anyone.

So my mother came here to Belo Horizonte because she was a daughter of the Portuguese . . . , and I stayed behind with my father. Papa couldn't come because they didn't want Indians going to the city to get educated.

We went to the plantation of Claudiomir Carneiro. My father only knew how to make straw baskets, [but] when he arrived he learned how to make other things. He learned to drive, he learned the skills of a mechanic, these types of things. He worked in the fields. But it was very difficult to continue on there because when the mother of that master was on another plantation, my father would have to follow her with a plank and towel to place on the ground where she walked so that she wouldn't have to step in the mud. . . . The work of a slave is what he did. But he did this because he didn't want to return because he discovered that the big landholders near the reserve had hired *ja-gunços* [paid killers]. So as not to be murdered, so as not to die, he stayed on the plantation.

My father was eventually able to leave that master of his, that Clau-diomir Carneiro. . . . He came to Belo Horizonte with another master. This is how my parents were reunited after three years of separation. Geraldo Vasconcellos brought him here to work as a mechanic be-cause he had learned how to be a mechanic on that plantation. . . .

We both spoke the indigenous language. But we would have to speak it in secret because his master didn't let him speak his indige-nous language. . . . He was afraid the other colonists were going to know that he came from the forest, that he was an Indian and not a colonist like them. The white man doesn't like the Indian in the city. So if they had known that there was one there, living among them, they could have sent him back.

We always heard, "Indians here are going to cause problems. They're going to give everyone problems. They'll always be trouble-makers." So my father told me that I couldn't play with the white kids. He said that I couldn't run after white kids "because if they fall and hurt themselves they will blame it on you." . . . My father also advised us to not respond to what they say. Even if we couldn't bear it, we were told to try, to do anything but respond.

I didn't encounter much discrimination because I didn't leave the house much. . . . Nevertheless, the few times I left, my classmates would always say, "She's an Indian. We're not going to play with her." Their parents were teaching them this, don't you think? This was very discriminatory because they wouldn't let us play together.

My parents didn't want me to marry an Indian. My father said, "It's better to marry here." . . . He didn't want me to return to that conflict that we had already lived through.

The story of Dorinha and her parents illustrates how the state's tacit support of the racist conventions of its citizenry helped lead to the production of non-Indian racial identities. This is not to say that the massacre, relocation, capacitation, and anti-Indian sentiments *caused* her family to leave their community, conceal their Indianness, and encourage their daughter to choose a white spouse; nevertheless, it surely provided powerful incentives for them to do so. Thus, by implicitly endorsing lynch mobs, slavery, illegal appropriation of territory, and other forms of anti-Indian racism, the state was clearly an important accomplice to the exorcising practices of its citizenry.

The Shift to a Postexorcist State

Ironically, the move away from the termination traditions can be traced to the military dictatorship that seized power in 1964. One of the principal justifications for ousting the democratically elected government, as with most authoritarian regimes in Latin America during this time period, was to rid the state of corruption. The military's legitimacy rested in large measure on the idea that it was more efficient and professional, less beholden to sectarian or special interests, and so, best able to rationalize and reform government and society.

To bolster this image, the military decided to indict SPI "as a symbol of all that was rotten in the state of Brazil before the coup." [74] Attorney General Jader Figueiredo was commissioned in 1967 by the minister of the interior to investigate corruption in SPI. After months of inquiries, interviews, and visits to Indian posts, Figueiredo held a press conference in March 1968 to publicize his 20-volume, 5,115-page report. He announced that

> evidence had been found not only of massive corruption, land-grabbing, and labor exploitation, but of massacres, enslavement, rape, torture and biological warfare against Indians. The crimes stemmed from the dereliction and, at times, collusion of SPI officials. The attorney general concluded that SPI had "persecuted the Indians to the point of extermination, the lack of assistance being the most efficient means of committing murder." [75]

With this, the military dismantled SPI and, in December 1967, created a new Indian bureau, FUNAI.

"Few believed," as Seth Garfield points out, "that long-neglected Indian rights were suddenly being safeguarded by the most unlikely of heroes — a regime set on the rapid development of the Amazon." [76] Instead of discrediting the populists, then, the Figueiredo report invited scrutiny of the military government's Indian policy. As a result, "scathing exposés on Brazilian Indian policy blanketed the European press." [77] A number of nongovernmental organizations, such as the International Red Cross, launched inquiries into the validity of accusations that suggested ethnic cleansing had not ended with the abolishment of SPI. To the chagrin of military officials, the report "would hound the government for years as denunciations of genocide continued to reverberate in the international arena." [78]

The Figueiredo report also attracted the attention of Brazilian politicians and activists who were opposed to the military regime: they seized the political opportunity that the document offered. "Politicians from the Movimento Democrático Brasileiro (MDB), the sole legal opposition party in Brazil . . . threatened to denounce the military government at the United Nations and to call for an international wardship system for the Indians—one of the regime's most dreaded nightmares." [79] Pro-democracy activists, moreover, learned from this incident that by attacking the government's maltreatment of indigenous people—which continued even after SPI was dismantled [80]—they could inflict political damage and even put the government on the defensive regarding its development initiatives in the Amazon. As a result, the indigenous cause was adopted as symbol (or cause célèbre) of the democratization movement, which enjoyed broad-based support in the late 1970s and early 1980s. Large segments of the Brazilian population, who might otherwise have been disinterested or ignorant of indigenous matters, became more cognizant of the Indians' struggle and sympathetic to their goals.

At about the same time, certain elements within the Catholic Church began to regard the church's traditional relationship with indigenous communities, which was "often to the Indians' detriment," as problematic. [81] As Thomas Bruneau writes, "Several bishops and missionaries acted to remedy this situation; the founding of CIMI [Indigenous Missionary Council] in 1972 with the support of the CNBB [National Conference of Brazilian Bishops] was the eventual result." [82] CIMI, as I will detail in chapter 5, represented a radical departure in church policy in that it rejected a centuries-long policy of Indian exorcism in favor of shoring up and defending indigenous peoples and their ways of life.

The question, then, is why did the practice of Indian exorcism suddenly become seen as a problem to be remedied? And what accounts for such a dramatic transformation in church policy? Most analysts, such as Bruneau, have attributed this change to the increasing influence of liberation theology at that time. But the close correlation between the dates that "the missionaries and bishops acted to remedy the situation" and the release of the Figueiredo report is deserving of further study. It seems highly probable that there was a causal relationship between these two events. Official confirmation of such egregious atrocities (oftentimes in communities where Catholic pastorals had worked and lived, which must have weighed heavily on the minds of church officials) may have provided the stimulus many needed to support a new policy and probably emboldened those who were already lobbying for change.

Precisely how significant this report was in shaping church policy will remain an open question until more data are available. It does seem certain, however, that it played some role in prompting the formation of CIMI, which in turn helped trigger indigenous mobilization. Alcida Ramos, like other observers, argues that CIMI "was the prime mover in launching a supralocal indigenous political movement in the early 1970s." [83] In 1974, for example, "CIMI organized the first in a long series of 'indigenous assemblies,' " bringing together people from extremely diverse and dispersed communities.[84] It was at these assemblies that Indians first articulated their grievances, developed and coordinated political strategies, built broader political alliances, and forged a sense of pan-tribal solidarity, as evidenced in the opening remarks of one of the first participants, Sampré Shernte: "My brothers, I call you brothers because I'm an Indian. I'm a brother of the same color, the same massacre." [85] By the late 1970s, the impact of CIMI's involvement in the creation of an indigenous movement was already being felt. Illegal forms of Indian exorcism—such as murder, enslavement, or forced appropriation of land—were greatly curtailed because indigenous people understood that their legal rights would be upheld, had a more sophisticated means of publicizing such atrocities when they occurred, and had an increasingly attentive international and domestic audience—thanks in large measure to the Figuereido report.

The Indian movement scored one of its most significant victories in 1988: it ended the state's "integrationist policy." [86] During the

1987–1988 Constitutional Assembly, "the Union of Indigenous Nations (UNI), backed by a coalition of the Catholic Church, NGOs, unions, professional organizations and pro-indigenous legislators, succeeded in negotiating a text containing strategic conceptual advances."[87] Despite a vicious and fraudulent media attack carried out by *O Estado de São Paulo*, a major national daily, and supported by powerful anti-Indian interests, the Indian lobby held and was able to ensure that the new Constitution rejected the notion of "natural assimilation."[88] The Constitution also recognized the rights of indigenous peoples to "their social organization, customs, languages, beliefs and traditions, and the original rights to the lands they traditionally occupy, it being incumbent on the Union to demarcate them, to protect and ensure respect for their goods."[89] The new Constitution further stipulated that the federal attorney general's office defend the interests of indigenous peoples in court and that indigenous groups could take legal action themselves.[90]

Figueirdo's public disclosures about SPI therefore represented, if nothing else, a watershed moment in state-Indian relations. Although state exorcisms did not suddenly come to a halt, the report nonetheless publicized and politicized the plight of indigenous people to a degree that would have probably taken the Indian movement, once it had emerged, many more years to accomplish.[91] Furthermore, the report helped set in motion a series of events that galvanized and coalesced various indigenous communities, environmentalists, journalists, human rights organizations, the Catholic Church, academics, and proponents of democratization (especially the labor-centered Left) behind an Indian movement. As the movement gained momentum in the 1970s and 1980s, it was gradually able to pressure the state to curtail its exorcist practices—at least the illegal articulations. Finally in 1988, the passage of "the indigenous peoples chapter" of the new Constitution successfully prompted the Brazilian state to legally reverse a course it had pursued for almost five hundred years. The idea of a multicultural state, at least with respect to indigenous people, had been officially sanctioned, and for the first time in Brazilian history, government policy was not directed toward civilizing, Christianizing, evolving, nationalizing, integrating, and whitening—in short, exorcising—Indians.

Brazil is a nation infamous for creating laws that are never or rarely enforced. In fact, the practice is so common that Brazilians have coined an expression to describe token laws: "for the English to see." [92] Have, then, these changes in state policy about Indian rights been matched by actual transformations in state practice? Moreover, how have these alterations affected, if at all, the lives of eastern Indians?

The terrorism and murders perpetrated in the Xacriabá community in 1987 offer a good case study since the official response reveals more than a legal shift toward a postexorcist state. Although the state moved too slowly to prevent the murders of several of the Xacriabá leadership, its reaction to the news of the deaths contrasts dramatically with its participation in the Maxakali, Pataxó, Krenak, and Pankararu incidents described earlier in this chapter. As José Xacriabá contends,[93]

> The Indians just wanted the land that was theirs and for this they were massacred. We only won a third of our land, and the rest is in the hands of the fazendeiros. We lost it to them, that which belongs to us. It says so in the benefaction of our land that was given to us by Princess Isabela—a document that had been made by the fazendeiros themselves a long time ago. Our document, to which we 6,000 abided by, is, however, in the end only one small document.
>
> There was a tension on the aldeia and Rosalino [the *cacique*], as representative of the area, confronted this tension. The area was almost completely invaded by fazendeiros. At the same time, FUNAI said that the land was ours. So Rosalino decided to fight them. He went fighting all the way to the courts there in Brasília and asked for the land to be demarcated. In 1985, CIMI began working with us, and we started to understand our rights, we began reacting to the fazendeiros. By 1986, the conflict was very grave between us. It was war. In 1987, the fazendeiros attacked Rosalino's home, and killed him and my brother-in-law. They also murdered Manuel Fiuza, my brother, José Teixeira, also a relative, and they had already killed José Pereira Lopes. Then after these murders, on 2 November 1987, the courts decided to remove the fazendeiros. Until the end of 1988, it remained very tense there. But at the end of that year, things started

The sons of Joselino Gomes de Oliveira (Xacriabá), who was murdered in 1987 in a land dispute with fazendeiros and posseiros. Otelice (left) is a doorman and José (right) works in a Coca-Cola bottling plant. In this photo they are on their way to church—Deus do Amor—not far from their home in Belo Horizonte.

to change. They learned to respect indigenous rights. Today, thank God, we have peace on our favela.

Unlike the aftermath of massacres in previous decades, the federal government did not ignore or condone the murders and pillage. Two of the killers were even sentenced to ten years in prison (rather than being allocated a slave or a section of Indian territory as the killers in the Pataxó massacre were). The state, moreover, did not use the conflict as a reason to incarcerate and relocate the Xacriabá leadership (as it did in the early 1970s). Finally, unlike in the Krenak and Pataxó conflicts, the government did not attempt to resolve tensions in the region by relocating the entire community and converting their territories into non-Indian settlements or a nature preserve. To the contrary, the government accelerated the demarcation of Xacriabá territory and FUNAI forcibly removed the fazendeiros from the Xacriabá lands.

Anti-Indian violence and threats of such violence, however, are still a fact of life for many Indian communities in eastern Brazil. For instance, fazendeiros have vowed to resist a superior court decision that orders them to surrender land back to the Krenak, and have threatened to murder Krenak leaders. The Maxakali also continue to be subjected to constant threats, both verbal and physical. I was told that the Maxakali children are so accustomed to being shot at that they run rather than walk from place to place. Leaders of the Kaxixó community also report having received death threats from local fazendeiros.

> On 23 January [1993], Jerry, nineteen, was threatened with death by the fazendeiro, Fabiano Fernandes Campos, carrying a large caliber rifle, on the road to the river where the Indians fish. On the 26th, Eva, fifty, was hunted by the fazendeiro Sebastião Barcelo. The Indian escaped by hiding in a nearby house. Such threats became more intense beginning in 1990 when the Indians began seeking ethnic recognition and demarcation of their land. Their land is 1,285 hectares, which was traditionally inhabited by the Kaxixó nation, and today is occupied by sixteen fazendeiros.
>
> On 8 April [1993], Jerry was beaten by Campos, owner of the Criciuma Plantation. . . . He grabbed the Indian and hit him in the head. He said that his father, Paulo Fernandes Campos, was going to kill him.[94]

Despite such continued violence, the state has stopped its endorsement of terrorist campaigns against eastern Indian communities and is much less apt to allow anti-Indian violence. Then, too, I have heard of no recent cases in which Indian leaders or activists have been imprisoned for their political work. Indeed, a number of indigenous communities have had their lands returned to them by the courts (for example, the Xacriabá, Krenak, and Pataxó Hã-Hã-Hãe), and it has been fazendeiros who have been forcibly removed.

Perhaps the best indicator of a substantive change is the perceptions of Indians themselves. Echoing José's remark that "they learned to respect indigenous rights. Today, thank God, we have peace on our favela." Zizi Pataxó, a thirty-five-year-old mother of four, describes a similar shift in her 1995 interview with me.

> We lost our language after the massacre at Pataxó. They killed lots of people. Whoever knew how to pray well, didn't die.[95] They spilled

Jerry, a vice cacique of the Kaxixó, and his mother, Eva, were attacked and threatened by neighboring fazendeiros because of their involvement in the recognition movement.

into the fine shrub brush, and fell into the forest. And those who didn't know, they died. Many hid their children there, in that jasmine there at Pataxó, creeping slowly to defend themselves from death. But they had no chance, they murdered so many. Because of this, many people there still have injuries. They cut everyone up, they amputated limbs. The whites beat and threw them against things. Some they killed at that moment. Others they kept alive so they could torture them. There were some that resisted and escaped. I remember one old Indian when I was a child. He had escaped but he was all scarred up. And the Indians who lived, they fled and scattered. Even as a child, I remember the cacique would say, "Listen, when a plane comes, do not go up there on top of the hill to see it, because they could be here to murder Indians!"

So everyone was scared. No one wanted to be Indian. If you said that you were a caboclo, they would take you and murder you.[96] So everyone was frightened. No one wanted to be Indian anymore—at that time we used the word *caboclo*—only if you were crazy. Only if you wanted to die. If you said that you were caboclo, the whites killed you. And if you spoke the language, they would kill you, too. That's why we lost our language. And you're seeing this mixture among the people. It's because of this as well. At that time my father was single; my uncles were single. So they mixed [married non-Indians], so they wouldn't have to be Indian, because if you said that you were Indian they killed you. No one wanted to be Indian so Indians married whites. The mother of my mother was a pure Indian, but her father was black.[97] The father of my father was pure, too. . . . But his mother already had other blood. She wasn't Indian. So the whole world ended up mixed up since the time of that massacre. Because there was this fear of being Indian. Today, we're no longer afraid of being Indian because now Indians have another value. Now they are starting to realize that Indians have a value, but at that time, Indians didn't have any value.

What Zizi's statements reiterate is how the state's legitimization of anti-Indian violence fomented a culture of fear. Because the state sided with the fazendeiros—rather than the victims of the massacres—Indians became (or remained) "open game." This fear of having your land

and body appropriated simply for being Indian clearly motivated many of the survivors to abandon or conceal their Indianness. Literally out of a fear of death, Indians were "enticed" to relinquish their language, marry non-Indians, and racially position themselves as non-Indians.

As Zizi's observations suggest, state practices have indeed changed, and that shift has had a dramatic impact on the valuation of Indianness. The fact that Zizi's description of the "fear of being Indian" is expressed in the past tense shows that this transformation has been actualized in many respects. Having racial status as Indian no longer compromises an individual's civil rights, in real terms, to life, liberty, and property— at least not to the same degree that it did just a few decades earlier.

4. Racial Stocks and Brazilian Bonds

In many countries of the world, there is a "cost" to being an ethnic or racial minority; for the few countries where the situation of the indigenous population has been investigated, a substantial cost in terms of earnings, poverty and social development has been estimated. — Harry Anthony Patrinos, World Bank economist, 1994

In 1972, after years of harassment by whites in southern Bahia, Manoel Pataxó killed a white man in a brawl. Since he was Indian, he fell under the jurisdiction of FUNAI, whose officials incarcerated him in the penal colony on the fazenda Guarani. By the time he was released from prison, Manoel's land had long since been confiscated, and so he and a few of his former fellow inmates fought to establish the fazenda as an indigenous reserve. In 1995, I interviewed sixty-nine-year-old Manoel who was one of Guarani's *caciques*, as well as the only Indian council member (*vereador*) of the Carmésia municipality—a position he won based on the political support of the Indian community. Manoel told me that outside of Indian spaces in eastern Brazil, he is usually not taken seriously as an Indian. In fact, he is frequently accused of being a racial charlatan.

> Sometimes when we go to conferences or meetings with Congress, or when we are invited by organizations to give presentations to the public, there's lots of criticism, there's lots of discrimination. They say, "Them over there, they're not Indians. They're pretending to be Indians so that the government will pay for their trips, so that they can eat for free, so that they can get land from the government on which to work or live. They have nothing to do with being Indians. They're just faking it."

Manoel's experiences underscore how posttraditional Indians—even individuals who have been terrorized as Indians for much of their lives—are often viewed as feigning Indianness for material gain.

In the previous chapter, I focused on one of the serious shortcomings of this huckster model of racial formation: the failure to address Indian exorcism. Yet such a criticism does not preclude the existence of Indianizing inducements. The fact that ethnic cleansing has waned only means that the analysis offered by racial hucksters is incomplete or oversimplified. It does not mean that there is no validity to the assertion that the indigenous population upsurge has been prompted by Indianness having become materially more advantageous. My objective in this chapter, then, will be to examine various facets of the materiality of Indianness to determine whether shifts in this terrain have been responsible, however partially, for the changed direction in racial formation.

Whitening Territories

In rural Brazil, large landholders are accustomed to controlling regions like personal fiefdoms. This plantation culture, according to David Hess and Roberto DaMatta, in which patriarchs exercise "a nearly absolute authority over their dominions in a way similar to that of a king over the realm," is rooted in Brazil's colonial legacy.

> Brazil is a product of a particular colonial legacy. That . . . plantation legacy was radically different from most of Canada and the northern parts of the United States. There, a more egalitarian society arose based first on small-scale or petty bourgeois capitalism: family farms, urban merchants, and small industries as well as a less centralized state with a more open decision-making process. Even in the South of the United States, where there was a plantation economy as in Brazil, there were many small farmers and urban merchants, as well as political, social, and religious structures that put a check on the power of the large landowners.[1]

As a consequence, fazendeiros have historically had little trouble in pressuring the sale of deed or simply confiscating the property from small landholders. It was this tradition that helped drive over eighteen million people from rural to urban areas between 1960 and 1980.[2] "Many internal migrants," Biorn Maybury-Lewis observes, "did not leave the countryside because of the proverbial bright lights and opportunities of the cities. Nor did the urbanization primarily reflect their desire to break away from the circumstances of the provincial poverty. Rural workers left because they were obliged to leave."[3] Hence, the story of how Karakana Canoeiro's grandparents lost their land is a history of "obligatory departures" likely shared by countless Brazilians.[4]

> My grandparents are Canoeiros from Araçuaí. They were born there. My mother was born there, too. That's why she is registered as "Indian Canoeiro Araçuaí." When my mother was two months old, their aldeia was taken by fazendeiros, so they had to leave. The fazendeiros invaded and asked them to leave, and said if they didn't they would be killed. They gave them three days to decide. So my grandparents were afraid and left. The uncles and cousins of my mother insisted on staying. They ended up being murdered. Everyone who stayed was killed. They killed many Indians. So they had to leave so they wouldn't be killed. So they fled, they fled to Bahia.[5]

The return to democratic rule in Brazil in the mid-1980s, among other factors, has meant that the strategy of appropriating a community's land simply by riding in on horseback and forcing people to leave at gunpoint has become less tenable.[6] The fazendeiros have had to become somewhat more subtle and sophisticated in their maneuverings with small landholders since they can no longer rely on the same degree of government support in eastern Brazil. Nonetheless, fazendeiros do have a number of other strategies — such as intimidation, blacklisting, and even terrorism — that they do not hesitate to wield against those, be they Indians or non-Indians, whose lands they desire.

I got a taste of the fear that the fazendeiros can instill when I was on the Kaxixó aldeia. The fazendeiros in the region are worried that the Kaxixó will be recognized as Indians by the federal government since this would mean the loss of not only certain small tracts of land but also a cheap source of labor. Given this, the local landholders actively work to subvert the recognition movement. As I noted in chapter 3, they have threatened the lives of some of the Indians involved in the movement and have prohibited them from securing employment in the area. Many members of the Kaxixó community are consequently reluctant to support the recognition drive or even talk about the issue.

One afternoon in July 1995, I interviewed a woman whose husband had been working that day on a neighboring plantation. Later that evening, after he returned and discovered that I had talked to his wife, he became infuriated. He came looking for me to warn me never to come near his home again. At first I erroneously assumed that he was upset due to some sexist notion that no one should interview his wife without either his permission or presence. Clearly this was a factor, but it also became evident, after he calmed down and explained to me why he was so irate, that he was fearful the fazendeiros would discover I had spoken with his wife about this subject and neither of them would ever be able to find work in the region again. He concluded his scolding by stating, "I know we are Indians, but this talk of recognition will only bring us trouble."

Thus the struggle for land, as the above quote suggests, can result in the suppression and potential erasure of Indian identities. This "whitening effect" is further intensified by the unequal distribution of land. The feudal culture, discussed earlier, coupled with the state's labor and development policies since World War II have prompted not only massive urbanization but also a dramatic increase in landless rural workers.[7] In his study of the Brazilian landless workers movement, Maybury-Lewis remarks that "the essential social fact of Brazil's contemporary rural political economy is the monumental concentration of land in the hands of a distinct numerical minority. . . . Indeed, Brazil has one of the most inequitable distributions of arable land in all the world."[8] Indians must often cope with a large, landless, non-Indian peasant population who see Indian land as easier to appropriate than that of the fazendeiros. Benvinda Pankararu explains it this way:[9]

We left Pernambuco because it was very dry there; it was also very crowded.[10] The *posseiros* [settlers or squatters] were there fighting with us over the land. So we left there and came here to the outside. So we went to the aldeia of others. We stayed eleven years in Guarani. There's still a lot of posseiros there today that fight with the Indians. The Indians build a fence and they destroy it. So it is very crowded

Paulo Pankararu was forced to move from his aldeia in Pernambuco to aldeia Apukaré in Minas Gerais due to the ongoing conflicts with posseiros.

> there, so we left. When I was little there were already posseiros there, but there were only a few. So they lived together with us. There was no conflict. But those posseiros went and brought their families, and so now there's no way. The posseiros want to control everything. There are three thousand Indians there. And the Indians and posseiros fight a lot. There on my aldeia FUNAI puts up a sign and those posseiros rip it down.[11]

In this situation, at least according to Benvinda, the posseiros acted without the assistance of fazendeiros. This is typically not the case. Posseiros or *lavradors* (landless agricultural workers) and landholders usually work in tandem to steal Indian land or prevent Indians from reclaiming land that has been illegally appropriated. In other words, a powerful anti-Indian fazendeiro-lavrador alliance often emerges, resulting in a climate of intense anti-Indian hostility.[12] The following excerpt from my interview with José Xacriabá offers a glimpse into the dynamics of this anti-Indian coalition.

> There was also a lot of danger in the cities. Today, we are still a little deferential in the cities. We're afraid . . . especially in Itacarambi,

where the majority of the landholders that were forced to leave our land live. We still walk with fear there. The court is there to protect us, to ensure that we have rights, that we have the freedom to walk in the city. But we still don't have much confidence. We still don't converse with them. To them, Indians aren't worth anything. Indians don't associate with poor field hands [lavradors] and small landholders [posseiros] because it was they who accompanied the big landholders. They beat us. They say they are going to kill us. This still scares us . . . this still frightens us Xacriabá. They don't like to see us there in the city, paying our bills. Those who murdered Rosalino, who murdered Fulgencio, don't like to see us mixing with the people.[13] They don't like us. They know who we are, that we are the family of the cacique. They know that. But they never enter our land. Never.

It is apparent, then, how land can be a de-Indianizing factor. The lack of land and concomitant struggles for it can fuel anti-Indian sentiments and violence, which in turn encourages the shedding of the signifiers of Indianness and Indian subjectivities.[14] In fact, one of the few remaining ways in which Indianness becomes a deadly identity in eastern Brazil is when it is combined with the land issue. Geralda Chaves Soares, a scholar and pro-Indian activist, notes that "clearly people are discriminated against as Indians [in eastern Brazil]. They say Indians speak poorly, that they are fools, that they don't understand things very well, and so on. But in general they don't kill anymore just for being Indian. They kill for land. Violence begins at the moment that Indians fight for land."[15] Thus territories, especially given their maldistribution, can be a whitening force because of the intense level of anti-Indian violence that land disputes still provoke.

The Terrain of Indian Resurgence

The impact of land on Indian formation, however, is not unidirectional. To complicate matters, territory can also have an Indianizing effect. The desire and struggle for land may induce non-Indians to reimagine themselves as Indians.

Indigenous communities are one of only two segments of the general peasant population that have special legal rights to land.[16] According to

Chapter VIII, Article 231 of the 1988 Constitution, indigenous peoples have a right to

> "their social organization, customs, languages, beliefs and traditions, and the original rights to the lands they traditionally occupy, it being incumbent on the Union to demarcate them, to protect and ensure respect for their goods." . . . By "original rights," the framers of the Constitution meant that indigenous peoples were the original owners of the land, and hence that their rights precede any administrative act of government. The government is obligated to demarcate their lands, but the rights of indigenous peoples are neither created by government actions, nor annulled by lack of it. Private land titles on indigenous lands are therefore nullified in the text. The new Constitution further stipulated that the Federal Attorney General's Office defend the interests of indigenous peoples in court.[17]

The process of legal land demarcation for indigenous communities is an extremely long and arduous one.[18] Even if a community has successfully gone through all of the various legal and bureaucratic stages, fazenderios and posseiros will usually only leave when forced to by police, and the police are often extremely reluctant to enforce such rulings. Furthermore, with the 1996 passage of Decree 1775, the Cardoso government made it much more difficult for indigenous communities to have their territories legally recognized.

> The government of Fernando Henrique Cardoso revised the rules for indigenous-land demarcation, ostensibly to protect due process of law for non-indigenous claimants. The effect, however, has been to give greater voice to the landed interests that have successfully blocked demarcations or illegally occupied indigenous lands in the past. Indigenous organizations and their allies suspect that the revisions aim to legalize theft. They argue that since the innovative 1988 Constitution nullifies private titles on indigenous lands, large landholders and ranchers have attacked and struck down government demarcation procedures in order to protect their illegal properties. Despite government assertions to the contrary, indigenous organizations—and private landowners—expect the revision to roll back the demarcation process.[19]

It would be incorrect, then, to assume that Indians can easily acquire land in Brazil. Nonetheless, there is no question that communities recognized as indigenous have a legalistic means of obtaining property, of achieving independence from local fazendeiros, that most non-Indians of the same class do not possess. Unlike black-, pardo-, or white-identified Brazilians, Indians have a constitutional right to land. This, in turn, affords Indians an institutional avenue for securing and maintaining territory.

Given, then, the paucity of land combined with this legal means for Indians to acquire and protect property, it should be evident how territory could act as an Indianizing incentive. I believe this is the effect that land had on indigenous resurgence among the Xacriabá of northern Minas Gerais. The Xacriabá with whom I spoke explained that prior to the 1980s, individuals in their communities self-identified as caboclos rather than Indians. In the words of Antonia Xacriabá, "There are lots of Indians [in Brazil]. There didn't used to be. I didn't know I was Indian. They called us 'caboclo.' But the 'caboclo,' I discovered, is the same thing as Indian."

The term *caboclo* has multiple, shifting, and often overlapping meanings in Brazil. It can be used to designate "a dark-skinned ruralite of indeterminate race, usually engaged in subsistence agriculture or day labor on plantations, and forming part of the rural *caipira* (peasant or backwoodsperson) culture." [20] Caboclo can also refer to a "civilized Indian or half-breed," or what Susanna Hecht and Alexander Cockburn named "the population of backwoods folk formed out of the long history of detribalization [and] miscegenation." [21] In this parlance, caboclos are considered culturally white (with perhaps a few tribal residues) and biological hybrids (the rough parallel of "mulattoness" vis-à-vis the Indian category). This was likely how a significant proportion of the Xacriabá originally interpreted "cabocloness." Finally, caboclo can be a synonym for Indianness. Such was the meaning Zizi remembered it having in southern Bahia and that it came to have for the Xacriabá whom I interviewed. [22]

In the mid-1980s, as the Xacriabá's struggle for territory came to a head, their fate hinged on a discursive battle around the legal definition of cabocloness. The Xacriabá and their lawyers chose to interpret cabocloness as a synonym for Indianness, and more important, this view was accepted and upheld by the courts.[23] As a result, the Xacriabá not only gained control over thousands of hectares of land but also "came to realize" that as caboclos they were Indians.

This is why I contend that land can have an Indianizing effect. Had the Xacriabá as caboclos (as distinct from Indians) been able to get their land demarcated, or if being Indian would not have facilitated their acquisition of property, it seems unlikely that the Xacriabá and their lawyers would have fought to equate caboclness with Indianness. It is doubtful, moreover, that the Xacriabá (at least the ones I interviewed) would have come to self-identify as Indians. Let me underscore that I am not suggesting in the reductive fashion of racial economism that land alone caused Indian resurgence in the case of the Xacriabá. Nor is my point that individuals like Antonia Xacriabá acted as racial accountants who simply select identities based on which one will bring them the most material reward. What I am arguing is that land *in conjunction with* other factors—such as the move toward a postexorcist state (chapter 3), the production and growth of alternative discursive and symbolic fields (chapters 5 and 6), and shifts in official definitions of Indianness (chapter 7)—can spur and has spurred Indian resurgence.

The Kariri-Xocó represent another instance of how land, and the struggle for it, can affect the direction of racial formation—even among communities already recognized as Indian. In November 1978, a group of Kariri-Xocó in the northeastern state of Algoas decided to reclaim a fazenda that they considered part of their ancestral territory. According to Vera Lúcia Calheiros Mata, this land acquisition prompted a "revitalization" of Indian subjectivities: "This conquest stimulated an [identity] politics" in which individuals "wanted to be 'Indian' (in the generic sense), one wanted to be Kariri-Xocó." [24] This new desire was reflected in the demographic growth that took place after this event. "In 1979, there were 728 Indians registered at the FUNAI post. In 1983, the number had elevated to 1,050." [25] By 1993, there were an estimated 1,700 Kariri-Xocó. Part of the newfound "want" to be Kariri-Xocó likely had a symbolic basis. The spectacle of such a bold and effective maneuver against the Development Company of the San Francisco Valley (Companhia de Desenvolvimento do Vale do São Francisco), the agency administering the fazenda at the time, must have inspired a sense of pride in being Kariri-Xocó—perhaps even prompting some to more overtly assert such an identity. But part of the desire no doubt had to do with land. As an anthropologist who has worked in the Kariri-Xocó community, Mata agrees, arguing that "the recuperation of the lands provoked a return of dispersed relatives to the aldeia and made beneficial a mixed marriage, in a region with scarcity of land."[26] Her inference to the increased cache of "a mixed marriage" is a bit vague, but it would seem to indicate that the promise of land encouraged individuals to embrace a Kariri-Xocó identity or ancestry. Moreover, a cultural orientation of Indianing (as opposed to whitening) was intensified in that an increasing number of individuals began practicing certain rituals associated with Kariri-Xocó culture, such as frequenting the Ouricuri, as a means of demonstrating the validity of their identity and concomitant land claims.[27]

It should be emphasized that the effect of land on Indian formation is complex and frequently uneven. In those instances where peasants fight for land *as Indians*, a powerful anti-Indian historical bloc tends to emerge, producing the types of anti-Indian violence that induce the production of non-Indian subjectivities. On the other hand, territory is a potential Indianizing factor because, *as Indians*, individuals and communities have a legal and institutional means not open to non-Indians of reclaiming and protecting stolen lands. In recent years, as definitions of Indianness have changed and Indian exorcism has been mitigated if not halted, the latter effect of land has intensified while the former has diminished. Indianness has, in a general sense, been transformed from a target to a shield. Historically, if a community was considered indigenous, it meant that its territory was defined as available if not empty. And certainly the conquest of Indian country prompted less public or official scrutiny than the appropriation of non-Indian lands. In fact, given so-called civilizing and later whitening projects, such acts of terror were likely legitimated as patriotic moments of nation building. Due to a number of the changes that are the subject of this book, however, Indian status has become, at least in some cases, a powerful subject position from which to claim, retake, and defend one's territory.

Despite its increasing potency as an Indianizing factor, it is important to keep in mind that land can still be influential, if not decisive, in encouraging individuals to imagine or reimagine themselves as non-Indians. Recall, for a moment, the Kaxixó. There are currently sixty-seven Kaxixó fighting for recognition. If they are successful, this would undoubtedly result in a dramatic upsurge in the Indian population given that there are approximately 7,000 persons in the region who could claim to be Kaxixó—many of whom are in need of land. Thus, as was the case with some of the Kariri-Xocó, individuals might start to assert indigenous identities if it entailed the promise of land; others, like Antonia, might come to realize they were Indian if their community were redefined as indigenous. It seems likely that none of this will come to pass, though. For the regional elite, because of their concern for land, will probably prevail in their efforts to torpedo the recognition movement by intimidating enough individuals into *not* mobilizing as Kaxixó.

FUNAI: *"A Change That Never Was"*

FUNAI, which consists of 47 regional administrations and 3,695 civil servants, is the government organ responsible for apportioning state services to Indians.[28] As such, it is supposed to foster "the build up of sanitation, medical assistance, and basic education for Indians."[29] For reasons detailed below, however, FUNAI often fails in its efforts.

As discussed in chapter 3, FUNAI was founded in 1967 after the release of the Figueiredo report that exposed the SPI as a "den of corruption and indiscriminate killings."[30] The Figueiredo Commission "found evidence of widespread corruption and sadism, ranging from the massacre of whole tribes by dynamite, machine guns and sugar laced with arsenic to the removal of an 11 year old girl from school to serve as a slave to an official of the Service."[31] FUNAI was thus supposed to mark a change from the crookedness and violence that had characterized SPI's tenure. Even with the atrocities of SPI as a reference, FUNAI was not an immediate improvement. In fact, FUNAI represents "a change that never was."[32]

At approximately the same time that FUNAI was established, the military leadership decided to intensify the colonization and economic development of the Amazon region as part of a broader political-economic strategy.[33] Tax incentives were offered and laws passed to promote settlement, mining, cattle raising, and agribusiness in the region.[34] Moreover, large-scale development projects were instigated with the assistance of huge international loans that resulted in, among other things, extensive highway construction.[35]

As a government agency, the military enlisted FUNAI as an accessory to its broader capital- and nation-building efforts. In October 1970, for example, "FUNAI signed a contract with the Superintendency for the Development of the Amazon (SUDAM) for the pacification of Indian tribes along the Trans-Amazon and Santarém-Cuiabá highways."[36] The Parakanân was one of the first of scores of tribes to be affected by this pact.

The Brazilian government revealed that the new Trans-Amazon Highway would pass through the Territory of the Parakanân. In late 1970, FUNAI agents attempted to pacify and attract the Parakanân tribe. . . . Immediately following their pacification, forty members of the Parakanân tribe were stricken with influenza. . . . By spring of 1971 . . . workers along the Trans-Amazon Highway began to invade the territory of the tribe. . . . In the course of these initial contacts, highway workers were reported to have given presents to the Parakanân men and to have raped several Indian women. Reports also noted that FUNAI agents had sexually violated some of the women of the tribe. In November 1971, a Brazilian physician named Antonio Madeiros visited a Parakanân village. . . . Madeiros . . . discovered that thirty-five Indian women and two FUNAI agents had venereal diseases. In addition, he found that eight children in the village had been born blind, and at least six others had recently died from dysentery. To make matters worse, in February 1972 another influenza epidemic struck the Parakanân tribe. . . . Several more Indians died. . . . [In July 1972], a four member team of the Aborigines Protection Society of London (APS) visited the Parakanân village. . . . In their report, the APS team wrote, "The hygiene was appalling, with excrement near the houses. . . . Eye disorders such as squints and (apparently) cataract [sic] were in evidence as were cysts and various growths, including a large tumor on a woman's head. Colds were also common and the risk of further infection from the nearby Trans-Amazon was painfully apparent." . . . Since their pacification and resettlement, the APS team reported, these Indians had sold their cultural possessions to outsiders in exchange for guns and ammunition and were living off the dole of highway workers along the Trans-Amazon Highway. Most revealing, the population of the Parakanân had been reduced to eighty persons and there was every indication that their culture was rapidly being destroyed.[37]

This is one of several similar instances illustrating how FUNAI "became a chief accomplice in the processes of ethnocide that were unleashed on the Indian tribes of the Amazon Basin." [38] Thus, far from representing some sort of break from SPI, "its 'reformed' Indian policy, to state the situation most simply, tended to speed up, rather than stop, the processes of ethnic destruction." [39]

The destruction that FUNAI helped perpetrate on indigenous communities in the Amazon was not nearly so severe in eastern Brazil principally because there was much less damage that could be done. When FUNAI was founded, centuries of discoveries had already dramatically affected eastern Indians. By the 1970s, they had immunities to many of the diseases that were devastating Indians in the Amazon. The highways and railroads had long been built in or near their territories. The vast majority of their lands and resources had been appropriated. Finally, eastern Indians already had hundreds of years of experience dealing with non-Indians, and therefore, they were not nearly as susceptible to being coerced, hoodwinked, or seduced by the exotica that non-Indians must have represented to people like the Parakanân. And so, unlike the Amazon where the pace of Indian exorcism was accelerated, FUNAI basically just picked up where SPI had left off in eastern Brazil—neither slowing down nor speeding up efforts to acculturate Indians and appropriate their lands.

For instance, FUNAI continued "the so-called renda indígena, or indigenous income, a special institution developed during the final years of SPI." [40] This system entailed forcing Indians to sell the products of their labor as well as to lease their lands and resources to outsiders for mineral, timber, and grazing rights.[41] The earnings were then used to subsidize the salaries of FUNAI agents and finance so-called government benefits for indigenous communities. Consequently, as with SPI, FUNAI represented a substantial fiscal loss for Indians given that their labor, lands, and resources were forcibly sold or leased away for a fraction of their net worth. Adding insult to injury, the small portion of these monies that actually found its way back to Indians was used to culturally exorcise them. According to General Bandeira de Mello, the president of FUNAI in 1970, "The money in this fund . . . [financied] government-initiated agricultural and industrial projects on Indian reserves [in order to] transform native hunting, fishing, and gardening economies and set the groundwork for the integration of Indians into the wider market economy and class structure of Brazil."[42]

FUNAI did not begin to fulfill its promise of change in eastern Brazil until the 1980s, when civilian rule was slowly restored and an Indian social movement emerged, thereby transforming government laws, institutions, and practices. Article 231 of the new Constitution, to take one example, "permits development of energy and mineral resources on native lands only by an act of Congress, and assures Indians royalties from these activities."[43] The practice of Indian agents profiteering from Indian resources — a policy practiced by both SPI and FUNAI — was thus made illegal. Furthermore, as discussed in chapter 3, FUNAI became much less complicit in anti-Indian violence. For instance, as early as 1982, "FUNAI filed a lawsuit on behalf of the Pataxó Hã-Hã-Hãe requesting the restoration of their original territory" and the concomitant removal of the fazendeiros.[44] And when the Pataxó Hã-Hã-Hãe recaptured 788 hectares of their territory in 1997, FUNAI did not attempt to block their action but instead intervened to ensure that the fazendeiros would not retaliate or attempt to retake the land.

Where the criticism of FUNAI as "a change that never was" still holds weight is with respect to corruption. As we have seen, FUNAI officials are no longer permitted to collude with mining companies, fazendeiros, and the military to appropriate Indian land, labor, and resources. Yet corruption of a more mundane, less conspiratorial sort continues unabated. I am referring to the wastefulness and gross misuse of resources that results when an institution is overly bureaucratic, lacking in transparency, unaccountable to its intended constituency, and managed by functionaries who are concerned primarily, if not exclusively, with their own self-interest.

Health care, the biggest social service that the government provides to eastern Indians, offers an excellent illustration of this particular brand of organizational abuse. Brazilians of all classes are guaranteed health care. Nevertheless, for those who cannot afford a private doctor, health care is deplorable. This would include *at least half* of the Brazilian population.[45] Those who have no option but to use the public health care system must attend hospitals that are sorely understaffed and lacking in basic equipment. Doctors and staff there are overworked and underpaid. It is, then, little wonder that these institutions of public health are notorious for being petri dishes of incompetence and malpractice.[46]

Virtually everyone I met described the public hospitals as a place of last resort. Brazilians reported long queues in which people would wait for hours with serious injuries such as severed limbs and severely fractured bones—some had even witnessed people dying in line prior to receiving medical attention. And then, once they were attended to, the horror stories continued. For instance, according to the Indians at aldeia Apukaré, a two-year-old Pataxó girl was killed in October 1995 by a doctor in Araçuaí who misapplied a routine shot. The following excerpt from an interview with Zizi Pataxó suggests that a similar "mishap" may have caused her daughter's death.

> I was one month away from giving birth when my other girl caught pneumonia suddenly, double pneumonia. It was seven in the morning when she suddenly became very sick. She wasn't sick at all. It was very sudden. When we arrived there [at the hospital], the doctor wouldn't see us until ten. He gave her some medicine and left.
>
> Just when it seemed that she was getting a little better, when I thought that God had answered my prayers and my daughter would not die—that's when he arrived. It was seven at night and he was really drunk, so drunk that his nose was red. I went to the bathroom and I could hear her coughing. When I returned she was coughing. I saw her. She had opened her eyes. She had opened her mouth. The doctor had sat down next to the crib. He was sitting, securing the girl's head and putting his hand deep into the girl's stomach. Then began those screams of the girl. Those wails. He ordered them to take me out of the room, and I grabbed the crib. The nurses dragged me out of the room and slammed the door shut. He stayed in there alone with the girl. Then I saw them preparing two shots to calm me down, and he stayed in there with her. I didn't want to lie down. I stayed there, sitting in the chair, knowing that he was probably killing the girl because I was poor, because I had no money to pay him. When he left, they applied another shot. They said, "The doctor ordered it." I

asked, "Doctor, where is my baby? Did she die?" He said, "She died." I said, "Why did you let my daughter die?" Then I collapsed and didn't see anything more.

Afterward, I don't remember what happened. I screamed. I cried. I was so disoriented. The people of Carmésia say that the most painful death, the one they felt the most, was that of that girl. There I was only one month short of giving birth again. I couldn't relate to anything. For me this world had changed. I was no longer in this world. Nothing made sense.

Regardless of whether this particular doctor was responsible for the death of Zizi's child, this passage offers an example of the sort of experiences I was repeatedly told about. In short, even if the public doctors and hospitals were of good quality, they certainly were not perceived as such. One can imagine, then, why the prospect of FUNAI might have been appealing to well over half the Brazilian population—as the racial huckster theorists argue it was—because, in theory, it was supposed to supplement the substandard quality of health care that poor Brazilians endured. The problem with this reasoning is that in practice, FUNAI provides very little by way of additional medical services. The only instances that I witnessed or learned about were a medical assistant who lived on the Tupinikim aldeia, an ambulance driver who took patients to the hospital in a neighboring city on the Xacriabá and Guarani aldeias, and a FUNAI hospital in Governador Valadares, Minas Gerais, that exclusively serviced Indians.[47]

I never visited the Indian hospital in Governador Valadares, so I have no firsthand knowledge as to what it was actually like. I have, however, been to a FUNAI hospital in Rondônia. That particular hospital, in the city of Porto Velho, was filthy. The stench of urine filled the air. Since the beds were without mattresses, the sick lay on bare springs. There was no staff there at the time, but the Indians assured me that there were doctors, nurses, and dentists on the payroll—all of whom were supposed to have been there. Still, added the Indians, "They sometimes do not appear for weeks at a time."

From what various people told me about the hospital in Governador Valadares, my sense is that it was not nearly as bad as the one I visited in Rondônia. Nonetheless, experiences such as Antonia describes below suggest that the actual services Indian hospitals provide to eastern Indians are not substantively better than those offered by public hospitals to all lower-class Brazilians.

They say that Indians don't work, that the government helps the Indian. That's a lie. The government thinks that it is helping the Indian, but who is benefiting are the whites who work for FUNAI. The richest association in Brazil is FUNAI. On the backs of Indians, they are getting rich. I saw firsthand how they operate. Indians are mistreated by FUNAI, they sleep on the ground, they eat bad food. I saw lots of things like this at FUNAI.

My aunt was in Governador Valadares and she called me to tell me that she was coming here to my house. So we went to the bus station to get her, and she had a baby and its mother with her. I got frightened because I had never seen such a thing in my life: the baby was wailing badly. So I asked what had happened with the baby. And the mother of the baby said that the people at Governador Valadares ordered the baby to die either at home or on the way home. And I wouldn't accept it.

That night that they arrived, the baby was wailing the whole night, and so I didn't think it was right to allow this baby to suffer. I took the baby to the hospital. The baby wasn't even registered. I explained to the doctor that the baby wasn't registered but on Monday she would have the registration. So then the doctor asked who was going to pay the bill. I said FUNAI would take responsibility for the baby. So the hospital took the baby. Then I telephoned FUNAI and I spoke with Helio. I explained the conditions of the baby and I asked how they were going to be paying the bill. The boy had to be operated on. A valve had to be inserted into his head. There in Governador Valadares, they didn't do this because the valve was very expensive and this valve was special. At that time, the valve was lots of money. So the people there [at FUNAI] went crazy because the valve, the hospital, and the care were going to be very expensive for FUNAI. But they operated on the baby. And the baby was good for eight days.

And when I returned the next day and looked for the baby, the baby wasn't there. I looked for the doctor, but the doctor was not in the hospital. Then they told me that the baby had died. So I became worried because after the operation the baby was well. On the death certificate they put that he had died of meningitis. They put him in a sealed case that they said they could not open because the disease was dangerous. At that point, I began to suspect that they had taken the valve out of the baby. I searched for the doctor so that she could explain it to me. But I only know that the doctor disappeared. I told FUNAI what had happened. They said that if they could have thrown a bomb at my house they would have done so to kill me because they spent a lot of money. So they ordered a nurse from Governador Valadares to take care of the baby. The undertaker came and had to take the baby to Xacriabá.

After that, everyone got mad at me, even my brother. Rodrigo [the cacique and chefe of the FUNAI post on the aldeia] said that I could never enter the aldeia again. And my brother said to Rodrigo that he would like to see who was going to stop her from entering. So I went there, to the house of my oldest brother. Afterward, I went to FUNAI to talk with Rodrigo and I asked him what right he had to stop me from entering the aldeia. He said that I had made lots of mistakes. And I said, "No, I simply tried to save the life of a child and the only reason I failed is because you prevented me from doing it." Then he shut up and never spoke to me again.

The above is but one story of how the health care provided to Indians varies little from what non-Indians of the same class receive in Brazil. Although it appears the boy could have been saved, he was sent away to die in Governador Valadares. He would have met the same fate in the public hospital had it not been for the promise of payment by FUNAI. And as soon as the hospital learned that the funds would not be forthcoming, the medical treatment was halted and the child died.

None of this should be interpreted as meaning that the government has not allocated significant amounts of money for Indian social services. In fact, according to FUNAI, the federal government appropriated nine million dollars to the agency in 1997 for Indian health care.[48] Subsequently, one can understand why, as Antonia notes, "the government thinks that it is helping the Indian" despite Indians receiving little health care assistance. A state congressional representative (*deputada*) of Minas Gerais, Maria José Haueisen, attributes this seeming incongruity to a regional disadvantage in which most of the budget has been funneled to the Amazon Indians due to environmental concerns.

> In recent years, international institutions have made financial contributions to proindigenous initiatives. However, the great majority of them, even the World Bank, direct their donations to the Amazon region because of the important accompanying matter of the environment. The Indians of Minas [Gerais] are almost completely forgotten. The same is true in relationship to federal assistance. The Ianomâmis receive a large quantity of resources for health care while the Maxakali haven't even received so much as the services of a nurse.[49]

Rodrigo Xacriabá, a FUNAI employee, cacique, and the individual whom Antonia mentioned above, has a similar reading. He believes FUNAI's failure to provide even a modicum of health care stems from a lack of resources.

> I'm the Cacique Rodrigo of the Xacriabá tribe, where approximately 6,000 Indians live. They live so far from [medical] assistance! I'm saying this because FUNAI, an organ that gives protection to indigenous communities, doesn't help us [*fica distante*] because it lacks the resources. Look at how all the indigenous communities of the state are in a lamentable situation because they lack medical assistance. The issue of health care on my reserve is a sad matter.[50]

There is perhaps some degree of truth to the claims that most of the resources are directed to Indians in other parts of the nation or that nine million dollars is an inadequate amount of money given the level of health care needs. In the final analysis, though, I concur with Antonia that the principal reason why Indians receive so little medical assistance—as well as other types of government aid for that matter—has to do with FUNAI's institutional culture. An ex-president of FUNAI, Márcio Santilli, describes this culture as "comatose" (*morta-viva*)—an organization that is "more bureaucratic than operational." [51] According to Santilli, FUNAI "neglects its own patrimony, paying hyper-inflated prices because of a lack of credibility and confronting an internal mutiny in the form of corrupt functionaries. In most cases, they are only motivated by their own interests—to the dissatisfaction of Indians." [52] In the opinion of its ex-president at least, rather than lacking resources, FUNAI poorly utilizes or even misuses its funds.

In my encounters, this "dissatisfaction" was by far the most prevalent sentiment toward FUNAI among eastern Indians. They, like Santilli, saw FUNAI as an institution that, due to red tape and "corrupt functionaries," was not operating in the interests of Indians. Antonia, for one, put it more bluntly: FUNAI, "the richest association in Brazil," is benefiting whites "on the backs of Indians." Such misgivings and ill will led the Pankararu to reject FUNAI's proposal to create an Indian post on their aldeia, despite the fact that it may have secured them a medical assistant and would have helped legitimate their aldeia as an authentic indigenous reserve. Similar feelings surfaced when I interviewed Domingos Pataxó in 1995 about his experiences as a FUNAI employee.

> I was already married and had a bunch of kids when I entered FUNAI. I worked in the fields, I made bows and arrows and sold them to buy things for the kids and my wife. The chefe was white and he saw that I was very interested in work. I worked hard with my parents. So he asked my mother if I wanted to work for FUNAI. And I said I didn't because afterward FUNAI would want to enslave me. He said, "No, it will help your future." He said I could work within FUNAI to help the Indian. I said, "That's not possible." We conversed like this until finally he won me over.
>
> I have worked for ten bosses of FUNAI already. So I know everything about being the boss of a post, about what is hatched. The money is seductive, and my passion is left behind. I am no longer able to do what I would like to do. Now I can't be a *paje* [spiritual adviser]. Now I can't go into any meeting in any place and resolve the problems that Indians face. If I was caught and put in prison, my life would end. So I think I was right in what I first said to that boss years ago. I can't fish or hunt. The boss says that we have to work here on the reserve. And the Indians here on the reserve think that if you're working for FUNAI, you can't resolve their problems. They question your alliances, your motives.

This, as mentioned earlier, was the community that the Italian anthropologist Oscar referred to in chapter 3 as a lot of racial hucksters who were simply identifying as Indian for the health care services that FUNAI provided. Interestingly, what comes through in Domingos's reflections is an extremely different image of FUNAI. It is not portrayed as a great patron of Indians—let alone a reason to self-identify as Indian. If anything, FUNAI is viewed negatively. Domingos saw it as inhibiting him from expressing his Pataxóness, as well as disempowering him from organizing and struggling for the interests of the Pataxó. And given that Domingos's employment with the agency led him to question his political alliances, it can be inferred that other Indians in this community felt likewise about FUNAI.

Note that I am not suggesting that FUNAI supplies no social services at all to Indians. Instead, I am arguing that the government assistance is not substantive. As we have learned, even in those cases where significant amounts of money have been allocated for certain services, once funneled through FUNAI the "real benefits" are scant. Moreover, the social services that actually materialize tend to do so in such a haphazard, distorted, and ineffective manner that it is often a stretch to refer to them as benefits.[53]

FUNAI, then, hardly fits the image of an institution that is such a windfall for Indians that non-Indians have been enticed to racially redefine themselves. To the contrary, FUNAI represents more of a liability than an asset for eastern Indians, racked as it is by cronyism, unmotivated functionaries, and an overly bloated, unresponsive bureaucracy. Yet despite the deep animosity that Indians hold toward FUNAI, few are in favor of its abolition. They instead support institutional reform and the appointment of an indigenous president.[54] Their logic is much like that of Senator Darcy Ribeiro's assessment of FUNAI: "It's bad with it, but worse without it."[55] It is feared that without this organization, Indians would no longer have an institutionalized voice in government. Even though both Indians and their allies realize that FUNAI is an extremely problematic agency, they are reluctant to call for the dismantling of an institution that is mandated to defend indigenous communities from "predators" as well as provide some basic social services. Still, in the era of neoliberalism and fiscal austerity programs, one can easily imagine why FUNAI, as many are predicting, may "become extinct."[56]

Except for the directors of FUNAI posts on the Xacriabá and Guarani aldeias, all of the Indians in eastern Brazil, at least prior to 1998, were lower class. That is, they belonged to that majority stratum of the Brazilian population that earns five or fewer minimum salaries (five hundred U.S. dollars or less) per month (see appendix C).[57] Employment opportunities for lower-class Brazilians are pitiful. Even in major cities, where the cost of living is equal to or higher than cities in the United States, the best one can hope to earn is the equivalent of three to four hundred U.S. dollars per month. In rural areas, where indigenous people are concentrated, prospects are even worse. As Cleonice Pankararu points out:

> Here in the rural areas, the people work in the fields. There's discrimination on the part of the fazendeiros. They only want manual workers. They give no value to people. They only want to exploit. The owners of the big mines in this region have lots of precious minerals. These mining companies really discriminate, too—they only want wealth. Many nations have to work only for a plate of food or bus fare. They give a week of work for a pittance.

Many "nations," meaning here "races," must indeed work for meager wages. Yet it is important to note that one's chances of being forced to work for insufficient pay increase if one is of a nonwhite "nation." This is because racism helps to concentrate and confine nonwhites to low-income jobs.

Employers oftentimes make a conscious decision not to hire nonwhites.[58] They do not explicitly state their racist hiring practices by putting up a sign or telling potential employees directly—although this does happen.[59] More typical has been the coding of racial preferences with advertisements such as "good appearance required" ("*boa aparência*"), which means "whites only need apply." [60] Or, of course, employers have simply refused to hire nonwhite applicants regardless of their qualifications.[61] This is particularly true "for any job involving direct contact with consumers or the public. As a result, jobs as receptionists, salespeople, and even waiters in better restaurants, are closed off to Afro-Brazilians." [62] It was common knowledge in the neighborhood where I lived in Rio de Janeiro that the stores in the Gavea and Rio shopping malls would not, except in extremely rare cases, hire Brazilians of color.

Many Brazilian employers, however, are probably not intentionally racist. They are instead heavily influenced by a culture in which whiteness is a powerful signifier of competency, trustworthiness, beauty, intelligence, and so on.[63] These insidious forms of white supremacy saturate Brazilian society. In many cases, employers may even see themselves as nonracist, but because they are immersed in ideologies that attach important symbolic meaning to certain phenotypes, they are likely to perceive individuals of diverse races yet equal caliber quite differently.[64]

It is no surprise that in terms of wage disparities, scholars have found a significant cost to being nonwhite—even after controlling for education and estimated experiences.[65] In fact, whites are "much more efficient in converting experience and educational investment into monetary returns," even as "nonwhites suffer increasing disadvantages as they try to scale the social ladder."[66] This is because white privilege has been found to be most ensconced vis-à-vis white-collar jobs. Racism certainly exists in the working-class sector of the economy, but "Brazilian employers discriminate at the middle-class level of the labor market far more than at the working-class level. . . . [Nonwhites] are hired for middle-class positions at rates much lower than those for whites, and once in those positions, they are paid much less."[67]

Among nonwhites, mulattoness has not been found to be an "escape hatch," as it was once believed. "On most statistical indicators," George Reid Andrews notes, "the pardo population as a whole ranks only slightly higher than the preto [black] population, and does not come close to occupying the position midway between whites and pretos that has frequently been asserted."[68] But what about Indians? Is it better in terms of employability, as some critiques of posttraditional Indians maintain, to be classified as Indian rather than black or pardo? Does the labor market benefit Indians, and therefore, might this asset be prompting indigenous resurgence?

My findings indicate that eastern Indians are not advantaged; indeed, in certain contexts, they are greatly disadvantaged. For instance, as Puhuí's comments suggest, Indianness compounds, rather than

Valdi Pataxó husking corn for chicken and pig feed.

mitigates, the enormous employment difficulties that lower-class non-whites confront in the municipality of Carmésia.

> The Indian doesn't have work, they don't have a good education—few even study, and whites [non-Indians] . . . can study, they have jobs.[69] Our people here, from our aldeia here, if they go to look for work here at the city hall, they won't find it because the mayor won't give them work. The Indian can't work because he [sic] has to have a person to represent him. A little while ago, in Carmésia, there came a person asking if fifteen Indians could go work in the eucalyptus plantation. Shortly thereafter, a message was sent that they needed a person that could "vouch for" [avalizar] the Indian so that the Indian could work. This shows a lack of respect, a lack of consideration. . . . So the Indian has to be dominated? It doesn't have to be this way. But because of this, the Indian can only work in the fields and produce a few things for his house and that's it. There isn't any future in that.
>
> I think differently. I sincerely don't like working in the fields. My work is artesenato. My livelihood is artesenato. My things were not bought with money from corn and beans, no. That would be a lie if I told you I bought those things with money from corn and beans. I help my father in the fields. I till the soil. I plant. I weed. I husk the corn. I shuck the beans. But I do not work in the fields, no. For me, the fields don't yield any money [comissão]. So we have to fight in another manner. I take my artesenato, leave this area, and sell my things just for myself. Sometimes I sell that of my family's instead of mine because I know the situation of the community. I have lots of relatives here who don't have the conditions for anything. So if I am with their artesenato, I have to do what I can to sell it for them as well. It is a struggle.

Indians, in Puhuí's view, have been locked out of even low-wage jobs—private and public. He explains that "the Indian can only work in the fields," and with this he means their own fields and not those of local fazendeiros where they could earn a wage, albeit a small one. Puhuí asserts that the reason Indians from his aldeia cannot even secure low-income jobs has to do with the "disrespect" shown them. What he means is that Indians, as I will discuss in detail in chapter 6, are seen by many in eastern Brazil as "lazy," "savage," "poor workers," "drunks," "dirty," and so on. To cite just one example, I was told by Jerry Kaxixó that the majority of non-Indians in Martinho Campos were "nauseated" by Indians.

> Many times whites are disgusted by Indians. Lots of time they'll even say it to our faces. One day I was in the city with my mother. And they said to us, "God, there's nothing more disgusting and ugly than an Indian." About 70 percent of the people in the region have this vision. They say that Indians are disgusting because they're pigs. They say they're dirty, that they don't like to take baths.

Obviously, if these sorts of imaginings of Indianness are prevalent, then it will be more difficult for Indians to find employment, let alone well-paying jobs. In the particular case mentioned by Puhuí, these derogatory stereotypes supposedly disadvantaged Indians in terms of both needing someone to "authorize" them (non-Indians probably would not have been required to obtain validation) and finding someone to provide such a recommendation (these notions of Indianness make it harder to do so). But how does this explain the fact that even though blacks and pardos also face a barrage of disparaging attitudes, they have not been shut out of the low-wage, manual labor sector of the economy? For instance, despite blackness being afforded little "respect," some (if not all) of the individuals who worked in lieu of the Indians on the eucalyptus plantation were without doubt blacks or pardos.

The answer rests with Puhuí's qualification "in these parts." Eastern Indians are concentrated in regions where they have been engaged, *as Indians*, in years of protracted, often bloody conflict with non-Indians for land, resources, and political power. Anti-Indian hostilities and sentiments are thus heightened. As a result, non-Indians in these regions, when constituting their imaginings of Indianness, draw most heavily from the more negative, mean-spirited, and vile notions of Indianness available to Brazilians.[70]

There is, then, much greater variability in the topography of anti-Indian as opposed to antiblack or antipardo imaginings. Conceptualizations of other racial subalterns are extremely derogatory and pervasive as well, but they are not elevated in certain municipalities. For instance, I found that the quality, degree, and tone of antiblack stereotyping does not shift much between Belo Horizonte, Carmésia, Vitória, Araçuaí, Vasalia, and so on. There are not specific microregions where it is dramatically augmented, as is the case with Indians. The reason for this stems from the fact that unlike Indians, few if any communities have mobilized *as blacks* for land rights, schools, public jobs, state resources, and so forth.[71] In other words, this particular sharpening of racism has not occurred because a viable black or pardo grassroots movement has yet to emerge, at either the local or national level, seeking the deracialization of power.[72]

This does not therefore mean that outside these zones of accentuated anti-Indian attitudes Indianness is an asset on the labor market. It is true that Indians residing in Belo Horizonte, a city where anti-Indian sensibilities are not magnified, were able to acquire low-income jobs, whereas in the rural regions they were locked out of this sector of the economy. Yet even here it did not appear that Indianness was an advantage on the labor market. By way of evidence, every Indian in Belo Horizonte told me that they concealed their Indianness from their employers. Remember that most posttraditional Indians do not signify Indianness. In the cities, in contrast to rural areas where there is little anonymity, it is possible to be closeted. One of their motivations for concealing their Indianness may have been to avoid the constant barrage of "curious" questions, such as "Do you eat people?" and "Why are you wearing clothes?" Or perhaps this decision to keep their Indianness a secret was driven by a concern that it could damage their employment chances since they might be viewed in light of anti-Indian stereotypes. Whatever the reasons, one would assume that if it were more advantageous to be Indian, then these individuals would have made their Indianness known to their bosses, managers, and coworkers.

Another feature of these microregions of Indian contestation that contributes to their almost complete exclusion from the paid labor force is the increased politicization of employment. In counties with Indian communities, jobs are deployed in a much more strategic and cognizant manner vis-à-vis indigenous people. Paid employment is used to express animosity toward the Indian community, consolidate anti-Indian alliances, or undermine the indigenous opposition. To take one case, it can be inferred from Jerry Kaxixó's statement below that the fazendeiros were wielding wage labor instrumentally as a tool to affect political aims—that is, the destruction of the indigenous movement in the region.

> To this day, in various families, [the Kaxixó] don't like to say that they're Indians because they're afraid. When they're close to a fazendeiro, working for them, they don't like to identify as Indian. Once they stop working, they return to identifying as Indian. This happens with about 90 percent of the people in the community. They're afraid of going hungry.

This more Machiavellian climate inhibits Indians from working in the public sector, too. As mentioned earlier, it is not just fazendeiros who are anti-Indian in regions where resources, and in particular land, has been contested by Indians. The local town dwellers and landless rural workers also tend to ally themselves with the fazendeiros, forming an anti-Indian bloc. This alliance is solidified and reinforced, in part, via private and public patronage. Consequently, elected officials in these districts, including those who might be inclined to be more meritocratic, rarely give Indians public jobs for fear of alienating their political and financial base. Even in Carmésia, where the anti-Indian bloc was not nearly as entrenched because there was never a struggle over land, "the mayor," as Puhuí pointed out, "won't give them work."[73]

One additional facet of these zones of struggle is that Indians often harbor enmity toward companies and fazendeiros who have for decades, if not centuries, occupied their lands, appropriated their resources, destroyed their environments, and threatened or murdered their relatives and friends. In the late 1960s, for example, Aracruz Forestry (Aracruz Florestal) began planting eucalyptus trees on and near several Tupinikim aldeias in Espírito Santo. Many of the Tupinikim's forests and areas of cultivation were almost entirely swallowed up by tree farms in the process. Moreover, the chemicals used in the paper factories went untreated (as they still do today), thereby devastating the regional waterways—traditionally a major source of food and income for the Tupinikim.

In 1971, the biologist Augusto Ruschi, who in the 1950s had studied the different ecosystems in the region and thus lamented the manner in which thousands of hectares of virgin forest had been destroyed, documented how seven hundred families had been dislodged from the area due to the "reforestation" carried out by Aracruz Florestal. Of course, the Tupinikim did not just passively accept the appropriation and destruction of their lands. Yet in an era of military rule and Indian exorcism, and in the absence of an Indian movement, the company—in cahoots with local and federal officials—was easily able to suppress any resistance. To this day, reports Carlos Augusto da Rocha Freire, the Tupinikim recount the horrific scenes of violence and disrespect that they suffered during this period of displacement, which resulted in the destruction of many Tupinikim aldeias: Araribá, Amarelo, Areal, Batinga, Braço Morto, Cantagalo, Guaxindiba, Lancha, Macaco, and Oho d'Água e Piranema.[74]

This history, not surprisingly, has generated ill will toward Aracruz Florestal as well as scorn toward those who might succumb to the pressures of poverty and go to work for this company. Although understandable, one effect is that the employment opportunities available to the Tupinikim are circumscribed. Similar sorts of legacies haunt Indians throughout eastern Brazil, helping to further constrain their wage-earning power.

The one niche that Indians have available for generating revenue that is not open to non-Indians is artesanato. In recent years, many tribes have been trying to develop this sector of their economy in conjunction with tourism. The Pataxó have probably been the most successful given the lack of conflict over land in their region and the local mayor's wish to capitalize on the Indians in the area to build up the tourist trade. Yet even on this aldeia, as Manoel Pataxó observes, selling artesanato is hardly a boon enterprise.

> One of the biggest problems that we face here is that of food because if you plant a large field, it will be lost to the forest. The people here need to make their artesanato, or work for someone who's stronger, to be able to buy a few staples. So the time comes when you plant, and then comes the time to weed [capinar] and you don't have anything to eat at home. Sometimes, then, you're forced to leave the field, spending the week making artesanato so that you can buy food. So you leave to sell what you've made, and when you return it's rained on your field. So suddenly the forest has taken over your field and there's no way to salvage it. So you have to make a small field. So because of this, food is our biggest problem.

Geselina Pataxó making artesenato in aldeia Apukaré.

Today I didn't have anything to eat. Sometimes you only have a little and there's not even enough for you to share with two or three people. Sometimes we don't get enough to be able to work during the week.

In short, as my research indicates, rural Indians are all but excluded from both the public and private sectors of the economy. Except for Manoel Pataxó, who was an elected official (vereador) in Carmésia thanks to the Indian vote, I never met or heard of another Indian in one of these microregions who was employed outside the aldeia.[75] Not coincidentally, I believe, only 8 percent of the Indians I interviewed (including those in urban areas) earned more than the equivalant of two hundred U.S. dollars per month. Furthermore, 48 percent of the interviewees had a salary of less than one hundred U.S. dollars per month as compared to 25 percent of pardos, 31 percent of blacks, and 14 percent of whites in southeastern Brazil.[76] And this despite the fact that my sample was skewed toward wealthier Indians given my overrepresentation of urban dwellers and the selection of aldeia Guarani as one of my research sites—the wealthiest aldeia in eastern Brazil. Therefore, with respect to employability, Indianness does not seem to be a plausible material reason for identifying as Indian.

Educational Gaps

The commitment to universal education in Brazil dates back to the corporatist state of the Vargas era of the 1930s.[77] Since that time, efforts to provide an education to all Brazilians—let alone a quality one—have been halfhearted at best. Most Brazilian children attend school for only four hours per day, and the majority do not complete eighth grade.[78] If one cannot afford to attend a private school and the one-year preparatory course for the *vestibular* (college entrance exam), then the chances of entering a university are basically nil. Not surprisingly, it is almost as rare to encounter students at the universities whose families are from the bottom half of the economic hierarchy as it is to see students of color.[79]

Because attempts to build a mass educational system are relatively new in Brazil, the only way that most children, especially in rural areas, could even learn to read and write was if they were supported by a patron—as was the case with Manoel Pataxó, who was born in 1925.[80]

I am very much for education. Where I grew up, we lived in the forest without a doctor; no one knew what a doctor was. All of my brothers were raised to be illiterate. They don't even know the letter *o*. Only I studied. When I was ten, my mother's godmother [was] in Salvador; she was the woman who raised my mother.[81] . . . So when momma married an Indian, she went to live in the forest. That's where we were all born. Her godmother said, "Look, when you have a son, your first son, I want you to give him to me." And my mother said, "Ah, no, I won't do it. If I have a son . . . the first one I won't give you." And her godmother said, "Ah no, you have to give him to me." And then she left for Salvador.

So ten years passed and she returned. She returned to see her promise. She arrived wanting to take Vava.[82] But Vava would have nothing to do with leaving. But I was more rebellious [*bandolero*]. So she said, "Do you want to go, Manoel?" "I want to," I said. I was to go on the condition that I couldn't return until I was seventeen. So momma sent me away. But with fifteen years she ordered me to return. So when I was in the fourth grade, I returned during holidays in July. I was going to spend my holidays at home. I was already fifteen, but I was only in the fourth grade because I began studying very late. So when I arrived, I went to cut some wood and I cut myself. The machete went right into my leg. So I couldn't return. I spent six months walking with a cane, and so I couldn't return anymore.

Later they sent me a message. The teachers asked me to return to study, but I decided not to return. I was the oldest . . . the other sons of papa were troublemakers . . . they were always messing around. So I decided to stay so that they wouldn't be alone. And my parents didn't know any better. They had no idea. If I knew what I know today I would have returned. "It's better that Manoel stay here," my mother said. "He's the oldest, he has to stay here to watch over the others, to help watch over the others." If I had returned to study, I would have gotten a job, which would have helped them. But I thought I was helping by staying. . . . All that intelligence that we didn't have, that we didn't have.

I tell my kids to study. "Here you have everything." I have these grandkids here, and I wish I had their opportunities . . . a school, materials, they can study whenever they want. The bus comes for them at their door every day—it comes in the afternoon and at night. So there are many that study, few drop out, but they study with little passion. When I was little I wanted so much to be able to study . . . but I couldn't because I didn't have the resources. After that time that I cut my leg, I never returned. Because I needed to buy books, to buy clothes, and my parents couldn't give them to me. But today these kids can study until high school.

The dependency of poor children on a patron for their primary education has lessened in recent decades with the gradual institutionalization of universal education. For instance, as Manoel notes, his grandchildren can take a bus to school, have their books paid for, and so on—all without the assistance of a godparent. They can also continue to live at home, which was not possible when he was a boy. Nevertheless, the educational options are still far from ideal for the vast majority of Brazilian children from the lower classes. The low wages paid to workers combined with the lack of child care often requires that older children work odd jobs or stay at home to watch their younger siblings while their parents work. And even when parents can afford to let their children remain in school, there are a number of logistical problems that these children and their families must overcome. In rural regions, for example, the majority of children must commute long distances by foot. In the region where the Pankararu live, both Indian and non-Indian children must walk two hours each way to school, and it is usually dark when they return home, making it dangerous as well as arduous.

Finally, public schools offer little by way of utilitarian value to students. These schools do not provide much technical training in skills that would enable students to acquire better employment in the future. As I have already mentioned, the public schools, especially those outside the major cities, are of such poor quality that students who wish to continue their studies cannot as their education ill equips them to do well on college entrance exams. Given this, many students try to attend private schools or move to urban areas where the quality of public education is somewhat better.

Two of the Indian students I interviewed were attending an agricultural high school in Espírito Santo in the belief that it might open up more job opportunities for them as well as give them some practical knowledge that could one day be used to improve the crop yield of their aldeias. As Bekoy Pataxó, a twenty-eight-year-old junior in 1995, said:

At the moment I study in an agricultural school. There are no such schools here in Minas Gerais, so they sent me to Espírito Santo, telling me they had an agricultural high school there. So I went to visit the school. It has been difficult. The problem is the money. The material for school is very expensive, and FUNAI doesn't give any assistance. The money that I receive—a grant that comes from nuns in Holland—is very little, and most of the time I go without things. It's very difficult. The money comes like this. . . . They send a quantity that has to last the whole year. Only it's not enough for the whole year. It's very little, and the things for school are very expensive. I have to buy clothes, shoes, and it's not enough. I pay at the beginning of the school year, for the whole year, and then I don't have any money for clothes, for food, for fare to see my family.

In February 1997, I received the following letter from Bekoy:

The year after you left was a year of much suffering. After I returned to Espírito Santo, my life was misery. I didn't have a place to stay with my daughter.[83] I lived from house to house, leaving my daughter with whomever I could find when I had to spend the fifteen days away from her at school. Only God knew of my suffering. The money that comes is little and it always arrives late. And by the time it arrives, I already owe the school and other persons so much that the money is never enough.

Right after the beginning of the year, a teacher and student of my school found a place where I could leave my daughter and spend my "alternatives."[84] It was an orphanage—a place where they leave destitute children. During the time that I wasn't at school, I stayed at the orphanage together with my daughter and helped to care for the other children. And the manager and the coordinator paid me sixty reais ($55) for my work. It was going very well until the orphanage went bankrupt.

Bekoy Pataxó and her daughter, Hwanahara Pataxó.

I wrote to Geralda [Chaves Soares] [85] asking her to write to the
Dutch nuns saying that I had passed the second year of high school
and that this year the grant would have to arrive sooner because I
don't have a place to stay with my daughter and this year, my third
year, I'm obliged to do an apprenticeship, and because of this I'm
going to need more money than in the previous years.

Classes begin the seventeenth of February, and I'm still on the
aldeia without any money. Honestly, Jonathan, I really want to drop
out of school. I can't take this situation any longer.

As Bekoy Pataxó's experiences illustrate, the problem that poor students frequently face if they hope to obtain a relatively good education
is not simply one of having to live away from family and community for
extended periods of time, but also having to cope with extreme financial
difficulties. Few grants or loans are offered by the government or philanthropists to poor students. For the majority of Brazilians, the only way
to acquire a quality education, regardless of one's skills, is via a patron-
client relationship. In the end, Bekoy's situation is little different from
that of her uncle Manoel when he was a student in the 1930s. True, she
is attempting to complete high school and not elementary school. Yet
she, too is dependent on a patron.

This dependency of lower-class Brazilians on a well-to-do patron for educational advancement has served to disadvantage Indians. As we have seen, Indians are concentrated in regions where they have been in direct conflict with non-Indians, particularly the local landed elite (that is, fazendeiros). Thus, they have tended to have an antagonistic relationship with precisely that stratum of Brazilian society that can afford to finance the educational dreams of poor, rural Brazilians. Not surprisingly, then, I did not meet a single indigenous person who had had their schooling supported by a local benefactor. Even in the two cases described above, it is telling that both individuals were assisted by persons outside their native region.

Indian Schools

Indians, like nonwhites in general, have been encumbered in their educational advancement by racism. For instance, in a study of Brazilian textbooks, Mauro Almeida found that

> every image of a family showed white people . . . always laughing, living in a well-furnished house, with a television, sofa, library. These families frequented country clubs and a Catholic church. There was not one image of a [nonwhite] family, not at any time. There were also no images of poor families. . . . The whites also monopolized the *community* and the neighbors. . . . Another arena dominated by the homogeneous presence of middle-class whites was the school. . . . And it is not necessary to say that "the authorities" (priest, military, businessperson, politician, etc.) were all white.[86]

Other scholars have also documented the paucity of nonwhite images in schools and textbooks; and the few representations of nonwhites that do appear tend to be pejorative.[87] Michael Hanchard notes that "numerous studies of children's primary school textbooks depict blacks as more sexually promiscuous and aggressive, intellectually inferior to whites, and rarely in positions of power."[88]

The images of Indians are equally troubling. As mentioned earlier, one of the most common tropes encountered is that of the antimodern. Understood as the antithesis of so-called modernity, Indians are represented and homogenized as timeless, naked forest people who are

Figure 1: Common images of Indians in primary and secondary school textbooks.

technologically primitive, and so must subsist via hunting and gathering. Indians qua primitives are most commonly portrayed as noble savages, although the more pejorative side of this stereotype also occasionally surfaces in school texts. Sometimes, Indians are caricatured as buffoons and sambos (see figure 1). Or, as ignoble primitives, their spiritual world is trivialized and belittled. One text described indigenous people as polytheistic because they "*could not give* scientific explanations for natural phenomenon."[89] And it would seem, at least according to Jerry Kaxixó, that the Indian as heathen has yet to vanish from some schoolbooks:

> The author in our textbook wrote that all indigenous religions worship the devil. He said that the Indian adores the things of the devil, that the Indians are demons because they worship with snakes. This book said that the indigenous religion is not a thing very pleasant, that it's deficient, that it's evil. Imagine all of Brazil reads this book, criticizing the Indian religion. For us this works to weaken our tradition, our culture. We already feel enslaved by these prejudices. And then a book that criticizes even more our religion—that complicates things even further.

The Brazilian tradition of Indian exorcism is, of course, rarely broached in school texts. When discussed, such matters as Indian colonization, slavery, and anti-Indian violence are denuded of any critique. To cite one example from a fifth-grade textbook:

> The slavers [bandeiras] originated because the economic activities would not permit economic growth without a better restructuring of the regional space of this part of Brazil. In order to try to get out of this situation, the Paulistas began to organize slavers to hunt Indians so as to sell them to fazendeiros who needed their labor.[90]

Echoing the military regime's justifications for the colonization of the Amazon during the 1960s, 1970s, and 1980s, genocide and slavery are characterized as an engineering problem—a "restructuring of the regional space." Slavery, moreover, is deemed morally acceptable, and even necessary, if the larger goal is economic development. Finally, when Indians are shown in the contemporary moment, something that is infrequent given their antimodern depiction as peoples of the past, they tend to be described as vanishing. As one sixth-grade book explained, "Rapidly, the Indian is being exterminated. Incapable of assimilating a material culture that is so much more evolved, their extinction is a sad truth that a few enlightened individuals and organizations are trying to combat." [91]

This is not meant to be an exhaustive review of the imaginings of Indianness in textbooks. The point, instead, is to provide a sense of the discursive and illustrative racism eastern Indians must negotiate in the schools. As will be seen in chapter 6, many of these same constructions of Indianness permeate popular thought. This, coupled with the above-mentioned fact that eastern Indians are concentrated in regions of heightened anti-Indian sentiments, means that these violent images are rarely, if ever, challenged by non-Indian students, teachers, or administrators in the white-controlled schools that many Indian children attend. Take, for instance, the indigenous students who study in the city of Pau Brasil. On 7 December 1999, fifty individuals—angered that the Pataxó Hã-Hã-Hãe had successfully reclaimed some of their traditional territory—stoned the Pataxó's school bus on its return to the São Lucas aldeia. The school bus driver managed to avoid an accident, but the bus was totally destroyed and four indigenous students were badly injured. Clearly, in such a politicized atmosphere, the derogatory images of Indians found in school texts are likely to have more significance.

Several of the Indians I interviewed described their classmates' and teachers' attitudes as dovetailing with the anti-Indian imagery found in school materials. This was even true of students in regions where conflicts over land were not nearly as intense as those faced by the Pataxó Hã-Hã-Hãe in southern Bahia. For instance, in the following passage, Cleonice Pankararu describes her school experiences in the city of Carmésia near aldeia Guarani (as noted before, given that the aldeia was previously an Indian penal colony, Indian land is not contested):

> There's a period in our culture in which the children are painted. So during this period, the kids don't go to school because the teachers don't accept them painted and the classmates harass them. So they just don't go to school. And on the reservation this is a ritual, this is something very important to the community. There's no respect for difference. When I was in school things like this happened often, but I didn't pay attention to it. My mother always said that we were from a different nation. So the people didn't understand us. So I would go to school and sit in the back row. Many didn't bother me, but others would say: "Look an Indian. Be careful or she will eat you." This was between the fifth and eighth grades. Their parents didn't accept an Indian studying with their children. They were afraid that I would attack their children because whites have this idea that Indians are aggressive.

Jerry Kaxixó had a similar evaluation of the teacher at the school the Kaxixó attended.

> The school is created with the idea of the white. Indigenous matters aren't dealt with. There is no discussion of our ancestors, how they lived, what we're trying to do today with the movement. The students have never been encouraged to think about these things. Beginning when the children are very little, the teachers criticize us. They say that the Indian walks around naked. This has a lot of negative repercussions. . . . These sorts of things happen all the time in the schools. The student is studying, trying to do well in school . . . but just for being Indian, he [sic] is criticized. And so we need a lot of changes. We need to seek help to end this racism within the [school]. We need to have persons who can pass on our culture.

Given the racism of non-Indian teachers, students, administrators, and textbooks, one of the principal agendas of indigenous people and the broader Brazilian Indian movement has been to pressure the federal government to create properly funded Indian schools complete with Indian teachers and an indigenous-centered curriculum. On the whole, this campaign has been extremely successful. Via a series of legislative decrees and constitutional articles beginning in 1988, the federal government has committed itself to the establishment of an Indian educational system that is *not* an apparatus of "civilization" and "nation building" operating to annul cultural differences.[92] These schools instead are explicitly designed to be antiracist. They are mandated to "recognize and valorize an indigenous community's particular social organization, language, values, and history" in order to reproduce and affirm ethnic cultures and identities.[93] For example, Article 78 of the Lei Darcy Ribeiro 9.394/96 passed in December 1996 orders

> the Instructional System of the Union to develop programs so that it can offer bilingual and intercultural education to indigenous people with the following objectives:
>
> I. The recuperation of indigenous peoples' historical memories, the reaffirmation of their ethnic identities, and the valorization of their languages and sciences.
>
> II. The guarantee to Indians of the freedom of information, and access to the technological and scientific knowledge of national society and of other societies—both indigenous and nonindigenous.[94]

Furthermore, the new set of laws requires that everything be done to hire Indian teachers for these schools, and that they be paid an equal salary to that of non-Indian instructors.[95]

The first effects of the new policy were being felt in eastern Brazil in 1997. In general, the states and municipalities are responsible for implementing these laws, and in 1995, at the initiative of the Federal University of Minas Gerais, Accord 3607/95 was passed by the state of Minas Gerais.[96] This accord was designed to establish Indian schools in the Xacriabá, Pataxó, Maxakali, and Krenak communities. As a part of this program, fifty-five Indian teachers were to be selected and trained so

Valmares Pataxó teaching adults math at the Indian School opened in aldeia Guarani in 1997.

Liro Garcia and Baiara Pataxó (back) learning math at the Indian school.

that they could teach in these schools at a high school level.[97] By September 1997, some of the first adult classes were just beginning to be offered on the Guarani aldeia.[98] Class subjects included math, geography, writing, art, history, and so on, with an emphasis, whenever relevant, on indigenous matters. The school was eventually to offer instruction in an indigenous language, probably Maxakali, but a teacher still had to be trained.

Unlike in North America, then, a parallel system of Indian education has only recently been established in Brazil. In the United States, one of the major tools of Indian colonization was education. During the nineteenth century, boarding schools were developed out of a "progressive" sense that Indians were not biologically inferior but simply culturally backward. The object was to "kill the Indian and save the person" via schooling. Accordingly, many Indian children were forcibly removed from their families and taken to schools, sometimes thousands of miles away from their communities, where every attempt was made to exorcise their Indianness. These children were compelled to speak English. Then, too, their names were changed, their hair was cut, they were given different attire to wear, they were indoctrinated into Christianity, and so forth.

Ironically, Indian boarding schools created numerous new and important means of resisting the colonization that the schools were trying to effect. For instance, boarding schools created a fairly large number of well-educated Indians who then formed the basis of an indigenous intelligentsia and professional class. This institutionalized tradition of Indian education, in conjunction with the antiracist movement of the 1960s, has also resulted in an extensive network of Indian colleges, fellowships and scholarships for Indian students, and the founding of American Indian Studies departments and affirmative action at non-Indian schools.

None of this exists in Brazil. Until recently there were no Indian schools, and there are still no Indian colleges or departments, nor financial aid for Indian students to attend school. At the 893 institutions that offer higher education instruction in Brazil, there were only 102 Indian students in 1997, and none were from eastern Brazil.[99] As a direct consequence, there are few if any indigenous novelists, filmmakers, anthropologists, literary critics, philosophers, essayists, lawyers, doctors, journalists, and entrepreneurs. High school attendance for Indians is startlingly low as well: in all of Brazil, as of 1997, only 1,009 Indians were enrolled.[100] Therefore, if all were to graduate—which is unlikely given Bekoy's experiences—this would mean a graduation rate of only .03 percent, as compared to 5.3 percent for blacks, 6 percent for pardos, and 13.9 percent for whites based on 1987 data.[101]

5. Prophetic Christianity, Indigenous Mobilization

The church must follow the example of Christ. She cannot exclude anyone and must offer to all, great and small, the means of salvation received from Christ. But her option and her preferences are the weak and oppressed. She cannot remain indifferent to the plight of the Indian forced from his land and the destruction of his culture. She cannot close her eyes in the face of the grave situation of insecurity in which the defenseless live, before the starvation of the poor, and the malnutrition of the children. —Representative Commission, National Conference of Brazilian Bishops, 1976

In *Prophetic Fragments*, Cornel West connects the "secular sensibilities" of the North American and European Left to one of its principal intellectual traditions: "Western Marxism."[1] To underscore his point, West observes that even though the major figures of this "Eurocentric" development of marxism were preoccupied with culture, none of them took religion seriously.

> Whether it was [Theodor] Adorno and [Herbert] Marcuse on the subversive character of highbrow music and poetry, [Jean-Paul] Sartre and [Louis] Althusser on the progressive possibilities of avant-garde prose and theater, or [Walter] Benjamin and [Mikhail] Bakhtin on the revolutionary potential of film and the novel—all rightly viewed the cultural sphere as a domain of ideological contestation. Yet none highlighted religion as a crucial component of this cultural sphere.[2]

In an analysis that would seem to confirm West's thesis, Roger N. Lancaster explains that his initial reluctance to recognize the links between popular religion and "class consciousness" in Nicaragua was rooted in his Marxian humanist "state of knowledge and theoretical position":

I will confess that my confrontation with Nicaraguan religion originally produced in me an intellectual dissonance. It is not that I am unfamiliar with strong religious feeling. I grew up in a poor rural Southern community, and was there reared to be a Baptist preacher. My path to atheism was not an easy one lightly taken, and it was certainly *not* one uninformed by strong religious experience in a working-class context. Nonetheless, religion and belief in God had long appeared to me in the terms of classical Marxian humanism: as *prima facie* evidence of alienation, and moreover as inherently alienating—and this conviction was all the greater for being tempered by direct experience with the phenomenon.[3]

Somewhat ironically, Lancaster had to travel to Nicaragua to discover a prophetic Christianity, given that one likely flourished in the community where he was reared. Put somewhat differently, I wonder whether Lancaster would have been surprised to find popular religion intimately wed to "revolutionary praxis" if he had been reared in a poor, rural, Southern, *black* Baptist church.[4] As a boy he would likely have known individuals whose Baptist faith empowered and compelled them to fight for social justice. He may even have become acquainted with some of the great stalwarts of the civil rights movement such as Reverend Fred L. Shuttlesworth of Alabama, who had his house bombed in 1956 on Christmas, was beaten by a white mob in 1957, and was hauled off to jail numerous times because of his antiracist activities. What sustained Shuttlesworth, what allowed him to remain "fiery and fearless," what enabled him to lay the groundwork for Martin Luther King Jr.'s successful campaign in Birmingham in 1963, were his Christian convictions.

> "I tried to get killed in Birmingham," [Shuttlesworth] says, his voice still urgent. "I tried to widow my wife and my children for God's sake, because I literally believed that scripture which says '. . . whosoever will lose his life for my sake shall find it.' I had no fear, you understand."[5]

Thus, had Lancaster been brought up in a black Baptist church, which according to West "fuses secular and sacred history and combines Christian themes of deliverance and salvation with political ideals of democracy, freedom and equality," he probably would have immediately recognized the prophetic Christianity he encountered in Nicaragua.[6] Had he come from such a religious background, he likely would not have experienced an intellectual discord as he encountered "the exact opposite relationship between religion and alienation" from what his marxist training had taught him to expect: "Religion and belief in God evinced a profound absence of alienation and acted as a means of overcoming it."[7]

Lancaster's biases were a mirror of some of my own. In the 1960s and 1970s, in a small, white town in rural Michigan, I was exposed to a very different version of Christianity than the prophetic form that had just transformed the social, political, and legal terrain of the United States. I attended a Congregationalist Church. Here, one did not encounter a prophetic Christ but rather accommodated oneself to the political and cultural status quo. I do not recall any discussions of social inequalities and injustices—let alone the offering of any substantive or systematic analysis of power, wealth and influence in society. "Instead," as West says, "as is the case with most religious Americans, . . . personalistic and individualistic explanations for poverty, occupational mobility and social catastrophe" were left unquestioned.[8] Much like Lancaster, then, I went to Latin America unprepared to find a prophetic church because of my personal experiences with organized religion rather than as a result of the secular sensibilities of certain intellectual traditions in which I was schooled.

A New Catholic Culture

After World War II, a new theology and concomitant religious culture arose in Latin America, which Michael Löwy refers to as "liberationist Christianity."[9] Instead of catering to the more elite sectors of society, as the church was seen as having done historically, adherents of this new kind of faith believed that the church should "look to the people (o povo) as its main focus and basis of support."[10] That is, rather than "the church [remaining] aloof, or even hostile, to the vast majority of the population," its role was "to use all possible means . . . to improve the miserable social situation" of the "people."[11]

As this prophetic Catholicism gathered momentum and gained followers, "a significant sector of the Church—both believers and clergy—in Latin America changed its position in the field of social struggle, going over with its material and spiritual resources to the side of the poor and their fight for a new society." [12] Perhaps nowhere was this shift more marked than in Brazil. According to Löwy, "the Brazilian Church is a unique case in Latin America, in so far as it is the only Church on the continent where liberation theology and its pastoral followers have won a decisive influence." [13]

An example of this "decisive influence" was the transformation of the church's position vis-à-vis the military dictatorship. Initially, in the early 1960s, the church supported and legitimated the 1964 military coup. By the end of the decade, however, the emergent liberation theology had affected the sensibilities of the church to such a degree that its stance regarding the state and military regime began to change. Subsequently, unlike in other parts of Latin America such as Argentina, as the military regime became more repressive, as the brutality directed against church people and even members of the clergy intensified, the Brazilian church became increasingly critical of the dictatorship and eventually became its main adversary.[14]

The rise of prophetic Catholicism also resulted in the church's neglect of its traditional pastorals and institutions in favor of creating new ones more in tune with the goals and values of liberation theology. One of the numerous ecclesiastical organizations that emerged from this theological/social movement was the indigenous pastoral CIMI. As Thomas C. Bruneau observes, "With the general development of a new approach to influence [that is, liberationist Christianity] in the late 1960s . . . elements in the church began to take stock of the situation and realized that they were at least partly to blame for the plight of [Indians,] and that if the church were not to defend them nobody would." Their concerns, he continues, resulted in the establishment of CIMI in 1972 "in an attempt to defend the few remaining indigenous Brazilians." [15] With the goal of "defending" rather than exorcising Indians, CIMI set out to build "the autonomy of Indians . . . [and] contribute to the strengthening of their organizations and alliances, in both Brazil and [on] the continent." [16]

As such, CIMI marked a significant change of course for the Brazilian church with respect to indigenous people. As was detailed in chapter 3, historically the church had been complicit with, and at times at the forefront of, Indian exorcism in eastern Brazil. Missionaries had actively worked for centuries to erase "ethnic" and "cultural" distinctions as well as to erode indigenous organizations and alliances. With the establishment of CIMI, however, the church began committing itself to precisely the opposite agenda.

This, then, brings me to the central question of this chapter: How has this new commitment, born in large measure from the theology that preached the gospel as a call for social justice, resulted in an increase in the number of individuals who self-identify as Indian?[17]

Liberationist Missionaries

One of the ways that CIMI has involved itself with eastern Indians has been via the placement of pastoral agents near, and if possible in, an indigenous community. This particular form of grassroots intervention—which was, of course, also the hallmark of the mission system—is referred to as "accompaniment." An interview with Geralda Chaves Soares, a former CIMI pastoral agent who accompanied the Maxakali between 1980 and 1986, is worth citing at length because it provides an excellent window into what such interventions can (and often do) entail in terms of dangers and hardships, objectives and goals, the immediate impact on a given community, and consequences for social and political mobilization.

In 1980, the violence against the Maxakali was escalating, and so the bishop, according to Geralda, asked CIMI to send some pastoral agents to the region to accompany the Maxakali:

> [The bishop] had become very concerned because it seemed that every day the violence intensified. There always arrived news of another Indian who had been assassinated. So we . . . I worked for CIMI at the time . . . we proposed the creation of a team that was to be made up of myself and another woman from the region.

Government officials, in particular FUNAI employees, were not pleased by the presence of these pastoral agents, forbidding Geralda

Geralda Chaves Soares standing next to a Maxakali totem on display in Belo Horizonte's city hall as part of a political drive, sponsored by CIMI and other organizations, to bring national and international pressure on the state government to halt the violence being leveled against the Maxakali and demarcate their land.

and her colleague from even visiting the Maxakali.[18] Geralda explains that

> at that time, FUNAI had the same authority as the police, so if you were found on indigenous land, they could expel you from the region or arrest you for two years. But of course this prohibition only applied to individuals who were involved in a particular popular movement because the fazendeiros could enter without any concerns.

And so during the first two years, the CIMI accompanists were compelled to live outside the aldeia and had virtually no contact with the Maxakali. Geralda and her associate thus initially focused their attention on non-Indians who were not large landholders—that is, on those individuals who did not have a direct conflict with the Maxakali over land. In particular, their goal was to counter anti-Indian stereotypes, better inform the surrounding population about Indian colonization in the region, and help the landless to unionize as farmworkers. As Geralda puts it,

We decided to try to help [those who were not large landholders] to understand why it was that Indians were fighting so hard for their land. Because there were lots of people who weren't fazendeiros, yet they sided with the fazendeiros. They had these racist ideas [about Indians]. They believed that Indians had invaded the territory, that the Indians had murdered lots of people, that they were treacherous and bad people.

Somewhat ironically, a number of these people who were siding with the fazendeiros against the Indians were also having to endure the same type of violence that was being brought against the Indians. There was a general violence. A number of rural workers were being expelled from the region. They would be banished without any warning or compensation. This was before there were unions in the region. So we tried to build coalitions with unions that were concerned with rural workers. So we began to help the people [o povo] to organize.

After a while, Geralda and her colleague began forging links with the Maxakali by befriending two elderly men who were not Maxakali but spoke the language "flawlessly" and had spent much of their childhood with the Maxakali. These men taught the pastorals the Maxakali language and introduced them to the Indians.

We eventually made contact with these two elderly men who were in their eighties. We talked at length with them. We asked them their advice. It was through them that we made lots of friends with Indians. That was in 1982. We gradually started becoming friends with the Maxakali. They'd come and visit our house. And their visits increased as well as the length of their stays. They would spend the night. And sometimes a group of them would come and spend a few days. If they were out fishing, they would stop by to ask for water or food. The chefe of FUNAI at that time didn't like this, so he started saying that we were prostitutes. He didn't want the Indians visiting us. The fazendeiros weren't too pleased with this either. Especially since at the same time the rural workers, with whom we were still working, started talking about land reform for the first time. So the fazendeiros were getting very upset with us as well.

It was right about during this same time period that FUNAI began a project there that I think was called the "Assimilation Project" — or maybe it was the "Integration Project." In any case, they wanted the Maxakali to learn the "external culture." But what they were really trying to do was break up their culture.

As the CIMI pastorals became better acquainted with the Maxakali, they began making brief visits to their village, especially when the Maxakali were in desperate need of food, clothing, or medicine. Despite this assistance, however, as Geralda describes below, many of the Maxakali remained suspicious of the pastorals.

One night it was raining very hard, but we left anyway for the aldeia because we knew they needed medicine. We walked two kilometers by foot. It was me, a priest, and another girl. We walked and walked, and finally we arrived so tired, we just wanted to sleep. We gave a shot to the girl who was sick and tended to some others who were ill. Then we asked if we could spend the night. But an old Indian woman said, "No, you can go now. The moon is coming out to show you the way." They already had had enough diseases, and so I could understand why they didn't want any more strangers around. But we were so tired. It felt like we didn't have our legs any longer.

A turning point came when Geralda and her associate sold the Maxakali's goods and did not attempt to cheat them of their proceeds, as others apparently had.

After the illness, they didn't have any food because they hadn't been able to attend to their fields since they'd been so sick. So they had nothing to eat. So they asked us to sell their artesenato for them, and with the money we brought back food and supplies. Afterward, everyone started telling stories. We spent that whole night celebrating. This was, I believe, when they first truly opened up to us. Our selling their artesenato and then bringing back things for them really built their confidence and trust in us. Other times people had taken their artesenato, but then had never returned with the money. Before this they weren't quite sure why we were there, what our intentions were. Even in the time of the disease we still weren't sure what they really thought about us. We didn't know what their vision of us was.

After this, we started to have more access. We started to learn and understand their perspective. And we also started to get them access to the media, to newspapers, to radio shows. When the fazendeiros murdered some Indians, we enabled them to denounce it, to publicize what had happened. All types of violence: beatings, killings, imprisonment, . . . we enabled them to publicly denounce it. It was the only way to bring attention to these atrocities. We had to put our mouth to the world. If we hadn't, they would have killed all the Maxakali off.

Then the Indians went to Brasília, and we went with them. They made a map of their lands. And this map showed their reality, it showed how there were invaders in the middle of their aldeia. What was their objective? They wanted to unify their territory. That was *always* their objective.

As Geralda and her colleague gained the confidence of the Maxakali—helping them to improve their standard of living with medicines and the sale of their artesanato, bringing greater visibility to the violence the Maxakali confronted, and linking them to the emerging pan-Indian movement—fazendeiros and their allies stepped up their efforts to terrorize the accompanists. Geralda's original colleague left in 1983 because of the intensity of the pressure. Then, one year later, in 1984, another pastoral was sent to work with Geralda. According to Geralda, he had been selected because he had been "very experienced with these types of high-pressure situations. However, it was too much for him too, and so he left." For a period of time, then, Geralda was "the only one who managed to hold out," but ultimately it became too dangerous for her to remain in the region.

I was forced to get a car because I could no longer walk. It wasn't safe any longer because I was so well-known. There was a jagunça [assassin] who had my picture in his pocket at all times because he wanted to kill me. I always kept my car parked right in front of my bedroom window so that in case anything ever happened, I could get up and flee in a hurry. One night, they tried to set my car on fire and blow it up. They tried to ignite the gasoline tank, but fortunately someone happened to pass at that time. The passerby yelled, and so they fled. The second time, this guy tried to enter my house, a former soldier, he tried to kidnap me so that he could murder me. In addition to these "attempts," the climate was such that I just couldn't stay any longer. I was threatened every day. I couldn't even go to the market because they could start a fight and I could "accidentally" get caught in the middle of it and [be] killed without anyone being able to say who did it. So [CIMI] proposed that I leave, and so I did.

As is evident from Geralda's account, the pastoral agents must sometimes hold out against great psychological and emotional hardship as well as risk to their physical well-being. This was particularly true in the 1970s and 1980s. During this period, conflicts in various parts of Brazil included "personal attacks on and intimidation of such bishops as Dom Pedro Casaldáliga and Dom Tomás Balduíno [president of CIMI], frontal attacks on CIMI by FUNAI elements, and the murder of Pe. Rodolfo Lukenbeing and Pe. João Bosco Penido Burnier in 1976," along with the assassination of the missionary Vicente Canas in 1987.[19]

The above excerpts also show that CIMI actually does represent a new brand of missionary work. As was detailed in chapter 3, for centuries the Jesuits and Capuchin monks were committed to civilizing and Christianizing eastern Indians. Their principal goal was to "bring culture" to a people deemed culturally deprived and backward. To accomplish this agenda, these missionaries—with, of course, some exceptions— sought to break down and erode tribal religions, languages, stories, kinship structures, songs, rituals, dances, symbolic orders, values, architectural styles, attire, and so on.

In sharp contrast to the objectives of civilizing missionaries, though, the CIMI pastoral agents have sought to reinforce tribal institutions, traditions, and identities. For instance, there was nothing in the interview with Geralda that suggested or even hinted she and her colleagues were attempting to "cleanse" Indians of their Indianness. One is instead left with the distinct impression that they were struggling to learn, understand, and publicize the Maxakali perspective so as to enable "Maxakaliness," as defined by Indians themselves, to survive and flourish. Further underscoring this point is the fact that non-Indians were targeted for "cultural change." Geralda specifically mentions efforts to challenge the "racist" perspectives and political alliances of the non-Indian peasants "who were siding with the fazendeiros against the Indians" despite the ironic fact that they "were also having to endure the same type of violence that was being brought against the Indians."[20]

One of the impacts that liberationist missionaries have had on indigenous communities, at least in some situations, is the curtailing of anti-Indian violence. This was apparently the impetus behind the bishop's request for someone to accompany the Maxakali. As non-Indian witnesses with greater knowledge of the legal system as well as more access to the media, these agents are better able to disrupt fazendeiros' efforts to destroy Indian communities and appropriate their lands. In Geralda's opinion, this was definitely the case. As she noted, if they had not started "putting their mouth to the world," the fazendeiros would have "killed all the Maxakali off."

A further effect of accompaniment stems from the manner in which these pastoral agents are able to act as resource persons. In much the same way that the older men who grew up among the Maxakali served as their consultants, the pastoral activists have the potential to play a similar role. They can, and often do, advise a given community on how to most effectively negotiate with the broader non-Indian world. Or as we saw with Geralda, they can function as intermediaries by selling and purchasing goods, taking children to the hospital, bringing medicine, forwarding requests for emergency funds, translating to and from legal and bureaucratic idioms, negotiating travel arrangements, and so forth.

One of the most difficult hurdles Geralda had to overcome was that of gaining the Maxakali's confidence. For reasons that should be readily apparent, the Maxakali were extremely suspicious of outsiders. Over an extended period of time and after a number of "tests," Geralda was eventually successful in earning their trust. She cites a particular turning point when they sold the Maxakali's artesenato, and instead of cheating them, returned with food and supplies. "Before this they weren't quite sure why we were there, what our intentions were," she remarks, but this action "built their confidence and trust in us."

Such trust has proved beneficial not only in affecting the degree of impact that a particular agent may have on a given community but also with respect to building a social movement. CIMI has almost single-handedly financed and coordinated the creation of pan-Indian organizations. If these activists were not situated in communities where they could build a tribe's confidence in them, and by extension CIMI, then the chances of members of a community like the Maxakali attending a function that has been orchestrated and financed by CIMI would be greatly diminished. This is especially true when one considers that these pan-tribal organizations often require travel to a location that is unfamiliar or hundreds of miles from home in order to meet and discuss strategies with other Indians in the greater region who are usually complete strangers. Hence, the formation of pan-tribal networks and a concomitant social movement may never have occurred, or at least not nearly as rapidly, had it not been for the relationships that these missionaries built at the grassroots level.

The other substantive outcome that I see accompaniment as having had on movement building is in keeping its parent organization, CIMI, well-grounded. For more than twenty years, CIMI-East has successfully avoided becoming overly remote, paternalistic, and "out of touch" with the concerns and needs of peoples it purports to support. It has not been undermined by an erosion of its popular base. Having agents who actually reside for several years in a given community has no doubt helped keep CIMI in tune with the realities, sensibilities, and desires of eastern Indians.[21]

Resource Mobilization

In chapter 3, when the Krenak discussed their forced removal or the Pataxó recounted the massacre their community suffered, nothing emerged from these interviews that suggested the presence of a broader social movement. There did not seem to be any communication channels or public relations infrastructure through which these events could be publicized. There was no mention of legal experts to challenge the murder of tribal members and appropriation of Indian territory. Links between indigenous communities were either nonexistent or so weak that Indians could not notify one another, let alone mobilize protest demonstrations, issue manifestos, lobby politicians, and the like. There did not even appear to be a larger pan-tribal community from which to draw encouragement and sympathy, as well as mitigate what must have been an almost overwhelming sense of isolation and powerlessness. The only available responses were to either hide in the forests and hills or beg assailants for some modicum of mercy.

Contrast the aftermath of these incidents with what occurred following the murder of Pataxó Galdino Jesus dos Santos at a bus stop in Brasília in 1997. Overnight, the story reached the regional, national, and international press. The publicity was so intense and immediate that the day after the murder, the governor of the federal district, Cristóvam Buarque, fretted out loud, "We are very concerned with the international repercussions of this episode." [22] Even President Cardoso, on hearing of the burning in the midst of a welcoming ceremony in Canada, interrupted the event to publicly condemn the murder, noting that he was "repulsed" by the crime.[23] The following week, numerous indigenous communities and leaders (especially in eastern Brazil) issued manifestos, held press conferences, visited schools, and organized mass demonstrations in response to the murder.[24] A day after dos Santos's burial, the Pataxó forcibly occupied five plantations—the 788 hectares of land that the regional federal court had ruled belonged to the Pataxó Hã-Hã-Hãe.[25] And finally, a month after the murder, a monument was constructed in honor of dos Santos and placed at the bus stop where he was slain.[26]

The juxtaposition of the degree of publicity, range of responses, and political gains that came in the wake of the murder of only one individual with the silence and disempowerment that followed the murder and forced relocation of whole communities is striking. It is testimony, at least in part, to the significant changes that have taken place in the broader society: Brazil has become more democratic, there is a freer and more open press, and non-Indian Brazilians as a whole are less tolerant of anti-Indian violence. But it is also a powerful example of the emergence of an Indian social movement.[27] Much, if not most, of the publicity, political pressure, public rallies, press conferences, and political gains were instigated and carried out by indigenous communities in conjunction with their national and regional organizations. It was Indians and their allies who accurately read public sentiment and seized the political opportunities created by dos Santos's murder to push for reform in FUNAI, permanently transform public space (for one, the construction of the bus stop monument), bring attention to the persistent problems of violence and poverty that Brazilian Indians confront, and recapture territories from fazendeiros (such as the Pataxó Hã-Hã-Hãe in Pau Brasil).[28]

As should be fairly evident, there has been a sea change in the quality and degree of pan-Indian collective action. Eastern Indians have moved from a state of political impotency to a position boasting a rather sophisticated and well-developed political apparatus. It is probably less clear, however, that NGOs, and especially CIMI, have been central to the creation of this social movement. In the late 1970s, UNI attempted to establish a pan-tribal movement in eastern Brazil complete with movement activists situated in each of the various indigenous communities, but this effort failed.[29] It was not until CIMI became involved in this region in the early 1980s that such a movement actually began to emerge.

CIMI's success in movement building can be attributed to a number of factors: the confidence that its agents have forged at the grassroots level, the development of democratic channels of communication between the organization and its constituency, and CIMI's willingness to allow indigenous peoples to define the organization's agenda (instead of vice versa). But the principal reason why CIMI was able to increase the political muscle of eastern Indians has been the "resources" it made available to eastern Indian communities. CIMI has been able to provide the capital, both material and cultural, that, as resource mobilization theorists have noted, is essential to the formation of any social movement.

For example, CIMI has made larger, pan-tribal political assemblages possible by paying for the cost of transportation, housing, and meals required to attend conferences and meetings. Eastern Indians could not afford to pay these expenses on their own, especially given how geographically distant indigenous communities are from one another. CIMI has also made available basic infrastructure such as conference halls, microphones, and overheads, thereby greatly facilitating meetings. Somewhat less critical but worth mentioning in this context, CIMI usually offers advice on how to carry out efficient and effective meetings — helping to draft conference agendas, suggesting ways in which to structure assemblies, and so forth.

One telltale sign that CIMI has been instrumental to the development of these organizations is their regional character. There are numerous levels of pan-tribal organizations operating in eastern Brazil: international, national, and regional. But the foundational pan-Indian organizations have been the regional ones. Without diminishing the significance of the other levels, it is important to underscore the fact that in terms of political mobilization, regional assemblages have proved to be bulwark institutions. Of some significance is the degree to which these regional organizations tend to correspond closely with regional divisions within CIMI. So, for instance, CIMI-East's jurisdiction is confined to the states of Minas Gerais and Espírito Santo. Not coincidentally, the key pan-tribal organization in this region, the Indians of the East, is composed of Indian communities exclusively from these two states.[30] This regional network could, in theory, include Indians from any number of surrounding states, or exclude Indians from all or part of Minas Gerais and Espírito Santo. Instead, it neatly parallels the geographic jurisdiction of CIMI, reflecting, in my opinion, the degree to which CIMI has been pivotal to the formation of pan-tribal assemblages.

In addition to providing a stable source of funding that has made it fiscally possible to develop pan-tribal organizations, CIMI has affected movement building in several other, albeit less crucial ways. It has been involved in extensively documenting and publicizing the issues that Indians confront—especially from an indigenous vantage point. CIMI publishes books and newspapers, maintains websites, and produces films to educate the general public about Indian history as well as current affairs. It also funds lawyers when needed, and solicits legal and political experts to help develop movement strategies and tactics. Moreover, CIMI organizes public campaigns, acts as a spokesperson, sets up press conferences, and lobbies politicians to amend, draft, and implement laws.[31]

One of the most common criticisms leveled against resource mobilization theorists in recent years is not supported by this study of CIMI. Based on analyses of the civil rights movement in the United States, the resource mobilization model has been criticized for portraying "protest groups" as being too reliant on "third parties" and "outside sources." As Aldon Morris asserts:

> Existing resource mobilization analyses of the civil rights movement have assigned heavy weight to the role played by outside elites and events. This view had been offered by such political scientists as Michael Lipsky, Howard Hubbard, and David Garrow and articulated by such sociologists writing outside the resource mobilization perspective such as Gary Marx and Michael Useem. . . . The approaches and analytical sophistication of these writers differ substantially, but they do agree that protest groups are dependent on outside resources

Reporters interrogating the head of CIMI-East, Luís Lobo, about the 1995 campaign for the demarcation of Maxakali territories. Seated around the table are Maxakali waiting to meet with sympathetic state parliamentarians.

because they lack organizational resources and skills. I contend that this view of the civil rights movement assigns undue weight to the role of outside elites and events.[32]

Morris's critique makes sense vis-à-vis the civil rights movement, where organizations like the Southern Christian Leadership Conference, Student Nonviolent Coordinating Committee, and Congress of Racial Equality developed much more independently of outside assistance. But in terms of the Indians of eastern Brazil, it is not an overstatement to claim, as Michael Lipsky does below, that political protest was contingent on the initiative and support of third parties:

> The "problem of the powerless" in protest activity is to activate "third parties" to enter the implicit or explicit bargaining arena in ways favorable to the protestors.... I have argued that the essence of political protest consists of activating third parties to participate in controversy in ways favorable to protest goals.... [R]elatively powerless groups cannot use protest with a high probability of success. They lack organizational resources by definition.[33]

This is not meant to imply that eastern Indians have been without agency or somehow tangential to their own social mobilization but rather that CIMI has been a necessary ingredient in movement building. Although, as Morris maintains, "the pace, location and volume of protest in various communities are directly dependent on the quality and distribution of local movement centers," indigenous communities in eastern Brazil would likely have remained disconnected and politically ineffectual had it not been for the intervention of CIMI.[34] Therefore, if prophetic Catholicism, along with other factors such as the Figueiredo report, had not prompted the church (that is, a third party) to intervene in ways favorable to Indians, it is extremely doubtful that an indigenous social movement would have emerged in the late 1970s in eastern Brazil.

A Race for Itself

I have situated CIMI's contribution to Indian social mobilization within the resource mobilization framework in order to pinpoint the manner in which CIMI has been involved in movement building. Nevertheless, this should not be interpreted as an endorsement of this analysis as the definitive explanation of this or any other social movement. As the "new social movement" theorists correctly observe, one of the major shortcomings of the resource mobilization model is that it fails to problematize identities and discursive practices. Much like structural-opportunist and rational choice proponents, resource mobilizationists erroneously presume that the "oppressed" have ready-made "hidden transcripts"—that is, there is an assumption that subalterns automatically have a critical understanding of their situation and possess the will to struggle. Consequently, they believe that all that is needed to produce social protest is the proper "objective" conditions, such as "political opportunity space, ideological and organizational resources, mobilization networks, leadership and so on." [35]

Resource mobilization theorists thus lack a concept of hegemony. They fail to realize that social inequalities are frequently sustained with the consent of the weak and not simply via repression. Moreover, identities appear in their model as preconstituted categories instead of as something to be invented and articulated. In this way, they mistakenly presume that a "class in itself" will reflexively become a "class for itself." None of this, of course, is meant to suggest that resources are an unnecessary component of protest mobilization, but only to concur with the new social movement theorists who note that collective identities and movement cultures cannot be taken for granted. [36]

Working with landless peasants in the 1960s in northeastern Brazil, Paulo Freire quickly came to this realization. He found that "the oppressed" were held in check not only via the brute force of the state and local fazendeiros but also through their own subjectivities. [37] Freire observed that the peasants had internalized the worldview of the fazendeiros: "The peasant feels inferior to the boss because the boss seems to be the only one who knows things and is able to run things," and they "see their suffering . . . as the will of God." [38] Echoing his contemporaries Franz Fanon and Albert Memmi, Freire argued that "the oppressed" are often unaware of the causes of their condition, and "fatalistically 'accept' their exploitation" because they have "internalized the image of the oppressor and adopted his [sic] guidelines." [39] Not surprisingly, Freire concluded that "the oppressed" must undergo *conscietização* (a raising of consciousness) if they are to mobilize to effect progressive change.

CIMI was, of course, not the only Catholic organization to emerge from the theological movement that transformed the Brazilian church in the early 1970s. A number of other orders were created to address a broad range of issues, including land reform, workers' rights, homelessness, and so on. Most of the clergy and activists affiliated with these associations reached a conclusion similar to that of Freire. They realized that if unionism were to flourish and a landless peasant movement to emerge, they would have to begin creating new forms of political vision and practice among "the people." Hence, tens of thousands of ecclesiastic base communities (Comunidade Eclesial de Base or CEBs) were established in an effort "to raise political and social awareness."[40] As John Burdick describes, "With the help of liberationist study guides and pastoral agents, members read the Bible together, discuss[ed] its implications for their everyday lives, and [were supposed to be] inspired by it to struggle for social justice."[41]

One of the serious problems with some of the consciousness-raising efforts of the CEBs has been their conviction that a "true" critical consciousness is a marxist one. For instance, Burdick discovered in his study of a suburb of Rio de Janeiro in the early 1980s that the pastoral activists were more concerned with imposing their "macro" class analysis onto working-class women's experiences than facilitating the development of a more organically based, critical understanding of their situation.

> Progressive Catholic discourse presents domestic problems as secondary to the "really important" issues of the world beyond the household. As one pastoral agent explained, "If there's something wrong at home, it's because the husband is unemployed. But why is he unemployed? That's the question we want people to think about." "Consciousness" in this view means an understanding not of inequality in the household but rather of the extradomestic realm of "politics and production." As the progressive priest justifying his discouragement of private confessions explained: "Women just talked about emotional stuff at home, there was very little space to raise their consciousness there."[42]

Burdick found that a number of women were indeed resentful of the pastoral agents' dismissal of their domestic concerns. As one former CEB member rebuked, "They say 'struggle, struggle, struggle!' . . . They mean unions, and neighborhood associations, and political parties, things like that. But I struggle here in my own home every day. They don't speak about that." [43] In attempting to impose a class-reductive interpretive framework onto these women's experiences with patriarchy, this particular CEB in effect undermined much of its potential base of support.[44]

Against this backdrop, it is noteworthy that CIMI (or at least CIMI-East) has not met with these same sorts of divisions between the pastoral activists and indigenous communities. This is partially due to the fact that CIMI, unlike several of the other Christian-based organizations, encountered communities and individuals at a very different moment of political mobilization. Eastern Indians could not be portrayed as ideologically "domesticated," to use Freire's term, in that a collective identity and an alternative form of common sense, which I call the "law of the Indian" (lei do indio), already existed within many tribal communities.[45] This does not therefore mean that CIMI has not helped the lei do indio to develop and spread; it instead suggests that an alternative system of knowledge, beliefs, behaviors and customs predated the intervention of CIMI. Unlike many of the other pastorals, then, CIMI did not need to sow a movement culture, and so was able to readily avoid the tensions, conflicts, and divisions that sometimes result, as Burdick documented, from consciousness-raising efforts.[46]

Another reason why CIMI has been much more successful in avoiding this sort of "banking" method of conscientização is because it has not been as encumbered ideologically as many of the other pastorals, or at least it has been ideologically encumbered in a different way. Although liberationist Christianity, the wellspring of CEDEFES, CIMI and the other popular pastorals, was heavily influenced by marxism, CIMI's agenda was to build indigenous organizations in order to help Indians develop a greater degree of political, economic, and cultural autonomy. This sort of political project—"defending ethnicities" and eradicating ethnic cleansing—is not as readily reducible to a marxist programmatic as, for example, attempting to get the working class involved in a workers' party or landless peasants engaged in mobilizing for land reform. The particular focus of CIMI inoculated it somewhat from the marxist strand of liberationist Christianity, and subsequently from the ideological authoritarianism that has historically plagued political projects heavily influenced by marxism.

NGOs and Indianization

The fact that NGOs throughout many parts of the Americas have been an important force behind indigenous mobilization has prompted some to argue that those individuals who receive assistance from such organizations are not real Indians. Instead, it is suggested, they are racial pretenders who have been stirred up by "outside agitators." As Edward Evans-Pritchard explains,

> The degree of international support for grass-roots social movements is sometimes a politically sensitive point, since target governments often attempt to discredit dissident groups with the claim that they are not authentically indigenous and have been mobilized by "outside agitators." However, nationalist claims of this sort inaccurately depict the domestic political system as closed when historically the state and dominant social groups themselves have usually drawn on significant outside resources. In the case of Indian movements, local Latino elites historically dominated Indian populations through the monopoly of access to markets, transport, state services, and other channels of contact with "outsiders."[47]

Clearly, outside influences do not somehow automatically prove the inauthenticity of those involved in a social movement or the identities created by such a movement. Historically powerful outsiders (the Catholic church, colonial governments, venture capitalists, and so forth), Evans-Pritchard notes, have been involved in the elimination of tribal subjectivities. As a result, many individuals of indigenous descent do not self-identify as Indian but rather as black, white, mulatto, moreno, and so on. Yet it would be incorrect to suggest that these people have acquired false identities simply because their racial/ethnic identities are partly a product of outside influences.

One version of the outside agitators argument that is a bit more nuanced contends that it is not external intervention per se that invalidates the identity claims of certain groups or individuals but rather the particular *ways in which* these outsiders have intervened. Paraiso, the anthropologist mentioned in chapter 3 who declared the Kaxixó racial hucksters after being contracted by the government to evaluate their Indianness, is representative of this stance. Elaborating on this idea, she added that the Kaxixó began to identify as Indian in order to achieve certain instrumental goals from governmental "entities of assistance." She portrayed the Kaxixó as having little or no agency—referring to them as "great victims," and asserting that certain expectations and hopes had been "transmitted" to them by these "entities of assistance"—and saw NGOs as manipulative, powerful racial hustlers.[48] In the final analysis, Paraiso concluded that the Kaxixó had been hoodwinked by NGOs into identifying and organizing as Indians.

The general contention that there has been a causal relationship between the influence of NGOs and Indian subjectivities is, however, correct. There is little doubt that without the intervention of NGOs, the Kaxixó (and many other eastern Indians) might not have come to identify and mobilize *as Indians.* The real problem with Paraiso's analysis is not the suggestion that there are linkages between NGOs and indigenous resurgence but rather her understanding of how these linkages actually operate. NGOs and their pastoral agents have not prompted racial reimaginings by somehow persuading naive and vulnerable individuals to adopt false indigenous identities; their effect on Indian formation, although crucial, has been less direct than Paraiso implies.

For instance, after Geralda Chaves Soares was forced to leave the Maxakali, she left CIMI as well and helped establish CEDEFES.[49] In the early 1990s, with the support of CEDEFES, she began working actively to find land for the Pankararu family discussed in the previous chapter. Eventually her efforts paid off. She was able to convince the local bishop, an Italian, to donate some of the church's land to the Pankararu. The following story indicates how such changes in identity can occur. A caboclo family—an elderly couple and their son, Pedro Índio—happened to live on the fazenda bordering the land given to the Pankararu family. According to Pedro, his grandfather, an Indian, had been a slave on the fazenda where Pedro still lived and worked. Even though Pedro's last name was Índio, prior to the arrival of the Pankararu family he did not self-identify as Indian. As chapter 7 will discuss, most Brazilians

Pedro Índio in aldeia Apukaré.

still consider Indians to be types of "wild animals"—and like others, Pedro feared living next to an Indian family.

But as he got to know the Pankararu, he realized that they were "just like him." He began to socialize with them on a regular basis, and they began to consider him an Indian based on his *jeito* (way of being). Gradually, over the course of a year, Pedro's identity shifted from moreno or caboclo to Indian. This transformation was probably best symbolized by something he did about a year after the Pankararu first settled on their new aldeia. When a local, non-Indian asked Pedro to be the best man at his wedding, Pedro agreed only on the condition that he could dress in "traditional Indian attire." His friend assented, and Pedro took part wearing the grass skirt, painted body, and necklaces that the Pankararu wear on such occasions.[50]

In the case of the Kaixó, the NGOs have affected racial formation in a similar manner. According to the Kaixó, due to anti-Indian violence, most individuals in their community stopped self-identifying as Indian by the early 1960s. In 1987, however, this trend began to reverse itself. As Jerry Kaixó remarked, "Many of us now identify as Indian, but before 1987 we said that we were the descendants of Indians." The question, then, is how historical circumstance changed in 1987. The Kaixó were involved in a struggle with local fazendeiros over land at the time.[51] To assist this community in their fight, the CPT sent a Portuguese priest called Padre Jeronimo to accompany the Kaxixó. It seems that during the course of his conversations with the Kaxixó and investigation into the history of the region, the Kaxixó revealed that they were the descendants of Indians. He heard stories of how the local fazendeiros had systematically destroyed tribal traditions and how there might still exist remnants of indigenous religious ceremonies. Moreover, he was shown the ruins of a number of indigenous archeological sites that the Kaxixó claimed were the villages of their ancestors. Padre Jeronimo, who may have been more sensitive to indigenous issues due to the Xacriabá conflict then at its apex, brought the matter of the Kaxixó to the attention of both CIMI and CEDEFES—a logical step given that they specialized in indigenous affairs.[52] Almost immediately after the Kaxixó became known to CIMI, members of its community were invited to pan-tribal conferences and meetings, and CIMI financed the travel of other Indians to the Kaxixó region.

Even if there were truth to Paraiso's belief that these NGOs and Padre Jeronimo schooled the Kaxixó into believing that they were Indians or convinced them that they should identify as such in order to regain their lost territories, such an argument is unsatisfactory at best. For instance, if someone had gone to Pedro before he had come to know the Pankararu and suggested that he was an Indian, he would have been either insulted or considered it a preposterous notion. What was transformative for him—as for the Kaxixó as a whole—was having close contact with an Indian community.

Although members of the Kaxixó community, on Padre Jeronimo's arrival in the late 1980s, described the archeological sites, explained that their people were the descendants of Indians who were enslaved until the mid-1970s, and were prohibited from referring to themselves as Indian by local fazendeiros, and so on, they did not really consider themselves Indian. The Kaxixó's criteria for Indianness, as well as that of others around them, were that a person was "of the forest," spoke a non-Portuguese language, used bows and arrows, was not of African or European descent, wore no clothes, and so forth. After CIMI introduced them to a world where individuals who self-identified as Indian looked like them, dressed like them, had similar histories, ate the same foods,

Eva Kaxixó attending her first pan-Indian conference in 1995. She told me in an interview that the Assembléia dos Índios Leste/Nordeste had had a significant impact on her identity.

José Candido Barbosa (Kaxixó) told me that he had been a slave for much of his life on the neighboring plantation. Since I interviewed him in his kitchen after dark, he held a kerosene lamp so that we would have light during our conversation.

were peasants like them, and had the same conflicts with fazendeiros, a transformation became possible. It is only with such exposure that racial identity shifts can be prompted and solidified. It is when someone actually comes into contact with a space that offers a different, yet tangible vision of Indianness, where someone's welcomed and recognized as Indian, that Indianness comes to seem like a realistic option. Furthermore, should an individual come to self-identify as Indian, it is this connection to an Indian community that articulates and affirms what is to the larger society a heretical identity claim, that sustains her or him in the face of the relentless challenges and even death threats that this new identity is sure to evoke.

NGOs have indeed been responsible for the production of Indian subjectivities, although not in the manner described by Paraiso. As an outgrowth of CIMI and CEDEFES's efforts to help indigenous communities build pan-tribal organizations and communication networks, survive and develop economically, publicize indigenous concerns and perspectives, secure territory, temper anti-Indian violence, assert themselves politically, and so on, they have facilitated the expansion of indigenous social, institutional, and geographic spaces. Contact between Indians and non-Indians has intensified as a result, and in some cases, it has led to a change in the racial identities of non-Indians. In certain instances, as with the Kaxixó, these NGOs have proactively attempted to increase interaction. But, as we saw with Pedro, such contact can occur through pure happenstance. By simply assisting the Pankararu to establish their own aldeia, CEDEFES, Geralda, and the bishop unintentionally brought Pedro into contact with a living indigenous community and that, in turn, led to his racial transformation. The presence of such a community has proven to be a catalyst for other identity shifts as well.[53] This is a vivid example of how NGOs, in their efforts to defend indigenous communities and improve their material conditions, can concomitantly, albeit inadvertently, generate Indian subjectivities. Clearly, then, these organizations have been a significant factor in the growth of indigenous resurgence, but it would be misleading to suggest that they are manipulators of racial categories even if they have sought to deliberately further connections between Indians and non-Indians.

6. The Common Sense of Racial Formation

[There is] some confusion about the word *Indian*, a mistaken belief that it refers somehow to the country, India. Columbus called the tribal people he met "Indio," from the Italian *in dio*, meaning, "in God." — Russell Means, Lakota activist, 1980

In the Dominican Republic, during the three decades of the Trujillo dictatorship (1930–1961), the government actively encouraged persons of African descent to self-identify as Indian. Many Dominicans do in fact have indigenous ancestors and cultural roots given the thousands of Indian slaves who were brought to Hispaniola from the other Spanish and English colonies — not to mention the descendants of the Taino, the original inhabitants of the island. This policy, however, was not motivated by the desire to recover tribal cultures or create a more Indian-centric nation. Instead, it was driven by antiblack racism. As Silvio Torres-Saillant describes this racial move, "The cultural commissars of the Trujillo regime preferred [the use of the term *Indian*] because it was devoid of any semantic allusion to the African heritage and would therefore accord with the negrophobic definitions of Dominicanness."[1] In other words, it was a white supremacist attempt to exorcise blackness from the nation — a strategy that has proved relatively successful. To date, no Dominican is officially classified as black, and the vast majority of nonwhites self-identify as Indian in lieu of categories with more African connotations.[2]

Given that the majority of posttraditional Indians are of African descent, it is sometimes suggested that a similar antiblack sentiment is behind their choice of racial identities. For instance, after I presented a paper at the 1996 Annual Anthropology Meetings in Washington, D.C., an anthropologist from Harvard University implied, in the form of a question, that these individuals were claiming an Indian identity so as not to be identified and associated with blackness. Carl Degler also insinuates that there might be a similar motivation behind assertions of Indianness when he writes, "It is not uncommon even in the Northeast for a mulatto, though clearly of Negro ancestry, to assert seriously and insistently that all his [sic] ancestors were Indians, for Indian blood does not carry the taint that Negro blood carries." [3]

It is understandable that persons even remotely familiar with Latin America would suspect that antiblack racism might underlie indigenous resurgence. Blackness, as countless observers of the region have noted, carries an immense stigma.[4] Even those scholars of race who have argued that the region is less encumbered with a so-called race problem than places like the United States have documented a plethora of derogatory notions of blackness.[5] As in other parts of Latin America, one of the principal ways in which African-descent Brazilians have attempted to deal with the negative connotations of blackness is via whitening. That is, many Brazilians of color have struggled to distance themselves—biologically, culturally, and symbolically—from blackness. The biography of Machado de Assis, one of Brazil's most renowned authors, offers a glimpse of the lengths to which African-descent Brazilians have oftentimes gone to avoid being associated with blackness.

> All his life, Machado had been haunted by three nightmares: his epileptic seizures, his modest origins, and his color—three sources of fear, anxiety, and shame. He seems to have become more reconciled to his epilepsy than to his origins and color. He visited his family at hours when he could not be seen; he married a white woman and maintained a discrete and reserved attitude toward abolition. In his novels he dealt with the personal tragedies of white individuals and rarely only marginally referred to slaves and blacks. He never confronted the issue of "blackness." He lived with the ambiguity of his situation and performed conscientiously the role he was supposed to play in the community of whites of which he had become a part.[6]

Against this backdrop of whitening, it seems reasonable to wonder whether Indianization may indeed be a product of the pervasive efforts to negate blackness. Perhaps the Indian resurgence in Brazil is a consequence, at least in part, of a symbolic terrain where Indianness, as Degler notes, carries less of a "taint" than blackness.

Common Sense as "Law"

In chapter 1, I mentioned that in 1995 the Folha de São Paulo sponsored a survey on racial identities and attitudes in 120 different cities throughout Brazil. Some of their findings were published on 25 June 1995, in a special section titled *Racismo Cordial*. Part of what was not published was the data on Indianness. Interestingly, of the five thousand urban Brazilians interviewed, 6.5 percent self-identified as Indian, while only 1.1 percent were identified by the interviewer as such. Of those individuals who self-identified as Indian, the interviewer classified 25 percent as white, 9 percent as black, .6 percent as Asian, 58 percent as pardo, and only 8 percent as Indian. And of those who were identified as Indian by the interviewer, 47 percent self-identified as Indian, 11 percent as white, 9 percent as black, 30 percent as pardo, and 2 percent as Asian. What these findings underscore, in rather dramatic fashion, is that the interviewer and the Indian-identified interviewees had very different ideas about who is Indian.[7]

In my research, I also found diverse notions of Indianness operating in eastern Brazil. These contrasting imaginings generally correlated little with an individual's gender or socioeconomic status, with where she or he resided, or with whether she or he was pardo, white, or black.[8] The distinction was instead between those who identified as Indian and those who did not. In other words, non-Indian Brazilians tended to operate within and reproduce a discursive and symbolic repertoire of Indianness unlike the one that most Indians shared.[9] Eastern Indians referred to these particular commonsense understandings as *leis*. A literal translation would be law, but eastern Indians used the term to suggest a general way of being and thinking. Thus, they named these competing cultural fields "the law of the Indian" and "the law of the white."

As I compare and contrast these laws below, it is important to keep in mind that popular thought is qualitatively different from more formalized thinking—such as legal, scholastic, or literary discourses. " 'Common sense,' " as Stuart Hall contends (paraphrasing Antonio

Gramsci), "is not coherent: it is usually 'disjointed and episodic,' fragmentary and contradictory. Into it the traces and 'stratified deposits' of more coherent philosophical systems have sedimented over time without leaving any clear inventory." [10] The following comments by Camillo —a university-educated, white dentist of Indian descent who also fashions himself as a lay historian—provide an excellent example of these characteristics of common sense. In the context of explaining the local history of northern Rio de Janeiro and southern Espírito Santo to me, he stated that

> around 1830, a French Padre, Guido Tomaz Mailiere, began attempting to get Indians to work on fazendas in exchange for food and clothing. His attempt failed because the Indians could not imitate the Portuguese because they needed to make up too much time too quickly. Indians were unable to make up 20,000 years and thus catch up with the Portuguese's technological superiority. For instance, they could not understand private property and the new forms of working relations that required long hours of work per day since they were only accustomed to hunting and fishing and not a competitive work relationship. The Indians wanted the Portuguese's goods (technology and goods like sugar, salt, knives, and spices), but they were not willing to work for them. . . . In 1877, Brethel, a plantation owner, purportedly witnessed the death of the last Indian in the region. He claimed that these last Indians were so drunk that they were defenseless against little animals, small onzas [jaguatirinhas], who ate them as they were passed out drunk.

As we will see, Camillo's account draws on a number of components of the conceptual field of Indianness typical of the law of the white in that Indians are defined as technologically inferior, lazy, people of the past, drunks, and unable to adjust to modernity. These notions are then articulated in such a way as to provide a power-evasive explanation of Indian exorcism. Colonization, slavery, and massacres are never mentioned. Instead, the culpability for the demise of the Indians is placed squarely on the shoulders of Indians themselves. They were simply too far behind technologically—"20,000 years," in Camillo's opinion. They could not adapt to slavery, which he euphemistically referred to as "new forms of working relations that required long hours of work per day." In fact, he maintains, they were so backward, so culturally inept, that they ultimately could not even defend themselves from being eaten alive by "little animals."

Camillo's narrative is also riddled with contradictory and specious reasoning. For example, later in the same interview, in an attempt to highlight the notion that Indians "lacked a market savvy," he told me in a patronizing tone, reminiscent of the "How-the-Indians-sold-Manhattan-for-a-handful-of-beads" manner, that "it was common for Indians to work for sixteen hours a day, just for some cachaça." He apparently forgot that he had just stated that the Indians were slaves, and so could not negotiate the terms of their "employment." Moreover, he seemed to be unaware that his assertion that they worked all day for a pittance completely contradicted his earlier, detailed discussion of how "Indians wanted the Portuguese's goods . . . but they were not willing to work for them."

Camillo's statements should serve to underscore how common sense, even the common sense of individuals with a high level of formal education, tends to be riddled with non sequiturs and highly questionable knowledge claims. Thus, in analyzing popular thought, the point will not be to evaluate these laws in terms of their accuracy and logical consistency — criteria against which common sense often fares quite poorly. Rather, the emphasis will be on analyzing the effects of these laws on Indian formation.

Lei do Branco (The Law of the White)

Most people in eastern Brazil are of African, indigenous, and/or European ancestry.[11] Thanks in large part to the legacy of scientific racism, these three lineages are imagined — by both Indians and non-Indians — as constituting the three primary racial groups of the nation: black, Indian, and white. The plethora of other racial categories that exist in Brazil are seen as derivatives of these three. In other words, mulatto, cafuso, moreno, pardo, and so on are all regarded as a combination or mixture of either two or three of these primary racial groups.

According to the law of the white, there is a set of phenotypic and non-phenotypic diacritics that position one racially. The physical markers of Indianness are "reddish brown skin color," "slanted eyes," "high cheekbones," "little body and facial hair," and "dark, coarse, straight hair." As a consequence, an individual with features that connote African or European descent is not likely to be considered or recognized as Indian (see chapter 1).

The corporeal criteria of blackness are equally, if not more rigid. In contrast to the United States, in Brazil a black must physically signify "racial purity." That is, a black must be extremely dark, have very kinky hair and full lips, and so on. In an attempt to illustrate this point, Angela Gilliam describes how the following well-known U.S. blacks would be classified in Brazil:[12]

Malcolm X: mulatto sarara
Mrs. Martin L. King Jr.: mulatto
Dr. Martin Luther King Jr.: black (or mulatto if he wore a suit and tie)
Harry Belafonte: mulatto
Lena Horne: white
Lola Falana: cafusa
Adam C. Powell: white
Sydney Poitier: black
Huey P. Newton: white (if he had the trappings of the rich)

Interestingly enough, the somatic boundaries for whiteness in Brazil are much more expansive than those for either blackness or Indianness. An individual can have curly or straight hair, brown or very fair skin, thick or thin lips, slanted or round eyes, and so on, and still be racially positioned as white. In other words, an individual may have certain physical characteristics that mark him or her as being of indigenous or African descent, but he or she can still be considered white. The physical signifiers of whiteness are much less contingent on putative "racial purity" than are blackness or Indianness.

The attitudes held by Maria, a white high school teacher of English in a rural town in the state of Rio de Janeiro, are typical.

JONATHAN WARREN: What happened to the Indians? Why don't they exist anymore here?

MARIA: Well, I believe that what must have happened—the marriage of Indian with the white—it made that mixture. And they lost their identity after that mixture, and no one spoke of Indians anymore. I believe that is what must have happened.

JW: Then an Indian with a white makes a white child?

MARIA: That's right.

JW: And an Indian with a black makes . . . ?

MARIA: Mixed. And then, in that mixture, I have the impression that no one spoke of Indians anymore.

These remarks offer a sense of how much more phenotypically encompassing the category of whiteness is than either Indianness or blackness. A child with one Indian and one white parent is thus predicted to be white—not Indian or mestizo. And someone with one black and one Indian parent is likely to be positioned as mixed—not as black or Indian.[13]

Besides pointing to the greater capaciousness of whiteness as compared to the other primary racial categories, Maria's assumptions also raise another relevant issue. These three primary racial groups do not make up a somatic triangle but rather are ranked along a continuum. Whites and blacks are considered to be the farthest apart physically— that is, at opposite ends of the continuum—with Indians occupying an intermediate position. This explains, then, why Indians, until the 1991 federal census, were classified as pardos (that is, mestizos or browns). It is because they are imagined along this somatic gradation in which they are considered to be whiter than blacks and blacker than whites. They are located on this continuum at a place similar to that of mixed-race Brazilians. Like mulattos and morenos, they are color coded as browns. Given this corporeal scale, non-Indian Brazilians anticipate that, on average, a white and an Indian (that is, pardo or brown) will produce a white child; a mestizo (pardo or brown) and a white would also be expected to have a white child; and a black and a white would be predicted to produce a mulatto (pardo or brown) child.[14]

Finally, this somatic continuum is aesthetically ranked with the black pole associated with ugliness and the white with beauty. Amelia Simpson, in her analysis of the Brazilian megastar Xuxa, offers a clear picture of this hierarchy.

Xuxa's promotion of a white ideal invests the old message of the superiority of whiteness with extraordinary power in the age of mass
media. She fits perfectly into a nearly universal mentality of privilege, one that endorses what Richard Dyer calls the "racial hierarchy
of desirability." Xuxa's fair skin, blond hair, and blue eyes, and the
replication of that look in the Paquitas and in the many products
connected to the "Xou," reinforce what most people in Brazil learn
about race from the time they are very young. These images circulate
in the society at large, but are especially pervasive through the mass
media and the advertising industry, which, as Carlos Hasenbalg has
observed, "reinforce the negative self-image of Afro-Brazilians who
are either invisible or portrayed in stereotyped roles." Anybody who
watches Brazilian television for half a day sees that it is dominated
by whites and by white images of power, success, intelligence, and
beauty. . . . This kind of treatment of blacks by the media in Brazil contributes actively to the formation of negative views such as
those found in another study. Here, a group of seven- to eighteen-
year-old youngsters, half of them black, were asked to attribute specific characteristics to either blacks or whites. The responses need
no decoding. The words "stupid," "ugly," "thief," and "pig" were associated overwhelmingly with blacks, while "pretty," "doctor," and
"rich" were attributed almost exclusively to whites.[15]

Since Indians occupy an intermediate position on this continuum, they
are considered uglier than whites but more beautiful than blacks. This
coupled with the fact that they can more easily produce white offspring
— given their location on this corporeal scale — means that Indians have
more "biological" capital than blacks and, of course, less than whites.[16]

THE ANTIMODERNS

Although an individual's phenotype, and the biological descent it signifies, is an important component of the law of the white, it does not
make one an Indian. In other words, it is a necessary but not sufficient
marker of Indianness. In 1993, I attended a conference in Salt Lake City
where I met a Navajo who was Mormon. As part of his religious duties,
he was obligated to go to São Paulo, Brazil, to proselytize for two years.
I asked him how he was "seen" (racially positioned) in Brazil. He said

that no one ever saw him as Indian, but oftentimes people would ask him if he were Oriental. In another instance, I asked the white person with whom I stayed on a couple of occasions in Rio de Janeiro if his daughter's mother (whom I had never met) was Indian. I raised the issue because his daughter appeared to be of predominantly indigenous descent and his apartment was filled with Indian paraphernalia. He was shocked by my question. After the few seconds it took him to regain his composure, he replied, "Oh no! She only looks Indian. Her mother must have some Indian blood in her."

What these stories should impart is that phenotype alone does not mark someone as Indian. In contrast, although whiteness and blackness are affected by nonphysical criteria, they are not as contingent on them. The symbolic markers of class and status play a role in determining whether one is perceived as being black, white, moreno, and so forth. Nevertheless, nonphenotypical criteria do not have the same power to trump the somatic criteria as they do for Indianness. Thus, the poorest person of exclusive Italian descent would still be seen as white, whereas someone like the soccer star Pelé is still considered black despite his wealth and power. Yet if an individual does not meet certain cultural criteria of Indianness, even if she or he meets all the physical requirements, then she or he will not be recognized as or considered to be Indian.

What, then, are the cultural criteria of Indianness à la the law of the white? As has been a typical feature of the discourses of dominance throughout the Western Hemisphere, Indians are imagined as "primitive/traditional" in the sense of being outside of and in binary opposition to "civilization/modernity." It is a representational order "predicated upon a structure of opposites" in which "the 'savage' [is] defined against what the perceiving" non-Indian Brazilians "[understand] themselves to be." [17] If Indians participate in professions, use technology, wear clothes, and inhabit urban geographies (which denote modernity), then they are not considered Indian, regardless of their phenotype. As Eliane Potiguara, a Potiguara Indian who resides in Rio de Janeiro, notes,

> Many people in Brazil were once torn away from their communities, and they later suffered much discrimination trying to recover their loss. For example, we spend most of our lives trying to reaffirm that

we are Indians, and then we encounter statements like, "But if you wear jeans, a watch, sneakers, and speak Portuguese. . . ." Society either understands Indians all made-up and naked inside the forest or consigns them to the border of big cities.[18]

Indians, then, are not imagined as catching the subway, drinking soda, piloting airplanes, using credit cards, watching television, and so on.[19] They are also *not* thought of as being doctors, college students, janitors, maids, factory workers, or lawyers. Indians are not considered to be residents of urban shantytowns, beachfront resorts, suburban homes, or plantation estates. To live in these so-called civilized spaces, to be in these allegedly modern occupations, to possess the latest consumer goods of the global economy, renders someone non-Indian.[20] Such a person is racially positioned as moreno, pardo, or Asian—but not Indian. To be an authentic Indian, one must live like a primitive in a traditional manner. One must embody the antiself of civilization, which in Brazil means living in a hut in the middle of the forest, naked, and with no contemporary technological conveniences. Or as Carlos, a white basketmaker told me, "An Indian walks naked, he wears a little woman's skirt and birdy feathers, and lives in the forest."

Throughout the Americas, the antimodern construction of Indianness has lent itself to two different symbolic orderings: as either "less than human" or "more than human." [21] Indians qua primitives can be esteemed as noble savages or derided as ignoble ones. In eastern Brazil, I often encountered the *bon sauvage* motif—especially outside the zones of contestation discussed in chapter 4. As a means of critiquing what were perceived to be the woes of Brazilian society, Indians would sometimes be invoked as being less individualistic, less driven by consumerism, free from the obligations of capitalist economies, and more in tune with nature.[22]

The more than human idea of Indians clearly affected this white practitioner of *umbanda* [an Afro-Brazilian religion] who explained, " 'The caboclo [Indian] is more powerful, he [sic] is purer than the *preto velho* [old black].' [This] greater 'purity,' he added, was due to the caboclo's connection to the pristine forest, away from the temptations of civilization." [23] This romanticized configuration of Indians as creatures of the forest—who are therefore more powerful, uncontaminated by civilization, stalwarts of nature, and so on—was the most prevalent articulation of noble savagery that I encountered in eastern Brazil. In fact, this trope surfaced with greatest frequency among non-Indians in the context of environmentalism. It seemed that any individual or organization that sought to further a green agenda invoked the creature of the forest à la noble savagery.[24] This was the case, for example, with the organizers of a parade I attended in Vasalia.

Every April, Vasalia has a festival that includes a parade, and in 1992, to commemorate the forthcoming international Earth Summit conference, this parade featured an environmentalist theme. The parade was broken up into three subsections, which were ordered accordingly: People of the World, Technology, and the Animal World. Dressed in green costumes and sporting darkly painted faces, carrying bows and arrows as well as torches, and periodically breaking into Hollywood-esque "Indian" cries and dances, the supposed Indians were situated not among the People of the World section (reminiscent of Disney's "It's a Small World") but rather in nature, in the domain of undomesticated animals, in what was called Animal World. Separated from the other peoples of the world, from technology (that is, modernity), Indians were thus defined as part of the wild animal domain.

Prior to the parade, its organizers (two gay white men—one a dentist and the other a high school teacher) had said, "Our goal is to not be carnivalesque. We want to be more political and less frivolous."[25] So when I saw the parade, I was surprised by how understated their environmental message was; the entire militant, green critique hinged on the audience, or at least a significant proportion of it, having a bon sauvage reading of Indianness. The organizers evidently assumed that merely by representing Indians as *bichos da mata* (creatures of the forest), they would evoke the imagery of an environmental paradise lost (or in danger of being lost) and create concomitant guilt or nostalgia around (as well as political opposition to) ecological disaster.[26]

The dark side of this noble savagery idea—the "less than human" articulation of the primitive—also emerges from time to time.[27] In Alcida Ramos's words, "Far from being relegated to the Middle Ages, the idea of the savage is alive and well in the minds and guts of civilized Brazilians."[28] Take for instance, the unsettling experience that José Xacriabá had when he visited the zoo in Belo Horizonte.

The Indian has more respect today in society, whereas before they were massacred. Today, we have more breathing room inside white society. There's still people who don't recognize our rights. There's still people who see us as lazy, as thieves, as animals. But we're humans just like the Portuguese, we're human beings, like any other nation that is human, but there are still people who see us as animals. I don't understand it. Yesterday, I saw a girl at the zoo run to the police saying, "Are they really Indians?" I felt like she saw us as a bunch of animals. It's crazy, don't you think? It made me think how many people still see us as animals, as buffoons. It seems that many people have not recognized the rights of Indians. . . . [W]e're humans that need our rights, that need to be recognized as human beings.

This girl was able to effectively dehumanize José and his colleagues via the tone of her voice and nonverbal cues. But there are also a number of other discourses deployed in eastern Brazil that convey the same message. In countless jokes, for example, Indians are portrayed as ignorant fools or Sambo figures. Indians are also frequently discussed as if they were slovenly or less refined than other groups—that is, as more primitive.[29] This was the opinion of Brazilian Army Minister Leônidas Pires Gonçalves, who on the National Day of the Indian in 1989 said before the House of Representatives' Committee for Foreign Relations in Brasília that "the Indians should not be protected because, after all, 'Indian cultures are very lowly and therefore are not respectable.'"[30] Moreover, as mentioned earlier, Indians are derided as being backward in terms of evolutionary development—tens of thousands of years as one layperson claimed. The former minister of science and technology, Jaguaribe, offered no estimate of how primitive Indians were, although he clearly concurred that they were too primordial to survive much longer. During a seminar titled "Education Policy for the Army: 2000," he predicted that "there will be no more Indians in the twenty-first century. The idea of congealing man [sic] in the primeval state of his evolution is, in fact, cruel and hypocritical."[31]

Notions of native savagery also surfaced during conversations with non-Indians when it was first learned that I was conducting research with Indians. The immediate questions would be whether I was afraid and whether the Indians were "tame" ("mansos"). Such language reveals, of course, an underlying assumption that Indians, like wild animals, are aggressive, uncontrollable, and dangerous. And even after they have been "domesticated," there is always the possibility that their true nature might emerge. Paulo Pankararu, for one, said that oftentimes on a bus when a child was misbehaving, the child's mother would point to Paulo and threaten to "sic that Indian" on the youngster if she or he did not straighten up.[32]

RELICS OF THE PAST

Thus imagined as antithetical to the modern, Indians become locked in time as static beings of a distant, lost past. Indians are not permitted to change and still remain Indian but instead are relegated to a fictionalized, homogenized pre-Colombian moment, as discussed earlier. The more someone deviates from this image of the past, the less Indian that individual is deemed to be. Change and adaptation are conceived of as racial contamination by non-Indians. According to this law, Indians are trapped in a simulated past not of their own making or choosing. Any attempt to adjust to a constantly changing world—a step required for any people's survival—brands them as racial charlatans.[33]

The temporal construction of Indians as both prehistoric and ahistorical is not unique to the common sense of non-Indian Brazilians. Lucy Lippard observes that similar sensibilities prevail in North America.

Even today, when Zunis wear rubber boots or sneakers at Shalako, or when an Apache puberty ritual includes a six-pack of soda among the offerings, tourists and purists tend to be offended. Such 'anachronisms' destroy the time-honored distance between Them and Us, the illusion that They live in different times than We do.[34]

Indians are the only racial group frozen in time, according to the law of the white. Non-Indians can adapt and respond to technological, social, and economic changes without being racially repositioned. For instance, white Brazilians can drive cars, listen to jazz, use laptops, wear watches, eat sushi, or drink martinis, and they are still considered white. They are not reracialized as blacks, Asians, or Indians when they purchase and consume these products. Not only do they remain untransformed but they can invoke modernity (racialized as white) as well as a transnational whiteness to claim that they are the "givers" of many of these goods to Brazilian civilization, despite the fact that they had nothing to do with their creation.

Finally, as relics of the past, Indians are often seen as irrelevant to contemporary Brazilian society. An example of this is the reaction Moema (a thirty-three-year-old white schoolteacher) had when asked to reflect on the issue of Indianness in Brazil. Moema asked the interviewer to turn off the tape recorder, and the interviewer complied.[35] Then she proceeded to tell the following story of what had occurred on the Day of the Indian in Espírito Santo.

> It was the Day of the Indian, so there were some Indians dressed up and putting on a dance in front of the stage. And on top of the stage was a rock band playing. The audience began watching the rock band and so they were ignoring the Indians. So the Indians complained, announcing sarcastically that "it was not the Day of the Indians but rather it was the Day of the Whites." Why do we have a Day of the Indian? They are finished. They are gone.

Even though they were obviously not "finished," given that they participated in this event, the idea of Indians being nonexistent, an artifact of the past, overrode Moema's actual experiences.

NON-BRAZILIAN

As has been typical of official and popular discourses in other parts of the Americas, Indians as primitives have been perceived as barriers to development, as cultures and gene pools of backwardness that must be exorcised if the nation is to progress and become modern. Ramos describes this aspect of the law of the white in the following manner: "Having primitives within national territory is like having embarrassing wilderness in one's backyard. If Brazil is to fulfill its self-ascribed prophecy of greatness, it first has to rid itself of all signs of primitiveness."[36] Adding to this all-too-familiar notion of Indians as obstacles to progress and modernization, the Brazilian military dictatorship of the 1960s through the 1980s constructed Indian communities as potential beachheads, as sites for alien encroachment, for the foreign takeover of the Amazon. This, in turn, prompted (or at least justified) the intensification of the surveillance, colonization, and exorcism of Amazonian indigenous communities that was carried out by the military government well into the late 1970s.[37]

In my interactions with non-Indians, none of them ever made any statements that suggested they viewed Indians as a threat to the security or progress of the nation — in short, as anti-Brazilians. Yet many of them certainly thought of Indians as non- or inferior Brazilians. According to the law of the white, Indianness and Brazilianness are mutually exclusive categories. The comments made to me by Sueli, a black maid whose grandfather was Indian, help illustrate this commonsensical notion.

> A few days ago, I saw in a Brazilian *Playboy* magazine an Indian who was interviewed as a model, and she was so beautiful. I said, "What?! She is a savage? Why are Indians savages? Huh?" So I wondered about it. I thought about how she was beautiful because she was posing like a person, like a real person, like a Brazilian. You get it? It is really interesting. You know? I thought it very beautiful. I think Indians are a very interesting thing.

As savages, as the antiselves of civilization, Indians are decoupled from modernity as well as from cultural practices that are not necessarily associated with modernity but are seen as key markers of Brazilianness. So, for instance, as mentioned earlier, Indians are believed not to speak Portuguese, practice Christianity, or play soccer. As such, Indians are not imagined as "real people," as Brazilians. Ramos analogized them to children.

> Because Indians are thought to be unable to speak the national language, drive cars, or put money in the bank, they are inferior, incomplete beings, just as children are in the national society. And when Indians show themselves capable of doing all these things, a certain widespread common understanding says they are no longer Indians.[38]

This final sentence underscores how Indians, within the confines of this law, cannot be both Indian and Brazilian/modern. To become the latter is to negate the former. It leads to a racial transformation.

One way that Indians' place outside the nation was articulated by non-Indians was by representing them as minor cultural contributors to Brazilian society. In general, I found that the law of the white paralleled the hierarchy that anthropologist Gilberto Freyre established in *The Masters and the Slaves* in the 1930s.

> The Negro's role [in Brazil] was a most impressive one. Along the agrarian seaboard it was, in my estimation, much greater than that of the aborigine. Greater in a certain sense than that of the Portuguese. . . . [T]he African, who was brought here by the Portuguese colonist, did possess a higher culture than the native. . . . [T]hey were in a better position than the Indians to contribute to the economic and social formation of Brazil. At times in a better position than the Portuguese themselves.[39]

Freyre positioned the Portuguese as the most significant national contributor, with blacks a close second. So as not to call into question white supremacy, though, Freyre hastened to add that even "the Negro's role" could be attributed to Portuguese influence since they "brought" this "most impressive" contributor to Brazil. In the final position, well below the Portuguese and blacks, were the Indians who, according to Freyre, lacked a high culture and thus were unable to contribute to the economic and social formation of Brazil.

The one modification of this order that I encountered among non-Indians was the relative position of blacks. Whereas Freyre placed blacks close to whites, and emphasized the distance between blacks and Indians, non-Indians tended to position blacks as closer to Indians. Asked which groups had influenced the cultural life in Vasalia, one white schoolteacher, Miguel, responded, "The Puris Indians had an influence but now if you consider the Italians, Portuguese, blacks—then the greatest influence is the Italian and Portuguese, then the blacks and Indians are last; they have had the least influence."[40]

Although I found little variation of this ranking among the non-Indians I interviewed, John Burdick recorded some differences between black- and nonblack-identified Brazilians.

> Negro mediums speak of the greater "civilization" of the slaves [blacks]. One *negra* medium insisted, "The *pretas velhas* [old blacks] brought gardening and seeds from Africa, but the *caboclos* [Indians] just hunted, they didn't know how to grow things. The preto velho

knew about manioc and banana. . . . The caboclos are powerful, OK, but they yell a lot, they have no *cultura* [manners]." [41]

Thus the blacks Burdick interviewed invoked a hierarchy of contributions that more closely approximated Freyre's in that blacks were positioned well above Indians. In fact, the suggestion that Africans already knew about manioc is intended to be a particularly devastating critique of Indians since this is one of the few contributions that non-Indians typically recognize Indians as having made to the nation.

In constructing Indians as minor patrons to the nation, not only is the non-Brazilianness of Indians reinforced but so too are notions of Indians as culturally and biologically inferior. In *Stains on My Name, War in My Veins*, Brackette Williams outlines how the status and worth of racial groups are reflected and discursively reproduced via their so-called contributions to the nation. The group that is defined as providing "the best source of social, cultural, and political practices . . . ought, therefore, to serve as the national standard—the homogeneous norm of civilized conduct—against which the conduct and the status of all [racial/ethnic groups] are judged." [42] And the "lesser givers" are not only expected to culturally conform to the norms and values of the premier benefactor but are also deemed to be culturally backward due to presumed genetic inferiority. Within the law of the white, then, discourses of primitiveness dovetail with those of significant historical contributions to leave Indians with little, if any symbolic value.

The Semiotics of Indian Formation

Given this sketch of the common sense of non-Indians, can one conclude that as supposedly traditional forest people of a premodern past who exist on the margins of the nation and time, the lei do branco is prompting indigenous resurgence? Is this demographic turnaround being spurred by "negrophobia," as is the case in the Dominican Republic? In other words, might the symbolic terrain of this law account for the shift in racial imaginings given that many, if not the majority of, eastern Indians are of salient African descent?

In all the interviews I conducted, I came across only one incident in which it appeared that the assertion of Indianness may have been linked to antiblack racism. Antonia, a fifty-three-year-old domestic servant in a working-class neighborhood in Belo Horizonte, suggested that her daughter, Rosinette, asserted her Indianness as a way to distance herself from blackness.

ANTONIA: Where my daughter studied, they thought that she was black, and because of this she was very much discriminated against. But after they discovered that she was Indian, they started to treat her well.

JONATHAN WARREN: How was she treated?

ANTONIA: She was discriminated against. They called her negra.[43]

JW: But what exactly happened?

ANTONIA: They isolated her—her teachers and her classmates. They wouldn't talk with her. They called her negra. They treated her badly until she told them that she was not negra, that she was Indian. After they found out that she was Indian, they started to treat her well.

Based on my outline of the law of the white, it could be surmised that in this case, her classmates saw Indian genetics as superior to that of blacks. They might have thought that she was "unlucky" in her physical appearance, and that if, for instance, she were to have children, then the probability of her having more attractive children would be enhanced if she were more than "just black." As discussed, Indians can at times be romanticized, idealized, and exoticised in eastern Brazil. This is especially true in regions where Indians pose little or no threat to white power—such as in Belo Horizonte, where Rosinette attended school. Outside the regions of Indian contestation, there is a greater tendency on the part of non-Indians to imagine Indians as friends of nature who, untouched by civilization, live in harmony with the environment, animals, and one another. In contrast, blackness is rarely, if ever, idealized or romanticized in eastern Brazil; thus, Rosinette's classmates could exotify her as an Indian other, but not as a black other. This factor, coupled with the biological capital of Indianness, probably accounts for Rosinette's enhanced treatment "after they found out that she was Indian."

According to Rosinette, she already self-identified as Indian before attending this school. Even though this symbolic context clearly prompted her to assert her Indianness, it would appear that she did not merely become Indian because it was better than being positioned as black among her colleagues. Nevertheless, her experiences certainly appear to suggest that contexts do indeed exist in eastern Brazil in which Indianness is "less of a taint" than blackness. These symbolic fields could, at least in theory, prompt the assertion of Indian identities.

While it is important to note that these spaces exist in Brazil, and that in certain instances they may be linked to indigenous resurgence, it seems unlikely that the law of the white is responsible for the recent shift in the direction of racial imaginings. One of the principal reasons has to do with the fact that this demographic turnaround has taken place in precisely those regions where Indianness tends to be the most stigmatized. That is, it has occurred in symbolic fields more like the one described below by Cleonice Pankararu, the twenty-four-year-old medical assistant I first met at the Environmental Summit in 1992.

> The majority of persons see an Indian as someone who has no value, who isn't a person, as a savage, something to be treated badly, who needs to be civilized, or who has to be taught to fit into society. Generally, the majority see the Indian as a thing that should be changed, that doesn't need its own characteristics. They think that they have to be civilized.
>
> When we go to a bar to have a soft drink, sometimes we have to go not very well dressed. If we use a different accessory, they don't accept it. Sometimes we can't even use a piece of jewelry from my culture. They criticize us. They don't respect us. They say, "Look there, an Indian. Look there, a savage. Look, a native." They don't respect us. They start making jokes. Some even physically attack us. I have an example of a friend who had never been in a city. So he went with a headband of feathers, and when he got to the city, the bar girl didn't want to let him enter because he was in shorts and had his body painted. Another went to the courthouse looking for a document, and the judge didn't want to help him. They ordered him to get dressed because he was naked. There are things like this that happen all the time.

If indigenous resurgence were symbolically driven, one would anticipate Indian identities to be emerging in those areas where Indianness was the least stigmatized and most esteemed. Yet Indian subjectivities have been arising principally in locales where anti-Indian sentiments have been sharpened because of Indian challenges to land distribution and political power.[44] Moreover, there was virtually no movement toward Indian subjectivities in those regions where there was a greater tendency for Indians to be idealized and romanticized—in those zones where Indians pose little threat vis-à-vis land reform, such as the larger urban centers.

Finally, as repeatedly noted, most eastern Indians are not even considered índios mesmos—neither phenotypically nor culturally. It would be difficult, then, for an individual to accrue the potential benefits of Indianness if he or she does not even signify Indianness. For example, Zizi Pataxó, the thirty-three-year-old seamstress who lost her child when she was eight months pregnant, hardly seems to be acquiring symbolic value by asserting an Indian identity.

> There are people who don't recognize what an Indian is. Because of this we still deal with a lot of jokes. We have to listen to all these jokes from whites. For instance, if we go dressed in our Indian clothing, they often call us witches and buffoons. It's things like this that they say to us, it's people who don't understand. They say, "You're not Indians, these people aren't Indians, you're clowns, you're a group of buffoons, you're witches." They criticize us like that. They say, "You're taking the feathers of chickens and leaving them naked so that you can dress."

And so even if the non-Indians described in this chapter had idealized notions of Indians as noble savages, these positive associations were obviously not being transferred to Zizi and her colleagues because they did not fit the lei do branco's criteria of what constitutes an Indian. Instead of reaping symbolic capital for asserting an Indian identity, eastern Indians tend to be ridiculed, harassed, and chastised as racial phonies, as the following remarks by Oswaldo Pataxó, a sixty-seven-year-old pensioner who had been driven from his land in Bahia by whites and thus brought his family to aldeia Guarani, indicate:[45]

> In this region [the municipality of Carmésia] we never had conflicts with the big landowners, with the people. There is a little discrimination, however. They say, "They're not Indians. They're northeastern-

ers. They're Bahians." We are Bahians, we're Bahian Indians. So they think that we're not Indians. So we suffer, we suffer because of this.

Lei do Índio (The Law of the Indian)

With respect to the diacritics of Indianness, there is a large degree of overlap between the law of the white and that of the Indian. The major difference is that the law of the Indian does not demand the same level of compliance. Rather than representing a radical departure from the law of the white, this common sense uses similar criteria, but applies them with greater flexibility. For example, both Indians and non-Indians are in agreement as to the somatic markers of Indianness. Straight hair, reddish brown skin, a round face, and slanted eyes signify Indianness to Indians and non-Indians alike. According to the law of the Indian, however, an individual does not have to embody these diacritics in order to be Indian. That is, unlike the law of the white, racial authenticity is not contingent on phenotypic conformity. The conversation I had with twenty-year-old César, a Pataxó who lived with the Pankararu on the Apukaré aldeia yet was preparing to leave to attend agricultural school in Espírito Santo when I arrived in 1995, clarifies the differences between these laws with respect to phenotype.

> JONATHAN WARREN: Are Indians who are the descendants of Africans treated differently here?
> CÉSAR: There is no difference—just the physical characteristics. One time here at school [in Coronel Murta] they were going to put on a play and they needed an Indian. Ivan was right there, but they didn't want him because . . . they said that he wasn't an Indian because he had curly hair. I think that is racism. They were wrong. Just because one has straight hair and the other curly doesn't mean he is going to quit being Indian.

As mentioned earlier, based on the common sense of non-Indians, a person of salient African descent is not considered Indian. Such a person would instead be categorized as moreno, cafuso, mulatto, and so on. This is why the whites described above did not want Ivan, an Indian who had physical features that marked him as mestizo and therefore non-Indian, to represent an Indian in their play. But it is evident that

Geselina Pataxó with her husband, Ivan Pankararu, and their nephew in aldeia Apukaré. Ivan, the cacique of the aldeia, had not been permitted to portray an Indian in the school play because his hair made him a racial impostor in the eyes of non-Indians.

César considers it a ridiculous notion that one would "quit being Indian" simply because of phenotype. His comments typify the racial logic of the lei do índio whereby mestizoness does not automatically signify non-Indianness. That is, one does not have to "look Indian" to be Indian.

The above should not be taken to suggest that phenotype is irrelevant vis-à-vis claims of Indianness. Even though those who do not approximate the somatic ideal of Indianness are not rejected out of hand as charlatans, this does not mean that appearances, and the genotype they signify, are insignificant. In fact, I found that the more "Indian" an individual appeared to be, the more credibility that person had as an Indian within posttraditional communities. In other words, the more an individual approximates the somatic diacritics of Indianness, the less likely she or he is to have her or his Indianness challenged. To cite but one case, Puhuí Pataxó had three children—two boys and a girl. His youngest child was viewed as "less Indian looking" primarily because of his blond hair. I would sometimes hear the other children, and even a few of his uncles, tease him by calling him a white person solely because of his phenotype—something that made him angry. Such aspersions were never cast against his siblings.

Given the relative tolerance for phenotypic diversity, it should be evident that eastern Indians did not demand that someone be of exclusive indigenous lineage. Nevertheless, they did require some degree of indigenous descent. As with the law of the white, to be considered Indian one must be of Indian ancestry. Yet unlike the lei do branco, someone does not have to be of exclusively indigenous descent in order to be seen as a legitimate Indian. In fact, for some eastern Indians, much the opposite position was taken. Often non-Indians would approach eastern Indians to boast about how they had a grandmother who had been pegado no lasso (taken by the lasso, enslaved).[46] Aside from the insensitivity revealed by those who told this story of conquest and rape with a strange mixture of humor and pride, some of the Pataxó told me that what disturbed them was how these individuals no longer identified with (or as) Indians. They referred to such individuals as "lost," "in denial," or as having "no respect for their ancestors." It was implied, then, that a person of even minimal indigenous descent should identify as Indian (or at least strongly ally her or himself with Indians), and work to reconnect with their tribal culture and other indigenous people.

As with phenotype and blood, Indians and non-Indians alike shared a similar set of cultural diacritics of Indianness. In particular, they saw traditions (such as language, dress, religion, ceremonies, architectural styles, and so forth) that were imagined as being derivative of preconquest cultures as authentic indicators of Indianness—the essential difference again being that the law of the Indian allowed for much greater deviation from tradition. As we have seen, the law of the white demanded intact traditions that had been uncontaminated by conquest, modernization, nation building, and capital formation. In contrast, the law of the Indian required only the fragments of the interpretive worlds and cultural practices that survived, albeit not unscathed, the influence of European discoveries.

The majority of posttraditional Indians understood their deviation from tradition as an indicator of their subaltern status. It served as a reminder that Indians live in a society controlled by non-Indians that prohibits them from practicing certain customs. For example, as Puhuí Pataxó explains:

> In Belo Horizonte, one woman came up to me and said, "Ah, you're not an Indian because if you were an Indian you would be naked." And I said, "If that is what it's about, then let's go over there so that you can see me naked." I asked her to go over there to see me naked. Then she got upset because she was trying to discourage me, but it wasn't working. So I said, "You think that here in the middle of the population, here in the center of the city, I am going to walk around naked? If I walk around naked, the police are going to beat me, thinking that I'm crazy. So that is going to end. . . . You see people naked there in the Amazon, but they don't go into the city naked." So I told her this, and she became angry. She wanted to start something, but I countered and that was that.

The fact that Puhuí can no longer live in a traditional manner, at least in terms of attire, in no way proves that he is not an Indian. Instead, it highlights to him—as it does for other Indians—his disempowerment as an Indian; it underscores the fact that he lives in a context where it would be impossible to live in accordance with certain tribal traditions, even if he desired to do so.

The absence of tradition, according to the law of the Indian, not only

Puhuí Pataxó and his wife, Eunice, who dressed for this photo and posed next to their *pintura* [portrait painting], common in many rural homes. Also note the picture of their eldest son dressed in his Pataxó attire (far right).

reflects a contemporary colonial reality but also the brutal colonization that Indians and their ancestors have endured. The logic works in much the same way that it does for the Irish, I suspect. Even though the Irish have lost a number of Gaelic customs and traditions through English colonization, they still very much consider themselves Irish. So, for instance, the fact that they speak English rather than Gaelic does not signify to them that they are not Irish but that they were colonized. Such is the logic of the law of the Indian, as reflected in the following interview statement by Gumercino Pataxó, the fifty-eight-year old who recently became a crente:

> I was raised speaking the Portuguese language because in our generation no one had the right to speak another language. And today the Pataxó hardly have a language. A while back, Captain Honorio, who was raised on the aldeia and so he had the language, he came to Pataxó. He tried to get the people interested in conversing in the language. But the Pataxó weren't interested in an Indian language because they were afraid.
>
> We have tried to find these old idioms. I went and spoke with a

priest in Belo Horizonte, and he told me that someone who might have a catalog of the old Pataxó language is the priests of Rio de Janeiro.

But today it is going to be difficult to learn our language because we associate so much with whites and our language is very complicated. [He then says aloud several words in Pataxó.] We don't speak like the Maxakali, who speak their language fluently.

Gumercino clearly recognizes that unlike the Maxakali, the Pataxó have lost their tribal idiom. But due to the law of the Indian, he does not interpret this to mean that he is no longer Pataxó. It simply highlights for him that the Pataxó were forced to relinquish their language and how difficult it will be to revive it—especially given its complexity. The loss of tradition functions as a sign of racism rather than racial inauthenticity. Ironically, as I will detail in chapter 8, as a symbol of conquest the absence of tradition serves to reaffirm and redouble, rather than discredit, an individual's sense of Indianness.

Another reason that the lack of preconquest practices is not necessarily seen as signifying inauthenticity is because modernization and change are not considered a contaminant per se. Most eastern Indians have rejected the binaries of the lei do branco that position Indianness in static opposition to modernity. As a result, cultural adaptations, inventions, and transformations are not interpreted as automatic indicators of racial erosion. Indeed, some of the individuals I interviewed, far from imagining Indians as vulnerable antimoderns, defined modernization as key to their survival as Indians. They saw, for example, education, economic development, and mastery of the latest technologies as complementing and enhancing Indianness—as opposed to polluting or detracting from it. This was why several Indians interpreted the failure of Indians to fully enjoy the fruits of modernity not as a consequence of them somehow being true to their Indianness or successfully resisting assimilation but rather as one more instance of anti-Indian racism, as João Tupinikim, a fifty-eight-year-old cacique and farmer, argues:

When I go to these meetings, people say that I'm not Indian. And to them, to be an Indian means to walk around naked. But that already ended. Today that is over. Today Indians should be well dressed, they should live in the best houses because they are the *Dono* (guardians or rulers) of Brazil. So why do they live in the worst houses? Why don't they dress well? Why don't they have cars? Some do have cars. Only the white population has the right to walk beautiful, to walk well dressed? The Indian has rights. The Indian should walk beautiful, should live in a beautiful house, should walk well dressed, should have a nice car also. But the Indian doesn't have these things. So we are very discriminated against. We are Indian and we need to learn that a real Indian is like myself.

It is crucial to underscore that cultural practices believed to be linked to preconquest cultures can and often do function as powerful indicators of racial authenticity. For example, if an individual worshiped a Pataxó god, spoke Maxakali, participated in a Pankararu religious ceremony, and so on, then a given community or individual's legitimacy as indigenous was enhanced. Nonetheless, such tribal traditions are not mandatory for most Indians. Eastern Indians in particular tended to be much less concerned with evidence of tribal continuance, for reasons discussed above, and were much more focused on an individual's cultural orientation or jeito. Pedro Índio, mentioned in chapter 5, had no tribal remnants to which he could point, but he was still considered Indian by other Indians. Eastern Indians saw him as Indian due to his jeito—or way of being. Although none of them were able to elaborate further, I believe they were referring to his orientation. I will develop this concept further in chapter 8, but in brief they meant that he privileged his social and political alliances with Indians—that is, Pedro sought to recover tribal memories and rebuild traditions from their ruins, embraced a different set of historical narratives, and asserted an Indian identity in both Indian and non-Indian spaces. Furthermore, Pedro valued and sought to master particular indigenous practices, ceremonies, and rituals.

In sum, Indianness according to the lei do índio is a complicated calculus of phenotype, blood, tradition, and orientation. As we have seen, indigenous phenotype and continuance of tribal traditions were not required by most eastern Indians but they have certainly entered into their calculations of Indianness. Individuals like the blond boy, who was teased and called a white person—that is, those who were further removed from the physical diacritics of Indianness—typically had to compensate in terms of tradition or jeito in order to have their identity as Indian recognized by the community. Conversely, the more an individual embodied the phenotypic ideal of Indianness, the more room that individual had to be less culturally, politically, or socially Indian. When Vera Lúcia Calheiros Mata notes that among the Kariri-Xocó there are "blacks [negros], blondes with blue eyes and individuals with an American Indian phenotype [biotipo]," one can assume that in order to have their identities affirmed by the community, the negro or blond, blue-eyed Indians would be under greater pressure than the more Amerindian-looking ones to participate in and master ceremonies such as the Ouricuri, a central cultural marker of tradition and jeito among the Kariri-Xocó.[47] On the other hand, the more an Indian is steeped in tradition, speaks the tribal language fluently, or has mastered the songs and dances of certain ceremonies, the more he or she can deviate from the diacritics of phenotype and jeito.

Although the boundaries of Indianness among eastern Indians are, in general, less exclusionary as compared to the law of the white, there have been intense conflicts at times over how inclusive or exclusive these alternative boundaries of Indianness should be. In fact, debates around the criteria of Indianness have erupted into fierce discursive and even physical battles in some communities. On the aldeia Guarani, for example, the Pataxó community divided over this issue, with one (the lower Pataxó) physically segregating itself from the other faction (the upper Pataxó). As a result of this division, there has been little dialogue between the two factions: parents forbid their children to date women and men from the other community, and physical violence sometimes breaks out. This conflict appeared to have started when the lower Pataxó, who were originally invited to the aldeia by the upper Pataxó, became dissatisfied with their ability to shape community practices and control resources. Since they could not win via elections — being in the numerical minority — they chose to attack the upper Pataxó's Indianness, asserting that since they were not real Indians, they had no right to dictate aldeia government. To support their claim that the upper Pataxó were charlatans or at best "less Indian," they invoked an even stricter criterion of blood and tradition than the one outlined above. This may prove a slippery slope for the lower Pataxó given that they did not seem any less "racially mixed" (for instance, the wives of the principal cacique of both groups were black) and their claims of being more traditional, aside from the fact that they were Catholic and not Protestant, were not perceptible to me. This seeming lack of real distinction on the axes they have politicized probably accounts for why the lower Pataxó sometimes invoked notions of Indians as antimodern to support their assertions of greater authenticity. During our conversations, for example, some of them would point out that they did not have satellite dishes for their televisions — unlike a few of the upper Pataxó — as proof of their truer Indianness.

Such conflicts may seem trivial and almost comical when framed in this manner, but it is important to stress that they are taken seriously by the people involved in them, and the ramifications are potentially a matter of life and death. In fall 1999, for instance, a brawl broke out between these two groups around this issue and an individual associated with the lower Pataxó, Salvinho, the thirty-six-year-old father of five who was always riding his bike, was severely wounded with a machete.[48] Moreover, when I was there briefly in 1997, it seemed that the critiques made by the lower Pataxó were gaining credence among non-Indians and organizations like CIMI, whose members made comments that suggested they considered the upper Pataxó to be "less Indian." Given the significance of CIMI to these communities, the partiality of its agents could have a series of disastrous consequences.[49] These internal conflicts over racial authenticity have also helped spark a cultural renaissance of sorts in that both communities, in order to prove their Indianness, have more aggressively sought to rejuvenate putative Pataxó traditions than they might have otherwise. Finally, how this and various other struggles that rage in countless indigenous communities throughout the hemisphere around precisely this same issue will be resolved, will likely have a profound effect on indigenous resurgence. That is, where the boundaries of Indianness are drawn by Indians themselves will, as we shall see, play a major role in determining the extent of the demographic turnaround.

THE WEALTH OF BRAZIL

There is another side of the common sense of the Indian that is also relevant to Indian resurgence. This facet is more deconstructivist in spirit

Zizi Pataxó with two of her three children and her husband, Benedito, a member of the lower Pataxó community, which considers itself more authentically Indian.

Salvinho Pataxó with his children and their friends in aldeia Guarani. In 1999, he was attacked and badly wounded by an upper Pataxó, in part because he had accused his assailant of being a faux Indian.

and so has less to do with proscribing or defining Indianness. This is the law of the Indian as cultural critique. It is aimed at unsettling the symbolic position of Indians and delegitimating mainstream articulations of Indianness, which as we have seen, define posttraditional Indians as non-Indian. That is, rather than serving as an alternative criterion of Indianness against which racial authenticities can be measured and policed, this aspect of the law of the Indian emphasizes the disruption of mainstream racialisms and representations of Indians. It is more akin to discursive terrorism than to canon building.

Eastern Indians contested and upset the law of the white in a number of different ways. One tactic was a frontal assault. This entailed making blunt statements such as "We're not animals, we're humans just like the Portuguese," "The Indian has manners," "The Indian is cultured," or "The Indian has worth, too." At times, although less frequently, Indians would drop the "too" or "also" and say things such as "Indians are not thieves, the whites are."

Another subversive maneuver was to provide "evidence." One notion that particularly irritated many Indians was the idea that "Indians are lazy." Posttraditional Indians offer a number of explanations as to why such a characterization is unfair. Some use a structural argument: "Indians cannot get bank loans like whites." Some employ a cultural justification: "That's not the way of Indians." And others, like Zizi offer counterfactual examples:

> Today you will see that Indians are still often called "lazy." There are whites that call the Indian "lazy." [Whites] say that "[Indians] don't like to work." Even when they came here for April 19 [the Day of the Indian] . . . the whites came here, and I took them to my little garden. I showed them everything and I said, "Are you seeing?!" Out there they say we are "lazy," that "the Indian doesn't like to work," that "the Indian only lives on the backs of others." So I took them there to show them *everything*. Then I gave them a bunch of produce from the garden. I said, "You see?! You say that Indians are lazy, but those are people who have never been here to this aldeia and seen the fields of the Indian." They say such things, that "the Indian is lazy, a dishonest worker." They're lots that still say that "the Indian doesn't like to work," that "the Indian only likes to beg for things," but this is because they don't understand.

A related line of criticism involved challenging the validity of the law of the white by questioning the speaker's authority. Puhuí, for example, attempts to undermine one woman's implication that he is not a real Indian by raising doubts about her expertise. Specifically, he demonstrates that she is someone who does not have a grasp of indigenous history and has never had any personal contact with actual Indians:

> People often say . . . like this one teacher I met at a conference, "You don't look like an Indian." Fine, in your vision I don't look like an Indian, but I am an Indian. It would be like me saying to the teacher, "Oh, you don't look like a teacher. I didn't know you were a teacher." Instead, she should say, "You're an Indian, but you don't have the characteristics." I would be more satisfied. But to come up to someone and say that they don't look Indian! We get shocked by certain things, by certain conversations. But because we have some manners, we remain patient. We converse with the person so that the person understands who we are because who knows better what it means to

be Indian than ourselves. We tell them where we live, how we live. Then one day that teacher said that to me, . . . and I said, "Do you know all of indigenous history?" She said, "I do." So I said, "I want you to tell it to me." And can you believe it, but she began telling me all these lies, telling me what she had learned in a book.

So I said, "Now I am going to tell you what happened to the Indian about which you know nothing. It's not enough to just base your knowledge in the literature. Do you know what happened to the Indian in '51 there in Barra Velha? Oh, you don't. You see, how can you say that you know all of Indian history. You don't even know a third of what happened to the Indian. You don't have a clue as to the suffering of the Indian. But I know. I know. Look, you know so much about indigenous history, . . . but of what really happened you know nothing. Because you have never been to an indigenous area. You don't know how an Indian lives, how an Indian eats."

Another strategy of critique that surfaced in the law of the Indian involved a transculturation of the law of the white. *Transculturation*, Mary Louise Pratt explains, is a term

ethnographers have used to . . . describe how subordinated or marginal groups select and invent from materials transmitted to them by a dominant . . . culture. While subjugated peoples cannot readily control what emanates from the dominant culture, they do determine to varying extents what they absorb into their own, and what they use it for.[50]

The point, then, is that eastern Indians often borrow heavily from the common sense of non-Indians and rework aspects of it to affect their own notions of what it means to be Indian. Take, for instance, the idea of the noble savage. Gumercino remarks that

an Indian is a person who was raised in the forest, in a savage nation; this is why we are Indians. The white only knows how to walk in the city. The Indian walks in the forest. He [sic] sleeps in the forest.

Here the people don't like the Indian. They are very jealous of our land. They hardly have any land. They say that we are lazy. "With all that land, they don't produce anything." But it's not like that. If we were to act like the whites, we wouldn't conserve the nature. And it is because of the forest that there exists game and birds. One's health depends on it because of the pure oxygen it creates. But the people don't like us because of this. The Indian is cultured, but he is not a field hand who cultivates the land like whites.

The Indian is independent. He lives in the forest. He doesn't depend on the hospital, but rather on the family. The doctor of the Indian was God, the family, and the forest. He didn't use clothes. Everything that he needed was in the forest. But today, unfortunately, the white has taken over the forest. My children already live in the rhythm of the white. I have a son who is a mechanic, and another who is a truck driver. The Indian has become more civilized, but he has always maintained his customs.

Plants are the medicine of God because it was him that made the floresta, the fauna. Our God is intelligent. With plants there is a cure. I believe that doctors often damage one's health. Everything that is in the forest is good. You can cure everything with tea. My mother had fifteen children, and none of them went to the doctor. Because of this I very much believe in our medicine.

Gumercino does not contest the basic categorization of Indians as primitives but instead simply ascribes a positive value to savageness in the tradition of noble savagery. It is clear that Gumercino considers Indians, as members of a "savage nation," to be equal to if not superior to those who are "civilized." Moreover, he emphasizes how Indians qua forest people are free from need and sickness, independent, more family oriented, protectors of nature, and so on. According to Gumercino, some of these qualities were lost or weakened due to deforestation and the appropriation of indigenous lands — "the white has taken over the forest." Interestingly, however, the main message is that most of the Indian's qualities have been retained. In Gumercino's opinion, one can adopt the technologies of modernity, occupy the professions of a capitalist economy, practice the religions of the white, and still be Indian. Such an individual remains Indian because many of the noble savage's sensibilities are imagined as incorruptible. That is, an Indian who takes up the "rhythm of the white" is believed to be capable of retaining the characteristics of the Indian. "The Indian has become more civilized, but he has always maintained his customs," proclaims Guercino. "Civilization," then, is not constructed as the polluting, racially transformative force it represents for most non-Indians; Indians can be truck drivers and mechanics yet still maintain their "customs."

Antonia Xacriabá refashioned the idea of noble savagery in a similar manner:

> The Indian is very simple, tenderhearted, but at the same time very intelligent. Look for yourself. If you see an Indian and he [sic] doesn't know how to read, he gets along just the same [convive com todos]. It's a mystery. He doesn't need to study to learn and be intelligent. He goes out into the world not knowing anything. All he has is his intelligence. Just like me. I came to Belo Horizonte not knowing anything. If it wasn't the intelligence, how could I have survived?

Again the echoes of noble savagery are evidenced in the idea that the Indian is tenderhearted and simple, while also possessing a superior knowledge, a higher sensibility. As in Gumercino's definition, this character of the Indian is perceived as immutable. According to the lei do branco, noble savagery is believed to be contingent on the Indian remaining outside of civilization, uncontaminated by urban landscapes and modernity. In Antonia's interpretive framework, however, there seems no danger of this greater intelligence being corrupted by the influence of civilization. The Indian character is an inherent quality, in her assessment. Therefore, even as Indians become civilized, they simply bring these superior instincts with them, just as she believed that she did when she moved to the city. By evoking notions of essentialism, then, Gumercino and Antonia were able to forge a discursive world that usurped the symbolic capital of the noble savage while simultaneously avoiding the discursive snare of inauthenticity.

The transculturation of the ideas of noble savagery and primitive essentialism in order to ensure tribal continuance if not resurgence is what Gerald Vizenor refers to as simulations of survivance.[51] That is, Indians are fighting fiction with fiction, deploying their own "models of the real without origin or reality" (the hyperreal) to counter the simulations linked to tribal erasures.[52] Gumercino's narrative of Brazilian history, detailed below, illustrates such trickster storytelling at its best. He manages to rework mainstream tales of nation building into fictions of persistence.

I consider myself a legitimate Brazilian with pride. I am proud because we were the first inhabitants of Brazil. The Indian is the wealth of Brazil. My father said the Portuguese arrived by boat with lots of grief and they only encountered the Indians. It was the 21st of April in 1500 that they anchored the boat Vera Cruz in Porto Seguro (which received its name because when they arrived they said, "What a safe port!").

Then the priest, Dom Henrique Soares Coimbra, celebrated the first mass in Brazil. For all the Portuguese, that priest was the same thing as God—some kneeled.

They took lots of pictures of Indians and took them to Lisbon. But there they said that they arrived in a land that didn't have any inhabitants. Yet they had already entered, devastating Indians, cutting and exporting wood—the redwood, the brazilwood.

My father told me a lot about the history of the discovery of Brazil. They colonized this land from Porto Seguro to Salvador. The Indians were badly treated because the whites wanted to finish them off so that they could be alone.

The whites said that the Indian doesn't know how to converse and because of this they are not people. They sent hunters to murder Indians.

Then there arrived a period in which Dom Pedro married Princessa Isabela, who was Indian. They had a child, who they named Dom Pedro II. It was him who became president.

In the war of the Canudo in the sertão of Bahia, the Indians fought hard on the side of Brazil. They helped to combat these invaders. It was because of this that [the whites] came to have better conditions in life.

Gumercino weaves together the discourses of "firstness" and "contributions" to define Indians as central to the making of the nation, and hence by implication, as anything but irrelevant and insignificant.[53] In his account, Indians were present for the first mass, they were there at the conception of the nation, even though the Portuguese tried to deny and cover this up. Princess Isabela, an important and often highly revered national figure (many Brazilians regard her as the individual responsible for the freeing of the slaves[54]) is defined by Gumer-

cino as Indian—even though she was not Indian. As such, he symbolically links Indianness with Brazilian national royalty, the freeing of the
slaves, and the subsequent political leaders of the republic. Finally, even
though the Canudo was a peasant revolt, Gumercino reconstructs it
and Indians' role in the subjugation of the revolt as a foreign invasion
in which the Indians saved Brazil. The message of Gumercino's history should be clear: Indians are neither inferior nor irrelevant. They
are instead the true Brazilians, the first Brazilians, who produced the
royalty, leaders, and great heroes of the nation. And despite having been
neglected, ignored, and murdered, they have always defended Brazil,
thereby proving themselves extremely loyal. Contrary to what whites
profess, then, Indians are anything but the insignificant savages of the
nation; rather, they are "the wealth of Brazil."

These examples, of course, do not exhaust the wide array of strategies and manners by which Indians have contested the lei do branco, but
they are intended to establish that one aspect of the lei do índio entails
a powerful critique of the common sense of the white. It is a foray into
a mixture of facts and fiction, a repertoire of simulations and truths,
intended to challenge and destabilize constructions of Indianness that
have characterized Indians' identity claims as bogus. It represents an
active effort to upset the symbolic hierarchies engendered by the law of
the white. It is a creative, ongoing maneuver to contest racial orderings
in which eastern Indians are derided as irrelevant, noncontributing, biologically inferior charlatans.

The Common Sense of Indian Formation

As we have seen, it is unlikely that the law of the white has prompted
Indian resurgence. Although in some contexts this discursive regime
may valorize Indianness, its overall effect, as measured by the testimonies of eastern Indians, is to dehumanize and stigmatize Indians.
Furthermore, its articulation of Indianness is so restrictive that few, if
any, human beings could actually qualify as Indian according to its criteria. The law of the white is thus an imagining that engenders non-Indian
subjectivities and the termination of tribal cultures. It is the common
sense of whitening rather than Indianing.

The law of the Indian, on the other hand, loosens the seams of Indianness and increases the discursive realms in which Indianness is valued, so that these survivors of the flood may assert and rebuild tribal identities. John Burdick, in his analysis of why there is so little popular support for the black movement in Brazil, notes that there are many persons of African descent who sympathize with the aims of the movement, "but feel dissatisfied with the option of adopting the 'black' label for themselves." Despite their "genuinely sincere" desire to valorize their African ancestry, he adds, these individuals "honestly cannot translate these sentiments into a conviction that they are black." [55] The law of the Indian affords persons of Indian descent these convictions vis-à-vis the so-called Indian label. To paraphrase the Maxakali's origin story reproduced in the introduction, it enables individuals who have endured the flood of European discoveries, who are pale and dirty after having been trapped in the Brazilian society for centuries, to feel as if Indianness is a legitimate option, that it is a "label" that can be adopted with satisfaction and confidence. The law of the Indian is, then, a vision that creates the possibility of securing tribal memories, traditions, and future realities. It is the common sense of Indian resurgence.

Let me detail the imaginings of one Indian woman and the racial identity of her children as a concrete example of how these laws are differently linked to Indian formation. As outlined in chapter 3, Dorinha Maxakali fled with her father to Belo Horizonte after a massacre of their community when she was a young child. With her father's encouragement, she eventually married a white man and had eight children— none of whom identify as Indian. When I interviewed Dorinha in 1995, she lived in a working-class suburb of Belo Horizonte, where she also worked part-time as a housekeeper for the Catholic Church parish. In many important respects, her common sense parallels the law of the white, as indicated in her response to my question about what it means to be Indian.[56]

It only means more difficulties, to be discriminated against. So we never spoke of it, and so it passed. Today everyone identifies [as Indian]. I think it has something to do with the new hairstyles and everything. But I think it's very difficult for everything: for work, for everything. I think it has to do with us having little education. It's because we don't have any studies that we can't find work. If we go looking for work, we don't have that degree that they ask for. So it's difficult. We're discriminated against because we have less cultura [manners, education] than whites. It's because of this.

The tone and content of her construction are quite distinct from the lei do índio with its emphasis on the equality if not superiority of Indians. For example, Gumercino portrayed Indians as being cultured and Antonia spoke of Indians' intelligence even in the absence of formal education. Dorinha, in contrast, focuses on Indians' weaknesses. In her words, Indians "have less cultura than whites." One senses that for her, Indianness is (or at least was) something to be ashamed of, to be kept concealed. In very much the spirit of the lei do branco, then, she essentially blames Indians for anti-Indian racism. As she maintains, Indians are discriminated against because they have less education and inferior manners. At a later point in the interview, Dorinha reiterates this same logic to explain anti-Indian violence.

> JONATHAN WARREN: There where the Maxakali live, do they only have problems with the fazendeiros or also with other whites?
> DORINHA: No, it was just with the fazendeiros. Those fazendeiros always ordered the deaths there. So it was always much more with the fazendeiros.
> JW: The reason I ask is because Ivan Pankararu told me that when he went there, the whites in the city often swore at the Maxakali, threw rocks at them, etc.
> DORINHA: But that is because when they go to the city they drink. They go there to drink. It is because of this. If they didn't drink, it wouldn't happen. If the whites get upset to the point of throwing rocks at them, then it is because of this. If they didn't drink, everything would be great because I am very loved here where I live.

This argument is reminiscent of that of the "historian" I cited at the beginning of this chapter. Camillo, like Dorinha, reproduced through his narrative *white innocence* by constructing the demise of Indian communities as being the fault of Indians. As he said, "They needed to make up too much time too quickly. . . . [T]hey could not understand private property and the new forms of working relations. . . . [T]hey were not willing to work." Those who more closely hewed to the law of the

Indian were much less apt to construct racism and Indian exorcism as something that Indians brought on themselves. For instance, Cleonice, Puhuí, and Gumercino all spoke of anti-Indian racism as being a product of white envy, ignorance, greed, lack of respect for difference, and so on. None of these individuals would have blamed the Maxakali for the rocks that were hurled at them. Dorinha's comments below further illustrate how her lei resonated with other aspects of the law of the white.

> JW: Are your children Indians?
> DORINHA: No, they are all mestizos. None of them are legitimate [Indians].
> JW: Why not?
> DORINHA: They're not because their father isn't. So they are mestizos, right?
> JW: But you had a mother who wasn't Indian and you are Indian.
> DORINHA: Yes, but I lived there [on the aldeia]. It is because of this. But these kids, no. Now they go there—the older ones. Sometimes I like to go there. But before, no one ever brought up the subject. Before, I never discussed the issue with my children, so that they could live here the life of the whites. We only talked about it after they were out of school. I was afraid they could be harassed, so I never brought up the subject—not once. I never spoke with them about the indigenous race because it could have come up with their classmates at school. And their classmates could have teased them. They could have called them bicho do mata (creatures of the forest) and everything else. And we already lived in the city, so what would have been the point. If they had known they were Indians, they might have dropped out of school because of the shame they would have felt. That is why I never said a word.

As seen in these remarks, Dorinha's "racial math" is quite different from that of César, who noted that just because an individual is "mixed" does not mean that she or he stops being Indian. For Dorinha, the child of an Indian and a white is a mestizo—not an Indian (at least not a "legitimate" one). As in the law of the white, racial identity is defined as a straightforward biological process. Moreover, to be Indian one must have lived "there," which seems to mean outside the city, on the aldeia. This is clearly an echo of the lei do branco, which defines Indianness as being in opposition to modernity, civilization, and urbanity. Dorinha also never discussed "the issue" with her children until they were adults. If she had believed that Indians were the "wealth of Brazil," that they had a superior intelligence, would she have concealed her Indianness? It seems she was at least partially influenced by the symbolic hierarchies that characterize the thinking of non-Indians.

Is it then coincidental that none of her children came to identify as Indian? Can we attribute the fact that she did not transfer an Indian identity onto any of her children to other factors? Perhaps one could explain her children's racial identity as a result of their not having been raised in an indigenous community, being "mixed," or Dorinha's justifiable fears stemming from her experience of having witnessed the massacre of her community and then having had to face racism in Belo Horizonte as a child? [57] I encountered other Indians in the same situation, however, who lived in the same neighborhood, who had endured similar hardships and atrocities, who were female and married to non-Indians, yet whose children identified as Indians.

What most distinguished Dorinha from these other Indians was common sense. Indians who abided by the law of the Indian and subsequently exposed their children to an alternative vision of Indianness, tended to raise children who self-identified as Indian. This is because, I believe, these parents gave their offspring a vocabulary that held out the possibility of viewing themselves as real Indians and allowed them to experience Indianness as something positive rather than something to be denied. Parents like Dorinha, on the other hand, who did not hold out to their children an alternative discursive world, typically reproduced children who self-identified as non-Indians.[58]

This analysis of Dorinha's common sense is by no means meant to belittle or chastise her as a self-hating Indian with false consciousness. In fact, such an image could not be further from the truth. She has, at least in the latter years of her life, become an important pro-Indian activist who is widely respected by the larger pan-Indian community in eastern Brazil. And of course her common sense, even though it certainly produces different outcomes than the law of the Indian, is no more true or false than that of any other individual. Instead, my intention in detailing her biography and vision, and the identities of her children, is to demonstrate the intersection between popular thought and racial formation.

As discussed in chapter 5, CIMI and other NGOs helped facilitate the spread of indigenous social, institutional, and geographic spaces, which in turn intensified the interaction between Indians and non-Indians. I hope that the means by which this contact may lead non-Indians to adopt Indian identities is now clear. Encountering individuals who self-identify as Indian yet are not "of the forest," who only speak Portuguese, were former slaves, have "lost their customs," "live in the rhythm of the white," and are of African and European descent, may be a disruptive experience, but it is not likely in and of itself to be transformative. In other words, this embodiment of a different vision of Indianness may call into question mainstream conceptualizations of Indianness, but it is unlikely to prompt radical shifts in racial imaginings. What makes contact so transformative is the law of the Indian that predominates in these realms. Non-Indians are thus exposed to different discursive articulations of Indianness, and a symbolic order in which Indianness can be experienced as something of worth and significance is thereby unveiled to them. In this way, they are provided with a repertoire of explanations that they can use to account for why they *are* Indians despite their physical appearance and posttraditional lifestyle. They are offered an alternative measure of Indianness, one that lends their assertion of an Indian identity discursive legitimacy, and then allows them to experience such an identity as authentic.

Put somewhat differently, it is doubtful whether formerly identified non-Indians—such as the Xacriabá, Kaxixó, or Pedro Índio—would ever have considered the Indian label a credible or serious racial identity, let alone felt comfortable or satisfied adopting such an identity, if they had relied on the law of the white. They, like other Brazilians, would have simply disregarded the eastern Indians they came to know as racial charlatans and buffoons. In addition, armed only with the law of the white, it is unlikely that they could have sustained an Indian identity in the face of the relentless taunting and incredulity that such an identity claim provokes in view of mainstream inventions of Indians. They too, would have instead considered such an identity preposterous. Thus, it is contact with Indians who physically look like them, have similar histories, live similar lives, accept them as Indian, *and* offer them a different common sense, that creates the potential—and perhaps even desire—for descendants of Indians to recognize themselves and others as survivors of the flood.

7. Indian Judges

Between the ivory tower and the real world are more bridges than meet the eye. —Alcida Rita Ramos, *Indigenism*

For more than a century, due to the social scientific division of labor in which Indians qua primitives have constituted the subject matter of anthropological study, anthropology has had an immense impact on shaping how Indians have been imagined throughout the world. Much of what is known and believed to be true about Indians is a consequence, then, of anthropological conceptual models and ethnographies. For instance, if one were to trace the genealogy of the laws detailed in the previous chapter, one would without doubt be quickly led to the writings of anthropologists.

In addition to disproportionately influencing how nonacademics such as taxi drivers, schoolteachers, filmmakers, lawyers, judges, maids, politicians, and doctors define Indianness, anthropologists in Brazil have played an even more direct role in the formation of ideas about who is Indian. Recall the anthropologist described in chapters 3 and 5, Maria Hilda Baquiero Paraiso, who was contracted by FUNAI to evaluate the Indianness of the Kaxixó. Her expert report (*laudo*) concluded that the Kaxixó should be regarded as charlatans—part racial hucksters, part duped pawns of activists and nongovernmental organizations. Not surprisingly, her "not-Indian" verdict was immediately contested by the Kaxixó and their supporters, who questioned her competency as an anthropologist. Suggesting that she was allied with the fazendeiros, they raised doubts about her objectivity. They also argued that she had ignored the archeological evidence and had spent insufficient time (one day) in their community. Nevertheless, they did not question the validity of an anthropologist having the authority to assess their racial authenticity, but simply requested that another, "more competent" and "less biased," anthropologist be hired.

The fact that an anthropologist—rather than a lawyer, planter, local politician, or schoolteacher—was solicited by the state to serve as an "Indian judge," coupled with the Kaxixó's failure to pose a more fundamental critique of a system in which anthropologists serve as arbiters of Indianness, points to the power that anthropologists enjoy in Brazil as Indian magistrates. According to Decree 1098 (Portaria PP/# 1.098), 6 September 1988, FUNAI is constitutionally required to contract with an anthropologist/sociologist, *sertanista* (a bush or backwoods specialist), and/or an Indian technician to supervise the creation of an expert report as to the authenticity (or level of acculturation) of an Indian community.[1] Yet because anthropology, unlike sociology for example, has historically devoted much more attention to indigenous issues, there are many more anthropologists who specialize in Indian affairs. Anthropologists—given their traditional focus on "the primitive"—are also generally perceived as more qualified with respect to Indian matters than individuals trained in other disciplines. As a result, FUNAI almost always calls on an anthropologist when the completion of an expert report is required. And when so-called expert witnesses are summoned by judges or lawyers to evaluate the racial authenticity of individual Indians or indigenous communities, it is in most cases an anthropologist who is asked to testify. Moreover, anthropologists— at the behest of politicians and state bureaucrats—are frequently influential in the drafting of laws that pertain to Indians. For instance, anthropologists and their scholarship were consulted by the lawmakers who composed the 1973 Indian Statute and those sections of the 1988 Constitution that define the legal criteria of Indianness.

The above is not meant to suggest that anthropologists are the only source of ideas about Indians or are fully responsible for how their imaginings are used by others. As compared with other professions or social scientific disciplines, however, anthropology has assumed a predominant role as a magistrate of Indianness. Given this, there is a link between the anthropological imaginings of Indianness and indigenous resurgence. As anthropological understandings of Indianness have changed in recent decades, so too have the racial rulings of Indian judges.

"In the second half of the 19th century," Adam Kuper writes, European intellectuals such as Karl Marx, Max Weber, Ferdinand Tönnies, and Émile Durkheim "believed themselves to be witnessing a revolutionary transition in the type of their society. Each conceived of the new world in contrast to 'traditional society'; and behind 'traditional society' they discerned a primitive or primeval society."[2] Until the 1970s, anthropologists viewed Indians through this same interpretive lens. That is, as in the contemporary law of the white, Indians were seen as the antithesis of the modern. Indians' interpretive framework was imagined as "the savage mind," to use Claude Lévi-Strauss's lexicon, which in effect usually meant the opposite of anthropologists' imaginings of themselves and their own society.[3] In Kuper's words,

> In practice primitive society proved to be [anthropologists'] own society (as they understood it) seen in a distorting mirror. For them modern society was defined above all by the territorial state, the monogamous family and private property. Primitive society therefore must have been nomadic, ordered by blood ties, sexually promiscuous and communist. . . . Primitive man [sic] was illogical and given to magic. . . . Modern man, . . . looked back in order to understand the nature of the present, on the assumption that modern society had evolved from its antithesis.[4]

Anthropologists did not "look at," as Kuper observes, but rather "looked back" at primitive societies. This is because in addition to the penchant for constructing Indianness and non-Indianness as globalizing oppositions, savage anthropologists tended to view Indians as members of societies of a very distant past.[5] They conceptualized the primitive as frozen in a timeless moment, and subsequently fashioned themselves, as the anthropologist Elman Service puts it below, as time travelers who visit societies such as the Arunta of Australia:

> What else can explain such a culture, then, but that there have been survivals into the present of ancient cultural forms which because of relative isolation have maintained a relatively stable adaptation. Many primitive societies have changed, assimilated, or obliterated, but that only makes the point more clear. Where an Arunta-like way

of life is not yet significantly altered by modern influences it is a culture that is primitive, ancient and preliterate. And it has a very long history, too, for the Arunta culture is paleolithic in type, although the paleolithic *era* ended when and where higher stages arose—a long time ago. . . . In this sense anthropology possesses a time machine.[6]

The particular moment into which Brazilian Indians were locked was that of the pre-European conquest. According to anthropologists, the authentic Indian lived in a manner that most closely approximated the ways in which fifteenth-century Indians were believed to have lived. The more an individual deviated from this alleged past—which like that of the Aborigines of Australia, was imagined as a fifteen-thousand-year-old holdover from the Paleolithic or Stone Age period—the less Indian she or he was deemed to be.

A corollary to the idea that Indians were members of static, pre-discovery societies was the notion that they lived in bounded, isolated communities located in peripheral regions. These "ancient cultural forms" were believed to have survived "into the present" due to their geographic "isolation." In other words, these islands of pre-Colombian culture, as they were imagined by anthropologists, had supposedly been preserved for several centuries due to their seclusion from capitalist economies, European colonization, and Brazilian nation building—that is, so-called modern influences. And so not only were Indians imagined as outside of history but also as removed from a broader regional, national, or international political-economic context.[7] This construction of Indianness, as Dennison Berwick notes, placed many tribes in a discursive catch-22.

> If they [remained] isolated . . . , they [were] cheated of their land; . . . But if they [learned] the languages of the newcomers, if they [took] the tools to use, if they [learned] to defend themselves according to the laws of newcomers, they [were] declared no longer Indians and their land [was] forfeited.[8]

Another tenet of the savage mind was the supposition that racial/ethnic identities were a direct outgrowth of culture. Peter Wade summarizes this position:

Each group [was] reified as a fairly homogenous entity with its own culture, the traits of which [could] be enumerated in a table. It [was] implied that moving from one group to the other [meant] a switch in cultural traits. . . . The implication was that the difference between "indian" and "mestizo" could be measured on a linear scale of the presence or absence of objective traits and attitudes.[9]

In short, it was believed that identities followed from prefabricated cultures, and thus "the possibility that . . . culture might change while ethnic boundaries persist . . . [was] not envisaged."[10] The fact that many Bolivian Aymara women, to use but one illustration, wear Spanish colonial dresses and English bowler hats would have been misinterpreted by anthropologists as a sign of their being less Indian. That is, given the assumption that cultural change resulted in the erosion of ethnic boundaries, they would have understood these cultural attributes as indicators of an erosion of indigenous culture and concomitant identities, when in fact the reverse is true. These items of clothing are important markers of Indianness in Bolivia, and they have the effect of reinforcing Indian subjectivities.[11]

Finally, the power of these dichotomous "cultural islands" (and the identities that were believed to follow mechanistically from them) was regarded as unequal. Primitive culture and concomitant identities were envisioned as weaker than modern culture/identities. Indianness qua primitiveness was constructed as the more vulnerable, less potent culture. It was the non-Indian/modern culture that had the power to contaminate, to racially transform Indianness, but not the reverse. As a pristine, ancient culture, Indianness could be polluted and spoiled. This is why whites were typically not perceived as being reracialized through cultural exchange with Indians, whereas Indians were believed to be de-Indianized by this same sort of interaction with non-Indians.

A useful analogy is the "one-drop rule" of the United States, whereby a white person was legally and socially redefined as black if they had any genetic ties or "black blood" at all. The operating logic of the savage mind merely substituted culture for blood: the slightest evidence of what is constructed as non-Indian culture resulted in an individual being categorized as non-Indian. Just as it did not matter how much white blood one had under the one-drop rule in the United States, so too the degree of Indian "retentions" was not considered the relevant variable. What was crucial was not whether one was 99 percent white in terms of "blood," or 99 percent Indian in terms of culture, but whether one was tainted (that is, had some black blood or non-Indian cultural influences). If the answer was affirmative, then one was racially transformed from an Indian into a non-Indian—just as an individual was changed from a white into a black in the United States.[12]

The following excerpt taken from Charles Wagley's *Amazon Town*, in which he was challenging nineteenth-century European naturalists' racial categorization of the Amazon population, should help to illuminate the interpretive framework of anthropologists and its impact on those whom they recognized as Indian.

> It is estimated that in 1852 as many as 57 per cent of the inhabitants of the Valley were Indians and that 26 per cent more were mamelucos or Indian-European mixtures; the rest were Europeans and Negroes. It is evident, however, that these "Indians" and mamelucos were not Indians in the social and cultural sense. Their way of life was more Iberian than native Indian. Although the nineteenth century visitors speak of "Indian custom" and "native life," they actually describe Portuguese customs. Mrs. Agassiz, the wife of the famous Swiss naturalist Louis Agassiz, who led an expedition into the Amazon, speaks of "a hideous old Indian woman who performed the strange rites of crossing herself and throwing kisses into a trunk which contained a print of 'Our Lady of Nazareth.'" H. W. Bates, the English naturalist whose account of the Amazon has become a classic, describes the festivals for the patron saint, St. Thereza, of Ega, the small village in which he resided for many months. . . . Biologically they were "Indians," but they were by culture Brazilians with more in common with the Luso-Brazilian world than with the autochthonous Indians still living in the isolated forests of the Amazon. Since the nineteenth century the Amazon caboclo has increasingly been brought into closer touch with the regional and national life. He [sic] is today a citizen of a national state, and his way of life is but a regional variety of a national culture.[13]

It is interesting to note how mainstream the Boasian decoupling of race and culture had become among anthropologists by the 1950s. By stating that "biologically they were 'Indians,' but they were by culture Brazilians," Wagley was no doubt making what he believed to be an antiracist move. For in suggesting that Indianness was not a matter of biology but culture, he was implicitly critiquing a racialism of his time in which it was assumed that blood determined personality, culture, behavior, and so forth. In other words, he was attacking one of the primary pillars of nineteenth- and early-twentieth-century racism: biological determinism.

If blood was not the basis of Indianness, then what did it mean to be Indian in the social as well as cultural sense? It is here that one witnesses the centrality of the savage mind on the verdicts of Indian judges. In Wagley's assessment, and in the opinion of many of his contemporaries, to be a "legitimate Indian" one had to closely approximate the imagined pre-Colombian generic Amazon Indian. Indians were the "autochthonous Indians still living in the isolated forests of the Amazon." Thus, the fact that these Amazonians had been touched by colonization and national society (which Wagley racialized as "Luso-Brazilian" —that is, white), that they lived in adobe homes outside the forest, that they had been affected by Catholicism (for example, they "crossed themselves" and offered a blessing "in good European style"), made them Indians only within the confines of quotation marks.[14] It did not matter that they were of Indian blood, that they "retained many patterns from native Indian heritage," because *they had changed*.[15] These individuals did not live as their forebears were thought to have lived in the fifteenth century. These Amazonians had been contaminated by white/modern/Western/Brazilian culture. Therefore, these individuals were caboclos, which in this context meant individuals of indigenous descent who were "clearly not Indian" because they had been culturally transformed.[16]

The savage mind remained the orthodox paradigm within anthropology until at least the 1970s. Prior to this time, anthropologists paid little attention to mestizo peasants and proletariat who claimed Indian identities. As Berwick observes, "Anthropologists did not want to investigate . . . Indians" who had "lost" their culture "by wearing the Whiteman's trousers" since such "Indians" were considered "inauthentic."[17] Seen through the interpretive lens of the savage mind, they were simply not taken seriously as Indians—let alone as worthy subjects of academic

A Pankararu Indian from Pernambuco, a state in northeastern Brazil, visiting his relatives in aldeia Apukaré. According to savage anthropologists, he would not be considered a legitimate Indian.

study. Instead, as José Augusto Laraneiras Sampaio points out, these Indians were thought of as the "residual" or "leftover" descendants of former Indian communities, whose extinction was just on the verge of taking place:

> The few authors, who took an interest in studying these peoples in the twentieth century prior to the 1970s, agreed that what stood out about these communities was their "obstinate resistance" in remaining Indian even though this was hardly viable. Their imminent dissolution and complete incorporation into the inferior sectors of national society was considered inevitable.[18]

What "stood out" to the few scholars who paid posttraditional, mestizo Indians any attention was their stubbornness in the face of the "inevitable." Denuded of their primitive culture, the presumed basis of Indian subjectivities, their complete submission to nation building was considered a foregone conclusion. To this generation of anthropologists, these were not real Indians but rather the residual descendants of Indians who were too backward, thickheaded, or uneducated to realize the inauthenticity, absurdity, and futility of their racial claims.

The Barthian Break

A review of the anthropological literature reveals that at the very moment that anthropologists were making ominous forecasts about the destiny of residual Indians, a completely different logic of Indianness began to emerge. This new logic would prove their predictions wrong, and by the 1970s, the anthropological criteria of Indianness were undergoing a substantive reformation. As I shall later detail, this emergent paradigm of Indianness would not only lend credibility to the racial claims of posttraditional Indians but would also create "racial options" for mestizos—in particular for caboclos—that simply did not exist while the savage mind reigned.

Beginning with the publication of Fredrik Barth's *Ethnic Groups and Boundaries* in 1969, there arose a fundamental redefinition of what constituted an ethnic group within the discipline of anthropology. As Barth explains,

> We are led to imagine each group developing its cultural and social form in relative isolation, mainly in response to local ecological factors, through a history of adaptation by invention and selective borrowing. This history has produced a world of separate peoples, each with their culture and each organized in a society which can legitimately be isolated for description as an island to itself.[19]

Ethnic groups, then, were imagined as static, preconstituted, culture-bearing units. Their basis was believed to be a simple matter of objective cultural differences. Or as Peter Wade describes the assumptions of this era, the underlying premise was that ethnic groups were

> relatively unproblematic entities: "there is a group, named X, which has given boundaries and a certain culture and social structure within those limits." The question of how those boundaries were constituted and re-constituted or the idea that the culture of the group might change while the boundary remained did not really enter the picture.[20]

With Barth, however, the boundaries not only entered the picture but became the critical focus:

> It is important to recognize that although ethnic categories take cultural differences into account, we can assume no simple one-to-one relationship between ethnic units and cultural similarities and differences. The features that are taken into account are not the sum of "objective" differences, but only those which the actors themselves regard as significant. . . . The critical focus of investigation from this point of view becomes the ethnic *boundary* that defines the group, not the cultural stuff that it encloses.[21]

Barth essentially turned the ontology of ethnic groups on its head, and in so doing, helped revolutionize anthropological views of ethnic groups. He argued that ethnic groups were not contingent on culture per se but rather identities and perceptions of sameness/difference. According to Barth, the cultural characteristics of various ethnic groups may be similar, "yet if one group says they are A, in contrast to another cognate category B, and they are willing to be treated and let their own behavior be interpreted and judged as A's and not as B's, then they will form an ethnic group."[22]

The allegedly objective cultural differences between Catholics and Protestants of Northern Ireland, for example, may vary little from the differences between their so-called kin in Chicago. In the U.S. context, however, these objective differences may not be regarded as crucial diacritics of ethnic/racial differences. In fact, given the saliency of the ethnic/racial categories of whiteness and blackness in the United States, they would likely minimize or not see such distinctions as relevant because they would imagine themselves as whites and thus "one people," whereas in the United Kingdom, these same cultural differences would be taken as relevant markers of ethnic difference. They would be perceived as evidence of their cultural, and probably biological, otherness. Furthermore, because of the significance given to this ethnic boundary in Northern Ireland, both the Protestants and Catholics (unlike their brethren in Chicago) would be continuously creating new cultural-symbolic materials (such as expressions, memories, parades, musical tastes, clothing styles, and housing decor) to emphasize and reinscribe this border. And so, although culture can be relevant as a marker of ethnic differences, as diacritics of an ethnic boundary, the cornerstone of ethnicity is not the degree of cultural differences.

Since the publication of *Ethnic Groups and Boundaries*, several scholars have criticized Barth for ignoring power, the ascriptive nature of certain ethnic categories, and the role of the state and phenotype in the construction of ethnic borders. Nonetheless, most contemporary anthropologists accept Barth's fundamental premise that there is "no simple one-to-one relationship between ethnic units and cultural similarities and differences." Anthropologist Kay Warren, for instance, states in *Indigenous Movements and Their Critics* that

> the goal of [my book] is not to document an invariant culture—though notable elements of the current mix have long histories—or to count only those elements we imagine as separate from the colonial process as "real" (read authentic) Maya culture. . . . Rather, in my view, Maya culture represents the meaningful selective mix of practices and knowledge, drawn on and resynthesized at this historical juncture by groups who see indigenous identity as highly salient to self-representation and as a vehicle for political change.[23]

Here, in what reads as a paraphrase of Barth's definition of ethnicity, Warren—as is typical of most contemporary anthropologists—envisions Indianness springing from identity rather than "the sum of 'objective' differences." The "cultural stuff" is no longer what anthropologists believe "makes" an ethnic group. Ethnic identities and communities—including Indianness—are no longer understood to be grounded in prefigured, objective cultural distinctions. It is instead recognized that if actors have ethnic identities and envision ethnic divisions, then ethnic groups can be maintained despite cultural change and in the absence of "real" cultural differences.

With the racial/ethnic boundary rather than the cultural content defined as the essence of Indianness, a number of the key criteria used by anthropologists to assess Indian authenticity have come to be considered irrelevant, if not fallacious. For instance, if it is presumed that an ethnic group can persist despite cultural change, then obviously the cultural continuation of the pre-Colombian world is no longer deemed necessary to substantiate Indianness. It has now become extremely rare for an anthropologist to assert or imply that an authentic Indian must be a sort of living, unaltered perpetuation of how one's ancestors were said to have lived five hundred years ago. Warren confesses that she still wrestles with such ideas, but what is noteworthy—what underscores a paradigmatic shift—is her view that such a vision is erroneous.

> In discussing Pan-Mayanism here, I have sometimes found myself struggling not to succumb to a portrayal of "Maya culture" as a static pre-Columbian essence; that is, treating the impressive persistence of preconquest knowledge and practices as "real" Maya culture and the rest as a distant colonial imposition or a recent extemporaneous add-on. Rather this book attempts to do justice to the various syntheses of Maya culture, elements of which have long and short histories, and their appropriation and recombination by local communities, religious confessions, social movements, and political groups in opposition to a variety of others.[24]

As the idea of the timeless Indian has given way, so too has the corollary notion of the isolated Indian. Real Indians are no longer conceived of as those who are removed from modernity. In fact, most scholars are careful to avoid having their work positioned as such. Stefano Varese, for one, cautions readers against such an interpretation of his work when he writes, "I do not wish to foster analytical naivete by including myself in the neopopulist anthropology that defines indigenous communities as uncontaminated citadels of precapitalist economy."[25] Another instance of the eschewing of the idea that Indian authenticity is contingent on being static and isolated is Jonathan Hill's description of his own book: "*Ethnogenesis in the Americas* decisively breaks out of the implicit contrast between static local cultures and dynamic global history. None of the indigenous and Afro-American peoples discussed in the following essays can be understood as isolated local cultures."[26]

As a further consequence of the Barthian break, the anthropological demand for the categorical purity of Indianness has been curtailed. Contemporary anthropologists are much less apt to regard cultural similarities between Indians and non-Indians—even a high degree of it—as a sign of non-Indianness. With ethnicity decoupled from culture, so-called cultural overlap is not immediately interpreted as a marker of Indian inauthenticity. Anthropologists ask instead whether an ethnic boundary exists in the form of identities and perceived borders. Like

Barth, they ask whether the group in question has a "membership which identifies itself, and is identified by others, as constituting a category distinguishable from other categories of the same order." [27]

Thus the adoption of European religions and rituals, modern technologies, Western dress, and so on, are no longer immediately taken as evidence of racial fraud. Dennison Berwick, a European anthropologist, describes this shift in perspective:

> Like millions of other fair-minded Europeans, I believed the social progress that came from contact with the Whiteman inevitably meant the destruction of the tribal Indians of South America. Indians in contact with Europeans are drawn irresistibly into the Whiteman's camp—begging for food or tools proves the superiority of our culture for it can supply items the Indians want; in time, they wear our clothes, pray in our churches, buy our radios and abandon their war paint and feathers. Disease can speed up this implosion, but the process of social evolution continues and inevitably, the Indian disappears. This is what I believed and it is a lie. . . . Most tribes want contact with their neighbors and want many of their tools; they want to "progress," but this is far from meaning the people want to give up being themselves or that they forfeit their traditional lands because they use a metal cooking pot or a video camera.[28]

In fact, in what represents a dramatic reversal of the savage mind, some scholars regard such adaptations as a testimony to Indian ingenuity in their effort to successfully negotiate colonization and racism. Where savage anthropologists would have and did read "indigenous people's appropriations of European symbols of rituals" as proof of their racial decay or growing fraudulence, contemporary scholars tend to see "a creative adaptation to a general history of violent changes—including demographic collapse, forced relocations, enslavement, ethnic soldiering, ethnocide, and genocide—imposed during the historical expansion of colonial and national states in the Americas." [29]

Even though I have emphasized Barth's role in disrupting savage anthropology, it is important to acknowledge that Barth's reconceptualization of ethnicity found an increasingly warm reception given that at this historical juncture, several liberation movements had emerged throughout the world—including Brazil—based on identities that were supposed to have disappeared due to cultural contact.[30] Moreover, these antiracist and anticolonial movements were leveling powerful critiques at nation- and empire-building projects premised on and geared toward the production of homogeneity out of racial and ethnic heterogeneity. Given this, when Barth published his thesis, state assimilationist efforts directed at whitening Indians into Brazilianness had lost much of the aura of inevitability and, more important, had come to be seen, in Thomas Skidmore's words, as "badly outdated."[31] One could argue, I suppose, that Barth's ideas, as well as his audience, were an outgrowth of these movements. Regardless of the precise linkages between Barth's thesis of ethnicity, the anticolonial and antiracist movements, and shifts in anthropological imaginings of Indianness, what is most critical to furthering an understanding of indigenous resurgence is that Barth's ideas represent a break from the trajectory of cultural anthropology until that time. If nothing else, then, his thesis of ethnicity marks a turning point in anthropological thought, which, given the centrality of that discipline to conceptions of Indianness, would eventually have significant ramifications for the direction of racial formation.

Postsavage Mind Rulings

In the early 1980s, João Carlos Nobre da Veiga, FUNAI's president, and Ivan Zanoni Hausen, director of FUNAI's Community Planning Department, unveiled a checklist of over fifty "Indian traits" to be used by FUNAI in assessing whether individuals were truly Indian. Self-identified Indians were to be rated on a scale of zero to one hundred. Those who acquired less than fifty-one points would fail the Indian test and be "emancipated" from their Indian status.[32]

FUNAI's "criteria of Indianness" proved short-lived, due in part to the strong rejection of this Indian scale by anthropologists. With savage anthropology on the wane, a number of the items on the scale—such as the requirement that Indians display a "primitive mentality"—offended the sensibilities of the anthropological community. Yet even if the savage mind had still been the orthodoxy of this time, it is highly unlikely that this vision of Indianness would have received academic approval. FUNAI's criteria biologized Indianness to such a degree that even savage anthropologists would have interpreted it as racist. For example, some of the Indian traits included evidence of a Mongolian spot and the presence of such genes as the Diego Factor.[33] As we saw in Wagley's description of real Indians (índios mesmos) above, even anthropologists who still subscribed to ideas about the savage mind had rejected, and even defined themselves in opposition to, such explicit expressions of scientific racism.

Hence, the postsavage mind was not central to the toppling of the criteria of Indianness because such anthropologists would have been equally opposed to such a yardstick. The same, however, cannot be said for the definition of Indianness encoded in the 1988 Constitution. Pro-exorcist forces such as the military and those with vested interests in Indian lands and resources fought unsuccessfully to make a distinction between acculturated and nonacculturated Indians, whereby only the latter would enjoy the rights guaranteed to Indians in the Constitution. Had this differentiation been approved, the territories of integrated Indians would have been opened up to colonization by non-Indians. Then, too, this would have laid the foundation for the appropriation of lands held by nonacculturated Indians as they would have eventually been ruled assimilated and therefore not Indian.

This concept of acculturated versus nonacculturated Indians dove-tailed and no doubt drew much of its inspiration from savage mind precepts of Indianness. As mentioned earlier, pre-1970s' anthropologists also embraced the idea that there were two categories of Indian: Indians with a capital I—those who lived in the forest, and were removed from national and global contexts; and "residual indians"—those whose culture purity had been contaminated by contact with national society, and so had to be qualified with a small i and quotation marks.[34] Had the savage mind continued to saturate anthropological thought in the mid-1980s, one can easily imagine how this distinction would have had much more legitimacy—perhaps even enough to have garnered the requisite political support to be enshrined in the Constitution. But in the post-savage moment, such a distinction did not coincide with the thinking of most anthropologists. And without the support of these Indian experts, it lacked the sufficient degree of credibility—despite the fact that it reverberated with popular understandings of Indianness—to ensure its passage into law.[35]

Although a constitutional distinction between integrated and non-integrated Indians was thwarted by the postsavage mind, no new articles of Indianness have been ratified as a result of this new imagining. For instance, the Indian Statute (Article 3 of Law 6001) enacted on 19 December 1973, continues to serve as the legal definition of Indianness in Brazil:

> [An] Indian or Silvícola is every individual of pre-Colombian origins and ascendancy who self-identifies and is identified as belonging to an ethnic group whose cultural characteristics are distinguished from those of the national society.[36]

This codification of Indianness was heavily influenced by savage mind anthropology as well as the law of the white.[37] Somewhat ironically, then, most contemporary anthropologists' operationalization of Indianness, definitions more informed by a postsavage framework, differ little from the Indian Statute. In 1994, for instance, Maria Hilda Baquiero Paraiso wrote in her expert report (laudo) on the Kaxixó,

> We consider an indigenous people to be a collective that, due to its categories and circles of integration, is distinguished from the national society and claims to be indigenous, and thus has a recognized social and collective character as well as assumes the sharing of certain consensual beliefs and values.[38]

Not only has the legal definition of Indianness remained unaltered but even anthropologists' more formal articulations differ surprisingly little from the Indian article crafted under the influence of the savage mind. Where one notes the effect of boundary anthropology is in the understanding of certain key terms and clauses. In other words, one of the most significant impacts of the postsavage mind paradigm has not been on the transformation of official definitions of Indianness— as might be anticipated—but rather the *interpretation* of certain ideas and passages. Most savage anthropologists likely would not have taken issue with Paraiso's definition of Indianness because they would have understood certain phrases to have very different meanings than do contemporary anthropologists. More specifically, they would have decoded "culturally distinct from the national society" in a completely different manner. This clause would have suggested to the savage mind a close approximation of how pre-Columbian Indians were believed to have lived. It would have meant evidence that the individuals or communities in question had been relatively untouched by European discoveries. Yet to postsavage anthropologists, such a phrase no longer has the same implicit meaning; it is no longer read as connoting that a present-day community must replicate a fifteenth-century one. Proof of Indianness today is not a matter of absolute purity or difference. Instead, Indians must only exhibit *some* cultural distinctions in order to be defined as culturally distinct from the national society.

This is precisely why posttraditional Indians (many of whom estimate that they are culturally "90 percent similar to national society"[39]) in the era of the savage mind would *never* have been recognized as Indian. Savage anthropologists would have dismissed these individuals as non-Indians, as simply a regional variation on national culture, as in Wagley's argument that even the Amazonians who "retained folk beliefs of aboriginal origin, visited *pajes*, used tupi terms, employed indigenous techniques, skills and rituals in hunting and fishing," should not be classified as Indians.[40] As such, it is highly unlikely that eastern Indians, who in general have even fewer "cultural distinctions" than Amazonians and are of "mixed biological ancestry," would have been recognized as Indians. But when "cultural characteristics . . . distinguished from those of the national society" was no longer read as "absolute differences" and was instead interpreted to mean "some differences," the legitimacy of their racial claims began to increase.

To take one case, note in the following excerpt how anthropologist Edwin Reesink does not hesitate to label as Indian those communities in the northeast who dressed, lived, and spoke "like others in the region." What is key for him, as a postsavage mind anthropologist, is not absolute difference but rather *evidence of a boundary*. It does not even seem to matter whether cultural distinctions were so-called retentions or adopted from other tribes. What he looks for is proof of the production of ethnic identities, solidarity, and distinctions. As he says,

> The Indians of the Northeast dress, live, and apparently speak like others in the region. . . . [Yet] they maintain some cultural traces. . . . [T]he principal difference resides in the world of beliefs and rituals. In Bahia, we have an example of the Kiriri of Mirandela, in the municipality of Ribeiro do Pombal. At the end of the 1960s, their profound

acculturation was documented, and it was verified that their religion consisted of a mixture of Catholic and indigenous elements. Some of those elements represented the only features of the Kiriri that were recognized as indigenous by the two groups in opposition [Indians and non-Indians], and the only source of pride for the Indians. Today they have adopted the Toré, as with the Pankararé, with the effect of reinforcing cohesion and an ethnic identity.[41] . . . The ritual serves as a diacritical sign of ethnicity and reinforces the cohesion of the ethnic group.[42]

Thus, posttraditional mestizos have been given a degree of recognition and credibility as Indians that far surpasses that which they had when the savage mind was prevalent. To the extent that groups like the Kiriri were accepted as Indians at all, savage anthropologists tended to consider them tainted, marginal, of little relevance, and ultimately facing extinction. They did not view them as real Indians but rather "stubborn leftovers" who were mixed biologically and culturally.[43] They had been corrupted by their contact with other "bloods," the Portuguese language, Christianity, modern technologies, and so on. Most contemporary anthropologists, however, take posttraditional mestizos seriously as Indians because they look at them through a completely different interpretive lens. Cultural similarities and overlap are now less important than the fact that they have "some cultural traces" (such as dances, songs, religious rituals, and so on) that are distinct from those of the national society. For postsavage anthropologists, the key criteria of Indianness are not cultural stasis, geographic isolation, and putative biological/cultural purity but rather the existence of Indian identities as well as perceived ethnic similarities and differences. With new understandings being brought to conventional definitions, then, many anthropologists have come to consider communities as Indian that earlier generations of so-called judges would have ruled "not Indian."

Caboclo into Indian

In addition to lending credibility to the racial claims of posttraditional Indians, boundary anthropology has created a racial option for mestizos that did not exist during the savage mind period. In the postsavage mind

Some of the participants of the 1995 Assembléia dos Índios Leste/Nordeste taking part in a Toré dance at the close of that day's meetings.

era, pardos who are of indigenous ancestry and in some way culturally distinct from the national society have a greater chance of being recognized by anthropologists and therefore the state as Indian if they choose to assert such an identity. This was, of course, not formerly the case: at one time a community had to demonstrate absolute, binary differences from national norms and continuance with simulated pasts.

The sector of the mestizo population that has been most affected by this evolution of anthropological thought has been caboclos. For instance, as mentioned in chapter 4, Antonia Xacriabá states that most of the Xacriabá identified as caboclos until the 1980s, when they recognized that they were Indian. A number of the Pataxó and Tupinikim told me that until the early 1980s, they too had self-identified as caboclos. Furthermore, many of the Indian communities in northeastern Brazil were previously known as caboclo communities.[44] In Bahia, for example, Josias Patricio (an elder councillor and ex-cacique of the Kiriri) observes, "We used to be known as 'caboclo.' Then 'caboclo' passed into Indian."[45]

As also noted in chapter 4 caboclo has had multiple, at times even contradictory, meanings in popular thought. It has been used to refer to an individual of mixed indigenous descent (a state analogous to that of the mulatto vis-à-vis Indianness), an acculturated Indian, a hick, and as a synonym for Indian, or some synthesis of two or more of these meanings. Such varied understandings of the category caboclo have also characterized social scientific and concomitant "official" discourses.[46] But only recently has the preferred reading of caboclo "passed into Indian." Prior generations of scholars, especially those more influenced by the racialisms of nineteenth-century science, regarded caboclos as half-breeds. Reflecting this thinking, anthropologist Edgar Roquette-Pinto gave the following estimate of the racial composition of the Brazilian population in 1922:[47]

brancos (whites)	51 percent
mulatos (mulattoes)	22
caboclos (primarily white and Indian mixture)	11
negros (blacks)	14
índios (indians)	2

As scientific racism went the way of phrenology, the association of caboclo with "biological hybridity" was increasingly overshadowed by a different interpretation. Caboclo came to indicate an acculturated or civilized Indian. It referred to an individual of discernible indigenous descent who deviated from anthropological understandings of Indianness, similar to the following Bahian notion of the distinction between Indians and caboclos as described by Harry Hutchinson: "When the Bahian of the Reconcavo speaks of índio, he [sic] usually thinks of the Indian of the interior of Mato Grosso or of the Amazon. When he wishes to indicate people of American Indian physical type in the Reconcavo, he generally says caboclo."[48]

Yet rather than simply the acculturated descendants of "forest dwellers," caboclos came to be envisioned as embodying a particular sort of civilization. Caboclos were thought of as rural people of indigenous descent who survived by hunting and gathering, undertaking subsistence agriculture, and working as day laborers on plantations. It was, then, the label given to exorcised Indians who lived as marginalized peasants and backwoodspeople. Thus, in the official view of the savage mind, caboclo referred to the Hoosiers of indigenous descent who had been stripped of most, if not all, of their tribal traditions. In other words, cabocloness was understood in much the same way that most non-Indians continue to define it to this day. It designated a "rustic, someone who was timid because of a preference for living in isolation, lazy, suspicious, tricky, like an Amerindian in having little body hair, and a number of other fragmentary attributions." [49]

For many savage scholars, caboclos retained so few of the physical and cultural attributes ascribed to Indians that they were considered to be only distantly connected to Indians. Most important, their "indigenous cultural retentions," so key to the savage mind definition of Indianness, were found to be minimal. Caboclo culture was perceived to be an outgrowth of peasant and "conquest" culture rather than an "unpolluted" continuation from the "pre-Colombian" period. And so caboclos were imagined as far "too contaminated" to be judged real Indians. Stephen Nugent, a contemporary anthropologist of "caboclo society" in northern Brazil, echoes these sentiments:

> The Indian from whom the caboclo is descended is itself a seriously compromised candidate for the focus of origin myth. Indeed, if there are significant continuities between Indianness and cabocloness (and few would deny any relationship between Indians and caboclos), these are continuities which obtain in a far more complex manner between Indian social formations undergoing a dramatic (if geographically uneven) conquest, and a neo-Amazonian peasantry which emerges despite the carnage around it. [50]

Although cabocloness was associated with Indianness, it was also clearly regarded as ontologically different. Savage mind anthropologists saw caboclos as non-Indians. The caboclo, in savage mind theory, was "like an Amerindian" but *not* an Amerindian. The "caboclo," Richard Pace observes, was "a sort of subset of mestizo" — not, significantly, a subset of Indian. [51]

The caboclo was thus constructed as one step away from Indianness toward whiteness, a "semisavage/rural" — halfway between "civilized/urban" and the "true savage" of the forest. [52] This notion of caboclo, as I mentioned earlier, still permeates the law of the white. Consequently, individuals and communities who fear Indian exorcism or consider Indianness a stain, sometimes employ this identity as a means of distancing themselves from Indianness.[53] Hutchinson describes such a person:

> One young girl who is almost a perfect American Indian type says she is a *mulatinha*. She vehemently denied there was any Indian blood in her family, but finally reluctantly admitted that a great-grandparent of hers had been partly Indian. This girl's niece would make a perfect double for the popular conception of Pocahontas, given a feather in her hair and a sarong, but she is considered a "mulata, almost morena."[54]

The caboclo category has great utility for such individuals, especially if they cannot "pass" as morena or mulatto. Although not ideal, it is "better" to be caboclo than Indian because it means that one is more civilized, as seen in João Pacheco de Oliveira's depiction:

> The process of detribalization is achieved by . . . convincing all of them that everything about their culture is backward—their language, their table manner, their cuisine, their housing, their rituals, etc. . . . that they are barbarians. Convinced gradually that their way of life is worthless, the Indian does not want to be called Culina, Kaxinaua, not even Indian, but instead, they would like to be called by the name of their oppressors, "Caboclo," which in this case represents the model of civilization.[55]

With the decline of the savage mind, the anthropological demands for absolute differences have given way, as we have seen, to the search for only some distinctions. The notion of the caboclo as synonymous with Indian has now come to the fore. As Patricio pointed out, the caboclo has passed into Indian. In fact, as Oliveira's comments reveal, the term *caboclo*, as culturally and biologically distinct from Indian, has come to have negative connotations. It is, says Oliveira, "the name of their oppressors," the sign of internalized hatred, and has come to be viewed as an inaccurate if not racist category. Edwin Reesink explains this process:

> The argument that "the caboclo isn't an Indian" is commonplace. As has been the case for several decades now, "caboclo" has been used to

deny the existence of Indians in various regions. To take one example, beginning in the 1850s, the Xocó Indians, who reside in Ilha de São Pedro, were officially declared mestizos in order to appropriate their land [as Indians, their land could not have been usurped by the state]. At that time, it was believed that "race" [as a biological construct] determined culture. Today, such a notion has been rejected by much of the scientific community. Nonetheless, the influence of these ideas of race and Indianness can still be felt, especially among nonacademics. For instance, because the Xocó are biologically "impure"— that is, because they are of European, African, as well as indigenous descent—they are frequently referred to as caboclo. They are considered "caboclo" and not "Indian" because they are "miscegenated" or "mixed race." As a consequence, it is widely believed, even in some academic circles, that communities like the Xocó do not deserve scientific attention as Indians and should not be granted Indian status. Behind the efforts to define these communities as caboclo, to prohibit them from identifying and being recognized as Indian, is a notion of Indianness that emphasizes biological purity. Thus, the struggle of the Indians of the northeast is above all else a struggle to free themselves from this biologized notion of Indianness, which has even affected their own consciousness. Indians have not become extinct simply because they have lost most of their culture and are of African and European descent. Indianness is a question of self-identity and identification by others. Nevertheless, the dominant culture, given its genetic idea of race and Indianness, oftentimes does not appreciate this fact. As a result, mixed-blood Indians, such as the Indians of the northeast, are frequently not recognized as Indians and instead must negotiate the pejorative category of "caboclo" that is imposed on them.[56]

Reesink's comments dramatically demonstrate how many contemporary anthropologists have come to see the term in a completely different light. It is interpreted as a category that is not only inaccurate but complicit with white supremacy. It is considered to be a product of an era in which it was erroneously believed that " 'race' determined culture." The term is seen as linked to the demands for racial (that is, biological) purity. It is also deemed a term employed to "deny the existence of Indians" in order to appropriate their lands and "legitimate their exploitation."[57]

With this turn in anthropological thought, the racial option of Indian has not only opened up for caboclos, it is even encouraged in some quarters. In other words, postsavage anthropology has increasingly made it a moral, political, if not scientific obligation for caboclos to assert Indian identities. According to at least some postsavage scholars, to identify as caboclo is to have internalized racism—it is a denial of one's "true identity."[58] Therefore, to shed a caboclo identity, "to free [oneself] from this imposed ideology" and assert one's Indianness, is defined as a proper and legitimate course of action.

It should be obvious that if caboclos elect to identify as Indian, to assert the notion of caboclo as synonymous with rather than distinct from Indianness, then their racial claims are more apt (as compared to the period when the savage mind was dominant) to be welcomed and affirmed by anthropologists. Given anthropologists' institutional authority as judges, as well as their impact on legal and judicial discourses about Indianness, this has also significantly enhanced the ability of caboclos to be recognized as Indian by the state. For example, during the trial to determine whether the Xacriabá were Indian, the lawyer representing "Amaro"—a fazendeiro who was attempting to prevent their recognition—attempted to support his client's position by alleging that they were caboclos and so not Indians. As Antonia Xacriabá, who observed the court proceedings, told me: "Then our lawyer asked him, 'What's a caboclo?' He didn't know how to respond. So then our lawyer explained to him that 'a caboclo is the same thing as an Indian.'"

In the days of savage anthropology, Amaro's lawyer's argument would very likely have won the day. Anthropologists and thus the judge, lawyers, members of NGOs, and FUNAI officials probably would have all understood the Xacriabá as caboclos rather than Indians. But in the postsavage mind, this line of reasoning, although it still holds sway in popular thought, was not persuasive in the courtroom. In the social scientific discourse and concomitant judicial, legislative, and state bureaucratic thought, Indianness and cabocloness have been reconstituted such that caboclos can reposition themselves as Indians.

As discussed in chapter 4, land was a material incentive for the Xacriabá to identify and politicize themselves as Indians, for had they been able to protect their territory as caboclos, they likely would not have pushed for government recognition as Indians. I hope it is now also evident that regardless of this material context, had there not been a discursive shift within anthropology, such a racial claim might never have been considered a legitimate option by the Xacriabá—and most definitely would not have been authorized by the courts and government. Although it is probably substantial, it is difficult, if not impossible, to assess the degree to which anthropologists' reconstruction of Indianness as the proper identity for caboclos has enabled communities like the Xacriabá to feel that an Indian identity is an appropriate one for them. Furthermore, were it not for the birth of postsavage anthropology, assertions of Indianness would have been politically infeasible. Without the endorsement of anthropologists—the so-called Indian judges—members of NGOS (so central to indigenous political mobilization) would most likely have been much more reluctant to support posttraditional Indians as Indians. FUNAI officials would certainly have considered such identities false, if not absurd. Finally, the courts would have rejected arguments that claim that "a caboclo is the same thing as an Indian."

It remains to be seen whether the postsavage paradigm will be taken to its logical conclusion. In theory, Brazilians of indigenous descent (and this category includes well over half the Brazilian population) who identify as Indian and are in some manner "culturally distinct from the national society" could qualify for Indian status. But there is evidence that the border or Barthian model may not be fully implemented and will instead stop with the Indianization of caboclos. For instance, according to this framework, the Kaxixó clearly constitute an Indian community. There is ample physical evidence that they are the descendants of Indians. They identify as Indians, and are sometimes counteridentified by non-Indians as such. And the Kaxixó are developing culturally distinct rituals. Nonetheless, as already mentioned, in her capacity as Indian judge, Paraiso ruled that they were not Indian. This is especially noteworthy given that she also drafted the expert report on the Xacriabá and approved their racial authenticity.[59] One of the main differences between the Xacriabá and the Kaxixó was that the latter were not caboclos before they sought recognition as Indians. As well, the Kaxixó were both attempting to rekindle old rituals that had died and borrowing rituals from other tribes. The Xacriabá, in contrast, had a few cultural traces in existence at the time of the expert report.

There is no question that an anthropologist like Reesink would have reached a different verdict than Paraiso; he would have had no difficulty in ruling in favor of the Kaixó Indians' authenticity. For instance, he notes that the Pankararé's key ethnic marker was borrowed from a neighboring tribe, describing how they "have recently introduced rituals of a parent group, the Pankararu, who live near them on the other side of the San Francisco River." He adds that this marker "serves as a diacritic signal of their ethnicity and reinforces the cohesion of their ethnic group." [60] Moreover, he regards the Kaimbé de Massacará, in the municipality of Euclides da Cunha (Bahia), as Indian simply on the grounds that they were discriminated against as such. As he says, there seem to be "no cultural differences between the Indians and their neighbors, except for the adoption of some negative ideas by the latter group about the former." [61]

Where the anthropological community decides to draw the line in a given racial terrain has significant consequences for the future size of an Indian population, for in eastern Brazil alone there are scores of communities similar to the Kaixó—that is, communities of indigenous descent with no living remnants of tribal traditions, but with the possibility of reviving or adopting them from other tribes. If anthropologists were, on the one hand, to construct Indianness as proper for these communities—as they have done vis-à-vis cabocloness—coupled with the continued spread of the law of the Indian and immense desire to acquire land in many rural communities, one could easily imagine the Indian population ballooning further in the coming years. On the other hand, if Paraiso's more narrow definition of Indianness—a definition more influenced by savage anthropology's notion that authentic cultural boundaries cannot be pieced together from the fragments of erased traditions or borrowed from other groups—becomes accepted wisdom, then the Indian population will still continue to grow, especially in northern Brazil where there are thousands of self-identified caboclos, but the scale will not be nearly as great.

How this discursive struggle is settled will have major ramifications, which may be revolutionary in proportion, for the future of Brazil. As discussed earlier, to be ruled authentically Indian gives peasant communities a constitutional right to land that might otherwise be ceded to the government or large landholders. The decisions of Indian judges will thus strongly impact the distribution of land and may help to rectify the existing skewed distribution of land for which Brazil is notorious. Furthermore, an increase in the number of mestizos who come to self-identify as Indian could have unanticipated implications for the politics of race in Brazil.

8. Contesting White Supremacy

Brazilian capitalism . . . has its origins in the racial question, in the enslavement of black and Indian peoples. — Benedita da Silva, "The Black Movement and Political Parties"

As I have mentioned and illustrated at various points throughout this book, white supremacy is an enduring tradition in Brazil. In a nation where at least half the population is nonwhite, actors on television shows, elected officials, university faculty and students, models in magazines, people in middle- and upper-middle-class occupations, and so forth, are almost exclusively white.[1] In fact, racial inequalities are so dismal that some observers have compared contemporary race relations in Brazil to those in the United States prior to the civil rights movement. Michael Hanchard, for one, has argued that

> the disparities in health, education, welfare, and employment between whites and nonwhites in Brazil, suggest, at the very least, bleak social conditions that rival or surpass those experienced by U.S. blacks in the 1950s and 1960s or colonized peoples of color in the Caribbean and elsewhere.[2]

Although the level of racism is startling, what is most noteworthy about Brazilian race relations is not the degree of white supremacy but rather the paucity of antiracist critique and political mobilization. Race has generally not been politicized, nor has it turned into a site of popular mobilization and national debate. To the contrary, it is widely believed that racism is not a serious or pressing matter.[3] Far from supporting or rallying behind antiracist politicians, activists, or organizations, most Brazilians — including racial subalterns — hold that Brazil is a racial democracy.[4] As such, Brazilian society represents an instance of racial hegemony in that racialized patterns of dominance and subordination are sustained less by force than consent.[5]

In the quest for a formula for a counterhegemonic common sense and concomitant politic, scholars of race have looked almost exclusively at subjectivities, communities, and movements that are situated in blackness. Moreover, and *without exception*, they have ignored Indianness. That is, within the subfield of critical race studies, there has been a pervasive, albeit unexamined, assumption that black identities are key to antiracism and Indian subjectivities are irrelevant. As a result, the focus has been on excavating African histories and genealogies, encouraging the production of negro subjectivities, generating greater popular support for the black movement, revalorizing blackness, and so forth. Absent have been discussions of the Indian movement, indigenous histories, of Indian identity formation, or anti-Indian racism.

For instance, in Howard Winant's analysis of the Brazilian racial terrain, Indianness is completely overlooked. In outlining what he considers the two aspects of racial politics in contemporary Brazil, Winant argues that the first

> is about racial inequality, mobility and redistribution along lines of race and racially based political action. The second is about the meaning of race, the nature of racial identity, the logic of racial categories, the centrality of African currents in Brazilian culture and history and the links between blacks in Brazil and elsewhere in the African diaspora.[6]

Note that the primacy of indigenous currents in Brazilian culture and history as well as the links between Indians in Brazil and elsewhere are not deemed relevant to the racial politics of contemporary Brazil. The politics of race is equated only with that of African-centered subjectivities, communities, and organizations. An antiracist project is situated exclusively within black identities and African cultural streams.

Another illustration of this restricted emphasis on blackness is Hanchard's *Racial Politics in Contemporary Brazil*. None of the chapters in his volume ever mention the flight from Indian subjectivities, anti-Indian stereotypes, or the Indian movement in Brazil. The focus is instead on black antiracist activists, the state of black social movements, the efforts of racial subalterns to distance themselves from black subject positions, the failure of Brazilians to appreciate their African heritage, the negative stereotypes associated with blackness, and so on. None of this is meant to suggest that a work must cover all aspects of racial politics or that it should not concentrate on blackness. Rather, the point is to show how analyses of racial politics—a subject that the title of this book promised to address—are usually studies of black politics exclusively.

Pardos as a Latent Black Population

Such a restricted stress on black identities, communities, and movements in discussions purported to be about antiracism is perplexing for several reasons. First, although it is five times larger than the Indian community, the black population in Brazil is relatively modest in size. That is, this bias in the literature could be better understood if blacks constituted a large segment of the national population. Yet countless surveys have documented the fact that only a small percentage of Brazilians self-identify as black. According to data compiled by IBGE in the 1991 census, for instance, 52 percent of Brazilians self-identified as white, 43 percent as pardo, and 5 percent as black.[7] Furthermore, the black population has declined throughout the twentieth century, whereas the Indian population, as already noted, has been increasing rather rapidly.[8]

This emphasis on blackness becomes even more confounding when one considers that the black movement has been much more dysfunctional than the Indian movement. For example, Hanchard contends that the *movimento negro* has been "episodic, fragmented and without self-sustaining organizations."[9] Although not without internal conflict and strife, the Indian movement, as we saw in eastern Brazil, has been fairly well unified, focused, and self-sustaining, not to mention remarkably successful. In contrast to the black movement, there have not been the same tendencies toward sectarianism and culturalism.[10] Instead, there has been a high level of ideological and organizational cohesion that has crystallized around land demarcation; measures to temper anti-Indian violence and discrimination; a devolution of political, educational, and cultural power to the tribal level; greater political power in county, state, and federal governments; and increased funding for indigenous health care, education, and economic development.

In addition to being in greater disarray, the black movement enjoys less popular support than the Indian movement. In 1992, John Burdick estimated that there were no more than twenty-five thousand active followers in the black movement nationwide, whereas in eastern and northeastern Brazil alone, I would place the number of Indian adherents in 1995 at somewhere near forty-five thousand.[11] Moreover, unlike the black movement's base—which consists primarily of professionals, intellectuals, and upwardly mobile students [12]—participants in the Indian movement are almost exclusively peasants and blue-collar workers. In short, the focus on black mobilization cannot be attributed to its having a broader, more organic base.

Why, then, do critical race scholars, such as Burdick in *Blessed Anastácia*, concern themselves exclusively with determining why the black movement does not attract ordinary Brazilians? Why are there never any comparable studies examining whether the Indian movement resonates with certain segments of the Brazilian population? Put somewhat differently, what accounts for scholars' restricted focus on blackness as an emancipatory subject position? Why this failure to consider the possibility of an antiracist movement being anchored, at least in part, in Indianness?

Beyond the fact that Indians tend not to be thought of in the context of race, a matter I will discuss shortly, there are at least three other reasons for this silence vis-à-vis Indians. First, as Jack Forbes has observed, there is a tendency to "insist upon translating *mestiço* and *pardo* as 'mulatto' which . . . results in a grave distortion of the tri-racial character of the *pardo-mestiço* group." [13] Pardos are not only of African and European descent but also boast indigenous origins.[14] Yet the fact that most pardos are part-Indian, that "perhaps a third of Brazilians . . . are at least part-Indian," is frequently overlooked "by modern writers who choose to emphasize only African and European components." [15] As a result, there is a proclivity "to lump all *pardos*, *mestiços* and *pretos* together as a 'colored' people (or as negroes), meaning by 'colored' *not* non-white but only negro or part-negro." [16] Scholars such as Maria Aparecida Silva Bento, for one, often assert that "blacks make up 44% of the population" because they categorize pardos as black.[17] This helps explain why "the perennial question of Brazilian racial politics" is frequently worded in the following manner: "If color prejudice and discrimination are indeed as pervasive and severe in Brazil as many observers have insisted, why is it that 'the great masses of the black population . . . are not receptive to the black movement's message of positive black identity and the denunciation of racism'?"[18] Surely Carlos Hasenbalg and Nelson do Valle Silva, whom Burdick is citing, are not referring to the 5 percent of the Brazilian population who self-identify as black as "the great masses" but rather to the other 43 percent who identify as neither black nor white and are officially classified as pardo.[19]

Another factor that explains the assumption, prevalent among scholars of race, that pardos are essentially a latent black population has to do with the fact that most of the observers of the Brazilian racial terrain are from or were trained in the United States. Given this, North American ideas about race and experiences with antiracism have had a major impact on Brazilian scholarship. Since the Brazilian pardo population fits North American constructions of blackness, and because most individuals of both African and indigenous descent eventually came to identify and mobilize as black in the United States, it is presumed that Brazilian pardos should follow a similar trajectory.[20] In other words, there is the teleological belief that pardos, if and when properly politicized, will come to identify with and privilege their "African heritage." This prognosis, if not prescription, is understandable given the successes of the black-led and centered antiracist movements in the United States. The most obvious pitfall associated with simply projecting a similar racial progression onto Brazil is that such a model ignores the particularities of the Brazilian context.

Racial categories and identities have been configured quite differently in Brazil. For instance, blackness tends to be more narrowly defined in Brazil than in the United States, where the one-drop rule has typically served as a legal and social benchmark of blackness. Although the difference between these two countries on this matter has often been exaggerated, it is undeniable that the hypo-descent rule of blackness has been much less salient in Brazil in both popular and official discourses.[21] Perhaps more important, a sense of community and identity associated with the idea of blackness has not developed to nearly the same degree in Brazil as it has in the United States, where blackness is clearly linked to a distinct cultural milieu. In the words of Marvin Harris, unlike in Brazil, "the Negro and the white of [the U.S.] census are 'social races,' groupings subjectively identified as culture carriers."[22] Thus, U.S. blacks often have different values, tastes, and interpretive frameworks than their white compatriots of a similar class.[23] As I will explain in more detail below, the same cannot be said for Brazilian blacks—nor for that matter, other non-Indian subalterns.[24]

One other possible reason why Indianness has not even been considered a racial option for pardos—let alone imagined as an antiracist subject position—is due to the way in which Indians have been constructed as bichos da mata, as antimodern forest people frozen in a premodern past.[25] In general, as I have outlined in previous chapters, Indianness is *not* thought of by non-Indians as a modern identity relevant to contemporary Brazilian politics—including the politics of race. On learning that I was interviewing Indians in Belo Horizonte, for example, a Brazilian sociologist who teaches in California immediately broke into laughter. The idea that there were Indians living in a city in one of the most economically developed regions of Brazil was a preposterous notion to him. For many, it may border on the inconceivable that pardos who live in cities or toil on plantations could one day become attracted to and engaged in an antiracist political project grounded in Indian identities.

Indians as "Ethnics"

Scholars of indigenous people, like the critical race scholars mentioned above, have also failed to explore the potential intersections of race and Indianness. That is, Indian researchers have not examined the possible impact of Indian communities on the issue of deracialization of power in Brazil. Although several of these scholars have emphasized how colonial conventions and Indian exorcism have been informed by racist ideologies and institutions, none to my knowledge have discussed the potential significance of Indianness for antiracism.

This principally has to do with the fact that throughout much of the academic community in Latin America, Indians are not considered germane to race matters.[26] Within the social sciences, as Peter Wade observes, "the virtually unquestioned assumption [prevails] that the study of blacks is one of racism and race relations, while the study of Indians is that of ethnicity and ethnic groups." [27] In Brazilian academic circles, whenever I encountered this belief that race meant black, I was reminded of a story that a Mexican colleague once told me. He was from an elite family in Mexico and looked white according to somatic constructions of whiteness in the United States. Apparently, he had a grandmother who had been Indian, and when he was around ten years old, his peers somehow discovered this fact and subsequently began to ostracize and harass him. As an outgrowth of these experiences, he decided to study issues of race and racism in college. Yet on inquiring at several Mexican universities as to how he could best pursue his interests, the frequent response was, "We [Mexicans] don't have that problem here because we have no blacks. You will have to go to the United States if you want to study race and racism. They have blacks there."

Wade suggests that the principal idea underlying this belief that race and Indians are separate and inconsequential matters "is that the category 'indian' does not depend on phenotypical signifiers. . . . In contrast, 'black' is often seen as a category defined by more fixed phenotypical criteria that cannot be manipulated in the same way." [28] It is of course incorrect, as Wade notes, to use " 'race' to talk of black identity and 'ethnicity' to talk about indian identity" as if blackness were only a matter of phenotype and Indianness only a matter of culture: "Such an opposition separates phenotype from culture, as if the former was not itself culturally constructed." [29] Furthermore, as discussed in chapter 6, the category Indian is dependent on physical signifiers, which is one of the reasons most eastern Indians are viewed as racial charlatans. Their African and European features mark them as inauthentic—as not "real Indians." Conversely, the category of blackness is often contingent on nonphysical markers. As Wade explains,

> The Latin American material shows that, for example, the same individual dressed shabbily and smartly will be identified with different colour terms that locate the person on a scale between black and white. These terms are not dependent on phenotype alone, because the context of somatic features alters people's classification—and even perhaps perception—of these features. [30]

One additional reason that it is inaccurate to conceptualize Indianness as a simple matter of "ethnicity qua culture" is because "the category 'indian' was an integral part of the colonial encounters within which the discourse of race emerged. . . . From a macrohistorical perspective, then, 'indian' was a racial category and retains strong elements of this history." [31]

In my discussions with Indian scholars in Brazil, none of them explicitly stated that Indianness was a matter of culture (rather than phenotype or descent) and that this was the reason why they did not explore the relevance of Indians to the politics of race. Instead, when they defended their analytic position, they did so on the grounds that this was how racial subalterns conceptualized their social world. As one Brazilian Ph.D. candidate of anthropology at the National Museum (Museu Nacional) in Rio de Janeiro remarked:

> When blacks refer to whites they mean another race, but Indians don't mean this. When Indians speak of whites, of the white man [sic] they are referring to a civilized man, and to his system of life, to a different cosmology, to a different mode of thinking and seeing oneself and the world. To the Indian, the white man could be of the white, black, or Asian race. The point here is that he is not an Indian and therefore is an other. This is the only reason that scholars don't think of Indian discourses as racialized discourses. [32]

Rather than claiming that Indianness is a matter of ethnicity (that is, culture) and not race (that is, phenotype/genotype), this young scholar justifies the failure of Indian scholars to deal with race by claiming that Indians imagine the differences between themselves and others in exclusively cultural terms. Although it is certainly true that Indians discern differences in cultural terms, they also take into consideration genotype and phenotype. [33] Moreover, discourses and other practices are rarely, if ever, "race neutral," regardless of whether individuals appreciate this fact. As I will illustrate later, Indians are producing different aesthetic hierarchies, narratives, symbolic orders, spatializations, political practices, and so on that, in the Brazilian context, have racialized meanings and potentially profound implications for the Brazilian racial order. Thus, even if Indians did not conceptualize differences in racial terms, this would not mean that their discursive and material practices were inconsequential to race matters.

Indianing

One of the principal pillars of white supremacy in Brazil is the concept of whitening. In the early part of the twentieth century, the Brazilian elite, as Thomas Skidmore details in the canonical work *Black into White*, formalized whitening as an official ideology in an attempt to rescue Brazil from the fate that biology, according to the tenets of scientific racism, had ordained for any nation in which whites were the minority. The creation of the whitening narrative enabled the Brazilian elite to reassure themselves and the world at large that Brazil could become a civilized nation despite its genetic deficiencies. Based on the presupposition that white blood was superior, it was argued that through miscegenation, white blood would cleanse Brazil of the negative features of its more primitive racial stock while maintaining the few positive attributes that these inferior races had to offer.

Sarah Radcliffe and Sallie Westwood claim that "this republican dream" of whitening, of salvaging genetically disadvantaged nations through el mestizaje, "has been contested by numerous indigenous and black groups throughout the [South American] continent." [34] Such statements tend to leave the false impression that whitening has been a practice instituted against the wishes of the ever-resistant subalterns of color. The reality in Brazil, however, has been much the opposite. Rather than resisting whitening, a large percentage of African- and indigenous-descent peoples have actively embraced it. [35]

It is commonplace, for example, for non-Indian Brazilians to whiten their racial categorization whenever possible, [36] that is, to select a self-identity that is whiter than how someone is in actuality racially positioned. [37] Individuals are constantly highlighting or emphasizing signifiers of whiteness — such as pointing to a white ancestor or indicating a feature such as "light eyes" — in order to assert a whiter subject position. As Rebecca Reichmann reports, "UN Rapporteur Maurice Glélé-Ahanhanzo . . . observed that when subjects were asked to identify their color in the 1991 national census, more than a hundred shades of color were 'used to describe themselves, out of a desire to distance themselves as far as possible from the colour black.' " [38] This desire might be more appropriately characterized as a wish to position themselves closer to whiteness. For instance, there are thousands, if not millions, of Brazilians of salient indigenous descent, many of whom have no African ancestry, who also engage in this ritual of managing the diacritics of whiteness in order to claim a whiter racial position. If it were merely a question of distancing oneself from blackness, then those without African ancestry would not need to indulge in categorical charades such as that described by Glélé-Ahanhanzo.

Another prevailing manifestation of this phenomenon entails the attempt to physically whiten one's descendants by selecting and pursuing mates who are white or whiter.[39] The following excerpt taken from an interview with Gabrielle (a thirty-two-year-old, mulatto/black maid and the mother of three) and her common-law husband Carlos (a twenty-eight-year-old, white day laborer and basket maker), illustrates this practice:

> It's not that I felt better than blacks, but I used to talk to my mother like this: "Mother, when I get married I will marry a white man." My mother used to ask me, "Why?" I used to answer, "Because I don't want my children to be dark like me." Then I used to say that, "If I found a white man to marry, I would marry him so that my kids wouldn't be little darkies." . . . This just reminded me that many darkies used to try to ask me out, but I wouldn't date them— no way. . . . I was only really thinking of the children. I used to think, "Okay, let me marry a person lighter than myself, because if I marry a dark person like myself, it's going to be all dark—the little children." But I was still thinking of the children, right? "So let me marry a lighter one because then my children will come out cuter."[40]

Edith Piza and Fúlvia Rosemberg argue that whitening "represents the mainstream expression of identity of subjects who have no links to the black movement."[41] To this definition I would add individuals with no connection to indigenous communities or organizations. Through an array of material and discursive practices, the eastern índios I interviewed often articulated, produced, and sustained a symbolic order that represented an alternative to the semiotics and orientations of whitening. Within this different cultural logic, which I refer to as Indianing, Indianness was the esteemed, the superior, the sacred, the ideal, and the desired. Consequently, it was Indianness, not whiteness, that acted as the gravitational force directing and shaping a number of attitudes, values, and actions.

For instance, in contrast to the expressed desires of the majority of non-Indians to partner with someone white or whiter, all but one of the Indians I interviewed claimed an adamant wish to date and marry an Indian, and to have their children partner with an Indian—regardless of tribe, as illustrated in the following interview with Benvinda Pankararu.[42]

> JONATHAN WARREN: Do you have a preference as to whether your son marries an Indian or a white?
> BENVINDA: I want him to marry an Indian.
> JW: Why?
> BENVINDA: Because all of my children are only married to Indians. And now there is only him, and he is going to obey me. I want him to marry an Indian so that our nation doesn't die.

Unlike most non-Indians, among whom there is a prevalent belief that whites are more physically attractive, this desire for an Indian partner was not framed as a question of aesthetics.[43] As a result of these racialized notions of beauty, or what Anna Lúcia Flovisbela dos Santos refers to as "aesthetic alienation," pardos and blacks often seek out partnerships with whites in order to "improve" the appearances of their children.[44] This attitude was expressed by Gabrielle, cited earlier, who claimed that she wanted to marry someone white because her children would be "cuter." Likewise, Henrique (a forty-three-year-old black who lived in Rio de Janeiro for fifteen years as a street vendor before returning to Vasalia) explained that he and most other blacks were motivated by aesthetic considerations when selecting a white spouse:

> [Blacks marry whites] because whites have good hair. . . . Their nose is not ugly [like ours]. Blacks normally have very large lips, like an animals and people think that this is ugly. I am trying to say that black

Benvinda Pankararu (right) with her grandson, Iuri, and Krenak daughter-in-law, Nilza da Graça.

people know that [their features] are ugly and white people also know that blacks are ugly.[45]

In this respect, then, Indianing does not constitute a simple reversal of whitening because Indians do not frame their motivation for Indian partners in terms of aesthetics. Although a few women told me that they found Indian men more attractive, appearance did not seem to be nearly as central a concern for partner selection as it was among non-Indians. Instead, the most frequent justifications for seeking an Indian partner were parental desire and a wish not to contaminate "the race" any further, as illustrated in this interview with César, the twenty-year-old student who was preparing to attend agriculture school in Espírito Santo in 1995.

> JONATHAN WARREN: Did you always think that you would marry a woman who was Indian?
> CÉSAR: Always!
> JW: If you had married a woman who wasn't an Indian, would your family have been sad?
> CÉSAR: I think so, yes.
> JW: Why do you think so?
> CÉSAR: Because of the race . . . so as not to mix the race.
> JW: Was it important whether the person was Pataxó [César's tribe] or just any Indian?
> CÉSAR: Just so long as she was Indian.

Like other eastern Indians I talked to, César, (who was married to a Pankararu), portrays mestizajem as a negative phenomenon—at least as it applies to Indians. This view represents a clear departure from the dominant discourse, which frames race mixing as a positive, progressive force because, as noted earlier, it is believed to lead to the erasure of blackness and Indianness, and the gradual production of whiteness.

THE POLITICS OF MEMORY

Indianing also emerged in what was and was not remembered by Indians. In the construction of family lineages and community histories, various researchers have observed that non-Indians usually stress their white ancestors and tend to characterize the past as conflict free, if not "unknown." [46] The responses of Consuela, a nineteen-year-old mulatto/black who lived in a favela in Rio de Janeiro, reveal this perspective on mixed ancestry.

JONATHAN WARREN: Who were your ancestors?

CONSUELA: I don't know.

JW: Do you know if you're the descendant of slaves?

CONSUELA: I don't know. Nobody ever said anything. All that I know is what I learned in school. Everything that I know about blacks is because of school because that is the stuff of history, so we have to learn about that, about blacks and slaves.

JW: Do you know if you're a descendant of Africans or Indians?

CONSUELA: No one here at home knows.

JW: Of Europeans?

CONSUELA: It appears that the father of my mother was Italian. Her mother was black and Spanish—something like that, but they never told me much about the black side. But she always talked about her father being Italian and her grandmother being Spanish.

Consuela's family, like most non-Indians with whom I spoke, appeared to focus exclusively on their white relatives and knew little about their nonwhite ones. Also absent from their family narratives was any mention of conquest, slavery, and apartheidlike practices. Other observers of the Brazilian racial terrain have found this lack of knowledge vis-à-vis historical forms of racial exploitation to be common among racial subalterns. For example, Nancy Scheper-Hughes remarks of the residents of a shantytown near Recife that "these people are the descendants of a slave and runaway slave-Indian (caboclo) population. Yet they do not think to link their current difficulties to a history of slavery and race exploitation." [47] Robin Sheriff observes that in a poor, urban community in Rio de Janeiro, "very few informants in fact, were able to recall hearing stories about the slavery era, although the grandparents and great grandparents of a number of the older people I knew had in fact been slaves." [48]

Most non-Indians I met simply asserted that they did not know if their ancestors had been slaves and claimed to have no knowledge of whether slavery had ever existed in the region where they lived. On some occasions, when the topic of Indianness was brought up, non-Indians would reproduce popular tropes of how their grandmothers had been pegado no lasso (abducted via the lasso; enslaved). Yet the antiracist critique inherent in these stories was always undermined by the fact that they told them in an offhand, humorous manner.[49] Furthermore, in the course of countless conversations with pardos and blacks, almost all of them eventually brought to my attention, with a tone of pride, that they had a relative who "looked like" me—who had olhos claros (light eyes) and cabelo bom (good hair).[50] As in Consuela's interview above, the genealogies that were salient to their personal and family memories were those of their white ancestors only. This was the lineage that was prized and highlighted, even if the white forebear had in all probability been their grandmother's slave master and rapist.

In contrast, posttraditional Indians never mentioned having relatives who physically resembled me. They generally minimized the presence of non-Indian relatives—especially white ones—in their remembrances and accounts of family and community histories, instead placing their Indian relatives at the center of their narratives. Moreover, memories often revolved around histories of conquest that their indigenous ancestors had suffered. When asked, "Who are your ancestors?" they would underscore their history of race exploitation by immediately invoking their community's history of struggle with anti-Indian racism.[51] And even when historical tropes were invoked, such as the pegado no lasso, they were clearly not told as jokes but were criticized or used to revalue Indianness. For example, consider Puhuí Pataxó's reading of this lasso story:

> You always hear people say that they have "Indian blood." You hear this all the time. There's also something they say that I think is a criticism [of Indians]. They will say, "My grandmother was hunted with dogs and captured by a lasso." This is an illusion. This is a big invention. If they said something like, "My mother, my grandmother, my great-grandmother was found in the forest"—then I would accept it. But to say they were taken by a lasso . . . they are suggesting that an Indian is game, that the Indian is an animal that can be caught in a lasso, that can be hunted with dogs. No, the Indian is human. An Indian can be encountered in the forest—a lost one. But it's really difficult to capture an Indian because he's [sic] familiar with

IVAN PANKARARU

Figure 2: "Indian 'Taken by the Lasso' " by Ivan Pankararu.

the forest. Probably lots of times they just found a person lost in the forest—deep in the heart of the forest, and then they would say that they took that Indian by a lasso and with dogs. But I don't believe this happened. It's a lie.

The suggestion that Indians could never be captured in the forest is a vintage, posttraditional foray of the sort discussed in chapter 6—one plainly aimed at upsetting the symbolic hierarchies engendered by the law of the white. Puhuí's statements also illustrate how eastern Indians did not consider the pegado no lasso trope a humorous matter. In fact, Puhuí viewed it as a myth that dehumanized Indians. Even those Indians who did not dismiss the validity of these stories, who did not consider it to be a myth, invoked this trope as critique of conquest. The drawings of Ivan Pankararu (see figures 2 and 3) are an excellent example of this. In keeping memories of indigenous conquest alive, he has obviously not romanticized it, nor has he portrayed the Indian as a savage or comical baffoon; rather, he has articulated it as a serious, if not critical, evaluation of anti-Indian violence.

THE MAXAKALI AS THE IDEAL

Another instance of this alternative logic of Indianing was the meaning and significance given to the Maxakali. The Maxakali, like all Indians in eastern Brazil, have been fundamentally transformed by colonialism. They have been forced to flee from their original territories and have been reduced to a handful of families—a mere fraction of their original

Figure 3: "Indian Hunted by Slave Catcher's Dog" by Ivan Pankararu.

population. Then, too, they must eke out an existence on a few acres of land where they are constantly terrorized (shot at, threatened, verbally abused, symbolically treated as nonhumans, and so on) by non-Indians.

Yet the Maxakali are extremely distinct from posttraditional Indians in that they are not trying to re-create a Maxakali world from the fragments and ruins of tribal traditions. For example, Maxakali is still their native tongue, and Christianity has not supplanted their religion. A number of the Maxakali's ceremonies, as well as their medicinal knowledge, spiritual insights, dances, architectural styles, hunting practices, and origin stories, have not been dismembered by discoveries.[52] Hence, in large measure because the Maxakali have managed to avoid the shattering of their tribal heritage, they more closely approximate the "real Indians" of Brazilian popular imagination than do posttraditional Indians who, as we have repeatedly seen, are typically considered racial impostors. For posttraditional Indians, the Maxakali also represent or more closely approximate the ideal of Indianness. As the ideal, however, they are not employed as a marker of the inauthenticity of posttraditionals but instead serve to underscore the degree of colonization posttraditionals have endured.

Furthermore, in contrast to non-Indians, the Maxakali represent a type of role model, an important community of reference. In a sense, the Maxakali function as a kind of racial/cultural mecca for posttraditional Indians. Many journey to their community, where they experience a type of spiritual reawakening. A number of Indians told me how they became "more deeply connected with their Indianness" by spending time with the Maxakali. Waldemar Krenak explained how after living and working with the Maxakali for several months he had been spiritually transformed. His time with the Maxakali gave him a glimpse into what the Krenak had lost, and what needed to be done if the Krenak were to survive and prosper as a people. As a result, he decided to devote his life to rediscovering and reviving Krenak theology.

The Maxakali function as the priests and nuns of Indianness. Post-traditional Indians do not expect to ever live precisely like the Maxakali; nonetheless they hold the Maxakali to be important guardians of tradition who should therefore be respected and consulted for guidance. They are revered as the keepers of a sacred knowledge, providing inspiration and direction for how other Indians can rejuvenate what has been lost through Indian exorcism.

As carriers of traditional ways, the Maxakali are highly regarded by posttraditional Indians. In 1995, for example, they were given disproportionate representation on the Indian Council of Minas Gerais by other Indians. All other tribes had two representatives except for the Xacriabá, who had three representatives because they were by far the largest tribe in Minas Gerais. The Maxakali, by contrast, were given four representatives, even though their population was no larger than most of the other tribes.

Another case of how the Maxakali are venerated within the greater pan-Indian community is the Maxakali influence on the posttraditional lexicon. The Kaxixó, Xacriabá, Pataxó, Krenak, Pankararu, Aranã, Canoeiro, and Tupinikim have all begun to incorporate Maxakali words into their everyday patois. The words most frequently used are those for Indian (tirri), non-Indian (andirrik), men (inpiar), women (inhex), child (kitoko), beautiful (bay), ugly (piba), rum (kaibok), tobacco (kurrak), money (kaiamba), horse (kamandu), cows (manãx), dog (kukey), and gays (manãite).[53]

The great lengths to which posttraditional Indians often went to defend, care for, and protect the Maxakali is a further example of how highly esteemed the Maxakali are by other Indians in eastern Brazil. In interactions with non-Indians, eastern Indians would almost always defend other Indians—even if they did not care for the particular

Indian who was being attacked or criticized, as indicated by Karakana Canoeiro's statement:[54]

> We went to the city the other night. There was a girl there with whom I'd just had a fight. Then another girl passes, a white girl, and she [the Indian girl] accidentally runs into this girl. So the white girl says that she is going to throw a cup of beer in her face. I immediately stood up for her (and this was the girl with whom I had just been feuding). Right away I said something like, "Then why don't you throw it?!" I defended her, and she defended me. It's because I'm Indian and she's Indian. How am I going to watch an Indian from my tribe get picked on and just stay quiet? That is how it is—one depends on the other. We may fight and argue among ourselves, but once we're off the aldeia and there's a person who's not Indian and who picks a fight with an Indian—we'll unite to defend the Indian.

In the above, a fight almost broke out because the one indigenous girl bumped into a white girl. The Maxakali, because they do not speak Portuguese and are less familiar with non-Maxakali customs and expectations, are even more prone to invoke the ire of non-Indians, and thus are often in greater need of defense than posttraditional Indians. That is, the Maxakali must negotiate a much greater cultural divide and as a consequence, unlike posttraditional Indians, more frequently fail to conform to what most Brazilians would consider acceptable behavior. For instance, when they visited the zoo in Belo Horizonte, the Maxakali could not understand why no one would kill the bears given such a splendid opportunity. Or, to cite another case, it did not make sense to them that they could not hunt the cattle from neighboring ranchers when they and their children were experiencing hunger. As one might imagine, then, outside of their communities the Maxakali often violate a number of expected mores and standards of interaction and comportment.

The majority of non-Indians are quick to interpret such behavior as evidence of the Maxakali's savagery. Posttraditional Indians, however, are just as quick to defend the Maxakali. For example, in May 1995, the Maxakali began visiting Geralda Chaves Soares's home, which was about a two-week journey by foot.[55] They traveled many miles to what was their original homeland. Given the number of people who had made the long journey (eighteen), many of them had to sleep outside in the courtyard. Inevitably, they tracked in and out of Geralda's home to use the shower, bathroom, and kitchen. This, of course, meant that the house was a lot dirtier than usual. As well, the young children did not wear diapers and so urinated on the floor. In their own homes, this would not have been a problem because they have dirt floors that quickly absorb the urine, but on the tiled floors it created a mess. Finally, the Maxakali have different norms of privacy and personal space. Their notions about personal possessions do not overlap with those of most other Brazilians. What a non-Maxakali might consider a personal possession, such as a watch or radio, could end up being taken by one of the Maxakali.

After a few weeks of trying to keep the place in the same order as when the Maxakali were not there, Geralda's housecleaner, a young white woman who was finishing high school and intent on finding a man of material means to marry, said in frustration, "I hate Indians! They are dirty and I can't stand them!" One of the posttraditional Indians, Valmares Pataxó, who had been staying with Geralda for several months so that he could complete his high school degree, heard what she said and became upset.[56] He argued, "When you speak badly of the Maxakali, it is like swearing at my parents. You don't understand anything about them and what they have endured. These are my brothers [sic] and I don't want to hear another negative word said about them." After this incident, he never spoke to the housekeeper again, although they had formerly been friends.

THE INDIANIZATION OF PLACE

Indianing also manifests itself in architecture and the management of space. As I noted in chapter 3, Benvinda Pankararu moved her family from their lands in Pernambuco to be near her father, who was imprisoned on what is today aldeia Guarani. As time passed, it became impossible for them to return to their aldeia in Pernambuco because it had been overrun by posseiros.[57] The Pankararu at Guarani—which consisted of five families, all the children and grandchildren of Benvinda— were profoundly unhappy at Guarani since it was not, in their words, "their space." The aldeia was controlled by the Pataxó. They became so dissatisfied and desperate to control their own territory that they considered leaving before any other location to settle was found. Finally, in

1994, they were granted a few hundred acres by an Italian bishop near Araçuaí in Minas Gerais.

Once there, with some financial assistance from NGOs and FUNAI, they eventually began constructing a new community according to what they defined as a "traditional Pankararu village." The six houses were placed to form a large rectangle about two hundred yards long and eighty yards wide. In the center of this rectangle was a large open area for religious and ceremonial dances, a spiritual house, and a building for community meetings. These communal structures were made out of so-called traditional building materials: small trees, and coconut palm (coqueiro). The houses in which they lived had red tile roofs, walls made out of clay bricks, and toilets and showers. They "Pankararuized," to use their words, these buildings by adding a large extended front veranda where they could socialize and make their artesenato (handicrafts). Finally, the village's entrance was specifically constructed to face east, where the sun rises. All these modifications and special designs — such as the extended veranda — were defined by them as important features of a traditional Pankararu home and village.

Most of the Indian communities in eastern Brazil had neither the land nor resources to reconstruct an entire community from scratch. Most had to live in houses that were abandoned or deserted by fazendeiros and peasants. Nonetheless, all the aldeias I visited had constructed or were in the process of constructing so-called ritual houses.[58] These structures were always built of natural material such as trees, bamboo, coconut palm, and tall grass (capoiera)–concrete, steel, or bricks were never used. To both Indians and non-Indians alike, physical structures such as these signify Indianness.[59] The Indianness of these buildings was further emphasized and reinforced by the fact that they were only used for rituals and ceremonies associated with Indianness: Indian weddings, holidays such as the Day of the Indian, and so forth. These houses were usually placed at the center of the village — as a church or bank often is in non-Indian towns and villages — and thus served as a conspicuous symbol of the Indianness of the community.

The interior decor of homes was also affected by Indianing. There were a number of parallels with the decor of non-Indians of the same class: images of saints, kitsch pictures from popular culture, as well as pinturas (paintings) of couples (in which the woman is wearing a dress

Cleonice Pankararu carrying tiles for the roofs of the new homes being constructed in aldeia Apukaré.

One of the homes being built in aldeia Apukaré.

A typical wall in Indian homes: indigenous artesenato and religious objects hang alongside Christian iconography.

and the man a suit).[60] How these homes differed was that they never placed the signifiers of whiteness at the heart of the home as non-Indian homes often did. For example, regardless of race, non-Indians almost always put the white or whitest relatives' photo — whoever that may be — in a central location in the house. The following Bahian quatrain succinctly captures this practice:

Of his white father, whom he never saw,
He has a picture in the parlor;
But of the Negro woman who gave him birth
He has no picture, nor does he even speak of her.[61]

In Indian homes, the photos of white relatives or friends of the family were not blown up and centrally placed; in fact, such photos would likely never be publicly displayed. Instead, on the walls there always hung explicit signifiers of Indianness, such as photos of themselves or family in "indigenous regalia." Indian artesenato that they had made themselves or been given as a gift — such as necklaces, bows and arrows, headbands or skirts used in ceremonies, and so on — *always* decorated the interior of Indian homes as well.

Indianing was also evidenced by the renaissance of interest in a number of indigenous deities, languages, and rituals. Until recently, as discussed in previous chapters, Indians were prohibited from speaking their language and performing their religious and festive ceremonies. According to historical accounts of the Pankararu, for example, "Indians who refused to speak Portuguese had their tongues extracted." [62] Due to the reduction in the amount of Indian exorcism, as well as anxiety about demonstrating Indian authenticity and "cultural distinctions from the national society" to achieve state recognition, there have been increased efforts to try to piece together traditions that had been shattered or forgotten. Elders have been asked to recall stories and show, whenever possible, how certain dances or rituals are performed. Archival evidence, which had been collected by anthropologists, missionaries, and government bureaucrats, is sought for consultation. And when there are no living memories or written records, ideas are sometimes borrowed and modified from other Indians, such as the Maxakali.

The first Pataxó wedding ceremony in fifteen years was performed in 1994; one year later, the first Krenak ceremony in twenty-five years took place.[63] A number of other religious or ceremonial rituals have since been rejuvenated, gaining a new vitality. The Tupinikim have revitalized the *Dança do Tambor*, the Kariri-Xocó the Ouricuri, and so on.[64] Various indigenous deities have taken on a new saliency within various tribes. For instance, the *Pai da Mata* of the Pataxó and *Tokón* of the Krenak have become household words again in these communities.[65] The toré, a basic round dance with singing, has become a stable ritual performed at most pan-Indian events and a hallmark of Indianness in the region.[66] As Vera Lúcia Calheiros Mata observes, after the Kariri-Xocó had retaken their land via an invasion, they "danced the *toré* to demonstrate to the authorities that they were 'real Indians'" and thus rightfully entitled to the disputed territories.[67]

Finally, there has been an attempt in several of the communities to recover their traditional languages. One manifestation of this is the serious effort to establish bilingual schools. As Manoel Pataxó (the sixty-nine-year-old municipal councilperson who decided not to continue on with his education when he injured himself as a boy) says of this desire to institute bilingualism,

It is one thing that we would really like here—a bilingual professor. The problem is that we can't find a teacher who is qualified, who knows our language well enough to teach it. We don't have the conditions yet for this, but we want to bring someone in who could really teach us the Pataxó language, someone who could put together a spelling book in our language.

One facet of the attempt to rejuvenate indigenous languages has been the move toward the use of indigenous names. Until recently, most post-traditional Indians either had just a "white" name or they had both an "indigenous" and a "white" name. In the latter instance, an individual's indigenous name tended to be kept secret because of the level of anti-Indian violence. Within the past ten years or so, most individuals have adopted their tribal name as their surname. There has also been a distinct trend toward giving children only an indigenous name. Furthermore, many adults who received just a "white" name at birth are beginning to adopt indigenous names. And those who were at one time much more secretive about their Indian names, now use them exclusively.

INDIAN-ONLY DOMAINS

A final illustration of Indianing—the articulation and reproduction of an alternative symbolic order to whitening—was the desire that most Indians expressed for exclusive Indian institutions or territories, such as schools, aldeias, soccer leagues, political associations, and so on. They organized so as to construct and maintain the physical and social boundaries between themselves and whites, which, of course, suggests a very different orientation, community of reference, and symbolic order—one in which whiteness is not privileged. Salvinho Pataxó's remarks (the bicyclist who was badly wounded by an upper Pataxó because Salvinho questioned the man's Indianness) were typical of the Indians with whom I spoke.[68]

Even though it is ultimately the community's decision, I personally believe that when an Indian decides to marry a white that they should leave the aldeia. If they don't do this, then each time an Indian marries a white, more and more whites are going to arrive and fill up the place. So if a person marries a white, they should live on the outside—not on the aldeia.[69]

Benvinda Pankararu showing me the Pankararu's religious attire. According to the Pankararu, the spirits of their deceased ancestors (the *Praiá*) frequently reside in this clothing. When one dons the Praiá clothing (*roupa do Praiá*), one takes on the spirits that inhabit them. Consequently, it is forbidden to refer to the individual wearing the roupa do Praiá by her or his name. Such a gesture not only shows a lack of appreciation for the transformative power of this attire but also may alienate or anger the Praiá.

Benvinda Pankararu instructing the young men how to perform ceremonial dances in front of a ritual cabana that was under construction.

Some segments of the black population have also struggled for non-white organizations or neighborhoods. In Salvador, Bahia, for example, Ilê Aiyê, the main black Carnival group in the city, forbids the entry of whites. As Antônio Carlos dos Santos, one of the founders of the twenty-five-year-old group and its current president, explains,

> We formed this group as a reaction to the separation of the races, to the perverse cultural apartheid that exists here, and we are not going to give up our black-only policy until we achieve our objectives and prejudice no longer exists. If we let whites and foreigners join, do you think that is going to improve conditions in the neighborhood or get the police to change their attitude toward blacks?[70]

Although there has been a long history of black organizations in Brazil, it is important to underscore how these groups and institutions have never enjoyed much support or active participation from the broader black and pardo populations.[71] As a result, these organizations have proven fragile in the face of elite or state opposition. To take one example, in the late 1930s when the authoritarian regime banned the Frente Negra Brasileira, a black political party, the organization quickly folded and never recovered. One need only compare this to the resilience of the African National Congress (ANC) in South Africa to get a sense of how little support black organizations attract in Brazil. Despite a much more violent and sustained assault, the ANC survived and eventually became the governing party. In Brazil, black-centered political parties that are committed to rectifying the racialization of economic and political power continue to attract very few black or pardo adherents. To date, various scholars have found that most blacks and pardos have little interest in black associations.[72]

In the rural towns of Vasalia and Araçuaí, as well as in two working-class, predominantly nonwhite neighborhoods in Rio de Janeiro and Belo Horizonte, I too never encountered anyone interested in creating all-moreno or all-black institutions or spaces. No one ever expressed any angst about whites participating in their organizations or living in their neighborhoods. In fact, the only comments I ever heard vis-à-vis this issue of residential or organizational segregation concerned cases in which subalterns felt that whites were attempting to exclude them from certain social or physical arenas. For instance, in the following interview, these kinds of concerns mobilized students of color who attended a working-class high school in Belo Horizonte.

JONATHAN WARREN: Do you think that there was racism in your school?

HELENA: The bourgeoisie sat in the back and those from the lower classes in the front. . . . In the bourgeoisie there were no blacks. There was not one black. They were all blonds — genuine blonds. I don't know if it was because they were rich and spoiled and therefore they just acted that way, but our class was completely separated. The whites were way in the back. And the blacks . . . and I don't mean just blacks who are dark like me but also morenos [mulattoes or light-skinned blacks] sat together. We all thought how absurd it was: "Why do they separate themselves from us? Why don't they want to work with us? Why do they act so arrogant toward us?" So we got together and we made a written statement [deposição]. And since I was one of the better students, I took the statement to the counselor, an excellent person. He gave us permission to hold a debate about racism in the school. . . . It took place during the last hour of class. So there wasn't a lot of debate. But it was good. It was great. Only the director spoke. She said that "in Brazil, it is impossible for racism to exist because everyone has blue blood, there's been a mixture of the races."[73] It was the only thing, the only part that interested me. All the rest was handouts on racism.

JW: Was the debate a success?

HELENA: Yes. This type [of racism] stopped in the whole school. Afterward it got better. For instance, the new year was arriving, and everyone started working together. We conversed with one another. It completely ended.

JW: Were there other forms of racism in your school or just that of your blond, bourgeois colleagues? For example, were your teachers or the curriculum racist?

HELENA: No! No. Only the kids. Only the colleagues in our class. But the teachers, the counselor, the curriculum . . . no. No, they weren't.

Helena was twenty-two years old when I interviewed her in 1995. She lived at home with her parents and earned a bit of spending money by tutoring high school students. It is clear that she and her colleagues, at least as she tells it, were not concerned with the creation of all-black subcultures or institutions. Indeed, they were driven by precisely the opposite agenda—their exclusion from their white classmates' informal networks. Although further research is required to determine the representativeness of my findings, it is of note that none of the Indians I interviewed ever expressed any concerns about access to whites and their social spaces. Instead, their anxiety pivoted on the absence of Indian teachers, the anti-Indian biases in the curriculum, and the anti-Indian sentiments of faculty and students. Thus, rather than fighting to be able to associate with whites, they were focused on creating all-Indian schools, making the curriculum less racist, challenging the anti-Indian attitudes of their colleagues and teachers, and struggling for more Indian faculty and administrators. Helena, as was the case with the other blacks and pardos I interviewed, did not even see the complete lack of black teachers or an all-white curriculum as racist, let alone seek to mobilize to transform these racializations of power.[74] It seemed that for students like Helena, as long as they could converse and nominally associate with whites, the race problem, in their minds, had been resolved.

In addition to being connected to a nonwhitening or Indianing orientation, I found that Indianness in eastern Brazil entailed a different language of race. Numerous researchers have observed that non-Indians
often work to avoid or minimize racism.[75] Their racial idiom parallels
in this respect what critical whiteness scholars have discovered to be
an aspect of race talk among many U.S. whites. According to Jennifer
Simpson, "educated whites" in the United States frequently attempt to
ignore, forget, or deny racism through what she terms "selective hearing," "creative interpreting," and "complicitous forgetting."

> I hear (White) people employ these rules in so many situations and
> with such ease that I realize the rules are not only unwritten, they are
> unrealized. "Oh, I didn't mean it that way," "Don't take my words so
> seriously," "I don't think that's what he was saying," are all ways of
> rewriting the story, writing racism out of the (remembered) story.[76]

Thus, "white talk," as Simpson calls it, is based on learning not to acknowledge or perceive the links between phenotype and power; on sup-
posing one has transcended the multiple ways one's ideas, values, expectations, emotions, and practices are shaped by race.

White talk describes the language of race spoken by the majority of
non-Indians in Brazil. White supremacy and privilege are, as numerous scholars have observed, "disallowed or submerged discourses."[77]
In the words of Rebecca Reichmann, "Racial discrimination is endemic
in Brazilian society. Yet mystification and denial of racial differences are
widespread."[78] The prevalence of race evasiveness, of white talk, is precisely why Antonio Sérgio Alfredo Guimarães warns that "any study of
racism in Brazil must begin by reflecting on the very fact that racism is
a taboo subject in Brazil."[79]

One of the reasons that racism is a taboo topic, that non-Indians
usually deny its existence, has to do with the fact that most "Brazilians
imagine themselves inhabiting an antiracist nation, a 'racial democracy.' This is one of the sources of their pride and, at the same time,
conclusive proof of their status as a civilized nation."[80] According to
Guimarães, it is difficult for Brazilians to acknowledge racism because
the idea that they inhabit a nonracist nation gives them ground to

claim moral and social superiority as Brazilians. That is, it is one of the few arenas in which they believe they have surpassed Europe and the United States—their benchmark of civilization. Given this belief and their satisfaction with it, they are reluctant to envision their society as racist.[81]

In large measure because of their emotional investment in the racial democracy imagining, there is a good deal of defensiveness vis-à-vis any implication that this may be a myth. The commitment to the racial democracy narrative is so tenacious that some Brazilians prefer to invoke essentialist ideas about black inferiority rather than acknowledge racism.[82] Note the response of Jorge, a twenty-two-year-old mulatto, to the question, "How would you explain the fact that all the bank employees [in Vasalia] are white?"

> I think that it must be because blacks haven't been able to obtain those jobs because they lack intelligence/knowledge. Their IQ is not high enough to get the job because they have the opportunity, because the exams are open to everyone. In the state of Rio, it's an open exam. If a black person passes the exam, he [sic] is hired. Blacks are not prevented from taking the bank exam.[83]

With disquieting ease, Jorge articulated a biologized notion of race rather than reexamining his belief that Vasalia is a town without racism. He also showed a remarkably naive understanding of how racism can operate. Summoning essentialized ideas of subaltern inferiority is just one of the countless discourses that non-Indians routinely practice to hedge the issue of racism. Many of the efforts to avoid or minimize white supremacy—practices that include the use of race-evasive categories such as moreno—have been mapped out and analyzed elswhere.[84] Below, I detail an instance of white talk in order to underscore the lengths to which non-Indians frequently go to sustain their imagining of Brazil as a society in which racism is not a serious or particularly relevant social force. Sonia was a thirty-two-year-old schoolteacher when I interviewed her in 1994. She "looked Indian" according to the other town residents and was likely a descendant of the Puris. I believe that she would have identified as Indian—much like Pedro in chapter 5— had she had contact with an indigenous community and its worldview.

SONIA: Here in Vasalia there is no racism. Nothing that I have observed.

JONATHAN WARREN: Then why are the majority of nonwhites poor?

SONIA: In Brazil? The majority of the Brazilian population is poor. The minority has [inaudible] power.

JW: But there are whites who aren't poor.

SONIA: There are whites who aren't poor and blacks who aren't poor. Pelé, for example.

JW: For example, how many black fazendeiros do you know?

SONIA: That's a good question because I don't know one [anxiously laughs].

JW: Why do you think that is so?

SONIA: [Anxiously laughs again.] My God . . . I don't know. Maybe it's a question of luck? It's an interesting question. But the majority of the population here is poor—whether they're white, yellow, or mixed.

JW: But no blacks have even a farm [sítio], right? There are no blacks [working as elected council representatives] in the mayor's office? And in the Brazilian government, there are only a few.

SONIA: I don't know if you noticed but there aren't many blacks [living here]. I think that marriage happens of whites with blacks, then through mixture—one doesn't remain black.

JW: All right, then do you know any mestizos who own a farm [sítio]?

SONIA: [More anxious laughter.] It's true. Now I understand. But honestly, I don't believe the fact that they don't own farms means that there's discrimination.

JW: Then it's because of luck?

SONIA: I think that rich people, that is what I think, that the majority come from inheritance. It's passed from father to son.

JW: Then [the complete absence of nonwhite farm owners] is a result of inheritance?

SONIA: I think so.

As I challenged her stated belief in a racial meritocracy, she employed the discourse of class. Racial inequality is often reduced to class inequality, and the examples of white poverty and Pelé are typically offered as proof of this interpretation. When her class explanation was tested with specific examples, such as the absence of black farm owners, she was momentarily trapped. Unable to invoke racism as an explanatory variable, but also with no alternative explanations, she had no answer, which was why she said "luck." After further thought, however, she recalled that there were few blacks in the region—they are, after all, mixed. But this also proved a cul-de-sac since pardos were not in positions of power in the region either. Finally, she resorted to another class explanation when she argued that the racialization of power was essentially a matter of inheritance. This account potentially suggests that historical forms of racism—such as slavery and conquest—might be the reason for whites having wealth to pass on to their descendants. Even so, such a discourse has the advantage of containing racism in the past, and it enabled her to construe the contemporary moment as free of racism— current racial inequalities could then be described as a product of historical, not present-day, racism.

RACIAL LITERACY

The Indians I met usually spoke a more race-cognizant idiom of race than pardos or blacks. I do not recall, for example, any Indians who attempted to deny or minimize racism. They were instead at ease discussing racial inequalities. In response to the same sorts of questions that I posed to non-Indians—such as, "Why is it that whites have all the political and economic power?"—they did not try to reframe or avoid my query. Rather, they would simply respond bluntly, much as Nilza da Graça (Krenak) did when she said, "They [whites] got rich on the backs of Indians."

In short, racism was not a taboo subject in Indian circles. I never observed any investment in maintaining or defending the validity of the racial democracy narrative. To cite just two cases, note the comfort with which Cleonice and Karakana responded when I asked whether racism existed in the region where they resided. Instead of trying to portray it as a question of class or subaltern inferiority, they promptly proceeded to provide me with some examples.

CLEONICE PANKARARU: Yes. Many whites don't like blacks and Indians. And there are more blacks and Indians who are poor. On television, every day there is a soap opera. And if a white appears, he is in the role of a lawyer, but if a black appears, he is in the role of a beggar or street person.

KARAKANA CANOEIRA: Here in Brazil, there are lots of persons who are racist. Sometimes simply because the person is black [negra], she is discriminated against and the white person is treated with more respect. It's like this. I was with a colleague of mine, and she is very dark. Then this guy comes and says that he'd like to get to know me. But in order not to have to interact with my colleague, he calls me over to him. So I asked her to come with me. He orders her to stay there—so I didn't go over to him. We left. There are lots of people who are racist.

JONATHAN WARREN: So you think that there is discrimination in Brazil?

KC: There's too much discrimination—racism.

JW: Where you live now, are they racist?[85]

KC: Yes. There's one girl there who is very dark [pretinha], and they talk about her in such a strange way—I don't think it's right. And the other day there was a woman at my friend's house. And she asked if I was a real Indian because I was clean and ate food just like them. Lots of people think that the Indian is a pig who doesn't like to work.

This is clearly not white talk. Besides the lack of defensiveness, what is noteworthy about their comments is their ability to recognize subtler forms of racism. In the absence of explicit racist statements, Karakana was able to perceive faint slights communicated nonverbally. This signifies a level of racial literacy that was uncommon among the non-Indians I interviewed.

Probably due to the general tendency to ignore or deny racism, non-Indians have fairly unrefined conceptualizations of the mechanisms and articulations of white supremacy—especially when they do not entail access to whites as partners, friends, or colleagues. France Winddance Twine implies such a linkage when she notes that "what is surprising is that even in [nonwhites'] homes . . . they still do not engage in discussions that could assist their family members and themselves in collectively coping with racism."[86] Thus, because there is an impulse toward white talk, there is little or no mention of experiences with and effective responses to racism. There are, in effect, few moments or spaces in which an individual could hone her or his abilities to perceive and negotiate racism. Moreover, little social or community knowledge is developed to be shared with subsequent generations. All of this contributes to a retarded level of racial literacy. It results in a situation where "even for folks who are indisputably black," to cite a black activist, "it's as though they had a lobotomized brain: a racist act goes in one ear, it gets processed there as something else, and comes out something entirely different." [87] Michael Hanchard puts it a bit more tactfully when he remarks that there is a "general inability of Brazilians to identify patterns of violence and discrimination that are racially specific" [88]

Most subalterns, then, given their racial illiteracy, do not even perceive racism. A 1987 study conducted in the largely black, poor municipalities of Volta Redonda and Nova Iguaçu in Rio de Janeiro found that "63.7 percent [of the respondents] said they had never experienced racism." [89] Confirming this survey research, John Burdick's qualitative interviews with eighty-three poor women in Rio de Janeiro revealed that except for "lifelong blacks," racial subalterns did not appear to recognize racism:

> [They] tended to view color prejudice in distant and nebulous terms. While most . . . said that they knew "racism" existed in Brazil, the word did not seem to have much personal meaning. Had they ever felt treated or looked upon unfavorably because of their color? Across the board, strong nos. When asked whether they had ever *person-ally* witnessed color prejudice or discrimination, we heard mainly nos; among those who answered yes, the offense had been witnessed *somewhere else*, not "here," and the examples given usually had to do with a dismissive attitude on the part of a wealthy white toward a poor black. Then informants would move on to insist that what such examples really illustrated was "social," not "racial" prejudice and that, after all, among the poor themselves there was neither. [90]

Burdick's findings also point to non-Indians' general inability to grasp how race and class intersect. Non-Indians are noted for their class reductionism. That is, they frequently frame inequality in exclusively class—or what Burdick referred to above as social—terms. Recognizing this, Edward Telles remarks that "in Brazil . . . race still is not considered an element underlying inequality." [91] Observe how Helena, the twenty-two-year-old black tutor I mentioned above, seemed to have no sense of how her class subordination might be connected to racism:

> If I were to rank my problems from one to twenty, with one being the worst of all my problems, racism would be number eighteen or nineteen. Racism just isn't something I'm greatly concerned about. I have bigger problems, such as putting food on the table, getting into a university, or getting a decent job.

Even blacks and pardos, who are overwhelmingly concentrated in the poorer sectors of the economy, rarely appreciate how their capacity to get a job and put food on the table are intimately entwined with racism. There is scant understanding of how white supremacy, both its contemporary and historical forms, is directly linked to the particular configurations of the labor market, social welfare, taxation policies, housing, educational opportunities, and so forth, which make meeting even basic economic needs extremely precarious for most racial subalterns. In short, they fail to grasp how white supremacy underpins their economic and social marginalization.

Another arena in which the low degree of racial literacy was illustrated was when I raised the issue of schools. Not one non-Indian whom I interviewed ever problematized racism in the curriculum or the fact that in the schools their children attended, the vast majority of the teachers were white.[92] Recall that Helena never brought these issues up in her discussion of racism in her school. These things were not seen as racist—just her exclusion from the social networks of her white peers.

Consuela, the nineteen-year-old mulatto/negra Carioca cited earlier in this chapter who was more knowledgeable of her white ancestors, exhibits a similar perspective,

> JONATHAN WARREN: Is there racism in your school?
> CONSUELA: No. In my school, no.
> JW: You never encountered any, neither in the private nor in the public school?
> CONSUELA: In the private school? I have not encountered much discrimination, no.

JW: You haven't encountered much or any?

CONSUELA: I don't know. I don't think there's any because it's a Catholic school. So because of God and these things . . . there isn't much . . . thank God . . . because if there was I wouldn't stay there. But they don't have any.

The Indians I interviewed, in contrast, were quick to identify the curriculum and absence of Indian teachers as problematic. This is demonstrated by José Xacriabá's expressed wish to have only Indian teachers.

On the aldeia, only two teachers are Xacriabá. The rest are white. But right now we're trying to promote a course for indigenous teachers so that we can get rid of those white teachers, so that only Indians will be working with Indians. In 1996, we want to replace all the white teachers.

Salvinho Pataxó echoes José's sentiments:

I am for Indian schools, for having our separate schools. Sometimes we have difficulties in the schools because they don't understand what's good for Indians. That's why I'm going to fight for an Indian school in our area. It is a way for us to break barriers and take a place in society. Look right now in the state of Minas Gerais, we don't have one Indian who has a high school degree.[93] So how is anyone going to make it to the university? That's why I'm in favor of fighting to organize and to build an Indian school here.

Salvinho clearly links the failure of Indians to make it to a university with the fact that primary schools are white-controlled—a link that the pardos and blacks I interviewed never made. The opinion of these two Indians is shared by most other posttraditional Indians. It is no coincidence, then, that they have successfully lobbied the state of Minas Gerais to establish all-Indian schools on four aldeias.[94]

Another example of what I regard as a more developed concept of racism, one that includes institutional racism, emerged in discussions of political power. When asked about racism, non-Indians rarely mentioned that whites control most positions of political power in Brazil. When it was brought to their attention, they would simply say that it had nothing to do with race. Because of this general attitude, pardos and blacks saw little need to vote for and support nonwhite politicians. They claimed that they voted for the best candidate, regardless of race. In 1995, however, when I interviewed Senator Benedita da Silva, a black who lost the mayoral election in Rio de Janeiro, she seemed to feel that pardos and blacks were not as color-blind as they believed themselves to be. She regarded race as a significant factor determining which candidate was seen as the best, the most competent, and in her case, the most human.

> I'm going to tell you something, and it's something I can't hide, in truth I enjoyed much more support from those blacks who had what's called a "consciousness," those who were a part of the "movement," than blacks who were not organized, not a part of the movement. I experienced explicit racism from those with the same color of skin as mine. The people on the street called me a monkey, gorilla. They said that I needed to eat bananas, that if I got elected the city would have to plant banana trees, would have to move the palace [the mayor's house] to the zoo. There were lots of barbaric things that I heard. The people would make such obscene gestures in my presence. And they would send letters. They still send letters. They're always sending letters.

Senator Silva's comments are a reminder that there is a big divide in consciousness between blacks who have been involved in the black movement and those who have not. As I have already mentioned, the number of blacks participating in the movement—in particular working-class blacks—is quite small. This lack of support for black political issues is underscored by the fact that candidates of color, even in districts where racial subalterns constitute an overwhelming majority, are rarely elected.[95] Even Silva must privilege her subject position as a favelado rather than a black or an antiracist if she wishes to be elected. As Ney dos Santos Oliveira notes, "Although she was active in the black movement and identified herself as 'a woman, a black, a favelado,' her political base was primarily among community organizations of the favelados and the Protestant church."[96]

Wanting to test my observations about blacks and their support of black candidates, I put the question to eastern Indians. That is, in the context of asking them about their own voting preferences, I asked them to confirm or challenge my perceptions about the voting preferences of blacks. Karakana Canoeiro's response is typical:

> JONATHAN WARREN: There on the aldeia, when there is an election, do the Indians vote for Indian candidates?
>
> KARAKANA CANOEIRO: They sure do!
>
> JW: Do you think blacks vote for black candidates the same way that Indians do?
>
> KC: No. For example, if there is a black candidate and a white one, they will vote for the white one — even if they're blacks they'll vote for the whites.

In contrast to pardos and blacks, posttraditional Indians considered white political power problematic, as evidenced by their support for Indian candidates.

> JONATHAN WARREN: When there is an Indian candidate, do the other Indians vote for the Indian candidate?
>
> PUHUÍ PATAXÓ: Yes. The other Indians here vote for Indian candidates. For example, my uncle was a candidate for city councillor, and we voted for him. Now in the 1996 election, we're going to select two candidates. We need two candidates because we have the conditions to elect two Indian candidates.
>
> JW: I have interviewed lots of blacks, and when there is a black candidate, some of them have told me, and I have witnessed this as well, that blacks don't support that candidate. Do you think this is true? Have you ever noticed this?
>
> PP: I have seen this, but I think it shows a lack of respect for one's kinfolk. If I were black, it's obvious that I have to vote for the black. It's my blood. I'm going to vote for a person that's not black? That's not of my blood? Just because they are going to give me a kilo of meat and a small sack of rice? If they give me these things, it's because they want to buy my vote. So I never accept these things. I vote for the person of my blood — the person that I like. But to vote for a person who has nothing to do with me — that's being against my people. That's really being against myself.
>
> JW: Why do you think Indians are different in this respect than blacks?

PP: The Indian is different in this respect because the Indian values his kinfolk more.

The above responses about supporting Indian politicians were typical of my conversations with posttraditional Indians. Race clearly had a different meaning for Indian voters than it held for most blacks and pardos in Brazil. It is interesting that, at least for Puhuí, race was the category of kin; hence, he was somewhat moralistic in his evaluation of blacks and their lack of political support for black politicians. In his view, this was a violation of blood, of family. The fact that he attributed this meaning to racial categories, and that blacks and pardos generally do not, offers a useful window into how Indian conceptions of race differ from those of most other Brazilians.

RESPONSES TO RACISM

One final feature of the racial idiom of non-Indian Brazilians is the failure to engage in "back talk." Because of the low level of racial literacy, they are less likely to interpret a particular event as racist, or given the attachment to the racial democracy idea, they are apt to reframe it as not racist. Even in those instances where a particular practice is recognized as racist, there is a tendency to leave it unchallenged.

As Carlos Hasenbalg and Nelson do Valle Silva argue, based on their analysis of a survey of the residents of the city of São Paulo, "There is a preference for avoiding conflict in dealing with racial discrimination." [97] A number of researchers report that blacks and pardos prefer to meet racism with silence.[98] That is, blacks and pardos tend to respond to perceived racism via withdrawal or by changing their behavior.[99] In one case, a black schoolteacher was humiliated by her godfather when he raised a banana at a public event and declared it her favorite food. Such a gesture is very offensive in Brazil because it infers that blacks are apelike. Instead of critiquing her godfather, such as by labeling the act racist in order to encourage him to apologize or change his behavior, she remained silent and consciously avoided bananas for the rest of her life—an aversion she passed onto her daughter.

Returning again to the 1987 survey study conducted in the predominantly poor, black communities of Volta Redonda and Nova Iguaçu in Rio de Janeiro, it was found that of the 32.7 percent "who said they experienced racism, 57.9 percent said they did nothing in response; 20.2 percent stated they reacted verbally or denounced the action in the press, and 18.9 percent said they left their jobs as a result of acts of discrimination in the workplace."[100] John Burdick notes in his interviews with non-Indian Cariocas of color that a typical response to racial slurs such as "monkey," as with the black schoolteacher described above, was to allow it to go unchallenged. As one interviewee told Burdick: "When we would play those games, the other kids would start right off: *macaco* [monkey]! . . . I would smile and laugh along with the rest of them."[101] The black Brazilian soccer player, Paulo César, protested the absence of resistance to racism in Brazil.

> In Brazil things are even worse than in the United States. There, prejudice is declared, and Blacks get together to free themselves from oppression. Here, no one admits that prejudice exists. Blacks themselves prefer to go through life trying to lighten their skins, instead of struggling for their rights. Prejudice is so great that mulattos don't like to be called Black. . . . That's what irritates me, the Black Brazilian cowers, he [sic] omits himself, he doesn't struggle for anything.[102]

The following response by Hemerson, a twenty-five-year-old, unemployed black who lives in Belo Horizonte, exemplified the passive response to racism of most of the non-Indian racial subalterns I interviewed.

> HEMERSON: One time, I was working as a representative selling books. I arrived at a house of a person and I offered him a book. Instead of politely taking the book, he asked what I wanted. He said to me, "Get out of my door, nigger. I don't like niggers." I left without saying anything and feeling sad.
>
> JONATHAN WARREN: Why did you stay quiet? Why didn't you challenge him?
>
> HEMERSON: I prefer to stay quiet. We [blacks] avoid discussion; it is much better. Because if he offends you and you feel offended, you are going to speak with him and he is just going to offend you even more. So it is preferable to just remain quiet. It is better to leave than to remain and listen to more. If you stay, you just get even more up-

set and then it could even become physically aggressive. You feel that pain in the heart, but that passes.

One of the noted features of the Brazilian racial terrain is what is referred to as *racismo cordial* (cordial racism).[103] Despite the inequalities, there is a palpable absence of tension or interracial animosity. George Reid Andrews suggests that race relations are cordial in Brazil precisely because nonwhites do not challenge racism:

> By persuading Afro-Brazilians to lower their expectations in life and not to create "disagreeable situations" by trying to push into places where they are not wanted (i.e., places which whites wish to reserve for themselves), the Brazilian model of race relations works very effectively to reduce racial tension and competition while maintaining blacks in a subordinate social and economic position.[104]

A well-known Brazilian expression accurately captures this idea: "There's no racism in Brazil, because blacks know their place."

Rebecca Reichmann and Roberto DaMatta contend that this proclivity for conflict avoidance vis-à-vis racism may be linked to a general tendency on the part of Brazilians to "avoid confrontation."[105] DaMatta describes this strategy as "an *encompassing* approach to conflict, intrinsic in national character."[106] Hasenbalg and Silva, however, question this explanation, pointing out that "this conciliatory attitude does not apply to work relations, since the majority accepts strikes as a legitimate means of pressure."[107]

If such conflict avoidance, at least in regards to racism, represents a national cultural pattern, then Indians can be said to be forging an alternative cultural practice. Indians are noted for engaging in what is known as back talk. For example, Burdick reports that "one white woman asked me rhetorically whether I ever saw a *negro* on TV going and saying, 'I am a *negro*, I want such-and-such'? No, they are ashamed of themselves. But the Indian, you see him [sic] go to Brasília on TV, to demand things from the government. They are proud."[108]

Antonio Sérgio Alfredo Guimarães refers to this sense of pride as a radical view of humanity that he sees as still lacking among most Brazilians of color.[109] I believe there is some truth to this perception that racial subalterns are ashamed of themselves, that they lack a full sense of their humanity. There are countless aborted interventions, offenses without outrage, and gestures of shame and embarrassment that do imply a lack of conviction that they are the equals of whites.

This was one of the dimensions that was so striking about Indians. They seemed to possess, to use Guimarães's phrase, a radical notion of their humanity. This was manifest in their body language, their air of confidence, and the degree to which they were intolerant of any sort of anti-Indian statement or comment. Instead of becoming silent or laughing to cover their shame, as if they at some level believed the derogatory statements being made, they were quick to take a proactive, critical response to perceived racism. Think back to Valmares's response to the housekeeper's comments about the Maxakali, Karakana's willingness to fight to protect even those Indians for whom she did not care, or how in chapter 6, Indians did not let stand, even momentarily, ideas of Indian primitiveness, let alone suggestions that they were racial impostors. The following quotes offer two further examples of how Indians rarely allowed pejorative statements, even slightly veiled ones, to go uncontested. First, Antonia Xacriabá observed,

> Whites see Indians as if they were rebels, savages that don't know anything and are lazy. One time, I got into a discussion with a man on the bus because he was talking badly about Indians. So I asked, "Why are you talking badly about Indians? I'm Indian. Why are you talking badly about Indians?" I didn't even let him respond. And then I guessed in front of everyone that he had worked on a reserve. He confirmed that he had. He apologized and sat down in shame.

And Gumercino Pataxó said,

> I was in Belo Horizonte and I saw a man mistreat the Indian. It was at the state capital. There were lots of big people there: teachers, city councillors, state representatives, etc. And one of them took the microphone and said, "In Brazil, as long as there exists this race of lazy people, [Brazil] will never progress." There was a teacher sitting next to me, and I said to him, "Just as there are lazy Indians, there are also lazy whites." With these words, the teacher went to the microphone and spoke. And that man [the one who "spoke badly about the Indian"] never said another word. He snuck out. When-

ever people speak badly about Indians, I tell them that we aren't any worse than they are and we deserve respect. I will give you another example of how they don't respect us. At that same conference in Belo Horizonte, Afonso Pena arrived there and said that we were lazy and that he didn't understand why they were giving us any assistance. I heard this and asked if he was from Brazil or from another country. He said that he was Brazilian, and then I said that he should then be ashamed of himself because he had our blood in him also. He then asked forgiveness and explained that the father of his father was an Indian.

This is not the racism evasive, conflict avoidance characteristic of white talk. This is not the posture of silence and lowered expectations. There is no indication that mistaken ideas about Indian primitiveness or inferiority would make Indian ancestry a dreaded secret or source of embarrassment. Nor is there the slightest hint that they have, at some level, internalized the derogatory imaginings of Indianness.

Antiracist Locations

My findings suggest that Indian identities in eastern Brazil *are* linked to a different "location," described by Charles Hale as "a distinctive social memory, consciousness, and practices as well as place within the social structure."[110] For instance, the Indians I interviewed were far less prone to adopt white talk than other nonwhites. As compared to other Brazilians, their language was that of race-cognizant back talk. They also tended to engage in a set of practices that represented a break from the whitening trajectory. By privileging Indian mates, ancestors, communities, symbolic materials, ceremonies, and spaces, eastern Indians were bringing into being alternative symbolic arenas in which whiteness was not hypervalued as the good, the beautiful, the desired, or the deserving.

Obviously, given my relatively limited sample, further research—both quantitative and qualitative—will be required to substantiate and assess the generalizability of my data. As the first in-depth study of the intersections of Indianness and racial politics, however, my principal aim in this chapter has been to initiate and inspire further serious study of Indians and race—a topic that has thus far been ignored.

Given the much more fully developed body of research on race and blackness, I have been able to speak with a greater degree of certainty about the racial situations of black-identified Brazilians and their organizations. The black movement, as numerous observers have pointed out, remains fragmented, has but a small base, and is clearly not on the verge of creating a historical moment. Furthermore, except for "lifelong" blacks and the small segment of the Afro-Brazilian population that has been affected by the black movement, black subjectivities are, at best, only loosely connected to a counterhegemonic racial politic. As Regina Pahim Pinto frames it, pardos and "blacks, although the object of discrimination and racism, are not really 'another' culture." [111] Thus, despite having a different position in the social structure, most non-Indian subalterns share the same memories, language of race, whitening orientations, and so forth, as whites of a similar class.

I wish to underscore that valuable as the study of black subjectivities is, it should not constrain the exploration or study of organizations and social movements situated in other subjectivities. If nothing else, I hope that my central finding that Indian subjectivities are linked to a different cultural politics of race than other racial identities in eastern Brazil will challenge critical race scholars and antiracist activists to expand their focus. In particular, I hope that it encourages them to think more creatively about antiracist projects in which blackness may not take the same forms as it has in other struggles for racial justice. Otherwise, if alternative trajectories toward racial justice are closed off, there is the risk that our visions of antiracism, shaped by experiences with battles against white supremacy in other national contexts, may lead scholars and activists to ignore or not take advantage of those sites where a new common sense, where competing discourses about race, inequality, and power, are being produced.

Epilogue

During the past five centuries, the racial hierarchies that European dis-coveries birthed in Latin America have changed little. The descendants of indigenous people, whether they self-identify as Indian or not, re-main economically, politically, and socially marginalized. In many coun-tries, the state of racism can be compared to apartheid in South Africa or Jim Crow in the United States. Until recently in Ecuador, for example, newspaper advertisements "offered haciendas for sale with Indians in-cluded, as if they were cattle or horses."[1] Moreover, as late as the 1990s, Indians were frequently prohibited from entering buses, and if they managed to board, were then subjected to verbal assault or, worse, were thrown from the buses and killed.[2]

Resistance to this marginalization is, of course, not a new phenome-non. Yet a number of indicators suggest that many of the changes de-scribed in this book—such as the growing shift toward Indian identi-ties, the intensification of indigenous mobilization, increasing efforts to revitalize indigenous cultures, and heightened racial literacy and antiracist practices—are occurring elsewhere in the region "in what some have termed 'the Indian awakening in Latin America.' "[3] In sev-eral countries, identities and movements have emerged that would have been virtually unimaginable as recently as the 1980s. For instance, in Guatemala, the majority of the contemporary leaders and intellectuals of the Pan-Mayan movement could pass as non-Indian, "given that they are educated, fluent in Spanish and economically mobile."[4] Many of these individuals, just one decade earlier, likely would have distanced themselves from Indianness and certainly would not have become in-volved in the *movimiento maya*. As Kay Warren notes, now "rather than becoming urban Ladinos, ... activists have turned to the difficult project of promoting the resurgence of 'Maya culture.' "[5]

Mexico offers another clear illustration of Indian resurgence. For most of the twentieth century, Indians were involved in popular struggles, but they did not fight as Indians.[6] Demands were usually "couched in class rather than caste terms."[7] Dominant understandings of power and conflict "pitted peasants against landlords, not Indians against whites or mestizos."[8] It was not until the late 1970s that a self-conscious Indian project began to reemerge with the establishment of El Movimento de Unificación de la Lucha Triqui and La Asemblea de Autoridades Zapotecas y Chinantecas de la Sierra in Oaxaca, the Totonac movement in Puebla, and of course the Zapatista National Liberation Army (EZLN) in Chiapas.[9]

Recognizing this change, Subcomandante Marcos, a leader of the EZLN, observes that "even though other . . . movements have had a strong indigenous component, only in the Zapatista movement is the [indigenous component] the guiding force and the backbone of the movement."[10] Concurring with Marcos, Dawn Hewett writes,

> Activism and mobilization, exemplified in the late independence and post-Revolutionary period of Mexico, were conducted exclusively under the banner of the traditional Left, which included peasants, workers and students as oppressed groups, but only included indigenous peoples as a member of one of the other aforementioned groups. By exhibiting a distinctly indigenous identity in their organization, [and] political objectives and in shaping their decision to rebel, the Zapatistas represent a shift in racial subjectivities, which is epitomized in a larger trend throughout Mexico toward mobilization galvanized around indigenousness.[11]

Considering the impact that a relatively small indigenous population has had on Brazilian society—furthering land reform, challenging the ideology that Brazil is (or at least should become) a "mono-ethnic" nation, establishing antiracist schools, countering hegemonic narratives of Brazilian history, placing Indians into political office, creating alternative discourses of race and power, and so forth—the potential for change is immense in those societies with larger Indian populations, such as in Bolivia, Ecuador, Guatemala, Mexico, and Peru.[12] Ecuador is a recent case in point. In less than fifteen years, Ecuadorian Indians—who are estimated to constitute between 10 and 40 percent of a population of approximately twelve million[13]—have built a vibrant pan-Indian social movement led and coordinated by a single national-level organization, the Confederation of Indigenous Nationalities of Ecuador (CONAIE). Some of CONAIE's achievements have included the creation of a national bilingual education program (designed so that indigenous students could study in their native language), the definition of Ecuador as a "pluriculture and multi-ethnic state" in the first article of the Constitution, the blocking of neoliberal agrarian reforms in 1994, and the creation of a relatively successful political party, Pacha-kutik.[14] The movement has also inspired and enabled other groups, such as Afro-Ecuadorians, to achieve certain political objectives, like territorial autonomy and greater self-determination.[15] Perhaps the most compelling evidence of the potential potency not only of the indigenous movement in Ecuador but also of Indian resurgence in nations with significant Indian populations was the pivotal role CONAIE played in the overthrow of the Ecuadorian government in 2000.[16]

Most analysts of Latin America agree that Indian resurgence is likely to continue, if not intensify, given the general movement of oppositional politics away from a reductive class-antagonism paradigm as well as several of the factors discussed in this book (for example, the curtailment of Indian exorcism as democratic rule becomes consolidated; the linkage of Indianness to certain material benefits such as land; the development and circulation of alternative definitions and valuations of Indianness in popular, legal, and academic thought; and the mainstreaming of antiracist discourses that more effectively overturn racist practices and undercut imaginings of nations as racial-ethnic melting pots with their emphasis on whitening through mestizaje).[17] There is little doubt, then, that the "Indian question" will be at the center of much conflict through out the hemisphere in the coming decades. Consequently, a number of matters addressed in this book—racial identity formation, notions of race and Indianness, political devolution, racial literacy, anti-Indian racism, cultural revitalization, land, health, and education reform, and so on—will be key sites of struggle in Latin America, at least for the foreseeable future. It is my hope that *Racial Revolutions* illuminates and furthers an understanding of these complex, highly charged, and extremely significant issues, especially for those committed to dismantling one of Europe's most crucial contributions to the region: white supremacy.

Appendix A: Questionnaire, 1995–1997

1. Describe a typical day in your life. What is your daily routine? Describe your activities from the time you wake up until the time you retire to bed.
2. From what sources do you receive the majority of your information about the world?
3. Do you have any close friends? If so, would you describe them for me?
4. Where were you raised?
5. What are your most vivid childhood memories?
6. Describe those physical characteristics that you find most attractive. Could you describe someone that you find beautiful?
7. From which racial/ethnic groups are you descended?
8. How do you self-identify? [If they didn't give a racial/color identity] How do you self-identify in terms of race/color?
9. Could you explain how you determine someone's racial identity.
10. What does it mean to be "———" [the color/race of how they self-identify]?
11. Are you seen as "———" [the color/race of how they self-identify] by persons who do not know you?
12. How do you determine if one is an Indian?
13. Are there differences between Indians and non-Indians? Explain.
14. Do you think an Indian has a different perspective than non-Indians?
15. In general, what do persons who are not Indians think about Indians?
16. How are Indians represented on television, in the schools, etc.? What do you think about these representations?
17. Do Indians encounter problems in Brazil? If so, explain to me what some of the primary ones are.
18. Is (was) it your preference to marry an Indian? Is (was) it your family's preference?
19. [Indians] If you had married a non-Indian, would your children have been Indian? [Non-Indians] If you had married an Indian, would your children have been Indian?

20. Do you self-identify as Brazilian? Explain.
21. What has been the importance of blacks, Indians, and/or whites to Brazilian society?
22. Do you think that whites encounter the same barriers in life as nonwhites?
23. Do you think that there is racial discrimination in Brazil? In the community in which you live?
24. How would you define racism? Could you provide specific examples of what you would consider an act of racism?
25. As a child growing up, what did you learn about racism from your family? From friends? Could you provide specific examples?
26. What were you taught about racial inequality at school? Explain.
27. Do you (or have you) ever discussed racism with your friends? Explain.
28. Is racism a subject of conversations today in your social circle or with your immediate family? Explain.
29. Have you ever witnessed or experienced racial discrimination? If yes, please describe the circumstances and then could you describe your response?
30. Can you recall any other examples of racism that you may not have personally encountered or witnessed?
31. How do you think your life would have been different if you were a woman/man?
32. Do you think that your race/color has affected your life? How do you think your life would be different if you were white/nonwhite? Indian/non-Indian?
33. What are your dreams for the future?
34. What advice would you give to young people?

1. Describe a typical day in your life. What is your daily routine? Describe your activities from the time you wake up until you retire to bed.
2. From what sources do you receive the majority of your information about events in Brazil?
3. Describe those physical characteristics that you find most attractive. Could you describe someone that you find beautiful?
4. Do you attend church? If yes, which church? How frequently?
5. How would you define the term *branco* (white)?
6. How would you define the term *negro/preto* (black)?
7. Could you explain how you determine someone's racial identity?
8. How would you define racism? Could you provide specific examples of what you would consider an act of racism?
9. As a child growing up, what did you learn about racism from your family? From friends? Could you provide a specific example?
10. What were you explicitly taught about racial inequality at school? Explain.
11. Have you thought about what you are going to teach your children about racism? If you currently have children, what have you taught them about racism?
12. Do you (or have you) ever discussed racism with your friends? Explain.
13. Is racism the subject of conversations today in your social circle?
14. Do you think that racism exists here in Vasalia? Why? Could you provide a specific example?
15. Have you ever personally encountered racism? Explain the circumstances. Have you ever encountered racism outside of Vasalia?
16. If yes to question 15, could you describe how you responded to this act of racism?
17. Do you have any other examples of racism that you have not personally encountered that you would like to share?

18. Do you know any wealthy people here? Are any of them nonwhite? Are any black?

19. Do you know any plantation owners? Are any of them nonwhite? Are any black?

20. Do you know any Catholic priests? Are any of them nonwhite? Any black?

21. Do you know any middle-class blacks?

22. Do you know any middle-class whites married to nonwhites?

23. Do you know any middle-class whites who married poor whites? Please provide specific examples.

24. How would you explain the absence of nonwhites among the elite of Vasalia?

25. Do you know any poor whites married to blacks or mulattoes of any class background?

26. Do you know any nonwhites who live on the main street?

27. Among the city council representatives, how many are white and nonwhite? Explain.

28. What problems do you think poor whites and nonwhites encounter? Are there any similarities or differences in the problems that poor whites and nonwhites face? Explain.

29. Do you personally know any blacks or mulattoes that are prejudiced against whites? Explain.

30. Do you know any blacks that are prejudiced against nonwhites? Could you provide a specific example?

31. Do you know any whites that are prejudiced against nonwhites? Could you provide a specific example?

32. How do you think that your life might be different if you were a woman/man?

33. How do you think your life might be different if you were white/black?

34. You are the descendant of which ethnic/racial groups? Explain.

Appendix C: Biographical Data of Indian Interviewees

Name/Tribe	Age	Occupation	Kids	Level of Education	Partner	Gender	Wage/Region
Vera/ Xacriabá	14	domestic	0	I:3	single	F	.5/1 urban
Eunice/ Pataxó	16	student	1	I:3	single	F	0 rural
Paulo/Pankararu	16	student	0	I:4	single	M	0/2 rural
Joaquim/ Pankararu	16	student	0	I:4	single	M	0/2 rural
Karkana/ Canoeiro	18	student/ domestic	0	I:7	single	F	1.5 urban
Lima/Pankararu	18	student	0	I:7	single	M	0/2 rural
Machado/ Xacriabá	19	soda packer	0	I:4	single	M	2/4 urban
Rosinette/ Xacriabá	19	student	0	I:8	single	F	0/6 urban
César/ Pataxó	20	student	0	II:1	Pankararu	M	0/4 rural
Ivan/Pankararu	21	cacique	0	I:4	Pataxó	M	0 rural
Audalio/ Xacriabá	21	baker	0	I:4	single	M	2/4 urban
Jerry/Kaxixó	22	vice cacique	0	I:4	single	M	0/1 rural
Valmares/ Pataxó	23	student	0	II:1	single	M	1/1 urban
Cornelio/ Xacriabá	23	truck loader	0	I	single	M	4.5/5.5 urban
Nilza/ Krenak	23	housewife/ artesenato	1	0:illerate	Pankararu	F	0 rural
Berto/Tupinikim	24	lavrador/ artesenato	1	I:4	Tupinikim	M	0 rural
Cleonice/ Pankararu	24	nurse	0	II	Pataxó	F	2/4 rural

Name/Tribe	Age	Occupation	Kids	Level of Education	Partner	Gender	Wage/Region
Marie/Pankararu	25	housewife/arte-senato	2	I:7	Pataxó	F	0 rural
Abdias/Xacriabá	27	doorman	2	I:5	white	M	1.5 urban
Aluijio/Pankararu	28	lavrador/arte-senato	1	I:5	Krenak	M	0 rural
Bekoy/Pataxó	28	student	1	II:2	single	F	.5 rural
Sergio/Krenak	30	FUNAI assistant	3	I:4	Pataxó	M	2/2 rural
Ursula/Pataxó	31	housewife	1	I:7	white	F	0/3 urban
Denise/Kaxixó	33	housewife/lavrador	5	I:1	Kaxixó	F	0/1.5 rural
Zizi/Pataxó	33	seamstress/arte-senato	5	I:1	Pataxó	F	.5/.5 rural
Waldemar/Krenak	35	FUNAI director	3	I	white	M	7/7 rural
Graça/Pataxó	35	housewife	6	0:illiterate	Pataxó	F	0/3 rural
Susana/Kaxixó	36	housewife	4	I:4	Kaxixó	F	0/2 rural
Puhuí/Pataxó	36	vice cacique/arte-senato	3	I:3	Canoeiro	M	1/1 rural
Salvinho/Pataxó	36	lavrador/arte-senato	5	I:5	Pataxo	M	.5/.5 rural
Balbina/Kaxixó	39	housewife	6	I:2	Kaxixó	F	0/3 rural
Pedro/Aranã	39	lavrador	0	I:3	single	M	0/2 rural
Domingos/Pataxó	44	FUNAI assistant	6	I:4	Pataxó	M	3/3 rural
José/Xacriabá	45	lavrador/arte-senato	2	0:illiterate	Xacriabá	M	0 rural

Name/Tribe	Age	Occupation	Kids	Level of Education	Partner	Gender	Wage/Region
Lucinda/ Krenak	46	housewife/ arte- senato	10	0:illiterate	Guarani	F	0 rural
Candida/ Xacriabá	47	janitor	1	0:illiterate	single	F	1/5.5 urban
Florinda/ Kaxixó	47	lavrador/ house- wife	3	I:4	Kaxixó	F	0/1 rural
Frederica/ Kaxixó	47	housewife	4	0:illiterate	Kaxixó	F	0/5 rural
Antonia/ Xacriabá	53	beautician/ domestic	2	I:2 illiter- ate	black	F	4/6 urban
Clemencia/ Pataxó	55	salesperson	3	0:illiterate	single	F	.5/.5 urban
Isaura/ Pataxó	56	lavrador/ house- wife	6	0:illiterate	Pataxó	F	0/1 rural
Djalma/ Kaxixó	57	cacique	0	I:1	Kaxixó	M	0 rural
Benvinda/ Panka- raru	58	pensioner	6	0:illiterate	Pankararu	F	1/4 rural
Gumercino/ Pataxó	58	lavrador	8	0:illiterate	Pataxó	M	1/1 rural
João/Tupini- kim	58	cacique/ lavrador	3	0:illiterate	Tupinikim	M	1/1 rural
Dorinha/ Maxakali	60	artesenato	9	I:4	white	F	.5/5 urban
Tancredo/ Kaxixó	60	lavrador	11	I:3	widower	M	1/1 rural
Tulio/Pataxó	67	lavrador/ pen- sioner	4	0:illiterate	Pataxó	F	1/1 rural
Manoel/ Pataxó	69	councilor/ cacique	4	I:4	black	M	2/2 rural
Nasciment/ Kaxixó	76	lavrador/ pen- sioner	7	0:illiterate	widower	M	1/1 rural

NOTES

Under the occupation column, an *artesenato* is a producer and seller of handicrafts, a *cacique* is the head or leader of a community, and a *lavrador* is a field hand or small farmer.

Under the education column, the roman numerals indicate the *grau* and the arabic numbers represent the *serie*. In Brazil, "the first grau" has eight series and would be the rough equivalent of kindergarten through eighth grade. "The second grau" has three series and its completion is comparable to a high school degree. Finally, "the third grau" represents higher education.

Under the partner category, I included persons who had steady partners as well as couples who lived together and/or were married. For instance, there were several couples who did not live together but had been slowly building their homes and saving money so as to eventually marry. I therefore decided to include these types of relationships in the partner category.

Under the "wage/region" column, the numbers refer to the quantity of minimum salaries. During most of the 1990s, the minimum wage was approximately one hundred U.S. dollars per month. For example, then, a three in this column would indicate a salary of three minimum wages or roughly three hundred U.S. dollars per month. The first figure in the column is the individual's income and the second is the household's. A North American reader should be careful not to assume a nuclear-type family when interpreting the household income. Oftentimes, distant relatives and middle-aged children make up the household and thus the household income. As well, I did not use the urban/rural distinction that census takers typically employ — for example, towns with a few thousand persons are generally considered urban. For me, urban meant a major city like Belo Horizonte or Rio de Janeiro. Individuals who resided in a small town, whose economy and culture were defined by its relationship to the surrounding rural communities, I classified as rural.

Appendix D: Biographical Data of Non-Indian Interviewees

Name/Color	Age	Occupation	Kids	Level of Education	Partner	Gender	Wage/Region
Zelia/black	16	student	0	n.a.	single	F	0/2 urban
Firmo/white (mul)	17	student	0	n.a.	single	M	0/6 urban
Gisa/white	17	student	0	n.a.	single	F	0 urban
Monisha/ white	17	student	0	n.a.	black	F	0/n.a. rural
Sueli/black	18	domestic	0	n.a.	white	F	.5/.5 rural
Miranda/ black	18	student	0	II	white	F	0/4 rural
Lulu/white	18	student/ tutor	0	II	single	F	3/6 urban
Margarida/ morena	19	student	n.a.	n.a.	white	F	0/n.a. rural
Conseula/ mulatto (bk)	19	student	0	II	single	F	1/n.a. urban
Dinoro/ white	19	student	0	n.a.	single	M	0/7 urban
Carla/ mulatto (bk)	21	teacher	0	n.a.	single	F	2/n.a. rural
Eduardo/ mulatto	21	military police	n.a.	n.a.	black	M	2/n.a. rural
Aida/ morena	21	housewife	n.a.	n.a.	black	F	.5/n.a. rural
Helena/ black	22	tutor	0	II	single	F	3/8.5 urban
Jorge/ mulatto	22	clerk	0	n.a.	white	M	1.5/n.a. rural
Carlucci/ mulatto (bk)	23	clerk	0	II	white	M	1.5/n.a. rural
Pedro/white	23	university student	0	III:2	n.a.	M	2 urban
Simeao/ white	24	civil servant	0	II	white	M	2/3.5 urban
Emina/black	24	receptionist	0	II	moreno	F	4/8 urban
Caetano/ black	25	salesperson	0	II	single	M	3 urban

Name/Color	Age	Occupation	Kids	Level of Education	Partner	Gender	Wage/Region
Hemerson/ black	26	unemployed	3	I	mulatto	M	0/7 urban
Camillo/ mulatto (bk)	26	gardener	n.a.	n.a.	single	M	n.a. rural
Carlos/white	27	basket maker	3	n.a.	black	M	.5/1 rural
Mani/black	27	domestic	1	n.a.	mulatto	F	n.a. rural
Valeria/ morena (bk)	27	housewife	n.a.	n.a.	white	F	0/n.a. rural
Catarina/ mulatto (bk)	27	teacher	0	n.a.	white	F	3/n.a. rural
Lula/white	28	photographer	0	II	mulatto	M	8/14 urban
Lorena/ black	28	domestic	n.a.	n.a.	single	F	3/n.a. rural
Beatriz/ white	29	artesenato/ manicurist	0	II	black	F	1/7 urban
Ariana/black	29	teacher	1	II	black	F	3/n.a. rural
Marcelo/ mulatto	29	unemployed	n.a.	n.a.	black	F	n.a. rural
Carmen/ mulatto	30	domestic	n.a.	n.a.	white	F	1/n.a. rural
Adriano/ mulatto	30	teacher	0	n.a.	white	M	2/n.a. rural
Cristiano/ mulatto	31	truck driver	n.a.	n.a.	white	M	4/n.a. rural
Flor/white	31	housewife	2	II	white	F	2/7 urban
Rozilda/ morena	31	unemployed	4	I:7	white	F	0/5 urban
Raquel/ white	31	teacher	n.a.	n.a.	white	F	3/n.a. rural
Zulmira/ white	31	housewife	2	II	white	F	0/5 urban
Sonia/white	32	teacher	0	II	n.a.	F	3/n.a. rural
Teodoro/ morena	32	salesperson	0	III:2	black	M	8 urban

Name/Color	Age	Occupation	Kids	Level of Education	Partner	Gender	Wage/Region
Alessandro/ white	33	pharmacist	2	n.a.	mulatto	M	5–10/n.a. rural
Gabriella/ mulatto (bk)	33	domestic	0	n.a.	white	F	.25/n.a. rural
Moema/ white	33	teacher	0	n.a.	white	F	5/n.a. rural
Manoel/ black	33	farmworker	n.a.	n.a.	white	M	n.a. rural
Isabela/ white	34	business owner	n.a.	n.a.	white	F	5/n.a. rural
Rodolpho/ mulatto (bk)	35	doctor	n.a.	n.a.	white	M	22 rural
Claudio/ white	37	dentist	n.a.	n.a.	single	M	8 rural
Agenor/ white	37	technician	2	II	white	M	7 urban
Francisco/ black	37	truck driver	n.a.	n.a.	black	M	5/n.a. rural
Vera/white	38	teacher	n.a.	n.a.	white	F	2/n.a. rural
Rogerio/ black	38	construc- tion	1	n.a.	white	M	3/n.a. rural
Lucienee/ mulatto (bk)	40	housewife	n.a.	n.a.	black	F	0/3 rural
Giovanni/ white	41	doctor	n.a.	n.a.	white	M	22 rural
Maria/ mulatto	42	teacher	n.a.	n.a.	white	F	2/n.a. rural
Leandro/ white	42	politician	n.a.	n.a.	white	M	25/n.a. rural
Henrique/ mulatto (bk)	43	clerk/ vendor	n.a.	n.a.	white	M	3/n.a. rural
Norma/ morena	45	domestic	3	I:2	white	F	3/7 urban
Mira/ mulatto (bk)	45	housewife	n.a.	n.a.	black	F	0/3 rural
Miguel/ white	45	teacher/ artist	n.a.	n.a.	white	M	5/n.a. rural

Name/Color	Age	Occupation	Kids	Level of Education	Partner	Gender	Wage/Region
Mario/white	46	plantation owner	n.a.	n.a.	divorced	M	10/n.a. rural
Luisa/ mulatto (bk)	46	teacher	n.a.	n.a.	white	F	1.5/n.a. rural
Tatiana/ mulatto (bk)	51	housewife	n.a.	n.a.	black	F	0/4 rural
Conceição/ white	52	historian	n.a.	n.a.	white	F	n.a. rural
Vittorio/ white	52	military/ poet	n.a.	n.a.	white	M	1.5/n.a. rural
Paulo/white	54	electrician	n.a.	n.a.	black	M	1.5/n.a. rural
Shayla/ mulatto	65	housewife	n.a.	n.a.	white	F	n.a. rural
Joãoquim/ white	66	farmworker	n.a.	n.a.	mulatto	M	3/n.a. rural
Fernando/ black	67	lawyer/ business owner	n.a.	n.a.	black	M	10 rural
Joaquim/ black	67	retired	n.a.	n.a.	mulatto	M	3/n.a. rural
Arturo/ white	72	plantation owner	n.a.	n.a.	white	M	20+ rural
Elena/white	73	telephone operator	n.a.	n.a.	widow	F	2/n.a. rural
Albertina/ white	93	pharmacist	n.a.	n.a.	widow	F	3/n.a. rural

NOTES

Under the color column, if a term is in parentheses, this means that there was a discrepancy between how an individual self-identified and how they were counteridentified by others in the community where they lived. The color located in the parentheses represents how they were counteridentified (mul = mulatto/mulatta and bk = black).

Under the education column, n.a. means that the data are not available. The roman numerals indicate the grau and the arabic numbers represent the serie. In Brazil, "the first grau" has eight series and would be the rough equivalent of kindergarten through eighth grade. "The second grau" has three series and its completion is comparable to a high school degree. Finally, "the third grau" represents higher education.

Under the partner column, I included persons who had steady partners as well as couples who lived together and/or were married. For instance, there were several couples who did not live together but had been slowly building their homes and saving money so as to eventually marry. I therefore decided to include these types of relationships in the partner category.

Under the "wage/region" column, the numbers refer to the quantity of minimum salaries. During most of the 1990s, the minimum wage was approximately one hundred U.S. dollars per month. For example, then, a three in this column would indicate a salary of three minimum wages or roughly three hundred U.S. dollars per month. The first figure in this column is the individual's income and the second is the household's. A North American reader should be careful not to assume a nuclear-type family when interpreting the household income. Oftentimes, distant relatives and middle-aged children make up the household and thus the household income. As well, I did not use the urban/rural distinction that census takers typically employ—for example, towns with a few thousand persons are considered urban. For me, urban meant a major city like Belo Horizonte or Rio de Janeiro. Individuals who resided in a small town, whose economy and culture were defined by its relationship to the surrounding rural communities, I classified as rural.

Notes

1. Posttraditional Indians

1 Holston, *The Modernist City*, 78.

2 The minister of war had granted the Pataxó Hã-Hã-Hãe legal title to 36,000 hectares of land in 1926. By 1997, this had been whittled down to just 1,079 hectares. In December 1996, a federal judge had ruled that an additional 788 hectares was legally theirs (Francisco, "Para Fazendeiro, Ocupação Foi Ilegal").

3 Rocha, "Mello Pede Justiça no Caso Pataxó."

4 "O Atentado Hora a Hora."

5 Ibid.

6 They would later claim that they had been inspired to commit what they referred to as a "joke" by an episode on television, but no evidence was ever found that such a show had aired (Bernardes, " 'Pegadinha' Deu Idéia de Queimar Índio").

7 "Carro foi Reconhecido na TV."

8 "Em 2 Anos, Brasília Teve 13 Queimados."

9 "Delegada Crê em Premeditação."

10 Felinto, "O Paciente Índio e Os Monstros da Classe Média."

11 Giraldi and de Freitas, "Acusados de Matar Índio."

12 "Índios Chegam a Brasília para Protestar."

13 "Surveys of the I.B.G.E., a Brazilian economic institute, suggest that the richest twenty percent of the Brazilian population still hold more than sixty percent of the nation's wealth, while the poorest twenty percent account for about two percent. In the United States, by comparison, the richest twenty percent take forty-two percent of the national income, and the poorest twenty percent have five percent" (Cohen, "Brazil Pays to Shield Currency").

14 Felinto, "O Paciente Índio e Os Monstros da Classe Média."

15 This is how they were described in court by a number of "upstanding citizens" (Bernardes, "Testemunha Afirma Ter Visto Pano Sobre Índio").

16 Ibid.

17 "Brasília Lembra."

18 This is also the name, as I mentioned, of the municipality from which dos Santos came.

19 Hemming, *Red Gold*, 88.

20 "In the harsh world of [the] sixteenth century, slavery was an accepted institution. It had been justified philosophically since Aristotle. Universities included slavery in the civil law inherited from the Romans. Most Europeans accepted slavery as a condition of certain inferior peoples. They were convinced of the superiority of Christianity and European civilization over all others. Some theorists argued that Brazilian Indians were inferior, since they were less sophisticated than Europeans

intellectually, technologically, and politically. They were therefore *natural* slaves" (ibid., 149; emphasis added).

21 Ibid., 37. King João III had divided the coastline into "fourteen 'captaincies,' each ranging from a hundred to four hundred miles of coastline and awarded to one of his subjects. Each recipient was called a 'donatory.' He became the hereditary lord of his huge stretch of territory, with considerable civil and criminal jurisdiction that included the death penalty for slaves, Indians and ordinary freemen" (ibid., 36).

22 Forbes, *Africans and Native Americans*, 36.

23 Hemming, *Red Gold*, 152.

24 Wagley, *Race and Class*, 12. The plantation and mountain regions roughly correspond to the northeastern and southeastern parts of contemporary Brazil.

25 Ribeiro, *Os Índios e a Civilização*, 56.

26 See Vizenor, "Ishi Bares His Chest."

27 Aldeia literally means a village or community, yet it tends to be used most frequently vis-à-vis indigenous communities. In fact, Indians and non-Indians in eastern Brazil almost universally referred to a particular Indian community as an aldeia. It is important to keep in mind that not all aldeias are federally recognized. That is, not all aldeias are labeled reserves (that is, reservations). As for the two indigenous penal colonies, they were established in Minas Gerais between 1966 and 1972. Numerous "insubordinate Indians" from various parts of Brazil were incarcerated in these prisons (see chapters 2 and 3).

28 On my most recent visit to Brazil in October 2000, I learned that since 1997 at least three other communities in this region have begun to self-identify as Indian. These communities include the Mukurim, Puris, and Tubinamba. The estimate of the eastern Indian population was arrived at from data compiled by CEDI in the late 1980s and early 1990s (Centro Ecumênico de Documentação e Informação, *Povos Indígenas no Brasil*, 515–516). I then phoned or visited a number of governmental and nongovernmental organizations (e.g., FUNAI, CIMI, CEDEFES) between 1997 and 2000 in order to get their most recent population estimates. Thus, with CEDI's data as my baseline, I updated its estimates using the most current numbers I was able to obtain from the various organizations involved in Indian affairs in this region.

29 Sampaio, "De Caboclo a Índio," 2–4. Postos indígenas (Indian posts) refers to the local administrative seats of the federal Indian bureau (FUNAI) that are located on most federally recognized indigenous reserves.

30 This excerpt is taken from a brief interview that I conducted with the Secretary at the 1995 assembly.

31 The estimate of the Indian population in northeastern Brazil was derived in the same manner that I established the number of eastern Indians. Using CEDI's figures as my baseline, I updated these figures using the most current estimates I was able to obtain from organizations such as CIMI, FUNAI, and CEDEFES (Centro

Ecumênico de Documentação e Informação, *Povos Indígenas no Brasil*, 371–373 and 515–516). There is some evidence to suggest that my estimate is too conservative. David Kennedy and Stephen Perz, for instance, predicted that northeastern Indians alone would number 76,241 by the year 2001. They arrived at this estimate using the 1991 census data from the northeast as their baseline and then they projected forward given the estimated fertility and mortality rates. Thus their projection excluded eastern Indians and did not include communities in the northeast that have emerged since 1991 (Kennedy and Perez, "Who Are Brazil's Indígenas?" 39).

32 Pardo is an official "color or race" category on the census. Individuals who treat it as a color variable think of it as the rough equivalent of brown. Those who employ it in a more racial (that is, genetic) sense usually mean mixed race. For darker-skinned Brazilians—individuals who generally are not seen as white—pardo qua race is thought of more in biological than sociological terms. Individuals who are considered white, but who may be of some non-European descent, tend not to embrace a pardo (that is, mixed-race) identity. Thus, they use this racial category in a more sociological manner.

33 Silva, "A Demografia e os Povos Indígenas no Brasil," 261.

34 Kennedy and Perz, "Who Are Brazil's Indígenas?" 10. On forced acculturation, see chapter 3.

35 Some observers of the census have criticized subsuming indígena under the color/race variable. They believe that if individuals interpret pardo as meaning "color" that it may create a confusion for some of the self-identified Indians who may not necessarily see skin color and being Indian as mutually exclusive. In other words, they may self-identify as indígena and yet also consider themselves to have a white, brown, or black skin color. The concern is that such a quandary may lead to an undercounting of the Indian population.

36 For example, "according to the Krenak leaders, while conducting the 1991 census, the enumerator responsible for the communities of the Rio Doce Valley, in Minas Gerais, . . . solicited the FUNAI identity cards from the Indians interviewed. Those who did not possess one were definitely counted by him as 'pardo' [brown]" (Silva, "A Demografia e os Povos Indígenas no Brasil," 263).

37 Kennedy and Perz, "Who Are Brazil's Indígenas?" 13. In the 1991 census, IBGE found a total population of 146,815,705. Of that, 75,704,934 self-identified as white, 7,335,116 as black, 630,633 as yellow/Asian, 62,316,045 as brown/mixed race, and 294,118 as Indian. In northeastern Brazil, 55,842 supposedly self-identified as indígena; in Minas Gerais it was 6,109, and in Espírito Santo 2,354. As should be clear from the above discussion, many observers believe the Indian population was undercounted due to such factors as the ambiguity of the term *indígena* as a color category and the failure of enumerators to rely on self-identification.

38 Kennedy and Perz, "Who Are Brazil's Indígenas?" 3.

39 Thornton, *American Indian Holocaust*, 160.

40 U.S. Census Bureau, *Statistical Abstract of the United States*, 14. Most experts believe

that similar increases have occurred in other parts of Latin America as well (see, for example, "Report on Indigenous Movements," 14–43). Unfortunately, except for Brazil, virtually no quantitative data is available for the region. One reason for the absence of even basic census data on Indians in Latin America is that most policymakers have resisted using "race" as a census category on the grounds that these societies are monoracial, mestizo nations, and so there is no need to document racial/ethnic diversity. Another common explanation for the resistance to gathering demographic information on race is that it only serves to reinscribe and heighten racial distinctions, a practice that is believed to cause racism. Thus the use of racial categories is considered both racist (an assumption that I will challenge in chapter 8) and prejudicial to the production of racially homogeneous, non-Indian nations.

41 Thornton, *American Indian Holocaust*, 223.

42 Momaday, *The Names*, 23–25.

43 Ibid., 25.

44 Ibid., 24–25.

45 Amorim, "Acamponesamento e Proletarização," 17.

46 In 1910, Francis E. Leupp, the Commissioner of Indian Affairs under Theodore Roosevelt, believed whitening to be so inevitable that he argued

> There will be no "later" for the Indians. He is losing his identity hour by hour, competing with whites in the labor market, mingling with white communities, and absorbing white pioneers into his own, sending his children to the same schools with white children, intermarrying with whites and rearing an offspring which combines the traits of both lines of ancestry. In the light of this new day which is now near noon, he need not be an inspired seer to discern the approaching end of his pure aboriginal type and the upgrowth of another which will claim the name "American" by a double title as solid as the hills on the horizon. (Quoted in Dippie, *The Vanishing American*, 256)

47 Oftentimes, the southern cone of Bahia is not considered part of eastern Brazil but rather northeastern Brazil. Like CEDI and most eastern Indians, I categorize it as eastern Brazil because of historical, geographic, and cultural links between the Indians of southern Bahia and those in Minas Gerais and Espírito Santo. A quick look at the map reveals that tribes like the Maxakali and Pankararu are but a few hundred miles upstream from the Pataxó of southern Bahia. Furthermore, most of the Indians on the Guarani aldeia are from southern Bahia.

48 Salvinho, thirty-four at the time of our interview in 1995, lives in the central part of aldeia Guarani (see chapter 2) with his wife and four young children. He was one of four Pataxó men who considered themselves leaders and attended many of the pan-tribal meetings. Although he was estranged from one of the families I stayed with while in Guarani, he agreed to be interviewed which was a bold and generous gesture on his part. It seemed that whenever I would walk somewhere I would see

him pass by on his bicycle, and he would always throw me his contagious smile (see his photo in chapter 6). As an aside, most Indians in eastern Brazil use their tribal name as their surname.

49 Sampaio, *De Caboclo a Índio*, 2.

50 Pratt, *Imperial Eyes*, 7.

51 Wolf, "The Vicissitudes of the Closed Corporate Community," 326.

52 Frye, *Indians into Mexicans*, 9–10.

53 Deloria, *Playing Indian*, 115. My notion of the term *traditional* is much more expansive than most. Oftentimes, traditional implies a putative biological and/or cultural purity. For instance, the Indians whom Gerald Vizenor (*The Heirs of Columbus*) refers to as "crossbloods" would typically not be considered traditional Indians because they are "mixed bloods" who utilize material cultures, technologies, and institutions not seen as indigenous in origin. Put differently, "the crossbloods" who appropriate "bingo halls, gambling casinos, radio transmitters and genetic research" in a manner that "support(s) traditional communal values" (Pasquaretta, *Tricksters at Large*, 230), would probably not be defined as traditional Indians. I, however, would categorize crossbloods as traditional since these individuals and their communities are able to manage "alien" material and symbolic realities in a manner that reinscribes traditional worldviews. In eastern Brazil, there are only two Indian communities (the Maxakali and Guarani) who would fit my definition of traditional.

54 Although some might interpret it ironically (a meaning with which posttraditional Indians do not imbue it), I am afraid that far too many would be prone to decode it in terms of conventional notions of Indians as "savages," "primitives," "nonmodern peoples," and so on. Ultimately, then, "more civilized" simply carries too much semantic baggage and so works counter to the concepts I am hoping to convey.

55 Wilson, *Maya Resurgence*, 7–13.

56 Tonkin, McDonald, and Chapman, *History and Ethnicity*, 17; and Wilson, *Maya Resurgence*, 9.

57 The exceptions to this are the Kaxixó and Aranã.

58 Freyre, *The Masters and the Slaves*.

59 Hemming, *Red Gold*, 18.

60 Ibid., 19.

61 See Gould, *The Mismeasure of Man*; and Horsman, *Race and Manifest Destiny*.

62 Gould, *The Mismeasure of Man*.

63 Quoted in Horsman, *Race and Manifest Destiny*, 71.

64 Ibid., 73.

65 The belief that there is a genetic basis to "racial/ethnic" groups, and subsequently that these imagined "genetically distinct races" have certain biologically determined attributes such as intelligence, criminal behavior, and mental illness, is unfortunately not limited to nineteenth-century scientific thought, nor to contemporary Brazilian popular thought. As Troy Duster details in *Backdoor to Eugenics*,

despite basic flaws in the assumptions of "genetic explanations" (let alone race-based genetic explanations), a presumed genetic basis of "races" and concomitant behaviors continues to be a fundamental premise of a great number of contemporary scientists and policymakers in North America and Europe.

66 It is similar to the fact that persons in the United States who are the offspring of a black and an Indian are frequently not recognized or seen as Indian by both non-Indians and Indians alike. In the United States, such individuals are likely to be socially defined and to self-identify as black.

67 See her photo in chapter 2.

68 Vizenor, *Manifest Manners*, 8.

69 Krupat, "Native American Autobiography," 174.

70 Brumble, *American Indian Autobiography*, 136.

71 Ibid.

72 Interview with Domíngos Pataxó, July 1995, aldeia Guarani.

2. Methodologial Reflections

1 Deloria, *Playing Indian*.

2 For examples of these arrival stories, see Hanbury-Tenison, *A Question of Survival*; and Maybury-Lewis, *The Savage and the Innocent*. The logic of this inference is contingent on the modernist dichotomy that posits traditional/primitive in binary opposition to modern/civilized. Within this framework, indigenous authenticity is contingent on a lack of contamination by the modern. Thus, this trajectory of the ethnographic expedition—from modern city to primitive interior—was a rhetorical strategy invoked to bolster the ethnographer's claim to scientific legitimacy given that his or her assignment was to document authentic indigenous (that is, primitive) cultures imagined as being outside the boundaries of modern time and place (Deloria, *Playing Indian*, 116).

3 While in Vasalia, we eventually conducted hundreds of informal interviews and fifty-two tape-recorded structured interviews (see appendix B) that served as the data for Twine's book, *Racism in a Racial Democracy*. For a detailed examination of our methodological approach in Vasalia as well as a specific discussion of some of the advantages and disadvantages of being an interracial research team in Brazil, refer to the methodological appendix in Twine's dissertation; and the introduction to Twine and Warren, *Racing Research, Researching Race*.

4 In much the same way that New Yorkers have a provincial view of the country and refer to any location between the East and West Coasts as "the hinterlands," *Cariocas* (residents of Rio de Janeiro) have a similar view of any place outside their city, especially if it is inland, and refer to it, usually with a note of derision, as "the interior" ("the outback").

5 See Twine, *Racism in a Racial Democracy*. Although none of the Vasalia residents self-identified as Indian, most of them claimed to be of Indian descent. Moreover, almost everyone who asserted an indigenous heritage said that they were the descen-

dants of Puris—the indigenous people who lived in this region when the Brazilians began colonizing it in the mid-nineteenth century.

6   During 1995, I also spent two weeks in Cabo Frio, Rio de Janeiro, where I conducted eight interviews with non-Indians, and six weeks in a *favela* (a low-income, predominantly nonwhite neighborhood) in the *zona sul* of Rio de Janeiro, where I conducted a total of six interviews (also with non-Indians).

7   I was ultimately unsuccessful in this endeavor primarily because I did not have the funding to stay long enough in São Paulo to establish the necessary contacts. According to Juliano Spyer ("Urban Indians," 438), more than one thousand Pankararu Indians live at least part of the year in Real Parque. Spyer also reports that one hundred Fulni-ô reside in another shantytown on the periphery of São Paulo and that there are at least three Guarani Nhandeva favela communities in this city of fourteen million (ibid., 440).

8   In chapter 5, I explain why Indians from these states tend to be more closely identified with northeastern Indians rather than those in Rio de Janeiro and São Paulo.

9   Figueira, "O Preconceito Racial na Escola," 64.

10 One potential pitfall of this heightened white privilege is that it may create a powerful incentive for white researchers to ignore or minimize the significance of race and racism in Brazil (see Warren, "Masters in the Field").

11 The same is not true for scholars who would be seen as black or mulatto. For example, France Winddance Twine ("Introduction", 3) notes that "I had expected to be treated as a professional researcher and was not prepared for the assumption by Brazilians of color that I was a maid, illegitimate sister of my white partner, or his whore."

12 See ibid.

13 North American or European "foreignness" seemed to enhance whiteness. One was imagined as whiter than domestic whites—in terms of genealogy if not physical appearance—and so had more symbolic capital.

14 To reiterate what I noted in chapter 1, pardo is an official term used on the Brazilian census to refer to individuals who have a supposedly mixed-race racial identity or locate themselves as brown in terms of color. It is important to keep in mind that few individuals actually identify as pardo. Instead, I am using it here to refer to that sector of the population that embraces one of several "intermediate" racial identities, such as mulatto or moreno.

15 I should add that for both Indians and non-Indians, the most difficult interviewees were women, especially married women with children. First, it was hard for Brazilians, particularly in rural areas, to imagine a relationship between a man and a woman that was not sexual. Given this, interviews with women were tough to negotiate because it was usually assumed that they might lead to a sexual liaison. Such a sexualized reading of the interview process by others in the community might have made women—and even more so, married women—reluctant to agree to an interview or uncomfortable during the actual interview. Another prob-

lem I encountered stemmed from the expectation that women were supposed to watch the children. Subsequently, it was much more difficult to find time when women could actually be interviewed on a one-to-one basis (see Patai, *Brazilian Women Speak*, 5).

16 On FUNAI, see glossary and chapter 5.

17 Quilombo, a community first established by runaway slaves, was also sometimes used by Brazilians I met to refer to an all-black neighborhood or village. As for landholders' "iron fist," it went back to the end of the eighteenth century. The region had been a stronghold of many large quilombos that inhibited Portuguese colonization. The quilombos also threatened slaveholders in neighboring regions because they served as a possible refuge for their slaves. In 1774 these concerns prompted the colonial government to send Captain Inácio de Almeida Campos and his wife, Joaquina Bernada de Abreu e Silva Castelo Branco, to the region in order to pacify the quilombos. To accomplish this goal, the couple forged an alliance with the Kaxixó, who served as their mercenaries. Once most of the quilombos were subdued and its residents re-enslaved, a number of the Kaxixó worked as overseers, slave catchers, and assassins (*jagunços*) for the captain and his wife as well as for other local planters. According to Geralda Chaves Soares and the Kaxixó with whom I spoke, the practice of slavery established in the region after the conquest of the quilombos was brutal even by Brazilian standards. The slaves, I was often told, were routinely beaten, required to work from sunrise to sunset, and fed just one kilo of corn per day. As a young girl in the early twentieth century, Antonieta Francisca da Silva remembered that she and her family were prohibited by the local fazendeiro from feeding the older slaves who could no longer work so that they would quickly die from hunger.

18 Of the Indian subsample, fourteen of the interviewees were urban Indians. The remaining thirty-six interviews were conducted in one of the three indigenous communities where I resided: Apukaré, Guarani and Kaxixó. See appendixes C and D. Also note that some of the interviews from Vasalia, a few of which I draw on in this study to help illustrate the interpretive framework of non-Indians, were conducted either exclusively by or in conjunction with France Winddance Twine.

19 After each interview, I would take notes summarizing important themes and comments that had emerged. Moreover, I would analyze my performance during the interview in an attempt to improve my skills as an interviewer. Although most of the interviews lasted approximately two hours, a few went as long as seven hours.

3. The State of Indian Exorcism

1 See Roosens, *Creating Ethnicity*; and Neely, *Snowbird Cherokees*.

2 Neely, *Snowbird Cherokees*, 103. Neely did not conduct her research with the Indians of more European descent, whom she referred to as "white Indians." Instead, she focused exclusively on the putative "full-blood Eastern Cherokees."

3   See chapter 1. Momaday, *The Names*, 24–25.

4   Quoted in Taussig, *Shamanism, Colonialism, and the Wild Man*, 32, 51.

5   Taussig, *Shamanism, Colonialism, and the Wild Man*, 53.

6   Ibid.

7   Ibid.

8   They were disillusioned because assimilationist solutions to ethnic relations gave way to more race-cognizant antiracist movements and government policies (Thompson, *Theories of Ethnicity*, 92).

9   Glazer, Introduction, 8–19.

10   Paraiso, *Laudo Antropológico sobre a Comunidade Denomidada Kaxixó*, 18–20. Notice that Paraiso displaces her power onto the government and nongovernmental organizations by expressing a concern that this community may be the pawn of a battle between the two. Paraiso does not choose to consider the possibility that the Kaxixó may be the "great victims," not only of the government and nongovernmental organizations but also of anthropologists such as herself who have the ability to dramatically affect their fate by ruling on their racial authenticity.

11   In 1954, at the urging of Senator Arthur Watkins, Congress adopted a "termination" program. Claiming that big government is inefficient, and Indians need to be free of it once and for all, anti–New Deal congresspeople and senators proceeded to cut federal services to Indians, place Indians under state jurisdiction, and encourage Indians to relocate from their communities to urban centers—to name just a few components of the termination policy (see Deloria and Lytle, *The Nations Within*).

12   "Canada Apologizes to Indigenous Tribes."

13   Leacy, *Historical Statistics of Canada*; and Statistics Canada, *1981 Census of Canada*.

14   Freyre, *The Masters and the Slaves*, 278.

15   Hutchinson, "Race Relations in a Rural Community," 16–17.

16   Hemming, *Red Gold*, 83.

17   The indigenous population along almost the entire Atlantic Coast of present-day Brazil and in the basin of the Paraná and Paraguay Rivers "can be divided into two large groups: the Tupi-Guarani and the Tapuia. . . . The Tupi, who were also known as the Tupinambá, dominated the coastal strip from the north down to Cananéia, in the southern part of the present-day state of São Paulo. The Guarani were located in the basin of the Paraná and Paraguay and along the coast, from Cananéia down to the southern reaches of . . . Brazil. In spite of their different geographic locations, the two subgroups are known as Tupi-Guarani because of their similarity in language and culture" (Fausto, *A Concise History of Brazil*, 7). Historians believe that when the Portuguese first began colonizing South America, "the Tupi-speaking nations, first the Tupinikim, then a wave of Tupinambá, . . . had recently migrated from the Paraguayan basin and were driving the tribes along the coast inland to seek refuge" (Hemming, *Red Gold*, 24). Thus, "at points along the littoral, the Tupi-Guarani population was interspersed with other groups: [for instance, the Aimoré

in southern Bahia and the northern part of Espírito Santo]. . . . These groups were called Tapuia, a generic word used by the Tupi-Guarani to indicate Indians who spoke a language different from theirs" (Fausto, *A Concise History of Brazil*, 7). Many of the peoples who were supposedly forced inland (such as the Tapuia) are today classified as belonging to the Macro-Jé linguistic and cultural group. The contemporary communities in eastern Brazil that are the descendants of the Macro-Jé are the Xacriabá, Pataxó, Krenak, and Maxakali. And those that are considered part of the Tupi-Guarani culture are the Guarani and Tupinikim (Teixeira, "As Linguas Indígenas no Brasil," 300–302).

18   Quoted in Hemming, *Red Gold*, 88.

19   At the time of this interview in 1995, Gumercino lived on the Guarani aldeia where his brother was one of the caciques. He and his wife have eight children, most of them adults. Their home, a five-room structure near a pond where they raise a few ducks, is removed from the main road by about two hundred yards. At that time, they had electricity but no indoor plumbing. The $100 per month pension that he and his wife received from the federal government sustained them, two of their children, and one grandchild, whom they were also raising. Gumercino had recently converted to Evangelical Protestantism after suffering a stroke. He confided that he did not really believe in it, but it helped him stop drinking and womanizing. A very warm and generous person, Gumercino was particularly proud of the fact that he knew all the Pataxó words for the local vegetation, and would rattle them off to me whenever we took walks or sat outdoors.

20   Gumercino suggested that this official was Captain M. S. Pinheiro. However, it is unlikely that this federal official was Pinheiro. At this time, he was in charge of the forestry service and its police force in Minas Gerais, not in Bahia. During his tenure with the forestry service and then later as the Chief of Assistance (*Ajudância*) Minas Gerais-Bahia for both SPI and FUNAI, Pinheiro played a central role in the appropriation of Krenak territories near Rio Doce and the establishment of the indigenous penal colonies in aldeias Krenak and Guarani. Thus given Pinheiro's centrality in Indian affairs in this region, especially as a potent force for Indian exorcism, it is understandable why Gumercino may have mistakenly woven Pinheiro into his account of the massacre in 1951.

21   Slaves and their descendants are frequently imaged as being predominantly, if not exclusively, of African descent. Yet this belies the historical realities of slavery and Indian colonization, as well as the memories of the descendants of slaves in Brazil (like those in the United States) whom I found to almost always attest to at least some known indigenous ancestry (see Forbes, *Africans and Native Americans*, 1993). I will return to this matter in greater detail in chapter 8.

22   This must have been several years later because the capital was not moved to Brasília from Rio de Janeiro until the early 1960s.

23   The Forestry Service (Serviço Florestal), established in 1934, often worked in tandem with SPI. Once lands were appropriated from Indians and declared "public forests," the subsoil rights could be leased to any number of mining companies

with, no doubt, substantial kickbacks for the directors of SPI or the Forestry Service. The possibility of confirming these sorts of financial arrangements was eliminated in 1967, when a "mysterious fire at the Ministry of Agriculture in Brasília destroyed the SPI's archive, with its correspondence and financial records" (Garfield, "The 'Greatest Administrative Scandal,' " 268).

24 Levine and Crocitti, *The Brazil Reader*, 13.
25 Hemming, *Red Gold*, 103.
26 Quoted in Hemming, *Red Gold*, 104.
27 Hemming, *Red Gold*, 99.
28 Ibid., *Red Gold*, 105.
29 Quoted in Hemming, *Red Gold*, 105.
30 Hemming, *Red Gold*, 105.
31 When Dom José I ascended to the Portuguese throne in 1750, he appointed Sebastião José de Carvalho e Melo, the future marquess of Pombal, his minister. "One of the most controversial measures of Pombal's government (1750–1777) was the expulsion of the Jesuits from Portugal and all its territories . . . , who were accused of forming 'a state within a state.' " It seems that Pombal was concerned with securing Brazil's northern and southern boundaries, which he believed was contingent on "integrating the Indians into Portuguese civilization. If there were no reliable inhabitants born in Brazil who identified with Portugal and its objectives, it would be impossible to assure Portugal's control over the vast, semi-populated regions of that colony." As a result, "Indian slavery was abolished in 1757. Many of the religious villages in the Amazon region were turned into towns with civil administrations. Laws were passed encouraging marriages between whites and Indians." And of course, the Jesuits were expelled because they were seen as inhibiting assimilation to the degree believed necessary via the creation of segregated, detribalized, semiautonomous, Jesuit-controlled indigenous colonies (Fausto, *A Concise History of Brazil*, 56–57).
32 Ibid., 481.
33 Ibid.
34 Itambacuri is located 350 miles west of Porto Seguro, Bahia, in northeastern Minas Gerais.
35 Ribeiro, *Lembranças da Terra*, 189.
36 Quoted in ibid., 196.
37 The Mucuri is a river running through Minas Gerais and southern Bahia. Its headwaters begin about two hundred miles inland (in the most eastern part of Espírito Santo) and enter the Atlantic approximately 100 miles south of Porto Seguro.
38 Interestingly, throughout his writings on Itambacuri, Pacó referred to himself in the third person. For example, in the above he did not write, "During *my* tenure *I* always" but rather, "During *his* tenure *he* always."
39 Hemming, *Red Gold*, 111.
40 Ribeiro, *Lembranças da Terra*, 189.
41 For most of these mission Indians, Pacó's writings came too late. The vast majority

of the eighteen tribes relocated to Itambacuri, even those not raised by priests, were decimated: their tribal traditions were terminated, and most of them (or their descendants) adopted non-Indian identities. Only a small percentage of those reared in Itambacuri, as well as in other eastern Brazil missions, retained even detribalized indigenous identities (such as diocese or church Indians) or identities nominally associated with Indianness (like Caboclos, Canoeiros, or Caciques).

42 Lima, *Um Grande Cerco de Paz*, 121.

43 Ibid., 254.

44 Ibid., 136.

45 Ibid., 127, 128.

46 Quoted in Horsman, *Race and Manifest Destiny*, 130.

47 Skidmore, *Black into White*, 65.

48 Ibid., 65–66.

49 Quoted in Skidmore, *Black into White*, 208.

50 The Krenak is the last remaining community descended from the Botocudos. The Botocudos always had a reputation for being a fierce people who resisted being missionized (see Soares, *Os Borun do Watu*, 48–50). The Pojichás described by Pacó as "the shadow and terror of the region" that the missionaries at Itambacuri had, as late as 1918, been unable to penetrate, was probably a Botocudo community (Ribeiro, *Lembranças da Terra*, 202).

51 Soares, *Os Borun do Watu*, 128.

52 Ibid., 129. The Totem Jonkyon was the center of the Krenak's principal religious ceremony. In brief, the Krenak's metaphysical world, which a number of Krenak are attempting to rebuild, consisted of the Maréts, who inhabited the superior realms and were the great organizers of nature. Among the Maréts was the Marét-Khamaknian, the creator of humans and the world. Another deity was Nanitiong, who was responsible for the fertility of women and advised when death was approaching. There were also the Tokóns who were responsible for selecting the earthly intermediaries, the shamans, with whom they stayed in contact during rituals. As well, there were six souls or spirits, which lived in the bodies of humans beginning at four years of age. For more detail on the Krenak religion see Paraiso, "Krenák."

53 Quoted in Soares, *Os Borun do Watu*, 132.

54 Maria's second husband, a Kaingang, had recently died at the time of our interview, and she was still in mourning over his death. Her son, Waldemar, was the administrator of the FUNAI post on the Guarani aldeia. Maria lived in a small, recently constructed, concrete house, not far removed from the administration building. A tiny, energetic, talkative woman, Maria was one of the interviewees who seemed most satisfied with her life—despite how incredibly difficult it had been. She was clearly pleased with the recent gift of a television from her son and deeply content that the Krenak had finally been given back title to some of their lands, which meant her years of exile would soon come to an end. Indeed, she was planning to return to the Rio Doce in a few months' time.

55 Soares, *Os Borun do Watu*, 132.

56 Ibid.

57 Ibid., 133.

58 Maria claimed that they traveled to Rio de Janeiro, but it is more likely that they visited Belo Horizonte. At that time, Pinheiro worked for the regional division of SPI that was responsible for Minas Gerais and Bahia and thus headquartered in Belo Horizonte, not Rio de Janeiro.

59 Soares, *Os Borun do Watu*, 139.

60 As I mentioned in chapter 2, I first met Cleonice in 1992 in Rio de Janeiro, and she was the person who invited me to live with her family on the Apukaré aldeia. Cleonice, who is intellectually and politically sophisticated, has a calm yet palpable presence. At the time of our interview in 1995, she was the most highly educated Indian in Minas Gerais, and was living part of the time on the aldeia Apukaré and the other part in Coronel Murta. A newlywed, she and her husband (a Pataxó) were not getting along well with her family (a matter that should not be too surprising given that about sixteen of us were living in a small house [see chapter 2]). So while I was there, they rented a small apartment in town as a way to have some privacy. After I left, she and her husband moved to Espírito Santo, where she was able to work as a medical assistant for FUNAI on one of the Tupinikim aldeias and be closer to her husband, who had just enrolled in an agricultural high school in that state (see chapter 4). They have since had two children, her husband completed his degree, and they are moving back to Apukaré.

61 The penal colony in Pensacola, where Indians were brought from as far away as New Mexico, was established and run by General Richard Henry Pratt, who used his experiences "training" the Indian prisoners to create a model for what eventually became the Indian boarding school system. And just as the prisons and boarding schools had the unintended consequence of fostering pan-tribal relationships and identities in the United States, it is likely that indigenous penal colonies in Brazil had a similar effect.

62 As far as I could determine from historical records and oral testimonies, only men were imprisoned.

63 This excerpt was based on interviews conducted by Geralda Chaves Soares (*Os Borun do Watu*, 140–41) with prisoners and their families from the Krenak penal colony.

64 The cuisine in Minas Gerais was distinct from that of Bahia, where people were accustomed to seafood, "spicier" seasonings, and a variety of dishes difficult if not impossible to make in Minas Gerais.

65 Ribeiro, *Lembranças da Terra*, 183.

66 Ibid.

67 Quoted in Ribeiro, *Lembranças da Terra*, 185.

68 Ribeiro, *Lembranças da Terra*, 185.

69 Ibid., 188.

70 Ibid., 190.

71 Ibid.

72   Ibid., 193. As with the assembled mission Indians, a number of the capacitated Indians became adamant Indian exorcists (see ibid.).

73   Some of her art is used in the schools to teach children about anatomy because of its physical accuracy. For example, she makes a female doll with a zipper for the vaginal area; using an umbilical cord, a baby can be pulled from the mother's womb.

74   Garfield, "The 'Greatest Administrative Scandal,' " 268.

75   Ibid., 269.

76   Ibid., 270.

77   Ibid., 271.

78   Ibid., 270.

79   Ibid., 271.

80   See chapter 6.

81   Bruneau, The Church in Brazil, 86.

82   Ibid., 87.

83   Ramos, Indigenism, 168.

84   Ibid., 169.

85   Ibid., 169–70.

86   Ibid., 172.

87   Schwartzman, Araujo, and Pankararu, "Brazil," 39.

88   Stephen Schwartzman, Ana Valeria Araujo, and Paulo Pankararu (ibid.) note that this was an attempted strategy of nationalists and the Right from the late 1970s on to legislate indigenous groups out of existence by making a legal distinction between "acculturated" Indians and "forest dwellers" (silvícolas), with different land rights applying to each. In this way, the obligations of the state toward the acculturated Indians would eventually cease or be severely limited. And since it was assumed that indigenous groups not yet assimilated would become so soon, the so-called Indian problem and any rights to land would ultimately become irrelevant (see also chapter 7). On the powerful anti-Indian interests, see Ramos, Indigenism, 177.

89   Quoted in Schwartzman, Araujo, Pankararu, "Brazil," 39.

90   Thus the way was paved for significant advances in indigenous land "demarcation." Demarcation consists of the identification of an area by FUNAI, establishment of the area's boundaries through a decree signed by the justice minister, physical demarcation, ratification by the president, and registration in the land office (ibid.).

91   During the 1970s, FUNAI proved to be little better (if not worse) than SPI (see chapter 4).

92   This expression dates back to the nineteenth century when the Brazilian government passed anti–slave trade laws to appease the English government, but did not comply with them. They were "for the English to see"; the laws themselves were neither enforced nor obeyed.

93   José, a tawny and extremely personable man, was forty-five in 1995. I interviewed him in Belo Horizonte when he was visiting for a pan-Indian conference. A small

farmer on the Xacriabá aldeia in northwestern Minas Gerais, José told me that he had recently married a Xacriabá woman in her early twenties and that they had two small children.

94 *Hoje em Dia.*

95 Zizi is a Baptist fundamentalist who attends weekly Bible meetings and sings in a church choir on the Guarani aldeia. Her faith is a source of tension on the aldeia because some Indians equate being Catholic with being "more Indian," and thus see her religious affiliation as "evidence" of how she has become "white" or "whiter." Zizi's statement about the power of prayer, therefore, represents her religious conviction, and is an attempt to illustrate the veracity and superiority of her faith by suggesting that only Crentes (Protestants/fundamentalists) survived.

96 In this instance, the term *caboclo* is a synonym for Indian. The meaning of this term and its relationship to Indianness has varied greatly (see chapter 7). Until the 1920s, it was an official census category at which time 51 percent of the population was identified as white, 22 percent as mulatto, 11 percent as caboclo, 14 percent as negro, and 2 percent as Indian (Roquette-Pinto, "Nota sobre os Tipos Antropológicos do Brasil," 309). In many ways, caboclo is to Indian what mulatto is to black.

97 Oftentimes, blacks are categorized and referred to as a subset of "whiteness." Within this conceptualization of whiteness, there are white whites, black whites, mulatto whites, and so on. When used in this manner, white means non-Indian.

4. Racial Stocks and Brazilian Bonds

1 Hess and Da Matta, *The Brazilian Puzzle*, 4–5.

2 Maybury-Lewis, *The Politics of the Possible*, 29.

3 Ibid.

4 During the early years of her childhood, Karakana (see photo in chapter 1) and her older sister were raised by their white father in southern Bahia. When her sister and brother-in-law (Pataxó) decided to move to aldeia Guarani, Karakana went to live with them. Karakana's father, a carpenter, eventually moved to aldeia Guarani to be near his daughter and grandchildren. At the time of this 1995 interview, Karakana was nineteen years old. Unlike her grandparents, she had been attracted away from the aldeia because of the excitement offered by the city.

5 According to Geralda Chaves Soares, the Canoeiros are the descendants of the Maxakali who worked for the various military outposts (*quartéis*) established in the Jequitinhonha Valley in the early nineteenth century to subdue and enslave the Indians of the region. Their job was to transport people, livestock and goods to and from the quartéis. Hence they were called Canoeiros (canoe-people or boaters).

6 To reiterate, this applies only to eastern Brazil. In the north, for example, it seems that this sort of violence is still commonplace.

7 "In 1940, 70 percent of the population still lived in rural areas; in 1997 only 20 percent did" (Schwartzman, "Brazil," 32).

8 Maybury-Lewis, *The Politics of the Possible*, 27. "In 1985, 50,105 property owners (indi-

viduals and legal entities), totaling only 0.84 percent of all property holders in Brazil, controlled 43.8 percent of the nation's farmland in holdings ranging from one thousand to several million hectares each. At the same time 52.9 percent of Brazil's property holders, numbering just over 10 million (probably mostly individuals), controlled 2.6 percent of Brazil's farmland in parcels of ten hectares or less" (ibid.). A decade later, this uneven distribution of land remained essentially unchanged. According to NACLA, in 1995 "the wealthiest 0.9 percent of landholders [owned] 44 percent of the land while the poorest 53 percent held just 2.7 percent" (NACLA, "Brazil," 16).

9   In 1995, Benvinda Pankararu was fifty-eight. She was a beautiful singer and intensely proud of the attire that the Pankararu used in their ritual dances. Benvinda would take me to see the clothing every few days, and each time she would stroke it with a nostalgic smile and remind me of what it was made. Both in appearance and personality, she was so strikingly similar to one of the daughters of the family I stayed with in Vasalia that I still cannot think of one without immediately recalling the other. A quick-witted, extremely kind woman whose tongue became too sharp if she indulged in a drink or two, Benvinda was the person who kept a mental record for the community of precisely how and when particular ceremonies should be performed.

10   Drought is a problem primarily affecting those living in northeastern Brazil. It is feared by some that this area could become Sahara-like as a consequence of the deforestation that continues at a rapid pace in the Amazon region.

11   "During the nineteenth century, Emperor Dom Perdo II ceded rights to 35,000 acres to the Pankararu. Decades later, in 1941, the reservation was mapped by the federal Indian Protection Service (SPI); by then it had shrunk to 20,000 acres. The shrinkage of their protected land—situated in the middle-lower São Francisco River Valley on the border of Bahia and Pernambuco—as neighboring farms and ranches expanded led to massive outmigration after 1950. . . . The continued pattern of migration south has emboldened 400 or so non-Indian squatter families to settle on or near Pankararu lands in Pernambuco. Migrant workers' siblings are left to maintain the land and prevent more seizures, although in general it is a losing battle" (Spyer, "Urban Indians," 437–38).

12   Thus far, this anti-Indian bloc has not emerged at the national or state levels (at least not in eastern Brazil). Nor has it formed, at least not to nearly the same degree, in regions where current Indian territory had been controlled either by the state (for instance, in aldeia Guarani) or the church (for example, in aldeia Apukaré) prior to it becoming the limited sovereign territory of Indians. This historical bloc has instead been restricted to the local politics of a city or county where Indians are struggling to reclaim land from fazendeiros and/or posseiros who have illegally confiscated it (such as in the Maxakali and Kaxixó aldeias), or where an Indian community has recently been successful in removing non-Indians from its lands (as in the Xacriabá, Krenak, and Pataxó Hã-Hã-Hãe aldeias).

13   Rosalino and Fulgencio were two of a handful of Xacriabá murdered in the mid-

1980s by fazendeiros and posseiros in the struggle for recognition and demarcation of their territory.

14 See chapter 3.

15 Soares, interview by author, Araçuaí, 1995. See also chapter 5.

16 The other segment are quilombo communities, whose members are descendants of runaway slaves. Article 68 of the Transitory Clauses of the 1988 Constitution assures the descendants of quilombos the possession of the land they occupy. In 1995, a community in Boa Vista was the first quilombo to receive title to its land as a result of this new law (Toneto and Lima, "O Axé de Zumbi").

17 Schwartzman, Araujo, and Pankararu, "Brazil," 36–43.

18 Guimarães, *Demarcação das Terras Indígenas.*

19 Schwartzman, Araujo, and Pankararu, "Brazil," 37.

20 Andrews, *Blacks and Whites in São Paulo,* 279.

21 Hecht and Cockburn, *The Fate of the Forest,* 167.

22 In chapter 7, I will revisit this issue of cablocness, illustrating how struggles around its meaning, especially academic debates, have created the space for communities like the Xacriabá to assert Indian identities and have these identity claims recognized by the state.

23 In chapter 7, I will explain how this interpretation came to be recognized and legitimated by the courts.

24 Mata, "Kariri Xocó," 2.

25 Ibid., 4.

26 Ibid.

27 The Ouricuri is practiced by various tribes in northeastern Brazil. The festivities last fifteen days in the months of January and February, with the ritual taking place in a forest clearing. Temporary shelters are built around the clearing to house people during the ceremony. The main part of the ritual of the Ouricuri consists of a combination of songs and dances coupled with the consumption of jurema (a wine made from the roots of a tree called the jurema). The ritual's climax is a trance that results from the dancing, singing, and drinking. In this state, participants say they are able to break the barriers between the past, present, and future, entering into a communion with their ancestors and deities. In 1978, after having been strengthened by the ceremony, the Kariri-Xocó left the Ouricuri to successfully retake their land from the fazenda Modelo (Mata, "Kariri Xocó," 11).

28 Fundação Nacional do Índio, "A FUNAI."

29 FUNAI is also "in charge of . . . demarcating, securing, and protecting those lands that have been traditionally occupied by Indians, stimulating the development of studies and surveys about indigenous groups" (ibid.).

30 Norman Lewis, quoted in Hecht and Cockburn, *The Fate of the Forest,* 154.

31 Paul Montgomery, quoted in Davis, *Victims of the Miracle,* 10–11.

32 Prezia and Hoornaert, *Esta Terra Tinha Dono,* 146.

33 Hecht and Cockburn argue that one of the military's principal agendas in launching what they referred to as Operation Amazônica was to legitimate their regime.

Their "legitimacy could be enhanced by the unifying appeal of a call for national integration under the aegis of manifest destiny, accompanied by the fervent ideology of modernization. *Esto é um país que vai prá frente*—this is a country that is going forward—became their war cry" (Hecht and Cockburn, *The Fate of the Forest*, 116).

34 To ease the pressure for land reform in other parts of the country, the military regime hoped that five million people would relocate to the Amazon by 1980. To this end, the Trans-Amazon Highway was constructed, and the Brazilian Institute for Agrarian Reform and Colonization was supposed to provide migrants (which it never did) with four things: a modest house with 5 acres of cleared land; at least 250 acres of land with provisional title making the peasant eligible to participate in a financing fund established by the Bank of Brazil and Bank of the Northeast; a minimum wage for at least six months; and guaranteed prices for agricultural production (Davis, *Victims of the Miracle*, 39). Then, too, the Superintendency for the Development of the Amazon created a far-reaching fiscal and tax-incentives program to promote more corporate farms in the Amazon Basin. For details, see ibid., 37. Overall, the development strategy failed to accomplish its goals of economic growth and resettlement. Its biggest legacy has instead turned out to be the large-scale destruction of vast tracts of Amazon forest and a massive national debt (see Hecht and Cockburn, *The Fate of the Forest*).

35 Between 1968 and 1972, the Inter-American Development and World Banks loaned Brazil a total of four million dollars for highway construction. "These loans represented the largest grants ever made to any country for highway construction in the history of the World Bank and were a major factor in the rapid growth of the Brazilian highway network" (Davis, *Victims of the Miracle*, 64).

36 Ibid., 65.

37 Ibid., 66–69.

38 Ibid., 76.

39 Ibid.

40 Ibid., 57.

41 Ibid.

42 Quoted in Davis, *Victims of the Miracle*, 57.

43 Hecht and Cockburn, *The Fate of the Forest*, 156.

44 Pedrosa, untitled.

45 I am assuming that most individuals who belong to families that earn five minimum salaries (in 1997, this was approximately five hundred U.S. dollars) or less per month cannot afford private health care. In 1990, this included 56 percent of the population (Fundação Instituto Brasileiro de Geografia e Estatística, *Côr da População*, 111).

46 The Economist Intelligence Unit reports that, "Public spending [in Brazil] on health is low, at 1.9 percent of GDP in 1990–97, according to World Bank statistics (compared with 4.3 percent in Argentina), and services inadequate. . . . The problems represented by low level of spending are compounded by the corrupt and inefficient nature of the health system: sophisticated treatments in São Paulo,

including heart surgery and organ transplants, consume a substantial proportion of public resources allocated to health while benefiting only a small minority of the population. Fraud in the refund system is extensive" (*Country Profile 2000*, 16).

47 A medical assistant is someone familiar with basic first aid, midwifery, and administering shots.

48 Fundação Nacional do Índio, "Histórico da Política Indigenista de Saúde a Partir da Década de 80," 1.

49 Quoted in *Diário do Lesilativo de Abril 28*, 10.

50 Ibid., 11.

51 "Funai Pode Ser Extinta," 1. Santilli was president of FUNAI from September 1997 until March 1998.

52 Ibid.

53 An additional service besides health care that I witnessed FUNAI furnishing eastern Indians was the provision of cement and tiling to the Pankararu aldeia. Because the Pankararu were not able to hire a carpenter to help them with the construction of their homes, however, most of these materials were destroyed by rain and heat. And as I was leaving, a long-awaited truck arrived from FUNAI carrying what was supposed to be badly needed staples. Unfortunately, they only brought starches such as pasta and cornmeal, neither of which was needed.

54 "Since 1967, when it was created, until 1991, FUNAI has already had eighteen presidents. Between the military rulers of the reservations, the career bureaucrats, and the *sertanistas* (ruralists/[wilderness or "hinterlands"] specialists), the organization has not managed to produce an official indigenous policy that takes into consideration the interests of indigenous peoples" (Centro Ecumênico de Documentação e Informação, *Povos Indígenas no Brasil*, 41).

55 Quoted in "Funai Pode Ser Extinta," 1.

56 "Funai Pode Ser Extinta," 1.

57 According to the World Bank, in 1995 43.5 percent of the Brazilian population earned approximately $200 per month (*Entering the Twenty-first Century*, 236).

58 See Andrews, *Blacks and Whites in São Paulo*; Hasenbalg, *Discriminação e Desigualidades Racias no Brasil*; Telles, "Industrialização e Desigualdade Racial no Emprego"; and Twine, *Racism in a Racial Democracy*.

59 See chapter 8.

60 See Andrews, *Blacks and Whites in São Paulo*; Damasceno, "Trabalhadores Cariocas"; and Twine, *Racism in a Racial Democracy*. This practice became illegal in the fall of 1997. In line with the general race evasiveness of Brazilian society, explored in chapter 8, there was no discussion of the racial subtext of these ads. Instead, debate around the law was framed as simply a matter of prohibiting discrimination against "ugly people."

61 Ibid.

62 Andrews, *Blacks and Whites in São Paulo*, 161.

63 See Damasceno, "Trabalhadores Cariocas"; Hasenbalg, "Race and Socioeconomic Inequalities"; Simpson, *Xuxa*; and Twine, *Racism in a Racial Democracy*.

64 See Andrews, *Blacks and Whites in São Paulo*; Damesceno, "Trabalhadoras Cariocas"; Hasenbalg, "Race and Socioeconomic Inequalities"; Telles, "Industrialização e Desigualdade Racial no Emprego"; and Twine, *Racism in a Racial Democracy*.

65 See Andrews, *Blacks and Whites in São Paulo*; Damesceno, "Trabalhadoras Cariocas"; Hasenbalg, "Race and Socioeconomic Inequalities"; Silva, "Updating the Cost of Not Being White"; Telles, "Industrialização e Desigualdade Racial no Emprego"; and Twine, *Racism in a Racial Democracy*.

66 Silva, "Updating the Cost of Not Being White," 43.

67 Andrews, *Blacks and Whites in São Paulo*, 166.

68 Ibid., 254.

69 As I noted in chapter 3, Indians frequently employ the term *white* to refer to anyone who is not Indian.

70 It is important to underscore that the particularities of constructions of Indianness in these contexts, as compared to other microregions in Brazil, is a consequence of emphasis rather than creativeness per content or unique syntheses. That is, there is a discursive and symbolic vocabulary of Indianness available to all Brazilians. And rather than adding new words or creating original symbolic sentences, non-Indians in these microregions tend to reduce this language to its most vulgar and spiteful elements, as well as increase the volume of this abbreviated lexicon so that it more profoundly informs material and discursive practices. While these components certainly form part of the societal idiom of Indianness outside these locations, the dialect is quite different in that the decibel level is lowered and the inflection on the more disdainful elements is further muted by being situated within a more expansive "word stock" of Indianness.

71 See chapter 8.

72 See Burdick, "The Lost Constituency"; and Silva and Hasenbalg, *Relações Raciais no Brasil*.

73 There is, nonetheless, still an anti-Indian bloc in Carmésia because Indians have mobilized, succeeding to a limited degree in affecting local elections, changing school curriculum, and acquiring public funds for such things as the paving of the road to their aldeia. As for Indians being excluded from the public sector, this has been found throughout much of Latin America. George Psacharopoulos and Harry Anthony Patrinos (*Indigenous People and Poverty*, 3) attribute this unevenness to "a lack of education." Although this may indeed play a part in causing these disparities, the inequalities in the public sector in eastern Brazil have much more to do with racial politics and patronage than educational credentials — and I suspect that the same holds true for much of Latin America.

74 Freire, "Tupiniquim."

75 Unfortunately, there were no economic studies or census data from which I could draw to confirm or nuance my observations. The first census data that included Indians — instead of subsuming them under the pardo category — was in 1991. As of 1997, though, this information had not been tabulated with respect to any economic indicators. And so as in the rest of Latin America, there is a "lack of empiri-

cal data of the socioeconomic conditions of [the] indigenous population" in eastern Brazil (Psacharopoulos and Patrinos, *Indigenous People and Poverty*, xxii–xxiii).

76 Fundação Instituto Brasileiro de Geografia e Estatística, *Côr da População*.

77 This commitment is relatively recent when one compares it to the United States,
which began implementing universal education in the mid–nineteenth century.

78 In 1990, only 25 percent of Brazilians ten years and older had completed *primeiro
grau*—the equivalent of junior high school in the United States (Fundação Instituto Brasileiro de Geografia e Estatística, *Côr da População*, 45).

79 At the University of São Paulo, for example, only one out every one hundred students was Afro-Brazilian ("Negro Briga por Mais Vagas na Universidade," 18).
George Reid Andrews (*Blacks and Whites in São Paulo*, 65) found that whites had a 480
percent better chance of attending a university than pardos. Approximately 9 percent of whites, 1 percent of blacks, and 2 percent of pardos attended university
(Warren, "O Fardo de Não Ser Negro," 115).

80 This was how Carolina Maria de Jesus, the best-selling author in Brazilian history,
was able to attend school in rural Minas Gerais. Her education was financed by a
white woman attempting to do penance for the fact that her ancestors had owned
slaves, thereby helping a number of Afro-Brazilian children who otherwise would
never have had the opportunity to learn to read and write (Levine and Meihy, *The
Life and Death of Carolina Maria de Jesus*).

81 Godparents in Brazil are much more important than they are in the United States
because so much of how individuals are able to study, buy a house, pay for medical
expenses, and the like is dependent on patron-client relationships. One way poor
people attempt to solidify such a relationship is through the strategic selection of
godparents. "Godmother" is a bit of a euphemism here because the claim that his
mother had been "raised" by this woman likely means that she was a live-in servant
(see Twine, *Racism in a Racial Democracy*).

82 "Vava" or Oswaldo Pataxó, is in a photo in chapter 1.

83 Her daughter, Hwanahara Pataxó, was two years old at the time.

84 At the agricultural schools, students attended classes for fifteen days, followed by
a fifteen day pause period. These pause periods were referred to as *alternativas*.

85 Geralda Chaves Soares accompanied the Maxakali in the 1980s and remained an
important activist for eastern Indians throughout the 1990s. See chapter 5.

86 Almeida, "O Racismo no Livros Didáticos," 18.

87 See Figueira, "O Preconceito Racial na Escola"; Pinto, "A Representação do Negro
em Livros Didáticos de Leitura"; Rosemberg, "Segregação Espacial na Escola Paulista"; and Silva, *A Questão Indígena na Sala de Aula*.

88 Hanchard, *Orpheus and Power*, 60.

89 Quoted in Almeida, "O Racismo no Livros Didáticos," 63.

90 Ibid., 49–50.

91 Ibid., 66.

92 Fundação Nacional do Índio, "Bases Conceituais da Educação Intercultural," 1–2.

93 Ibid.

94 Ibid., 4.

95 Ibid., 2.

96 Fundação Nacional do Índio, "Programas de Formação e Capacitação de Professores que Lecionam nas Escolas Indígenas," 1. Those responsible for working with indigenous communities to establish indigenous schools are FUNAI, state and municipal secretaries of education, or NGOs (Fundação Nacional do Índio, "Bases Conceituais da Educação Intercultural," 2).

97 Fundação Nacional do Índio, "Programas de Formação e Capacitação de Professores que Lecionam nas Escolas Indígenas," 1.

98 Education for the children was to be slowly phased in as soon as enough teachers and facilities were made available.

99 Fundação Nacional do Índio, "Programa de Formalização de Parcerias," 3. In 1991, of the 1,985,825 applicants, 426,558 students were admitted to one of these institutions of higher education (Fundação Instituto Brasileiro de Geografia e Estatística, Brasil em Números, 46).

100 Ibid., 4.

101 Warren, "O Fardo de Não Ser Negro," 115. The graduation rate for Indians is based on an Indian population of 330,000 — as estimated by FUNAI in 1997 (Fundação Nacional do Índio, "A FUNAI," 1).

5. Prophetic Christianity, Indigenous Mobilization

1 West, Prophetic Fragments, 13–16.

2 Ibid., 15.

3 Lancaster, Thanks to God and the Revolution, 3.

4 I assume Lancaster attended a white Baptist church given that he did not racialize the church he attended — this despite the fact that he did situate it in terms of class, rurality, and region of the country.

5 Quoted in Davidson, "Brave Heart," 42.

6 West, Prophetic Fragments, 4.

7 Lancaster, Thanks to God and the Revolution, 3.

8 West, Prophetic Fragments, x.

9 "Usually this broad social/religious movement is referred to as 'liberation theology,' but this is inadequate, in so far as the movement appeared many years before the new theology and most of its activists are hardly theologians at all; sometimes it is also referred to as the 'Church of the Poor,' but this social network goes well beyond the limits of the Church as an institution, however broadly defined. [I prefer] to call it liberationist Christianity, this being a wider concept than either 'theology' or 'Church,' including both the religious culture and the social network, faith and praxis" (Löwy, The War of Gods, 33).

10 Bruneau, The Church in Brazil, 18.

11 Ibid., 18, 50.

12 Löwy, The War of Gods, 5. As we will see later in this chapter, John Burdick (Looking for God in Brazil) found that the construction of the "oppressed" as "the poor" —

thereby effectively ignoring or minimizing other axes of power such as gender, race, sexuality, and so on—has adversely affected who has been attracted to the so-called Church of the Poor.

13 Löwy, *The War of Gods*, 81. "The Roman Catholic church does not recognize national churches per se but, rather, aggregations of dioceses located in specific national units. The recent proliferation of national Episcopal conferences and international councils might lend some credence to the idea of national churches—and the CNBB does claim to speak for all Brazilian bishops [there are almost three hundred in Brazil]—but cooperation among the members of the church hierarchy in terms of goal implementation comes down to the actions of the individual bishop. [The bishop] has absolute power in his diocese; only the pope is superior" (Bruneau, *The Church in Brazil*, 9–10). Therefore, even though one can speak of the "position" or "stance" of the national church based on what the council of bishops decides, it must always be remembered that certain dioceses may have radically different positions on a range of issues given that it is the bishop, not the national church, who sets the "policies" of any given diocese (see ibid.)

14 Löwy, *The War of Gods*, 87.

15 Bruneau, *The Church in Brazil*, 86.

16 This statement was taken from a CIMI brochure distributed by the organization in 1997.

17 Although I am emphasizing the role of liberation theology in the production of different institutions and orientations vis-à-vis Indians, I think it crucial to bear in mind that the antiracist and decolonization movements that had touched much of the world in the 1950s and 1960s must have influenced the Brazilian church to reconsider its relationship and responsibilities to indigenous peoples. And, of course, the publication of the Figueiredo report in 1967 was probably another contributing factor (see chapter 1).

18 Writing in the early 1980s, Thomas C. Bruneau (*The Church in Brazil*, 88) remarked that "attacks are common at the local level, where CIMI personnel are frequently denied access to Indian reserves, at the regional level, where CIMI people, because of harassment or blocked communication, are not permitted in meetings of Indians hosted by FUNAI, and at the national level, where the organization is directly denounced. Since the government controls the reserves, CIMI can only protest these incidents of bad faith."

19 Bruneau, *The Church in Brazil*, 88. "Canas lived with the Enawene-Nawe people, from whom he received the name Kiwxi, and he defended the indigenous area Saluma [in Mato Grosso]. It is believed that this was the principal reason for the assassination because the fazendeiros accused him of being responsible for the Indians' resistance against invasions onto their territories" (Mundo Católico, "Governo Cria Secretaria Nacional de Direitos Humanos," 2). Mysteriously, given that he was residing in Mato Grosso at the time of his disappearance, his cranium was not found until two years later when a child came across it in a public plaza in the city of Belo Horizonte (ibid.).

20 See chapter 4.

21 This has not been the case with some of the other Christian-based organizations. Although beneficial, having agents working at the grassroots level is no safeguard against an organization becoming out of step with its constituency.

22 Quoted in "Violência Maucha a Imagen do Brasil."

23 Quoted in "FHC Diz no Canadá que Morte Causa Repulsa."

24 For example, "The Pataxó . . . in Carmésia . . . carried out a rebellion in response to the murder of their 'kin' Galdino Jesus dos Santos. . . . Painted for war, they danced in protest in the city hall and demanded the punishment of the five youth responsible for the crime (Célia, "Guerra na Câmara"). Then, too, a rally, which included Indians and Movement of Rural Workers without Land activists, took place in Brasília a few days after the murder ("Índios e Sem-Terra Protestam").

25 Francisco, "Para Fazendeiro, Ocupação Foi Ilegal." This was, of course, the reason dos Santos had been in Brasília — to force the government to remove the fazendeiros from this land that the courts had ruled was rightfully of the Pataxós.

26 Giraldi, "Índio Recebe Homenagem."

27 It should be evident at this point that by "social movement," I am not referring to the politics of "everyday life" — something I will focus on in chapters 7 and 9. Instead, I am using the term in the more conventional sense: a social movement is the extent to which an attempt to gain control over the conditions of one's life "takes the form of organized, collective actions based on solidarity and confrontation while being conscious of the expressive and strategic goals" being pursued (Veber, "The Salt of the Montaña, 383).

28 On bringing attention to persistent problems, see "Índios Sofreme Fome e Miséria."

29 By the late 1980s, UNI had fallen apart not only in eastern Brazil but in the country as a whole. Alcida Ramos (Indigenism, 140) suggests that UNI's leadership moved away from its original focus on "grassroots, unspectacular, long-term work at consciousness raising . . . emphasizing Indianness as a value to be preserved. . . . Its command changed hands, its headquarters moved to the city of São Paulo, its ties with local communities gradually severed, and by the late 1980s it ceased to exist. In turn, myriad local and regional indigenous organizations had cropped up, mostly in the 1990s and especially in the Amazon."

30 The other important regional organizations are the Indigenous Council of Minas Gerais and the Assembly of Indians from the Northeast, Minas Gerais, and Espírito Santo. Both have been financed and coordinated by CIMI-East (the latter co-sponsorship with CIMI-Northeast).

31 For example, in November 1995, CIMI (in conjunction with the Indigenous Pastors of the Maxakali, Intervalo Cinema e Vídeo, the Union of Professional Journalists of Minas Gerais, and the State University of Minas Gerais) organized an international campaign to motivate the federal and state governments to demarcate the Maxakali's land. As a part of this campaign, CIMI put together a picture journal of the Maxakali; paid for the Maxakali and other Indians from Minas Gerais to

come to Belo Horizonte for a meeting with sympathetic state representatives and to hold a press conference; and constructed a model of a Maxakali home in city hall, where a benefit party to help raise political and financial support was then held. As a consequence of this campaign, hundreds of thousands of signatures were amassed from around the world, and the state government was eventually persuaded to work out a compromise with the fazendeiros so that the land of the Maxakali will be demarcated.

32 Morris, *The Origins of the Civil Rights Movement*, 280–81.

33 Quoted in ibid., 281.

34 Morris, *The Origins of the Civil Rights Movement*, 284.

35 Escobar and Alvarez, *The Making of Social Movements in Latin America*, 14.

36 As will become much more evident in chapter 8, most racial subalterns in Brazil do not have an antiracist "common sense."

37 Contemporary theorists of social movements no longer imagine political space as being divided into two clearly demarcated camps such as "the oppressed" and "the oppressors." Instead, it is assumed that "a multiplicity of social actors establish their presence and spheres of autonomy in a fragmented social and political space. Society itself is largely shaped by a plurality of these struggles" (Escobar and Alvarez, *The Making of Social Movements in Latin America*, 3).

38 Freire, *Pedagogy of the Oppressed*, 48–49.

39 Ibid., 31, 51.

40 "By the early 1980s the number of CEBs in Brazil was estimated at around 80,000" (Burdick, *Looking for God in Brazil*, 2).

41 Ibid.

42 Ibid., 176–77.

43 Quoted in ibid., 177.

44 Burdick, *Looking for God in Brazil*, 176.

45 For more on the lei do índio, see chapter 6.

46 The fact that a fertile subjective terrain existed, that a movement culture was already in place, helps explain why CIMI was so effective in building a movement by simply providing the organizational skills and resources.

47 Quoted in Brysk, "Turning Weakness into Strength," 42.

48 Paraiso, *Laudo Antropológico sobre a Comunidade Denominada Kaxixó*, 18–20.

49 CEDEFES does much of what CIMI does—just to a smaller degree given that it has fewer resources and is focused on more than indigenous issues. One of the arenas into which CEDEFES has ventured to a greater extent than CIMI is economic development. Many Indian communities are in need of capital investment that would enable them to develop their economic infrastructure. Given their low salaries, and the fact that Indians cannot use their territories as collateral the way that private landholders can, eastern Indians are dependent on outside funding for development projects. Like CIMI, CEDEFES does not provide communities with investment capital directly but has been invaluable in assisting indigenous communities in writing grants and linking them up with philanthropists or funding

organizations. Some examples of what they have helped to finance are a community garden (with funds donated by Franciscan nuns from the Netherlands), the materials and contractors needed to build a few small houses (funded by an Austrian NGO), a small irrigation system (financed by Manes Unidas, a Spanish NGO), and some ritual houses (paid for by Father Jeronimo, a Portuguese priest).

50   The significance of such a gesture is heightened when one considers what a stigma it is for men to wear necklaces, let alone a skirt, in rural Brazil. Today, Pedro self-identifies as an Aranã Indian (he was able to determine his background when an archive was discovered in 1999 by a priest in Rome describing what Pedro believes to be the history of his people, the Aranã) and is accepted as one by Indians throughout eastern Brazil. For example, the Pankararu invited Pedro to live on the aldeia with them. He has thus far declined their invitation, but he does participate in their dances and sacred ceremonies, which are usually reserved for Indians only. Benvinda, the matriarch of the aldeia, who does not believe that Indians should marry non-Indians (see chapter 8), keeps promising to find a Pankararu wife for Pedro the next time she visits her homelands in Pernambuco. In the various interviews I conducted with eastern Indians who knew Pedro, I would ask them whether they considered him to be an Indian. No one ever hesitated to answer in the affirmative. When pressed to explain why he was an Indian, they all said it had to do with his jeito, which they assured me was distinctly Indian—a way of being they could never elaborate on, and that I could not distinguish from the behavior of other rural Brazilians. Most indicative of Pedro's complete acceptance into the eastern Indian community is the fact that he attends state and regional pan-Indian assemblies as an Indian representative. At the handful of assemblies I attended when he was present, he appeared to be treated no differently than other posttraditional delegates.

51   That same year the courts ruled in their favor, granting the Kaxixó title to twenty-eight hectares of land. This land, the courts decided, had been illegally appropriated from them by the local fazendeiros.

52   Recall from chapters 3 and 4 that a number of Xacriabá were murdered at this time in a similar struggle over land. Then, too, the courts ruled during this same year that the Xacriabá were Indians and thus entitled to several thousand hectares of land, prompting the forced removal of fazendeiros from the region.

53   On a brief visit to aldeia Apukaré in October 2000, I learned that the presence of the Pankararu has encouraged several of Pedro's kin to take seriously "Indianness" as a possible identity. In fact, since I was last in the region in 1995, more than one hundred individuals have come to self-identify as Aranã. They consider themselves Aranã because they have determined via oral histories, church records, municipal archives, and planters' documents that they are the descendants of Pedro Sangê, an Aranã who in the late nineteenth century had been brought from the Itambacuri mission to be a slave on the plantation where Pedro and his immediate family still live and work. As Indians, the Aranã have been sending representatives to the various Indian meetings and conferences in eastern Brazil and have petitioned the

bishop in Araçuaí to grant them land to begin building aldeia Pedro Sangê, adjacent to aldeia Apukaré.

In addition to the Aranã, there are a number of caboclo families who live near and wish to have more contact with the Pankararu and Aranã. These families are believed to be descendants of either the Maxakali—who consider the region where the Pankararu now live their original homeland—or, like the Aranã, mission Indians of Itambacuri. When I was recently there, the Pankararu and Aranã debated their status and decided to intensify their association with these families. This does not mean that these individuals or their children will develop an Indian identity, but it is possible, especially considering what has happened with the Aranã.

6. The Common Sense of Racial Formation

1   Torres-Saillant, "The Tribulations of Blackness," 139.

2   Alarcón, "Racial Prejudice."

3   Degler, *Neither Black nor White*, 167. Karen Blu (*The Lumbee Problem*) found that the same type of critique is frequently leveled against the Lumbee Indians of North Carolina, many of whom are of African, indigenous, and European descent. It is argued that they are alleging an Indian identity so as not to be categorized as black.

4   Warren and Twine, "Critical Race Studies in Latin America."

5   See Wagley, *Race and Class in Rural Brazil*.

6   Costa, *The Brazilian Empire*, 241–42.

7   I am grateful to Edward Telles for his generosity in making this data available to me.

8   This may, at first glance, seem to contradict what I argued in chapter 4, when I discussed how in certain regions, in particular where Indians have been engaged in struggle with non-Indians over land and other resources, anti-Indian sentiments are heightened. Recall, however, that I described the common sense of these regions of contestation as a more odious articulation of the precepts of Indianness invoked by non-Indians in general—thus, not an alternative set of precepts. Furthermore, one of the principal emphases in this chapter, unlike chapter 4, is on the diacritics of Indianness. In terms of *who* is considered Indian, there was little variability among non-Indians regardless of region.

9   This, of course, does not mean that these two discursive fields are neatly contained. As I will show, there is overlap, synthesis, dialogue, critique, exchange, transculturation, and so forth between the two laws. Moreover, these differing common senses are not automatic or mechanistic outgrowths of an individual's racial position or identity. This will be illustrated later in this chapter when I examine the experiences of Indians who adhere more closely to the law of the white.

10 Hall, "Gramsci's Relevance for the Study of Race and Ethnicity," 431.

11 In eastern Brazil, "Asians" were neither numerically nor symbolically relevant. This is partly due to the fact that Japanese Brazilians are concentrated in São Paulo. It also likely has something to do with the fact that Asians are not considered to be one of the primary races of the nation.

12 Gilliam, "From Roxbury to Rio," 177–78.

13 It is worth noting how this differs from the United States, where individuals of both African and indigenous descent have historically been constructed as black (see Forbes, *Africans and Native Americans*).

14 There are numerous sorts of mestizos, some of which are considered closer to the black end of the somatic continuum. The two major mestizo categories used in everyday parlance are moreno and mulatto. A rough definition of the distinction is to think of morenos as closer to the white end of the continuum and mulattos as closer to the black pole. Thus, a white and a moreno would be predicted to produce a white child, whereas a white and a mulatto would either have a moreno or a white child—although it might take one more mixing, in the minds of non-Indian Brazilians, to produce a white child given mulattos' greater distance from whiteness. Within this conceptual schema, Indians are thought of as more closely equivalent to moreno than mulatto.

15 Simpson, *Xuxa*, 37–38.

16 By biological capital, I mean both phenotype and genotype. "Indian looks" are considered more desirable than "black looks." And even if one does not "appear Indian," if one is viewed to be of Indian descent, one will have more "genetic capital" than an individual with the same appearances, but who is considered to be of exclusive African descent. That is because such a person will be thought of as more likely to produce whiter offspring than an individual of putatively pure African lineage.

17 Fothergill, "On Conrad, Cannibals, and Kin," 49.

18 Potiguara, "Harvesting What We Plant," 46.

19 This is why, in recent decades, a common visual trope of Indians in Brazil is that of them watching television or drinking soda. To a non-Indian Brazilian, such an image is symbolically disjunctive and so an attention grabber—"an interesting photo."

20 See Ramos, *Indigenism*; and Warren, "The Brazilian Geography of Indianness."

21 Taussig, *Shamanism, Colonialism, and the Wild Man*.

22 See Ramos, *Indigenism*; and Warren, "The Brazilian Geography of Indianness."

23 Quoted in Burdick, *Looking for God in Brazil*, 163–64.

24 See Ramos, *Indigenism*; and Warren, "The Brazilian Geography of Indianness."

25 Informal conversation with Camillo Vasalia, 1992.

26 See Ramos, *Indigenism*, 163. Indians are often territorialized as creatures of the forest, which has the effect of reinforcing the notion of Indians as antimoderns, especially given that modernity tends to be imagined in opposition to nature. The irony is that this iconography undermines, rather than promotes, a green agenda. The Brazilians I met symbolically linked modernization with a physical terrain that excludes nature. Therefore, as long as nature is considered antithetical to modernity, as "in the way of progress," then the environmental movement will likely encounter difficulties in generating grassroots support. Yet instead of naturalizing modernity, the creature of the forest iconography, however noble it may be, simply

reinforces the idea that nature is the topography of primitive, nonmodern peoples. It thus reinscribes the notion that nature is a space separate from civilizations (the People of the World) and modernity (Technology), which in the end cannot but impair a green politic given how anxious most Brazilians are to modernize (see Warren, "The Brazilian Geography of Indianness").

27 Again, this is especially true in the zones of contestations mentioned in chapter 4.

28 Ramos, *Indigenism*, 163.

29 For example, I sometimes heard non-Indian parents berate their children's poor table manners by demanding they "stop eating like an Indian."

30 Quoted in Ramos, *Indigenism*, 46.

31 Ramos, *Indigenism*, 48.

32 See photo of Paulo in chapter 4.

33 This facet of the law of the white is enshrined in the Brazilian Civil Code: "Although the Constitution grants Indians the right to remain Indians, the Civil Code . . . declares that such status will eventually be suspended. The expectation is that the Indians will 'adapt' to Brazilian civilization and hence stop being Indians. The assumption is that one cannot be 'adapted' and continue to be an Indian. Adaptation would mean a change in ethnic identity" (Ramos, *Indigenism*, 19).

34 Lippard, Introduction, 26–27.

35 The interviewer was France Winddance Twine.

36 Ramos, *Indigenism*, 47. The meaning of this analogy hinges on the Brazilian notion of wilderness (or nature) as antimodern (see Warren, "The Brazilian Geography of Indianness"). Such a territorialization of modernity poses, of course, a substantive challenge to the Brazilian environmental movement as well as the Indian movement (given that Indians are constructed as creatures of the forest).

37 See chapter 4.

38 Ramos, *Indigenism*, 23.

39 Freyre, *The Masters and the Slaves*, 279–81.

40 Note that along the symbolic continuum of contributions to the nation, Indians rank below blacks and concomitantly so too does their Brazilianness.

41 Burdick, *Looking for God in Brazil*, 164.

42 Williams, *Stains on My Name, War in My Veins*, 171.

43 To call someone black (negro) in Brazil is generally considered rude and offensive in much the same way that it was an insult to refer to a person as black in the United States prior to the civil rights movement.

44 See chapter 4.

45 See photo of Oswaldo in chapter 1.

46 A common trope in Brazilian popular thought is the story of the grandmother who was supposedly caught with a lasso and then civilized. I will return to this narrative, and eastern Indians' response to it, in chapter 8.

47 Mata, "Kariri Xocó," 4.

48 According to Geralda Chaves Soares, "Salvinho's sister was dating one of the men from the upper Pataxó. On discovering the relationship, Salvinho forbade his sis-

ter from seeing her lover on the grounds that he was not an Indian. Escalating the dispute, he then confronted his sister's lover. Salvinho not only accused [the upper Pataxó of being a racial charlatan] but also called him 'negro feo' [the equivalent of 'nigger']. In retaliation, the young man brutally attacked Salvinho, who nearly died from the machete wounds and remains partially paralyzed. In the aftermath of this assault, tensions between the two communities have heightened and nearly erupted, in a few instances, into further violence" (telephone conversation with Geralda Chaves Soares, 15 August 2000.)

49   See chapter 5.

50   Pratt, *Imperial Eyes*, 6.

51   See Vizenor, *Manifest Manners*. There are, of course, dangers involved in these sorts of symbolic incursions. Such transculturations could be reappropriated and used for anti-Indian racism. Moreover, political alliances built on these ideals can prove extremely precarious. For example, claims to territories based in part on the noble savage imagining can prove tenuous when a community wants to develop or use its resources in "nonharmonious manners" (see Warren, "The Brazilian Geography of Indianness"). The weakness of this trope also surfaces when a whale or nature preserve—rather than a plantation—is at stake. For instance, in defense of not returning the national park, Monte Pascoal (some of the land that was stolen from the Pataxó in 1951), to the Pataxó, the park's director, Silvio da Cruz Freire, immediately attacked the idea of the noble savage: "A significant portion of the depredations this park has suffered are due to the Indians, so for them to suddenly present themselves as protectors of the environment flies in the face of reality. I can't remember a time when there haven't been Indians inside the park burning trees to plant their crops or cutting them down to use in making handicrafts" (quoted in Rohter, "Indian Tribe Wants Brazil's Plymouth Rock Back," 3). Thus, claims to land based on faux representations rather than history and ethics can prove perilous indeed (see Cook-Lynn, "Land Reform").

52   Jean Baudrillard, *Simulacra and Simulations*. Quoted in Vizenor, *Manifest Manners*, 9.

53   Again, for a detailed analysis of how the discourses of firstness and contributions are intertwined with the cultural politics of race, see Williams, *Stains on My Name, War in My Veins*.

54   The historical reality was, of course, much more complex. For instance, George Reid Andrews (*Blacks and Whites in São Paulo*) argues that slavery was brought to an end by one of the few, if not the only, examples of mass popular revolt in Brazil.

55   Burdick, "The Lost Constituency of Brazil's Black Movements," 151.

56   It should be stressed that no one individual perfectly exemplifies the lei do índio or lei do branco. This is because most individual leis of Indianness are influenced to varying degrees by these different leis, as well as by other, often seemingly unrelated, ideas and notions, which are then fused and combined in idiosyncratic and sometimes creative ways. Furthermore, although I said that Indians tended to construct their own common sense more closely to the lei do índio, this was only a tendency and not something that could be generalized to all Indians or whites. There

were, of course, Indians whose views more closely paralleled the lei do branco, just as there were whites whose views more closely approximated the law of the Indian.

57 With respect to her own encounters with discrimination in school, see the excerpt from Dorinha's interview in chapter 3.

58 The likelihood of being exposed to the law of the Indian increased if one lived in an Indian community or had more frequent contact with such a community. In such cases, children were not as dependent on their parents to provide them with an alternative repertoire. This is probably why I found that children raised in Indian communities were likely to identify as Indian, even in those few instances where their parents had a common sense that more closely paralleled the law of the white. Children who grew up away from such a community were much more dependent on their parents for exposure to such a lei, and as such, there was a much stronger correlation between the parent and children's lei outside of Indian communities.

7. Indian Judges

1 This governmental decree represented the regulation of Article 2, Decree (Decreto) 94,946, 23 September 1987 (Conselho Indigenista Missionario, Legislação Indigenista Brasileira, 67–68).

2 Kuper, The Invention of Primitive Society, 4.

3 Lévi-Strauss, The Savage Mind.

4 Kuper, The Invention of Primitive Society, 5.

5 On globalizing oppositions, see chapter 1.

6 Service, Primitive Social Organization, 8–9.

7 Wade, Race and Ethnicity in Latin America.

8 Berwick, Savages, 3.

9 Wade, Race and Ethnicity in Latin America, 43, 46.

10 Ibid., 46.

11 See Portillo, Mirrors of the Heart.

12 This idea of modern culture being stronger than primitive culture, coupled with the notion that identities followed from culture, helps explain why cultural contact was presumed to lead to the erosion of Indian subjectivities but not non-Indian ones. In other words, cultural interchange was believed to erode tribal identities, whereas non-Indians went unaffected. And so a Yanomami, as Berwick (Savages, 4) suggests, would be considered less Yanomami if she carried a metal pot, but the white would not be considered less white if he used quinine to cure malaria.

13 Wagley, Amazon Town, 39–40.

14 Ibid., 39.

15 Ibid., 40.

16 The savage mind is, I believe, one of the reasons that Darcy Ribeiro wrongly prophesized that Indians would become extinct by the end of the twentieth century (see chapter 1). Alcida Ramos attributes his prediction to the realities of Indian exorcism. She writes, "Ribeiro's pessimism was understandable, given the constant

depopulation, loss of territory, exploitation of resources and labor, and armed persecution. For nearly five centuries people after people faced the same problems, which led many to extinction and others to precarious survival" (Ramos, *Indigenism*, 119). But much of his forecast likely also rested on the notion that Indian identities were grounded in contained, unpolluted, antimodern cultures. As Indians were culturally transformed by the expanding contact zones, it was assumed that they would become Indian only in phenotype (and stigmatized as such), but devoid of any specific cultures or traditions (Ribeiro, *Os Índios e a Civilização*, 222).

17 Berwick, *Savages*, 2.

18 Sampaio, *De Caboclo a Índio*, 3.

19 Barth, *Ethnic Groups and Boundaries*, 11.

20 Wade, *Race and Ethnicity in Latin America*, 44.

21 Barth, *Ethnic Groups and Boundaries*, 14–15.

22 Ibid., 15.

23 Warren, *Indigenous Movements and Their Critics*, 12.

24 Ibid.

25 Varese, "The Ethnopolitics of Indian Resistance in Latin America," 63.

26 Hill, *History, Power, and Identity*, 2.

27 Barth, *Ethnic Groups and Boundaries*, 11.

28 Berwick, *Savages*, 1–2.

29 Hill, *History, Power, and Identity*, 1.

30 On liberation movements in Brazil, see chapter 3.

31 Skidmore, *Black into White*, 214.

32 Ramos, *Indigenism*, 249. A few years earlier, Interior Minister Maurício Rangel Reis had proposed an "emancipation decree" that would have given FUNAI the authority to terminate indigenous special status. It was an attempt to appropriate Indian lands and "integrate" Indians into national society—that is, exorcise Indians from the nation. Due to intense international and national protests, however, the proposal was never enacted.

33 Ibid.

34 See Reesink, "Índio ou Caboclo," 123.

35 See chapter 6.

36 Conselho Indigenista Missionario, *Legislação Indigenista Brasileira*, 38. Silvícola literally means "inhabitant of the forest." This continues to be an official category of Indianness and illustrates how Indians are territorialized (see Warren, "The Brazilian Geography of Indianness").

37 See Reesink, "Índio ou Caboclo," 122.

38 Paraiso, *Laudo Antropológico sobre a Comunidade Denomidada Kaxixó*, 5.

39 See chapter 1.

40 Wagley, *Amazon Town*, 40.

41 The Toré is a circle or round dance, often accompanied by singers and rattlers, performed by Indians throughout eastern and northeastern Brazil.

42 Reesink, "Índio ou Caboclo," 128–29.

43 Ribeiro, *Os Índios e a Civilização*, 56.

44 See Reesink, "Índio ou Caboclo"; and Sampaio, *De Caboclo a Índio*.

45 Quoted in Sampaio, *De Caboclo a Índio*, ii.

46 By official, I am referring to judicial, state bureaucratic, and legislative discourses. Again, since anthropologists are recognized as Indian experts, they play a powerful role in shaping these official constructions of Indianness.

47 Quoted in Skidmore, *Black into White*, 277.

48 Hutchinson, "Race Relations in a Rural Community of the Bahian Reconcavo," 28.

49 Nugent, *Amazonian Caboclo Society*, 23.

50 Ibid., 45.

51 Pace, *The Struggle for Amazon Town*, 145.

52 Ibid.

53 On fear of Indian exorcism, see chapter 3.

54 Hutchinson, "Race Relations in a Rural Community of the Bahian Reconcavo," 31.

55 Oliveira, "As Facções e a Ordem Politica em uma Reserva Tukuna," 157.

56 Reesink, "Índio ou Caboclo," 133–34.

57 Ibid., 134.

58 Reesink clearly saw the purity requirement as ridiculous. Instead, the emphasis is placed on "boundaries"—identities and counteridentities. And in the last sentence of the above-quoted passage, Reesink even implies that a caboclo identity is a form of internalized racism.

59 Paraiso, *Laudo Antropológico sobre a Indentidade Etnica dos Xacriabá*.

60 Reesink, "Índio ou Caboclo," 128.

61 Ibid., 129.

8. Contesting White Supremacy

1 For an overview of the literature on racial disparities in Brazil, Andrews, *Blacks and Whites in São Paulo*; Burdick, *Blessed Anastácia*; Hanchard, *Orpheus and Power*; Reichmann, *Race in Contemporary Brazil*; Silva and Hasenbalg, *Relações Raciais no Brasil Contemporaneo*; Simpson, *Xuxa*; and Twine, *Racism in a Racial Democracy*.

2 Hanchard, *Orpheus and Power*, 5–6.

3 See Barcelos, "Struggling in Paradise," 156.

4 See Hanchard, "Black Cinderella?" 71.

5 See Hanchard, *Orpheus and Power*; and Twine, *Racism in a Racial Democracy*.

6 Winant, *Racial Conditions*, 146.

7 These are rounded-off percentages. Out of a total population of 146,815,705, 75,704,934 Brazilians self-identified as white, 7,335,116 as black, 630,633 as amarelos (Asian), 62,316,045 as pardos, 294,118 as indígena, and 534,859 were undeclared (Fundação Instituto Brasileiro de Geografia e Estatística, *Censo Demográfico 1991*, 178–80).

8 On the decline in black population, see Hanchard, Introduction, 9.

9 Hanchard, *Orpheus and Power*, 100.

10 See ibid.

11 Burdick, "Brazil's Black Consciousness Movement," 25. In eastern Brazil, virtually every Indian I met could be considered an active follower. That is, they were
sympathetic to the agenda of the movement, sometimes participated in movement
organizations, and when possible, took part in political actions. To make a conservative estimate, at least two-thirds of those who identified as Indian could be considered active followers. Given that approximately seventy thousand individuals
identified as Indian in eastern and northeastern Brazil (see chapter 1), that would
put the number of participants in this region at roughly forty-five thousand.

12 See Burdick, "Brazil's Black Consciousness Movement"; and Andrews, *Blacks and
Whites in São Paulo*.

13 Forbes, *Africans and Native Americans*, 244.

14 See Piza and Rosemberg, "Color in the Brazilian Census," 51.

15 Buckley, "Native Struggle to Keep Identities," 2; Forbes, *Africans and Native Americans*, 245.

16 Forbes, *Africans and Native Americans*, 244.

17 Bento, "Silent Conflict," 110.

18 Burdick, "The Lost Constituency of Brazil's Black Movements," 138.

19 It should be added that not only do many pardos not self-identify as black but they
would be deeply offended, given their derogatory notions of blackness, by even
the suggestion that they were black (see Gilliam and Gilliam, "Odyssey," 76; and
Penha-Lopes, "What Next?" 823).

20 Most U.S. blacks—like pardos in Brazil—are of indigenous, African, and European descent. In fact, much of slave culture, the antecedent of U.S. black culture,
was heavily influenced by the thousands of indigenous people who were part of
the general slave population. These sorts of cultural and biological components of
blackness have largely been ignored or minimized because blackness has come to
be imagined as an African-only category (see Forbes, *Africans and Native Americans*).

21 On the exaggerated differences between the two countries, mulattoness is a good
example. Although certainly less prevalent than in Brazil, it has always been a part
of the U.S. racial landscape. Until the 1920s, the U.S. census used it as an official
racial category. Moreover, many nineteenth- and twentieth-century laws used the
term *mulatto* (as distinct from black), and it continues to figure as a self-identity for
some individuals of African descent (see Twine, Warren, and Ferrandiz, *Just Black?*).
Several researchers have found that there is little difference in Brazil between mulattoes and blacks in terms of employment opportunities, returns for education,
symbolic violence, and so on.

22 Harris, "Racial Identity in Brazil," 22.

23 See Warren, "O Fardo de Não Ser Negro"; and Warren, "Masters in the Field."

24 See Pinto, "Movimento Negro e Educação do Negro," 33.

25 See chapter 6.

26 Wade, *Race and Ethnicity in Latin America*.

27 Ibid., 37.

28 Ibid.

29 Ibid., 39.

30 Ibid., 38.

31 Ibid., 37.

32 E-mail correspondence with Sonia Travassos on 17 March 1999.

33 See chapter 6.

34 Radcliffe and Westwood, *Remaking the Nation*, 18.

35 See Andrews, *Blacks and Whites in São Paulo*; Bento, "Silent Conflict"; Burdick, *Blessed Anastácia*; Hasenbalg, *Discriminação e Desigualdades Racias no Brasil*; Piza and Rosemberg, "Color in the Brazilian Census"; and Twine, *Racism in a Racial Democracy*.

36 The ubiquitous nature of whitening in Brazil is underscored by how a number of nongovernmental organizations chose to expend their energies and resources in the year prior to the 1991 census. With funding from the Ford Foundation, several NGOs launched a campaign under the slogan "*Não deixe sua côr passar em branco. Responda com bom censo*" ("Don't let your color pass into white. Respond with good sense").

37 In Brazil, there is a social etiquette operating that instructs everyone to "lighten" one's description of others. Even if an individual saw someone else as black, for example, they would rarely refer to them as such, unless they wanted to offend the person. Instead, if the subject could not be completely avoided, the preferred strategy would be to refer to the person as mulatto, moreno, or white as a matter of courtesy (see Guimarães, "Measures to Combat Discrimination and Racial Inequality in Brazil," 142).

38 Reichmann, Introduction, 8; see also Carneiro, "Black Women's Identity in Brazil."

39 See Burdick, *Blessed Anastácia*, 39.

40 Quoted in Twine, *Racism in a Racial Democracy*, 93.

41 Piza and Rosemberg, "Color in the Brazilian Census," 47.

42 Benvinda, a fifty-eight-year-old Pankararu spiritual leader for the Apukaré aldeia, is described in fuller detail in chapter 4.

43 See Burdick, *Blessed Anastácia*; Harris, "Racial Identity in Brazil"; Twine, *Racism in a Racial Democracy*; and Warren, "Masters in the Field."

44 Santos, "Women and Racism," 52. See also Andrews, *Blacks and Whites in São Paulo*; Burdick, *Blessed Anastácia*; and Twine, *Racism in a Racial Democracy*. Another explanation less frequently offered was that "opposites attract."

45 Quoted in Twine, *Racism in a Racial Democracy*, 91.

46 See Scheper-Hughes, *Death without Weeping*; Sheriff, " 'Negro Is a Nickname That the Whites Gave to the Blacks' "; and Twine, *Racism in a Racial Democracy*.

47 Scheper-Hughes, *Death without Weeping*, 90.

48 Quoted in Twine, *Racism in a Racial Democracy*, 118.

49 "Folkloric to a fault is the much repeated story (by all sorts of people, including São Paulo taxi drivers) of the Indian grandmother who was caught with a lasso. It is a little half-joke usually told in the most candid of moods and as if it were highly original to people who are perceived as having anything to do with Indians or even to Indians themselves. It goes without saying that the joke never involves an Indian

grandfather or father (too humiliating for a man) or an Indian mother (too close for comfort) who was lassoed. To have a wild Indian grandmother is reason for pride; it is a valid passport to authentic Brazilianness" (Ramos, *Indigenism*, 69).

50   I have hazel eyes and straight, black hair (see the photo of me in chapter 2).

51   See chapter 3.

52   See the introduction for their origin story.

53   In some ways, these words are a window into the principal categories of difference, desire, and anxiety in eastern Indian communities. Gay is the word perhaps most in need of explanation. Among both Indians and non-Indians, suggesting that a man was gay was a prevalent means of insulting men, of questioning their masculinity. The importance of gayness, as a negative referent, to most Brazilian men's masculinity and sense of self probably accounts for why the Maxakali word for gay was widely known. The other likely reason is that the word for gay, *manãite*, is similar to that for cow (*manãy*).

54   See photo of Karakana Canoeiro in chapter 1.

55   Geralda Chaves Soares was the CIMI pastoral who accompanied the Maxakali in the 1980s until she was forced to leave due to death threats (see chapter 5).

56   See photo of Valmares Pataxó in chapter 4.

57   See chapter 4.

58   See photo of ritual cabana in chapter 2.

59   To non-Indians these structures also signify poverty, backwardness, primitiveness, and so on (see Wagley, *Amazon Town*). Consequently, non-Indians would never dream of conducting important rituals or ceremonies (such as a wedding) in such structures. In rural areas, these cabanas are where poor people live, or they are used for storage and to house animals. In tourist areas, variations on these structures are used as bars.

60   See the photo of Puhuí and his wife, Eunice, in chapter 6; to their right is their pintura.

61   Degler, *Neither Black nor White*, 167.

62   Spyer, "Urban Indians," 437.

63   Both of these ceremonies included the construction of particular structures with special rituals — such as a male carrying a heavy rock for a long distance to symbolize the burdens he would be expected to bear during marriage — and the wearing of "traditional" clothing — such as grass skirts, body painting, and necklaces and rings that were made in the community. To conduct the Krenak wedding, a specific ritual house had to be carefully built according to the recollections of Krenak elders.

64   In the early twentieth century, the Dança do Tambor used to last two to three days. The captain of the tambor, all dressed up in ritual attire and wielding a staff, would go from house to house gathering Indians to participate in the dance, which was supposed to call forth the master of the forest. For the occasion, Indian women would prepare a drink, *a coaba*, made from fermented cassava. The percussion instruments used were a rattle (*a matraca*) and a leather drum (*o tambor*). In the past,

the captain of the tambor enjoyed a position of high status, and was recognized as a healer and community leader. The dance of the tambor reinforced an exchange between Tupinikim communities as well as their symbolic integration. It was the "residual culture" that gave support to indigenous resurgence, and made possible the establishment of a distinctive culture and the Tupinikim's recognition as distinct by the wider regional population. The ritual almost disappeared because it signified cabocloness to non-Indians in the region and thus attracted anti-Indian violence. In the postexorcist era, the dance of the tambor has made a gradual return, especially in the Caieiras Velhas community (see Freire, "Tupiniquim"). For a brief description of the Ouricuri, see chapter 4.

65   Pai da Mata, literally Father of the Forest, is sometimes regarded as a sort of trickster figure. For example, many hunters would warn about the Pai da Mata intentionally confusing them so that they would become lost. Others spoke of Pai da Mata as a more vengeful, rather than playful, God. It was common to hear Pataxó warning others to not mistreat the forest, otherwise Pai da Mata would make sure they perished in the forest. Also, a number of Pataxó were interested in reviving a dance that is intended to call forth the Pai da Mata—a dance that sounded similar to the Dança do Tambor described in the previous note. As for the Krenak, according to Maria Hilda Baqueiro Paraiso, the *Maréts* ("responsible for female fertility and for delivering notices from the dead") have lost their importance, but the *Tokón* ("the spirits of nature; they are responsible for the selection of shamans, the earthly intermediaries to the Tokón") have assumed a central place in the contemporary Krenak religious universe. The *Nanitiong* ("the great organizers of natural phenomena") and spirits of death continue to be significant as well. There is also a vibrant movement among the Krenak to revive the Borun language, traditional songs, dances, rituals, child rearing, hunting and medical practices, as well as to recover the sacred totem that was stolen from them in the 1930s (see Paraiso, "Krenák," 2, 10).

66   See the photo of a Toré dance in chapter 7.

67   Mata, "Kariri Xocó," 11.

68   See photo of Salvinho Pataxó in chapter 6.

69   Exactly like in Canada until 1985, an Indian woman in Brazil who takes a non-Indian partner is required to leave the reserve. Men, in contrast, can marry non-Indians and still live on the aldeia. This ordinance is particularly irksome to most Indian women, who see it as a clear case of gender bias. The men were more divided over this issue. Unlike the Indian men in Canada, who defended such an ordinance by arguing that it was based on "Indian traditions" (see Silman, *Enough is Enough*), posttraditional Indians who were in favor of the ordinance never invoked such a justification. They clearly believed it to be a construction of FUNAI, not a continuation of any tribal tradition. Instead, they employed sexist constructions of men and women to support their position. Those in favor of it argued that it was "because men are more powerful" and therefore a white man on the aldeia could completely transform the society, whereas women, "as the weaker sex," would not have such

an impact. Those men against the ordinance were so not because it was sexist or unfair but rather because they saw it as a means of letting more non-Indians onto the aldeia—something they strongly opposed.

70 Quoted in Rohter, "Brazil Carnival's Fabled Amity May Hide Bigotry," 3.

71 On the history of black organizations, see See Andrews, *Blacks and Whites in São Paulo;* Barcelos, "Struggling in Paradise"; Nascimento, *Brazil;* and Pinto, "Movimento Negro e Educação do Negro."

72 See Burdick, *Blessed Anastácia;* Reichmann, *Race in Contemporary Brazil;* Twine, *Racism in a Racial Democracy;* and Wagley, *Race and Class in Rural Brazil.*

73 In Brazil, to have "blue blood" means to be of racially mixed descent.

74 In the interview, she said that all of the teachers in her school had been white. Helena also showed me one of her textbooks. Like other high school texts in Brazil, the only images of nonwhites were as servants, buffoons, or sports players. Moreover, racism and the realities of slavery and conquest were never even broached.

75 See Andrews, *Blacks and Whites in São Paulo;* Reichmann, *Race in Contemporary Brazil;* and Twine, *Racism in a Racial Democracy.*

76 Simpson, "Easy Talk, White Talk, Back Talk," 377.

77 Scheper-Hughes, *Death without Weeping,* 90.

78 Reichmann, "Brazil's Denial of Race," 35.

79 Guimarães, "Racism and Anti-Racism in Brazil," 208.

80 Ibid.

81 See also Barcelos, "Struggling in Paradise."

82 See Bento, "Silent Conflict"; Hasenbalg, *Discriminação e Desigualdades Racias no Brasil;* and Twine, *Racism in a Racial Democracy.*

83 Quoted in Twine, *Racism in a Racial Democracy,* 77–78.

84 See Burdick, *Blessed Anastácia;* Guimarães, "Measures to Combat Discrimination and Racial Inequality in Brazil"; Hanchard, *Racial Politics in Contemporary Brazil;* Piza and Rosemberg, "Color in the Brazilian Census"; and Twine, *Racism in a Racial Democracy.* Since virtually everyone in Brazil could technically be classified as moreno, except for whites who are blond, Nancy Scheper-Hughes suggests that this term has the effect of blurring racial hierarchies: "[Nonwhites] call themselves simply *os pobres* [the poor] and they describe themselves as *moreno* [brown], almost never as *preto* or *negro* (black). They are 'brown,' then, as all Brazilians, rich and poor, are said to be 'brown.' In this way, the ideology of 'racial democracy,' as pernicious as the American ideology of 'equality of opportunity,' goes unchallenged, uncontested, into another generation" (*Death without Weeping,* 90).

85 Karakana, as I mentioned above, was a nanny for a wealthy family in Belo Horizonte. See her photo in chapter 1.

86 Twine, *Racism in a Racial Democracy,* 139.

87 Quoted in Burdick, *Blessed Anastácia,* 139.

88 Hanchard, *Orpheus and Power,* 6.

89 Ibid., 63.

90 Burdick, "The Lost Constituency of Brazil's Black Movements," 141–42.

91 Telles, "Início no Brasil e Fim no EUA?" 194.

92 On racism in curricula, see Hanchard, *Orpheus and Power*, 60; and Silva, *A Questão Indígena na Sala de Aula*.

93 Cleonice Pankararu was the only high school graduate at this time and she had moved to Espírito Santo.

94 See the photos of an Indian school in chapter 4.

95 See Barcelos, "Struggling in Paradise," 164.

96 Oliveira, "Favelas and Ghettos," 84.

97 Quoted in Barcelos, "Struggling in Paradise," 164.

98 See Burdick, "The Lost Constituency of Brazil's Black Movements," 142; Hanchard, *Orpheus and Power*, 63; Sheriff, "Negro is a Nickname"; and Twine, *Racism in a Racial Democracy*.

99 See Twine, *Racism in a Racial Democracy*.

100 Hanchard, *Orpheus and Power*, 63.

101 Quoted in Burdick, *Blessed Anastácia*, 143.

102 Quoted in Nascimento, Brazil, 84–85; taken from "an interview given to Christina Lyro for the influential *Journal do Brasil*."

103 "Racismo Cordial."

104 Andrews, *Blacks and Whites in São Paulo*, 175.

105 Reichmann, Introduction, 18.

106 Ibid., 5.

107 Quoted in Barcelos, "Struggling in Paradise," 164.

108 Burdick, *Looking for God in Brazil*, 148.

109 Guimarães, "Review of *Racism in a Racial Democracy*," 192–93.

110 Hale, "Cultural Politics of Identity in Latin America," 568.

111 Pinto, "Movimento Negro e Educação do Negro," 33.

Epilogue

1 Rohter, "Bitter Indians Let Ecuador Know Fight Isn't Over," 2.

2 Ibid.

3 Warren, *Indigenous Movements and Their Critics*, 36.

4 Ibid., 11.

5 Ibid., 7.

6 See Knight, "Racism, Revolution, and *Indigenismo*," 76.

7 Ibid.

8 Ibid.

9 El Movimiento de Unificación de la Lucha Triqui was founded in the late 1970s. Currently this organization, composed of ninety-eight villages, is fighting for the release of political prisoners, a demilitarization of the Triqui region, and assistance with education, health, and economic development (Hewett, "Challenging the 'Mestizo Nation,' " 7). La Asemblea de Autoridades Zapotecas y Chinantecas de la Sierra was founded in 1979 to promote cultural revitalization, teach indigenous languages in public schools, improve health and education in indigenous commu-

nities, protect the civil rights of indigenous peoples, and achieve greater political autonomy for indigenous communities (ibid., 8). "The Totonac movement was formalized in 1989 and its goals include 'self-determination and autonomy, enhancement of culture, health, and nutrition, development of organic and sustainable agriculture, democratization of government through a People's Council and the restoration of traditional religion and customs.' One of the movement's recent successes includes procuring a loan from the municipal treasury for the establishment of its own bilingual school" (ibid., 8; see also Wahrhaftig and Lane, "Totonac Cultural Revitalization"). Finally, Ejército Zapatista Liberación Nacional (EZLN emerged on the national and international scene in 1994. As occurred in Ecuador the same year, the EZLN mobilized in response to neoliberal agrarian reform that entailed the official abandonment of land reform—a key promise of the Mexican Revolution. The other aims of the EZLN include the release of political prisoners, redefinition of Mexico as pluricultural, recognition of indigenous collective rights of "autonomy" (that is, political devolution), and promotion of indigenous culture (such as support for bilingual education) (see Collier, "Zapatismo Resurgent").

10 Quoted in Hewett, "Challenging the 'Mestizo Nation,' " 6.

11 "Hewett, "Challenging the 'Mestizo Nation,' " 7; see also Collier, "Zapatismo Resurgent," 22.

12 "Demographically, 90 percent of the indigenous population in the Americas—which totals approximately 36 million people—live in Mexico, Guatemala, Ecuador, Bolivia and Peru. While Mexico has the largest number of indigenous citizens, more than 10.5 million, they represent only 12.4 percent of the national population. . . . There are indigenous majorities in Guatemala, where 5.4 million indigenous citizens make up 60.3 percent of the population, and in Bolivia, where 5 million indigenous citizens make up 71.2 percent of the population" (Warren, *Indigenous Movements and Their Critics,* 8–9).

13 See Collins, "A Sense of Possibility," 48.

14 On the blocking of neoliberal agrarian reforms, see Pacari, "Taking on the Neoliberal Agenda," 23. As for the Pachakutik movement, it "is a coalition with non-indigenous social movements and thus is not solely an indigenous party. In both [the] 1996 and 1998 elections Pachakutik candidates won seats at all levels of government, from town councils to Congress. Currently there are 53 indigenous politicians elected on the Pachakutik ticket holding local and provincial seats, and four holding seats in Congress. With two mestizo deputies, there are a total of six Pachakutik members within the 123-member Congress. Pachakutik members also won seven seats to the National Constitutional Assembly, established in 1998 to reform the Constitution" (Collins, "A Sense of Possibility," 44).

15 In the United States, many of the conceptual shifts, legal changes, and political strategies that helped the Indian movement advance were created or coined by the black movement. In Latin America, the influence seems to be in much the opposite direction. For instance, in Ecuador, Adam Halpern and France Winddance Twine observe that the black movement has "modeled [its] strategies after suc-

cessful approaches used by other indigenous peoples in their claims for territo-rial autonomy in the early 1990s." They add that "as Blacks have adopted many of the same 'strategy' and 'identity' issues of Indians, they have also conceptualized and framed their movement as an 'indigenous' movement" (Halpern and Twine, "Antiracist Activism in Ecuador"). For a similar example of the linkages between indigenous peoples' organizations and black mobilization in Colombia, see Wade, "The Cultural Politics of Blackness in Colombia."

16 Although eventually abandoned by its principal ally in the coup, the military, indigenous leaders have warned that they are "tired of being marginalized and treated as orphans by the government," and said the day might soon come when the talking would have to end. "This was not an armed uprising, and that may have been a mistake that will have to be rectified in the future," one leader said. "We do not even have weapons, and this is not the time to take up arms. But I want to tell you clearly and emphatically that if this system is not changed in the next five years, then you are going to see our people take up arms" (Rohter, "Bitter Indians Let Ecuador Know Fight Isn't Over," 2).

17 A marxist view of power, in which class was seen as the foundational identity of oppositional politics, dominated the Latin American Left until recently. The de-centering of this paradigm, which created greater possibilities for other sorts of emancipatory projects such as the indigenous movement, is often attributed to the end of the cold war. Although no doubt a factor, it is more likely the final straw rather than *the* cause for the dislodgment of this understanding of power. Clearly, other political and intellectual movements (feminism, queer politics, antiracism, the environmental movement, postcolonialism, and so on) had been at work for decades prior to the collapse of state socialism in Eastern Europe, complicating, if not eroding, many of the precepts of identity politics that privilege class.

Glossary

aldeia: an indigenous reserve or community; a village

artesenato: handicrafts (for example, bows, arrows, necklaces, rings, combs, rattles, and so on); the production and selling of these arts and crafts is one of the main sources of income for Indians in eastern Brazil

bicho da mata: animal or creature of the forest; Indians are often imagined as such in Brazil

branco: white; in general, "whiteness" is more inclusive than how it is socially defined in North America; for Indians, white oftentimes means "non-Indian"

caboclo: a synonym for Indian; an individual of predominant or salient indigenous descent who in cultural terms is considered to be only loosely connected to Indians (a "detribalized" Indian); a person of indigenous and European and/or African descent (a "mixed blood"); a backwoodsperson or "hick" (*caipira*)

cachaça: a Brazilian rum

cafuso: a person of African and indigenous parentage; a term rarely used in colloquial speech in eastern Brazil

cacique: the leader of an indigenous community

Canoeiros: descendants of the Maxakali, who worked as canoers or boaters for the military outposts (*quarteis*) in the Jequitínhonha Valley in the nineteenth century

chefe: a boss or director; Indians usually used it to refer to the director of FUNAI on any given aldeia

Crentes: Protestants, typically evangelicals

empregada: a maid, domestic servant

favela: a low-income, predominantly nonwhite neighborhood; typically, the residents do not own their property; usually located in the higher elevations of cities

fazenda: plantation, farm, or ranch

fazendeiro: owner of a plantation, ranch, or farm; usually considered to be large landholders, but not necessarily

índios mesmos: "real" or "authentic" Indians

jagunço: hired assassins; in rural areas, they are usually contracted by fazendeiros to buttress their authority

lavrador: an agricultural worker; typically landless or owning a very small plot of land; usually a tenant farmer, sharecropper, or peon

leis: literally it means laws; colloquially used to refer to a patterned way of being and thinking

mameluco: an individual of Indian and European parentage; rarely used colloquially

mestizo: an individual of parentage from at least two of the "primary races," defined as Indian, black, and white; includes caboclos, morenos, mulattos, cafusos, mamelucos, and so on; the official categorization of mestizo is pardo

moreno: a polite term used to refer to blacks, mulattos, and Indians; nonwhites in opposition to whites; whites who are brunettes or who have more olive-colored skin; often used as a race-evasive term because of its great inclusiveness (most Brazilians could be classified as moreno); the official categorization of morenos is pardo

mulatto: an individual of European and African parentage; a polite term for someone who is considered black; a person of predominant African descent who can claim to not be of exclusive African ancestry and/or who is a professional or middle class; the official categorization of mulato is pardo

negra/negro: the rough equivalent of the North American usage of black, but in general it is less inclusive; can be used to refer to an individual of exclusive, predominant, and/or some noticeable African parentage; considered a pejorative term by many, but less so than the term preto

Pai da Mata: literally Father of the Forest; a godlike figure of the Pataxó

pajé: spiritual expert or adviser; shaman

pardo: the official term for mestizo; individuals who self-identify as moreno, mulatto, caboclo, and so on are classified as pardo.

posseiros: roughly translated as squatters or homesteaders; Indians used it to refer to whites who were not large landholders (fazendeiros), even though technically speaking a posseiro need not be a small landholder

povo/povão: literally, the people; it often has the class/race connotations of the non-elite, poor/working classes, as well as nonwhites; it is also used to suggest "the true Brazilians"

preto: like negro, it can be used to refer to an individual of exclusive, predominant, and/or some noticeable African parentage; in colloquial use, it is more pejorative than negro; said in a particular tone, it carries the meaning roughly equivalent to the term nigger

quilombo: maroon communities; individuals and communities that can demonstrate they are the descendants of quilombos enjoy similar constitutional rights to land as the Indians

sertão: arid or desert-like wilderness, wilds, bush, hinterland, backwoods

sertanista: an individual who is an expert on the sertão

Bibliography

Alarcón, Antonio V. Menendez. "Racial Prejudice: A Latin American Case." *Research in Race and Ethnic Relations* 7 (1994): 299–319.

Almeida, Mauro W. B. "O Racismo no Livros Didáticos." In *A Questão Indígena na Sala de Aula: Subsídios para Professores de Primeira e Segunda Graus.* São Paulo: Editora Brasiliense, 1993.

Amorim, Paulo Marcos de. "Acamponesmento e Proletarização das Populações, Indígenas do Nordeste Brasileiro." *Boletim do Museu do Indio: Antropologia* 2 (May 1975): 1–19.

Andrews, George Reid. *Blacks and Whites in São Paulo, Brazil: 1888–1988.* Madison: University of Wisconsin Press, 1991.

"O Atentado Hora a Hora." *Folha de São Paulo* 3 (22 April 1997): 2.

Barcelos, Luiz Claudio. "Struggling in Paradise: Racial Mobilization and the Contemporary Black Movement in Brazil." In *Race in Contemporary Brazil: From Indifference to Inequality,* edited by Rebecca Reichmann. University Park: Pennsylvania State University Press, 1999.

Barth, Fredrik. *Ethnic Groups and Boundaries: The Social Organization of Culture Difference.* Boston: Little, Brown and Company, 1969.

Basso, Ellen B. *The Last of the Cannibals: A South American Oral History.* Austin: University of Texas Press, 1995.

Bento, Maria Aparecida Silva. "Silent Conflict: Discriminatory Practices and Black Responses in the Workplace." In *Race in Contemporary Brazil: From Indifference to Inequality,* edited by Rebecca Reichmann. University Park: Pennsylvania State University Press, 1999.

Bernardes, Betina. " 'Pegadinha' Deu Idéia de Queimar Índio." *Folha de São Paulo* 3 (22 May 1997): 10.

———. "Testemunha Afirma Ter Visto Pano Sobre Índio." *Folha de São Paulo* (6 June 1997).

Berwick, Dennison. *Savages: The Life and Killing of the Yanomami.* London: Hutchinson, 1992.

Blu, Karen I. *The Lumbee Problem: The Making of an American Indian People.* Cambridge, Mass.: Cambridge University Press, 1980.

"Brasília Lembra Morte de Índio Pataxó." *Estado de Minas,* 28 April 1997, 1.

"Brazil: The Persistence of Inequality." *NACLA Report on the Americas* 26, no. 6 (1995): 16.

Brumble, H. David, III. *American Indian Autobiography.* Berkeley: University of California Press, 1988.

Bruneau, Thomas C. *The Church in Brazil: The Politics of Religion.* Austin: University of Texas Press, 1982.

Brusco, Elizabeth E. *The Reformation of Machismo: Evangelical Conversion and Gender in Colombia.* Austin: University of Texas Press, 1995.

Brysk, Alison. "Turning Weakness into Strength: The Internationalization of Indian Rights." *Latin American Perspectives* 23, no. 2 (1996): 38–57.

Buckley, Stephen. "Native Struggle to Keep Identities." *Washington Post* (21 December 1999): 2 (www.sltrib.com:80/1999/dec/12211999/nation_w/8308.htm).

Burdick, John. "Brazil's Black Consciousness Movement." *NACLA Report on the Americas* 24, no. 4 (February 1992): 23–27.

———. *Looking for God in Brazil: The Progressive Catholic Church in Urban Brazil's Religious Arena.* Berkeley: University of California Press, 1993.

———. *Blessed Anastácia: Women, Race, and Popular Christianity in Brazil.* New York: Routledge, 1998.

———. "The Lost Constituency of Brazil's Black Movements." *Latin American Perspectives* 25, no. 1 (1998): 136–55.

"Canada Apologizes to Indigenous Tribes." *New York Times*, 8 January 1998, A1.

Carneiro, Sueli. "Black Women's Identity in Brazil." In *Race in Contemporary Brazil: From Indifference to Inequality*, edited by Rebecca Reichmann. University Park: Pennsylvania State University Press, 1999.

"Carro foi Reconhecido na TV." *Folha de São Paulo* 3 (24 April 1997): 3.

Célia, Maria. "Guerra na Câmara." *Hoje em Dia*, 4 April 1997.

Centro Ecumênico de Documentação e Informação. *Povos Indígenas no Brasil, 1987/1988/ 1989/1990: Aconteceu Especial, no. 18.* São Paulo: Centro Ecumênico de Documentação e Informação, 1994.

Cohen, Roger. "Brazil Pays to Shield Currency, and the Poor See the True Cost." *New York Times*, 5 February 1998, A1.

Collier, George A. "Zapatismo Resurgent: Land and Autonomy in Chiapas." *NACLA Report on the Americas* 33, no. 5 (March/April 2000): 20–25.

Collins, Jennifer N. "A Sense of Possibility: Ecuador's Indigenous Movement Takes Center Stage." *NACLA Report on the Americas* 33, no. 5 (March/April 2000): 40–48.

Conselho Indigenista Missionário. *Legislação Indigenista Brasileira.* São Paulo: Edições Loyala, 1989.

Cook-Lynn, Elizabeth. "Land Reform." *Wicazo Sa Review* 14, no. 1 (spring 1999): 103–12.

Costa, Emilio Viotta da. *The Brazilian Empire: Myths and Histories.* Chicago: University of Chicago Press, 1985.

Country Profile 2000: Brazil. London: The Economist Intelligence Unit, 2001.

Damasceno, Maria Caetana. "Trabalhadoras Cariocas: Algumas Notas Sobre a Polissemia da Boa Aparência." *Estudos Afro-Asiáticos* 31 (October 1997): 125–48.

Davidson, Joe. "Brave Heart." *Emerge* (September 1998): 40–47.

Davis, Shelton. *Victims of the Miracle: Development and the Indians of Brazil.* New York: Cambridge University Press, 1978.

Degler, Carl. *Neither Black nor White: Slavery and Race Relations in Brazil and the United States.* New York: Macmillan Publishing Co., Inc., 1971.

"Delegada Crê em Premeditação." *Estado de Minas*, 4 April 1997.

Deloria, Philip J. *Playing Indian.* New Haven, Conn.: Yale University Press, 1998.

Deloria, Vine, Jr., and Clifford Lytle. *The Nations Within: The Past and Future of American Indian Sovereignty.* New York: Pantheon Books, 1984.

Diário do Lesilativo de Abril 4, 1994 (www.almg.gov.br/dia/L280494.htm).

Dippie, Brian W. *The Vanishing American: White Attitudes and U.S. Indian Policy*. Lawrence: University of Kansas Press, 1982.

Duster, Troy. *Backdoor to Eugenics*. New York: Routledge, 1990.

Dweyer, Jeffrey, and Peggy Lovell. "The Cost of Being Nonwhite in Brazil." *Sociology and Social Research* 72 (1988): 136–42.

"Em 2 Anos, Brasília teve 13 Queimados." *Folha de São Paulo* 3 (8 May 1997): 9.

Entering the Twenty First Century: World Development Report 1999/2000. Washington, D.C.: The World Bank, 2000.

Escobar, Arturo, and Sonia E. Alvarez, eds. *The Making of Social Movements in Latin America: Identity, Strategy, and Democracy*. Boulder, Colo.: Westview Press, 1992.

Fausto, Boris. *A Concise History of Brazil*. Translated by Arthur Brakel. Cambridge, U.K.: Cambridge University Press, 1999.

Feagin, Joe. R., and Melvin Sykes. *Living with Racism: The Black Middle-Class Experience*. Boston, Mass.: Beacon Press, 1994.

Felinto, Marilene. "O Paciente Índio e Os Monstros da Classe Média." *Folha de São Paulo* 3 (22 April 1997): 2.

Fernandes, Florestan. *The Negro in Brazilian Society*. New York: Columbia University Press, 1969.

"FHC Diz no Canadá que Morte Causa Repulsa." *O Tempo*, 22 April 1997.

Figueira, Vera Moreira. "O Preconceito Racial na Escola." *Estudos Afro-Asiáticos* 18 (1990): 63–72.

Forbes, Jack D. *Africans and Native Americans: The Language of Race and Evolution of Red-Black Peoples*. 2d ed. Urbana: University of Illinois Press, 1993.

Fothergill, Anthony. "On Conrad, Cannibals, and Kin." In *Representing Others: White Views of Indigenous Peoples*, edited by Mick Gidley. Exeter, U.K.: University of Exeter Press, 1992.

Francisco, Luiz. "Para Fazendeiro, Ocupação Foi Ilegal." *Folha de São Paulo* 3 (27 April 1997): 2.

Freire, Carlos Augusto da Rocha. "Tupiniquim." In *Povos Indígenas*. São Paulo: Instituto Socioambiental, 1998 (www.socioambiental.org/epi/tupiniq/tupiniq.htm).

Freire, Paulo. *Pedagogy of the Oppressed*. New York: Continuum, 1989.

Freyre, Gilberto. *The Masters and the Slaves: A Study of the Development of Brazilian Civilization*. Translated by Samuel Putnam. 2d ed. Berkeley: University of California Press, 1986.

Frye, David. *Indians into Mexicans: History and Identity in a Mexican Town*. Austin: University of Texas Press, 1996.

"Funai Pode Ser Extinta." *O Estado de São Paulo*, 21 November 1998 (www.estado.com.br/edicao/encarte/xingu/xing20.html).

Fundação Instituto Brasileiro de Geografia e Estatística. *Censo Demográfico 1991: Resultados do Universo Relativos de Caracteristicas da População e dos Domicilios*. Rio de Janeiro: Fundação Instituto Brasileiro de Geografia e Estatística, 1991.

———. *Brasil em Números*. Rio de Janeiro: Fundação Instituto Brasileiro de Geografia e Estatística, 1994.

———. *Côr da População Síntese de Indicadores, 1982–1990*. Rio de Janeiro: Fundação Instituto Brasileiro de Geografia e Estatística, 1995.

Fundação Nacional do Índio. "Bases Conceituais da Educação Intercultural." (www.funai .gov.br/edind2.htm).

———. "A FUNAI" (www.funai.gov.br/funai.htm).

———. "Histórico da Política Indigenista de Saúde a Partir da Década de 80" (www.funai .gov.br/saude.htm).

———. "Programas de Formação e Capacitação de Professores que Lecionam nas Escolas Indígenas" (www.funai.gov.br/edind3.htm).

———. "Programa de Formalização de Parcerias" (www.funai.gov.br/edind5.htm).

Garfield, Seth. "The 'Greatest Administrative Scandal.' " In The Brazil Reader: History, Culture, Politics, edited by Robert M. Levine and John J. Crocitti. Durham, N.C.: Duke University Press, 1999.

Gilliam, Angela. "From Roxbury to Rio — and Back in a Hurry." In African-American Reflections on Brazil's Racial Paradise. Philadelphia, Pa.: Temple University Press, 1992.

Gilliam, Angela, and Onik'a Gilliam. "Odyssey: Negotiating the Subjectivity of Mulata Identity in Brazil." Latin American Perspectives 26, no. 3 (1999): 60–84.

Giraldi, Renata. "Índio Recebe Homenagem." Folha de São Paulo, 6 April 1997.

Giraldi, Renata, and Silvana de Freitas. "Acusados de Matar Índio Não Irão a Júri." Folha de São Paulo 3 (13 August 1997): 5.

Glazer, Nathan. Introduction to Ethnicity: Theory and Experience, edited by Nathan Glazer and Daniel P. Moynihan. Cambridge, Mass.: Harvard University Press, 1975.

Gould, Stephen Jay. The Mismeasure of Man. New York: W. W. Norton and Company, 1981.

Guimarães, Antonio Sérgio Alfredo. "Racism and Anti-Racism in Brazil: A Postmodern Perspective." In Racism and Anti-Racism in World Perspective, edited by Benjamin Bowser. London: Sage Publications, 1995.

———. "O Recente Anti-Racismo Brasileiro: O Que Dizem os Journais Diarios." Revista USP 28 (December–February 1996): 84–95.

———. "Measures to Combat Discrimination and Racial Inequality in Brazil." In Race in Contemporary Brazil: From Indifference to Inequality, edited by Rebecca Reichmann. University Park: Pennsylvania State University Press, 1999.

———. "Review of Racism in a Racial Democracy: The Maintenance of White Supremacy in Brazil." Transforming Anthropology 8, nos. 1 and 2 (1999): 192–94.

Guimarães, Paulo Machado. Demarcação das Terras Indígenas: A Agressão do Governo. Brasília: Conselho Indigenista Missionário, 1989.

Hale, Charles H. "Cultural Politics of Identity in Latin America." Annual Review of Anthropology 26 (1997): 567–90.

Hall, Stuart. "Gramsci's Relevance for the Study of Race and Ethnicity." In Stuart Hall: Critical Dialogues in Cultural Studies, edited by Stuart Hall, David Morley, and Kuan-Hsing Chen. London: Routledge, 1996.

Halpern, Adam, and France Winddance Twine. "Antiracist Activism in Ecuador: Black Indian Alliances." Race and Class 42, no. 2 (October–December 2000).

Hanbury-Tenison, Robin. A Question of Survival: For the Indians of Brazil. London: Angus and Robertson, 1973.

Hanchard, Michael. *Orpheus and Power: The Movimento Negro of Rio de Janeiro and São Paulo, Brazil, 1945–1988*. Princeton, N.J.: Princeton University Press, 1994.

———. "Black Cinderella? Race and the Public Sphere in Brazil." In *Racial Politics in Contemporary Brazil*, edited by Michael Hanchard. Durham, N.C.: Duke University Press, 1999.

———. Introduction to *Racial Politics in Contemporary Brazil*, edited by Michael Hanchard. Durham, N.C.: Duke University Press, 1999.

———, ed. *Racial Politics in Contemporary Brazil*. Durham, N.C.: Duke University Press, 1999.

Harris, Marvin. "Racial Identity in Brazil." *Luso-Brazilian Review* (1964): 21–28.

Hasenbalg, Carlos. *Discriminação e Desigualdades Racias no Brasil*. Rio de Janeiro: Ediçoes Graal, 1979.

———. "Anotações Sobre a Classe Média Negra no Rio de Janeiro." *Revista de Antropologia* 26 (1983): 53–59.

———. "Race and Socioeconomic Inequalities in Brazil." In *Race, Class, and Power in Brazil*, edited by Pierre-Michel Fontaine. Los Angeles: Center for Afro-American Studies, University of California, 1991.

Hecht, Susanna, and Alexander Cockburn. *The Fate of the Forest: Developers, Destroyers, and Defenders of the Amazon*. New York: HarperPerennial, 1990.

Hemming, John. *Red Gold: The Conquest of the Brazilian Indians, 1500–1760*. Cambridge, Mass.: Harvard University Press, 1978.

Hess, David, and Roberto DaMatta, eds. *The Brazilian Puzzle: Cultures on the Borderlands of the Western World*. New York: Columbia University Press, 1995.

Hewett, Dawn. "Challenging the 'Mestizo Nation': The New Face of Popular Movements and Indigenous Identity in Mexico." Unpublished manuscript, 2000.

Hill, Jonathan D. *History, Power, and Identity: Ethnogenesis in the Americas, 1492–1992*. Iowa City: University of Iowa Press, 1996.

Hoje em Dia, 16 April 1993, 13.

Holston, James. *The Modernist City: An Anthropological Critique of Brasília*. Chicago: University of Chicago Press, 1989.

Horsman, Reginald. *Race and Manifest Destiny: The Origins of American Racial Anglo-Saxonism*. Cambridge, Mass.: Harvard University Press, 1981.

Hutchinson, Harry. "Race Relations in a Rural Community of the Bahian Reconcavo." In *Race and Class in Rural Brazil*, edited by Charles Wagley. Paris: United Nations Educational, Scientific, and Cultural Organization, 1952.

"Índios Chegam a Brasília para Protestar." *Folha de São Paulo* 3 (20 August 1997): 4.

"Índios e Sem-Terra Protestam Contra Assassinato de Pataxó." *O Tempo* (22 April 1997).

"Índios Sofrem Fome e Miséria." *Hoje em Dia*, 4 April 1997.

Kennedy, David P., and Stephen G. Perz. "Who Are Brazil's Indígenas? Contributions of Census Data Analysis to an Anthropological Demography of Indigenous Populations." Unpublished manuscript, 1999.

Knight, Alan. "Racism, Revolution, and *Indigenismo*: Mexico, 1910–1940." In *The Idea of*

Race in Latin America, 1870–1940, edited by Richard Graham. Austin: University of Texas Press, 1990.

Krupat, Arnold. "Native American Autobiography and the Synecdochic Self." In *American Autobiography: Retrospect and Prospect*, edited by Paul John Eakin. Madison: University of Wisconsin Press, 1991.

Kuper, Adam. *The Invention of Primitive Society: Transformation of an Illusion*. New York: Routledge, 1993.

Lancaster, Roger N. *Thanks to God and the Revolution: Popular Religion and Class Consciousness in the New Nicaragua*. New York: Columbia University Press, 1988.

Leacy, F. H., ed. *Historical Statistics of Canada*. 2d ed. Ottawa: Statistics Canada, 1983.

Levine, Robert M., and José Carlos Sebe Bom Meihy. *The Life and Death of Carolina Maria de Jesus*. Albuquerque: University of New Mexico Press, 1995.

Levine, Robert M., and John J. Crocitti, eds. *The Brazil Reader: History, Culture, Politics*. Durham, N.C.: Duke University Press, 1999.

Lévi-Strauss, Claude. *The Savage Mind*. Chicago: University of Chicago Press, 1966.

Lima, Antonio Carlos do Souza. *Um Grande Cerco de Paz: Poder, Indianidade e Formação do Estado no Brasil*. Petrópolis, Rio de Janeiro: Vozes, 1995.

Lippard, Lucy R. Introduction to *Partial Recall: With Essays on Photographs of Native North Americans*, edited by Lucy R. Lippard. New York: New Press, 1992.

Löwy, Michael. *The War of Gods: Religion and Politics in Latin America*. New York: Verso, 1996.

Mata, Vera Lúcia Calheiros. "Kariri Xocó." In *Povos Indigenas*. São Paulo: Socioambiental, 1999 (www.socioambiental.org/epi./kariri/kariri.htm).

Maybury-Lewis, Biorn. *The Politics of the Possible: The Brazilian Rural Workers' Trade Union Movement, 1964–1985*. Philadelphia, Pa.: Temple University Press, 1994.

Maybury-Lewis, David. *The Savage and the Innocent*. London: Evans Brothers Limited, 1965.

Momaday, N. Scott. *The Names: A Memoir*. Tucson: The University of Arizona Press, 1976.

Morris, Aldon D. *The Origins of the Civil Rights Movement: Black Communities Organizing for Change*. New York: Free Press, 1984.

Mundo Católico. "Governo Cria Secretaria Nacional de Direitos Humanos." *Notícias e Comunicados do Conselho Indigenista Missionário* 255 (28 August 1998) (http://www.redemptor.com.br/~catolico/mc/cimi.htm).

NACLA. "Brazil: The Persistence of Inequality." *NACLA: Report on the Americas* 28, no. 6 (May/June 1995).

———. "Gaining Ground: The Indigenous Movement in Latin America," *NACLA: Report on the Americas*, 29, no. 5, (March/April 1996).

Nascimento, Abdias do. *Brazil: Mixture or Massacre? Essays in the Genocide of a Black People*. Dover, Mass.: Majority Press, 1989.

Neely, Sharlotte. *Snowbird Cherokees: People of Persistence*. Athens: University of Georgia Press, 1991.

"Negro Briga por mais Vagas na Universidade." *Democracia* 107 (October/November 1994): 18.

Nugent, Stephen. *Amazonian Caboclo Society: An Essay on Invisibility and Peasant Economy*. Providence, R.I.: Berg Publishers, Inc., 1993.

Oliveira, João Pacheco de. "As Facções e a Ordem Política em uma Reserva Tukuna." Master's thesis, University of Brasilia, 1977.

Oliveira, Ney dos Santos. "Favelas and Ghettos: Race and Class in Rio de Janeiro and New York City." *Latin American Perspectives* 23, no. 4 (1996): 71–89.

Pacari, Nina. "Taking on the Neoliberal Agenda." *NACLA Report on the Americas* 24, no. 5 (March/April 1996): 23–32.

Pace, Richard. *The Struggle for Amazon Town: Gurupá Revisited*. Boulder, Colo.: Lynne Rienner, 1998.

Paraiso, Maria Hilda Baqueiro. *Laudo Antropológico sobre a Identidade Etnica dos Xacriabá*. Salvador: Universidade Federal da Bahia, 1987.

———. *Laudo Antropológico sobre a Comunidade Denomidada Kaxixó*. Salvador: Universidade Federal da Bahia, 1994.

———. "Krenák." In *Povos Indígenas*. São Paulo: Instituto Socioambiental, December 1998 (www.socioambiental.org/epi/krenak/ krenak.htm).

Pasquaretta, Paul Andrew. "Tricksters at Large: Pequots, Gamblers, and the Emergence of Crossblood Culture in North America." Ph.D. diss., State University of New York at Stony Brook, 1994.

Patai, Daphne. *Brazilian Women Speak: Contemporary Life Stories*. New Brunswick, N.J.: Rutgers University Press, 1988.

Pedrosa, Rafael. Untitled. *Estado de Minas*, 22 April 1997.

Penha-Lopes, Vania. "What Next? On Race and Assimilation in the United States and Brazil." *Journal of Black Studies* 26, no. 6 (1996): 809–26.

Pinto, Regina Pahim. "A Representação do Negro em Livros Didáticos de Leitura." *Cadernos de Pesquisa* 63 (1987): 88–92.

———. "Movimento Negro e Educação do Negro: A Ênfase na Identidade." *Cadernos de Pesquisas* 86 (August 1993): 25–38.

Piza, Edith, and Fúlvia Rosemberg. "Color in the Brazilian Census." In *Race in Contemporary Brazil: From Indifference to Inequality*, edited by Rebecca Reichmann. University Park: Pennsylvania State University Press, 1999.

Portillo, Lourdes. *Mirrors of the Heart: Race and Identity*. Part 4 of *Americas*. South Burlington, Vt.: Annenberg/CPB Collection, 1993. Video.

Potiguara, Eliane. "Harvesting What We Plant." *Cultural Survival Quarterly* (fall 1992): 46–48.

Pratt, Mary Louise. *Imperial Eyes: Travel Writing and Transculturation*. London: Routledge, 1992.

Prezia, Benedito, and Eduardo Hoornaert. *Esta Terra Tinha Dono*. São Paulo: FTD, 1991.

Psacharopoulos, George, and Harry Anthony Patrinos, eds. *Indigenous People and Poverty in Latin America: An Empirical Analysis*. Washington, D.C.: World Bank, 1994.

"The Quilombos." Http://www.brasil.emb.mw.dc.us/ndsg/textos/quilom-i.htm, 14 December 1997.

"Racismo Cordial." *Folha de São Paulo*, special supplement (25 June 1995).

Radcliffe, Sarah, and Sallie Westwood. *Remaking the Nation: Place, Identity, and Politics in Latin America*. London: Routledge, 1996.

Ramos, Alcida Rita. *Indigenism: Ethnic Politics in Brazil*. Madison: University of Wisconsin Press, 1998.

Reesink, Edwin. "Índio ou Caboclo: Notas sobre a Identidade Étnica do Índios no Nordeste." *Universitas* 32 (1983): 121–37.

Reichmann, Rebecca. "Brazil's Denial of Race." *NACLA Report on the Americas* 28, no. 3 (December 1995): 35–45.

———. "Introduction." In *Race in Contemporary Brazil: From Indifference to Inequality*, ed. Rebecca Reichmann. University Park, PA: The Pennsylvania State University Press, 1999.

———, ed. *Race in Contemporary Brazil: From Indifference to Inequality*. University Park: Pennsylvania State University Press, 1999.

Ribeiro, Darcy. *Os Índios e a Civilização: A Integração das Populações Indígenas no Brasil Moderno*. 2d ed. Petrópolis, Brazil: Vozes, 1977.

Ribeiro, Eduardo Magalhães. *Lembranças da Terra: Histórias do Mucuri e Jequitinhonha*. Belo Horizonte, Minas Gerais: Cedefes, 1996.

Rocha, Pedro. "Mello Pede Justiça no Caso Pataxó." *Estado de Minas* (26 August 1997).

Rohter, Larry. "Indian Tribe Wants Brazil's Plymouth Rock Back." *New York Times*, 3 December 1999 (www.nytimes.com/library/world/americas/120199brazil-indians. html).

———. "Brazil Carnival's Fabled Amity May Hide Bigotry." *New York Times*, 12 December 1999 (www.nytimes.com/library/world/americas/121299brazil-racism.html).

———. "Bitter Indians Let Ecuador Know Fight Isn't Over." *New York Times*, 27 January 2000 (http://www.nytimes.com/library/world/americas/ 012700ecuador-indians. html).

Roosens, Eugeen E. *Creating Ethnicity: The Process of Ethnogenesis*. Newbury Park, Calif.: Sage Publications, 1989.

Roquette-Pinto, Edgar. "Nota sobre os Tipos Antropológicos do Brasil." In *Archivos do Museu Nacional, XXX*. Rio de Janeiro: Museu Nacional, 1928.

Rosemberg, Fúlvia. "Segregação Espacial na Escola Paulista." *Estudos Afro-Asiáticos* 19 (1990): 97–106.

Sampaio, José Augusto Laraneiras. "De Caboclo a Índio: Etnicidade e Organização Social e Política entre Povos Indígenas Contemporâneos no Nordeste do Brasil, o Caso Kapinawá." Master's thesis, UNICAMP, Campinas, 1986.

Santos, Anna Lúcia Florisbela dos. "Women and Racism." In *Women in Brazil*, edited by Caipora Women's Group. London: Latin America Bureau, 1993.

Scheper-Hughes, Nancy. *Death without Weeping: The Violence of Everyday Life in Brazil*. Berkeley: University of California Press, 1992.

Schwartzman, Simon. "Brazil: The Social Agenda." *Daedalus* 129, no. 2 (2000): 29–56.

Schwartzman, Stephan, Ana Valeria Araujo, and Paulo Pankararu. "Brazil: The Legal Battle over Indigenous Rights." In *NACLA Report on the Americas* 24, no. 5 (1996): 36–43.

Service, Elman. *Primitive Social Organization: An Evolutionary Perspective*. New York: Random House, 1962.

Sheriff, Robin. " 'Negro Is a Nickname That the Whites Gave to the Blacks': Discourses on Color, Race, and Racism in Rio de Janeiro." Ph.D. diss., City University of New York, 1997.

Silman, Janet. *Enough Is Enough: Aboriginal Women Speak Out.* Toronto: Women's Press, 1987.

Silva, Aracy Lopes da, ed. *A Questão Indígena na Sala de Aula: Subsídios para Professores de Primeiro e Segundo Graus.* 2d ed. São Paulo: Editora Brasiliense, 1993.

Silva, Benedita da. "The Black Movement and Political Parties." In *Racial Politics in Contemporary Brazil,* edited by Michael Hanchard. Durham, N.C.: Duke University Press, 1999.

Silva, Marcio Ferreira da. "A Demografia e os Povos Indígenas no Brasil." *Revista Brasileira de Estudos Populacionais* 11, no. 2 (1994): 261–64.

Silva, Nelson do Valle. "Updating the Cost of Not Being White in Brazil." In *Race, Class, and Power in Brazil,* edited by Pierre-Michel Fontaine. Los Angeles: Center for Afro-American Studies, University of California, 1991.

Silva, Nelson do Valle, and Carlos Hasenbalg. *Relações Raciais no Brasil Contemporaneo.* Rio de Janeiro: Rio Fundo Editora, 1992.

Simpson, Amelia. *Xuxa: The Mega-Marketing of Gender, Race, and Modernity.* Philadelphia, Pa.: Temple University Press, 1993.

Simpson, Jennifer S. "Easy Talk, White Talk, Back Talk: Some Reflections on the Meanings of Our Words." *Journal of Contemporary Ethnography* 25, no. 3 (1996): 372–89.

Skidmore, Thomas. *Black into White: Race and Nationality in Brazilian Thought.* 2d ed. Durham, N.C.: Duke University Press, 1993.

Soares, Geralda Chaves. *Os Borun do Watu: Os Índios do Rio Doce.* Contagem, Minas Gerais: Centro de Documentação Ely Ferreira da Silva,

Spyer, Juliano. "Urban Indians." In *The Brazil Reader: History, Culture, Politics,* edited by Robert M. Levine and John J. Crocitti. Durham, N.C.: Duke University Press, 1999.

Statistics Canada. *1981 Census of Canada: Summary Guide, Total Population.* Ottawa: Statistics Canada, 1983.

Taussig, Michael. *Shamanism, Colonialism, and the Wild Man: A Study in Terror and Healing.* Chicago: University of Chicago Press, 1987.

Teixeira, Raquel F. A. "As Linguas Indígenas no Brasil." In *A Temática Indígena na Escola: Novos Subsídios para Professores de 1 and 2 Graus,* edited by Aracy Lopes da Silva and Luís Donisete Benzi Grupioni. Brasília: MEC, 1995.

Telles, Edward. "Racial Distance and Region in Marriage: The Case of Marriage among Color Groups." *Latin American Research Review* 28, no. 28 (1993):141–62.

———. "Industrialização e Desigualdade Racial no Emprego: O Exemplo Brasileiro." *Estudos Afro-Asiáticos* 26 (September 1994): 21–51.

———. "Inicio no Brasil e Fim no EUA?" *Estudos Feministas* 4, no. 1: 194.

Thompson, Richard H. *Theories of Ethnicity: A Critical Appraisal.* New York: Greenwood Press, 1989.

Thornton, Russell. *American Indian Holocaust and Survival: A Population History since 1492.* Norman: Oklahoma University Press, 1987.

Toneto, Bernadete, and Paulo Lima. "O Axé de Zumbi." *Sem Fronteiras* (November 1995).

Tonkin, Elizabeth, Maryon McDonald and Malcolm Chapman, eds. *History and Ethnicity.* London: Routledge, 1989.

Torres-Saillant, Silvio. "The Tribulations of Blackness: Stages in Dominican Racial Identity." *Latin American Perspectives* 25, no. 3 (1998): 126–46.

Twine, France Winddance. *Racism in a Racial Democracy: The Maintenance of White Supremacy in Brazil.* Rutgers, N.J.: Rutgers University Press, 1998.

———. "Racism in a Racial Democracy: The Cultural Politics of Everyday Racism in Rural Brazil." Ph.D. dissertation. University of California at Berkeley. 1994.

———. "Introduction: Racial Ideologies, Racial Methodologies, Racial Fields." In *Racing Research, Researching Race: Methodological Dilemmas in Critical Race Studies,* edited by France Winddance Twine and Jonathan W. Warren. New York: New York University Press, 2000.

Twine, France Winddance, Jonathan W. Warren, and Francisco Ferrandiz. *Just Black?* New York: Filmmakers' Library, 1991.

Twine, France Winddance, and Jonathan W. Warren, eds. *Racing Research, Researching Race: Methodological Dilemmas in Critical Race Studies.* New York: New York University Press, 2000.

U.S. Census Bureau. *Statistical Abstract of the United States: 1999.* 119th ed. Washington, D.C., 1999.

Varese, Stefano. "The Ethnopolitics of Indian Resistance in Latin America." *Latin American Perspectives* 23, no. 2 (1996): 58–71.

Veber, Hanne. "The Salt of the Montaña: Interpreting Indigenous Activism in the Rain Forest." *Cultural Anthropology* 13, no. 3 (1998): 382–413.

"Violência Maucha a Imagen do Brazil." *Estado de Minas* (21 April 1997): 3.

Vizenor, Gerald. *The Heirs of Columbus.* Hanover, N.H.: University Press of New England, 1991.

———. "Ishi Bares His Chest: Tribal Simulations and Survivance." In *Partial Recall: Essays with Photographs of Native North Americans,* edited by Lucy R. Lippard. New York: New Press, 1992.

———. *Manifest Manners: Post-Indian Warriors of Survivance.* Hanover, N.H.: University Press of New England, 1995.

Wade, Peter. "The Cultural Politics of Blackness in Colombia." *American Ethnologist* 22, no. 2 (1995): 341–57.

———. *Race and Ethnicity in Latin America.* London: Pluto Press, 1997.

Wagley, Charles. *Race and Class in Rural Brazil.* 2d ed. Paris: United Nations Educational, Scientific, and Cultural Organization, 1952.

———. *Amazon Town: A Study of Man in the Tropics.* New York: Macmillan Publishing Co., Inc., 1958.

Wahrhaftig, Albert L., and Bruce (Pacho) Lane. "Totonac Cultural Revitalization: An Alternative to the Zapatistas" (http://www.sonoma.edu/anthropology/Totonac_Revival/Totonac_Revival.html).

Warren, Jonathan W. "O Fardo de Não Ser Negro: Uma Análise Comparativa do Desempenho Escolar de Alunos Afro-Brasileiros e Afro-Norte-Americanos." *Estudos Afro-Asiáticos* 31 (October 1997): 103–24.

————. "The Brazilian Geography of Indianness." *Wicazo Sa Review* 14, no. 1 (spring 1999): 61–86.

————. "Masters in the Field: White Talk, White Privilege, White Bias." In *Racing Research, Researching Race: Methodological Dilemmas in Critical Race Studies*, edited by France Winddance Twine and Jonathan W. Warren. New York: New York University Press, 2000.

Warren, Jonathan W., and France Winddance Twine. "Critical Race Studies in Latin America: Recent Advances, Recurrent Weakness." In *The Blackwell Companion to Racial and Ethnic Studies*, edited by John Solomos and David Theo Goldberg. London: Basil Blackwell, 2001.

Warren, Kay B. *Indigenous Movements and Their Critics: Pan-Maya Activism in Guatemala*. Princeton, N.J.: Princeton University Press, 1998.

West, Cornel. *Prophetic Fragments*. Grand Rapids, Mich.: Eerdmans, 1988.

Williams, Brackette F. *Stains on My Name, War in My Veins*. Durham, N.C.: Duke University Press, 1991.

Wilson, Richard. *Maya Resurgence in Guatemala: Q'eqchi' Experiences*. Norman: Oklahoma University Press, 1995.

Winant, Howard. *Racial Conditions: Politics, Theory, Comparisons*. Minneapolis: University of Minnesota Press, 1994.

Wolf, Eric. "The Vicissitudes of the Closed Corporate Community." *American Ethnologist* 13 (1986): 325–29.

Index

Constitution (1988): definition of Indianness, 208, 221; the indigenous people's chapter, 86; indigenous people's legal rights to land (Article 231), 99, 106, 208, 221; See also Decree 1775; Emancipated Indians, Indian Statute (1973)

Contact zone, 22

Contagem (Minas Gerais), 27, 52

Coronel Murta (Minas Gerais), 44, 48, 184

Congress of Racial Equality (CORE), 153

Costa, Emilio Viotta da, 165

Cree (Indian community; Canada), 35

Crocitti, John, 64

Crossbloods, 301

Culina (Indian community), 228

Cunha, Euclides da, 232

DaMatta, Roberto, 94, 276

Darcy Ribeiro Law (1996), 132

Davis, Shelton, 103–6, 314 nn.34, 35

Decree 1098 (1988): process for determining authenticity of an Indian community, 208

Decree 1775 (1996): land demarcation process, 99, 310 n.90

Degler, Carl, 165–66, 257

d'Evreux, Yves, 26

Dippie, Brian, 300 n.46

Diretório missions. See Capuchins

Distribution of wealth, 297 n.13, 315 n.57

Doce River (Sweet River), 40, 71, 73, 299 n.36

Dom José I, 307 n.31

Dom Pedro II, 199, 312 n.11

Dominican Republic: and negrophobia, 164, 180

Durkheim, Émile, 209

Duster, Troy, 301–2 n.65

Dyer, Richard, 171

Eastern Indians: linguistic and cultural groupings, 306 n.17; population, 12; reasons for regional categorization, 36–37, 300 n.47. See also Posttraditional Indians

Ecclesiastic base communities (comunidade eclesial de base; CEB), 155, 321 n.40

Education, 123–36; bilingual and intercultural education to indigenous people, 132, 258–59; establishment of Indian schools, 132, 271; graduation rates, 135–36, 316 n.73, 317 nn.78, 79, 318 n.101, 335 n.93; Indian boarding schools (Canada and U.S.), 60, 135, 309 n.61; racism in schools and school textbooks, 128–31, 263, 271

Emancipated Indians, 220, 328 n.32

Escobar, Arturo, 154, 321 n.37

Ethnic groups: ontological assumptions of, 215–17

Ethnic Groups and Boundaries (Barth), 215–17

Ethnogenesis in the Americas (Hill), 218

Ethnography: as antiracist intervention, 39

Evans-Pritchard, Edward, 157

Fanon, Franz, 154

Fausto, Boris, 305 n.17, 307 n.31

Federal University of Minas Gerais (UFMG), 54, 132

Figueira, Vera Moreira, 37

Figueiredo, Jader (general): investigation of corruption in SPI (Figueiredo Report), 83–84, 103, 153, 319 n.17

First Universal Races Congress (London), 70

Fiuza, Manuel (Xacriabá), 87

Florida: Indian penal colony, 77

Folha de São Paulo: racial attitudes among urban Brazilians (Racismo Cordial supplement), 12–13, 16, 166

Forbes, Jack, 10, 237

Ford Foundation, 331 n.36

Forestry Service (Serviço florestal), 64, 72, 74, 306 nn.20, 23

Indians and Indianness: as alcoholics, 167; as antimoderns, 160, 167, 172–73, 175, 192, 203, 210, 211, 239, 302 n.2, 324 nn.19, 26; biological capital, 181, 324 n.16; as bounded communities (isolated cultural islands), 210–13, 221, 225, 227; as buffoons, 129; census definitions, 16, 170; as compared to national society, 223; creatures of the forest (bichos da mata), 158, 160, 173–74, 196–97, 203, 221, 239, 328 n.36; as defined by eastern Indians (law of the Indian), 184–200; as determined by gender, 233 n.69; as devil worshipers, 129; as an ethnic boundary, 215–20, 229–33; as a habitable identity, 201–6, 276; "I-am-We" sense of self (a critique), 30–31; as irrelevant to race matters, 235–40, 278–79; as lazy, 118, 167, 194–95, 277; legal definitions and interpretations, 221–24, 230–31; as modern, 189; as naked, 187, 160; as noble savages, 129, 173, 181, 183, 196–98, 326 n.51; as non-Brazilians, 160, 177–80, 325 n.40; as orientation (jeito), 190–92; competing definitions in popular thought, 166–68, 323 n.9, 326 n.56; as "purebloods", 28, 160, 168–69, 177–80, 203, 229, 240; racial categorizations of, 36–37; as savages (primitives), 174–76, 178, 182, 207, 209, 211, 228, 131; the semiotics of, 180–84; simulations of, 29; somantic markers of, 184–86, 324 n.15; as static (ahistorical), 23, 129, 167, 175–77, 209, 211; as stigma (stain), 82, 203, 227–28; topography of anti-Indian attitudes, 118–19, 183–84, 316 n.70, 323 n.8; as vanishing, 11, 18, 130; as wealth of Brazil, 199–200

Indian populations (demographics): in Brazil, 5, 11–18, 165, 236, 298 nn.28, 31, 299 nn.36, 37, 329 n.7; in Canada, 60; in Ecuador, 281–82; in Latin America, 300 n.40, 336 n.12; in U.S., 17

Indian resurgence and: anthropological thought, 230–33; antiblack racism, 164–66, 180–82; common sense, 200–6, 327 n.58; land, 98–103, 182–83; non-governmental organizations (NGOs), 157–63. *See also* Indianing; Indian populations (demographics)

Indian Statute (1973), 208, 222

Indians into Mexicans (Frey), 23

Indígena: as a census category, 16, 299 n.35, 316 n.75

Indigenous Movements and Their Critics (Warren), 217, 280–81, 280, 336 n.12

Indigenous penal colonies, 40, 75–78, 298 n.27, 309 n.61

Índio, Pedro (Aranã) 158–63, 190, 205, 265, 322 nn.50, 53

Interracial research team, 302 n.3

Interviewees: class background of, 114, 123; and gender of, 303 n.15; number of, 52, 302 n.3, 303 n.6, 304 n.18

Ishi, 11

Itambacuri (mission), 66–68, 71–72, 307 n.34, 308 n.41, 322 n.53

Jeronimo (Portuguese priest), 160

Jesuits: colonizing missions, 10, 64–68, 78–79, 146; expulsion from Brazil, 307 n.31

Jesus, Carolina Maria de, 317 n.80

Jequintinhonha Valley, 47, 49, 78–80

João III (king), 8, 10, 298 n.21

Kaingang (Indian community), 40, 308 n.54

Kariri-Xocó, 101–3, 191; religion (Ouricuri), 191, 313 n.27

Kaxinaua (Indian community), 228

Kaxixó (Indian community), 12, 14, 19–20, 49–51, 59, 102–3, 118–20, 158–63,

United Nations (UN), 84
University of São Paulo, 71, 317 n.79
Urban population, 311 n.7

Van den Berghe, Pierre, 57
Vasalia, 34–35, 37, 39, 47, 119, 174, 177–79, 243–46, 262, 265–67, 302 nn.3, 5, 312 n.9
Varese, Stefano, 218
Veber, Hanne, 320 n.27
Veiga, João Carlos Nobre da, 220
Vizenor, Gerald, 29, 198, 301 n.53

Wade, Peter, 210–11, 215, 239–40
Wagley, Charles, 11, 212–13, 221, 223
Warren, Jonathan, 38, 136, 239
Warren, Kay, 217, 280–81, 280, 336 n.12
Watkins, Arthur, 305 n.11
Weber, Max, 209
West, Cornel, 137–39
Westwood, Sallie, 242
Whitening, 18, 68–71, 165, 282; campaigns against, 331 n.36; on census, 242–43; and common sense, 200–206; and dating preferences, 243–46; and interior décor, 257; and land issues, 94–98; and memory, 246–49; as outdated, 220; in U.S., 300 n.46
White privilege: consequences for employment, 115; methodological effects because of, 37–38
Whites and whiteness: contributions to

the nation, 177–80; as physical ideal, 171; positive attributes associated with, 171; as racial position, 57; somatic boundaries of, 169, 172, 303 n.10; white innocence, 202
White talk, 264–69, 274–78, 334 n.84
Williams, Brackette, 180, 326 n.53
Wilson, Richard, 24
Winant, Howard, 235
Wolf, Eric, 22
World Bank, 111, 314 n.35, 315 n.57

Xacriabá, Antonia, 101, 108–10, 181,198, 202, 225, 277, 230
Xacriabá, Cristiano, 15
Xacriabá, José, 19, 29, 87–88, 97–98, 174–75, 271, 310 n.93
Xacriabá, Rodrigo, 111
Xacriabá, Rosinette, 181
Xacriabá (Indian community), 12, 15, 19, 29, 52, 87–88, 97–98, 100–3, 108–11, 132, 160, 181, 174–75, 202, 198, 205, 225, 230–33, 271, 277, 310 n.93, 312 nn.12, 13
Xocó (Indian community), 228–29
Xuxa, 170–71

Yanomamis. *See* Ianomâmis

Zapatista National Liberation Army (EZLN), 281, 336 n.9
Zunis (Indian community; U.S.), 176

Jonathan W. Warren is Assistant Professor of Latin
American Studies at the Henry M. Jackson School of
International Studies at the University of Washington,
and will join the departments of African and African
American Studies and Cultural Anthropology at Duke
University. He was born and raised in St. Johns, Michigan.

Library of Congress Cataloging-in-Publication Data
Warren, Jonathan W.
Racial revolutions : antiracism and Indian resurgence in Brazil /
Jonathan W. Warren.
p. cm. — (Latin America otherwise)
Includes bibliographical references and index.
ISBN 0-8223-2731-7 (cloth ; alk. paper)
ISBN 0-8223-2741-4 (pbk. : alk. paper)
1. Indians of South America—Brazil—Ethnic identity.   2. Indians
of South America—Brazil—Mixed descent.   3. Indians of South
America—Brazil—Social conditions.   4. Indians, Treatment of—
Brazil—History.   5. Brazil—Race relations.   6. Brazil—Ethnic
relations.   7. Brazil—Politics and government.   I. Title.   II. Series.
F2519.3.E83 W37   2001   305.898081—dc21   2001033783